Beside Still Waters

A Daily Devotional for Men

Beside
Still
Waters

A Daily Devotional for Men

Jim Grassi, D.Min.

Serving Our Lord Since 1981

Beside Still Waters

ISBN: 978-1-7358693-1-5

Published by Men's Ministry Catalyst
www.mensministrycatalyst.org

Dedication and Thank You

Dedicated to all the faithful partners, participants, and friends of Men's Ministry Catalyst (Let's Go Fishing Ministries, Inc.) who have helped inspire our team for over forty years.

I especially appreciate and acknowledge the support and encouragement I've received from my bride of 56 years - Mary Louise Grassi, a Proverbs 31 woman.

In the end, what makes a book shine is not the paper it's printed on, nor who the publisher is, nor even the story-telling ability of the author, but the skill, patience, and wisdom of a good editor and graphic person. My friend and co-laborer Rob Fischer of Fischer Publishing has helped make this work possible. Thanks Rob.

A special shout-out to our twin sons, pastors Daniel James and Thomas William who bless our lives as we see them serve our Lord. I've learned a great deal about life by watching them mature in their faith.

William Shakespeare said: "Thinking of friends and family and their worth is often enough to drive away an army of fears, regrets, and enemies." When you take on a project of this magnitude you occasionally wonder if it's going to matter. Then you think about the friends and acquaintances you encountered over the years who testify how a certain devotional helped them through a difficult time. Praise God!

It is my prayer that this book will inspire and better equip you to wade through the chaos and frustrations of life by leaning on God's Word.

Introduction

Some thirty years ago, I began writing weekly devotionals to help inspire business leaders, ministry partners, and sports personalities who desired to grow in their faith but couldn't go to church on a regular basis. My normal way of inspiring others is by story that connect with biblical principles. Storytelling was used by our Lord as a teaching tool and a way to explain His plan for mankind. People relate to story. It was natural for me to share some observations and metaphors from my experience as a chaplain, businessman, outdoorsman, and men's ministry leader that help direct people to God's Word.

For almost three decades many of those receiving these devotionals have sent them to family and friends around the world. The devotionals are designed to be both provocative and practical on an array of topics that stimulate you to think over a concept or biblical truth throughout the day.

On Day 7 of each week I encourage you to reflect on and pray over the previous devotionals as you look forward to another week with new spiritual quests. In fact, some days when you simply sit with God you will experience "fullness of joy" in His Presence (Psalm 16:11 NKJV) or receive the peace only He can provide.

The most precious gift you can give anyone is "Time." Our loving Lord wishes for us to spend time with Him. He established an example of this with His disciples in Mark 6:30-32, *Then the apostles gathered to Jesus and told Him all things, both what they had done and what they had taught. And He said to them, 'Come aside by yourselves to a deserted place and rest a while.' For there were many coming and going, and they did not even have time to eat. So, they departed to a deserted place in the boat by themselves.*

We can become so consumed in trying to fulfill all the demands on our lives that we forget the most important thing – time with the Master. I once heard a pastor say the following: "Never get so caught up in the work of the Kingdom that you don't have time for the King."

Where did Christ and His disciples often go to seek God's peace and presence? So often they went "to the water". There is a mystical healing property associated with water. On a quiet lake, a placid stream, or sitting by a babbling brook you can often hear God whisper His truth and wisdom into your mind and soul.

The flowing water sound can eliminate abrasive sounds and confusion. It also brings calmness and a sense of tranquility to your spirit – transforming chaos into a relaxing and soothing experience.

Enjoy the journey and share the adventure with others. "Grow in the grace and knowledge of the Lord and Savior Jesus Christ." (2 Peter 3:18) May the time you spend reading *Beside Still Waters* calm your spirit and inspire your soul so you can hear and follow God's voice in your life.

In His Service,

Jim

Jim Grassi, D. Min.

contact@mensministrycatalyst.org

Week 1, Day 1: Are You Fearful?

*"'Do not fear; I will help you. Do not be afraid... for I myself will help you,'
declares the LORD, your Redeemer, the Holy One of Israel."*
– Isaiah 41:13b–14

Our research indicates fourteen areas of major concern for most people in the country. Men's Ministry Catalyst developed booklets on each of these topics. The booklet on fear is requested more than any other topic.

Fear is something that can absolutely extinguish the joy in life. It can make the healthiest person sick to their stomach. It can paralyze your ability to think clearly. Those who regularly experience fear know too well its byproducts — discouragement and doubt.

Sometimes we focus on our fears instead of on the rich promises of God. We fear financial ruin because of the unstable global economy. We fear the loss of our job. We fear for our health or that of a loved one. We fear for our children. We fear for our relationships. We fear global war and terrorist acts. We fear what will happen to America because of its moral decline.

For about thirteen years of his life, David fled from Saul as a fugitive. Saul went to great lengths to kill David because God had chosen him to be the next King. At one point, David was so fearful of Saul that he fled into enemy territory and barely escaped with his life. Following that incident, David wrote Psalm 34. In the opening verses of that Psalm David declared:

I will extol the Lord at all times; His praise will always be on my lips. I will glory in the Lord; let the afflicted hear and rejoice. Glorify the Lord with me; let us exalt His name together. I sought the Lord, and He answered me; He delivered me from all my fears.

Those who look to Him are radiant; their faces are never covered with shame. This poor man called, and the Lord heard him; He saved him out of all his troubles. The angel of the Lord encamps around those who fear Him, and He delivers them. (Psalm 34:1-7)

It is easy to look at our circumstances and feel afraid. Jesus reminds us not to fear man or circumstances but God alone. Jesus said, "Are not five sparrows sold for two pennies? Yet not one of them is forgotten by God. Indeed, the very hairs of your head are all numbered. Don't be afraid; you are worth more than many sparrows." (Luke 12:6–7)

Scripture Reading: Read Isaiah 40:25-31; 41:10

Personal Application:

- From the above passages in this day's devotion, how do we overcome our fears?
- What will you do today to displace fear in your life with trust in God?

Week 1, Day 2: Watch Out for Decoys!

"But there were also false prophets among the people, just as there will be false teachers among you. They will secretly introduce destructive heresies, even denying the sovereign Lord who bought them—bringing swift destruction on themselves."
— 2 Peter 2:1

For most of our marriage we have enjoyed living in areas surrounded by open space. From ground and tree hunting blinds I have viewed and filmed many creatures to better understand their habitats, behaviors, and characteristics. Manufacturers have provided me with attractants to test in my outdoor laboratories. I've tried an assortment of game calls, chemical scents, and life-size decoys to lure various animals into my area. The gullibility of some animals is quite surprising.

I soon realized that by combining certain game calling techniques and decoys, I could tempt game to let down their guard and give in to their lusts. For instance, a single decoy may not tempt a trophy buck. However, several 3-D decoys strategically placed had a positive effect on the unsuspecting animal. As a big buck stomped its feet and snorted at the small decoy herd, he became bold and proud letting down his guard. His arrogance and desires overruled his protective instincts and caused him to take risks that he would not have considered otherwise.

Today, we find scores of tarot card readers, sorcerers, fortune-tellers, false prophets, cultic teachers, and some slick politicians. They too are "decoys" who are very appealing to the gullible and lonely, the lost and weak, the mis-informed and unchurched. The fake media and perverse television programs pitch anti-biblical, immoral themes and add to the confusion.

Christ warned His young disciples several times to beware of false teachers, "Watch out for false prophets. They come to you in sheep's clothing, but inwardly they are ferocious wolves." (Matthew 7:15). False teaching will lead us away from God's Word and the promptings of the Holy Spirit. It will cause us to disobey His teachings and disregard our spiritual convictions.

Sometimes we are no different than that poor unsuspecting buck. Our greed, passion, lusts, and driven spirits cause us to forget about the temptations and decoys that will lure us away from our beliefs. Once we sacrifice our character and God's Word we end up with an arrow of regret in our side. While the wounds may eventually heal, the pain, scars, and remorse linger.

The Apostle Paul warned young Timothy, "But you, man of God, flee from all this, and pursue righteousness, godliness, faith, love, endurance and gentleness. Fight the god fight of the faith." (1 Timothy 6:11-12)

Scripture Reading: 1 Timothy 4:1-5

Personal Application:
- Who are the obvious deceivers impacting your life?
- What steps will you take to guard your heart and that of your family?

Week 1, Day 3: No Pain, No Gain

"For our light and momentary troubles are achieving for us an eternal glory that far outweighs them all."
— 2 Corinthians 4:17

Every year twenty-one Ironman Triathlons take place around the world. From those qualifying events 80 athletes are chosen to compete in the coveted Ironman Triathlon in Kona Hawaii. Five of those qualifying events are held in the United States, including one in the community in which I live, Coeur d'Alene, Idaho.

Having volunteered at this event for years, I have been privileged to meet many of the dedicated men and women athletes who compete in the triathlon. I couldn't help but be impressed with their dedication, perseverance, discipline, and self-motivation. They understand pain and suffering, working as much as 8-10 hours a day on their fitness, form, and skills.

An Ironman Triathlon is about as grueling as it gets. It involves a 140-mile course in which athletes swim, bike and run. The best athletes complete this arduous feat in eight-and-a-half hours, but for many the day is much longer, lasting up to 17 hours.

In the Ironman Competition, success comes to those who are conditioned, focused on the goal, and persevere through pain. In reflecting on this, I couldn't help but see the similarities between the Ironman Triathlon and living the Christian life.

Someone once said, "The highest award for a person's toil is not what he/she gets for it, but rather what he/she becomes by it." That quote speaks to the kind of pain and suffering so many followers of Christ experience and testifies to the importance of the *process*, not the reward.

This is true not only for those suffering with a terminal illness, deep relational wounds, persecution, or other trauma, but also for the pain of simply enduring the trials of daily living. The Apostle Paul reminds us, "For it has been granted to you on behalf of Christ not only to believe in Him, but also to suffer for Him." (Philippians 1:29)

That word "granted" literally means "graciously given." Our Lord knows that suffering is a necessary element in the process of our becoming more like Him. For how could we develop patience, perseverance, and unswerving trust in the Lord without suffering? "And after you have suffered for a little while, the God of all grace…will Himself perfect, confirm, strengthen and establish you." (1 Peter 5:10)

Scripture Reading: Hebrews 11:35-40; 12:1-3

Personal Application:

- In what areas of your life are you suffering right now?
- In what ways can you leverage your suffering to become more like Jesus?
- If the Lord has graciously granted you with such trials, spend time worshiping Him and asking for His strength and perseverance.

Week 1, Day 4: Preserving Unity

Unity is essential to a healthy team, organization, church, and family. Unfortunately, it's hard to come by and difficult to maintain. Too often strife rules over peace. We've all experienced it: office spats, family feuds, and church splits. Strife is dominant in politics and among rivals representing opposite positions. King Solomon had much to say about the cause of strife, conflict, and dissension:

"Hatred stirs up conflict, but love covers over all wrongs." (Proverbs 10:12)

"Where there is strife, there is pride." (Proverbs 13:10)

"It is to one's honor to avoid strife, but every fool is quick to quarrel." (Proverbs 20:3)

"A greedy man stirs up conflict, but he who trusts in the LORD will prosper." (Proverbs 28:25)

Hatred, anger, greed, pride, self-centeredness, and a contentious spirit all stir up conflict and threaten unity. By contrast, Paul wrote, "As a prisoner for the Lord, then, I urge you to live a life worthy of the calling you have received. Be completely humble and gentle; be patient, bearing with one another in love. Make every effort to keep the unity of the Spirit through the bond of peace." (Ephesians 4:1-3)

The attitudes and actions that build unity are love, humbleness or selflessness, gentleness, patience, and bearing with one another. Unity of the Spirit is what Christ has called us to. You and I are indwelt by the same Holy Spirit. If we don't have peace and unity among ourselves, why would unbelievers look to us to find peace with God?

This doesn't mean that we'll agree with each other all the time, but we must love, bear with, accept, and extend grace to each other. "Accept the one whose faith is weak, without quarreling over disputable matters." (Romans 14:1)

Selflessness is the foundation of Christian love and required for unity to flourish. It's Jesus' selfless sacrifice on the cross that allows us to claim His unmerited grace and mercy. If we are to be truly Christlike in our attitudes, we must humble ourselves and focus on the needs of others — not in our own strength, but with complete dependence on God.

Let's not let our minor differences on theology, style, or approach create division in the body of Christ. Let's not let our own ambitions, frustrations, or preferences create conflict. Let's recognize our inability to do this on our own and press into God for His strength, unconditional love, and perspective.

Scripture Reading: Philippians 2:1-11

Personal Application:

- What one thing stands out to you most from this devotion or the Scripture reading?
- What will you do today to cultivate unity in your relationships?

Week 1, Day 5: Where Is Your Focus?

With so much chaos and commotion around us we can easily become distracted or sidetracked from God's calling and purpose in our lives. This should weigh heavy on our hearts. One of my favorite teachings Jesus gave His disciples is about keeping focused on Him in times when trials threaten to distract us.

In Matthew 14 we read about the disciples having a tough night while trying to row across the Sea of Galilee. They had made their way far from shore but were being buffeted by the wind and waves. In fact, they had been struggling at the oars all night and now it was just before dawn.

The disciples had already been tired before this rowing marathon, so by now they must have been totally exhausted. The night before, Jesus had urged His disciples to get in the boat and row to the other side and wait for Him there. Meanwhile, Jesus went up on a mountain to pray.

Now, out on this rough inland sea, at the point of their greatest need, they saw Jesus approaching them walking on the water! "When the disciples saw Him walking on the lake, they were terrified. 'It's a ghost,' they said, and cried out in fear. But Jesus immediately said to them: 'Take courage! It is I. Don't be afraid.'" (verses 26-27)

Peter was so impressed with this miracle that he said, "Lord, if it's you, tell me to come to you on the water." Peter is a lot like many of us—impulsive, direct, and a risk taker! Jesus told him to come, so he *fixed his gaze* upon the Lord and stepped onto the water and headed toward Jesus.

But Peter became distracted by the wind and waves, and taking his eyes off Jesus, he began to sink. He cried out, "Lord, save me!" "Immediately Jesus reached out His hand and caught him. 'You of little faith,' He said, why did you doubt?" (Matt. 14:31)

With his gaze fixed on Jesus, Peter stayed on top of the water. But when he let the wind and waves distract him, he lost his focus on the Lord. Many things can distract us today from keeping our eyes on the Lord, things like trials and difficulties, fleshly pleasures, hobbies, toys, money, a job or career, and the list goes on. These things can draw our attention away from the most important thing in life—an ever-deepening relationship with Jesus.

When you feel distracted by the circumstances of life or the materialistic trappings of this world, keep your gaze (concentration) upon Him. To be effective disciples with relevant impact we need to "fix our gaze and concentration on the Lord."

Paul urged Timothy, "Be diligent in these matters; give yourself wholly to them, so that everyone may see your progress. Watch your life and doctrine closely. Persevere in them." (1 Timothy 4:15-16)

Scripture Reading: Hebrews 12:1-3

Personal Application:

- What things in your life are most likely to distract you from focusing on the Lord?
- What will you do differently today to maintain focus on the Lord throughout the day?

Week 1, Day 6: Priorities for a Father

Our nation continues to move toward what is known as a "fatherless society." One-third of children are born out of wedlock; twenty-four million kids don't live with their biological fathers; half of all marriages end in divorce.

Fatherlessness is rampant and a well-documented problem in this society. Children who come from fatherless homes are five times more likely to experience poverty, emotional problems, teen pregnancy, and substance abuse. Fatherless children are also more likely to drop out of high school and experience problems with the law. It's no wonder that 85 percent of male prisoner's report having had no father figure in their lives.

Fathers who allow their ambitions, hobbies, and passions to become more important than their primary role as a husband and father also present a form of fatherlessness. The term "NASCAR fathers" describes an approach to parenting that is all too common in modern times. This is the image of a race car driver roaring around the track at two hundred miles an hour, zipping into the pit to refuel, then roaring off to rejoin the race with just a wave good-bye.

This is just too close to what fatherhood looks like in many homes in America today. There is certainly a cost to the men who live this way, but the greater cost, in my opinion, is paid by the wives and children of such NASCAR fathers. A man who makes a quick "pit stop" at home, on his way between commitments and work, is shirking his responsibilities as a godly husband and father.

God wants men to be husbands and fathers first, and good providers second. When a man switches these priorities, he damages himself and others around him.

Certainly, society is no friend to men. The media continues to play down the God-ordained leadership role of the husband and father. Most sitcoms degrade men by portraying them as unmotivated, ignorant beings with little vision or passion for anything that is intellectual or spiritual. Men are portrayed as expendable fools.

In *The Promise Keeper at Work* by Bob Horner, he writes, "When a child comes to faith, nine percent of the time they can influence an unchurched family to become Christians. When a woman comes to faith in the same situation, only 13 percent of the time will her influence cause the family to come to faith. But when a man comes to faith, 93 percent of the time the entire family will come to faith and become participants in church."

Men, we are charged to "Follow God's example…and walk in the way of love, just as Christ loved us and gave himself up for us." (Ephesians 5:1-2) We are to love our wife and children with the same kind of love God lavishes on us.

Scripture Reading: Ephesians 5:25-32; 6:4

Personal Application:
- What things in your life supplant the time you want to spend with your wife and children?
- What tangible steps can you take to be a present, godly influence in your family?

Week 1, Day 7: Weekly Recap and Prayer

On the seventh day of each week, use the **ACTS** acronym to spend time with the Lord reviewing and assessing your week and praying to God. (**A**=Adoration; **C**=Confession; **T**=Thanksgiving; **S**=Supplication)

First, look back over the previous six days for this week to remind yourself what you read and agreed to. Then, follow the ACTS pattern for prayer below. Finally, use the space below to journal what God is doing in your life and share this with a trusted spiritual partner.

Adoration: Simply spend time in adoration of the Lord. Praise Him and glorify His name. (See 1 Chronicles 29:10-13; Psalm 100; Romans 11:33-36.)

Confession: Confess your sins and shortcomings before God. ("If we confess our sins, he is faithful and just and will forgive us our sins and purify us from all unrighteousness." – 1 John 1:9) To confess (or agree with God) about your sin, implies that you are repentant and desperately want Him to change you.

Thanksgiving: Thank God for what He has done and is doing in your life and the life of your family. Give Him credit, for everything you have comes from Him. (See Psalm 136.)

Supplication: Supplication is just a fancy word for making your requests known to God. Based on the devotions of this past week and the things going on in your life right now, what do you want to ask Him for? "If you, then, though you are evil, know how to give good gifts to your children, how much more will your Father in heaven give good gifts to those who ask Him!" (Matthew 7:11)

Journal: What is God doing in your life right now?

Week 2, Day 1: A Bitter Pill

I have a friend who gives her oldest dog pain medication each morning for his arthritis and it seems to really help. It's a bitter pill, and he won't take it if she gives it to him alone. No matter how much he needs it or how far back in his mouth she puts it, he just spits it out. So, she wraps it in a thin piece of ham or turkey to cloak the taste.

Sometimes she gives the other dogs a bit of meat too, but not always. When the other dogs don't get meat, they look dejected...as if they're unloved. Even if she gives them a biscuit, they still feel slighted because they didn't get meat. They don't understand. They don't know about the bitter pill that the other dog must swallow. And so, it is with us.

When faced with something unpleasant, we usually do everything we can to avoid it. We'd spit it out if we could. Even when we know it would be good for us and we need it, we often resist. How about dental check-ups, spring cleaning, or studying for an important exam? How about confronting that guy at work, asking for forgiveness, or forgiving?

And sometimes we just don't understand. We don't really know what we need. God does though, and sometimes it's a bitter pill. Sometimes it's graciously wrapped with comfort, peace, and even blessings, but at times it's just raw suffering. But He is always there to love us and minister to us.

Sometimes when we see others' blessings, we wonder why we can't have some too. But we don't always see the struggles others face. Maybe that free trip to Hawaii is just the blessing she needs to temper a hidden grief. Maybe that raise is just what he needs to help him through his son's drug-rehab expenses. Only God knows the troubles we each face, the burdens we carry, and what lies ahead. Only God knows exactly what we need.

Obviously, not every blessing is to cover pain. God is generous and loves His children. "If you, then, though you are evil, know how to give good gifts to your children, how much more will your Father in heaven give good gifts to those who ask him!" (Matthew 7:11)

God doesn't always cover over the bitter things in life, but His grace is always sufficient. He always offers hope and unconditional love. Let's be thankful in everything, knowing God is in control. His blessings aren't equal, but when we really step back and take a good look, they're always abundant!

Scripture Reading: 2 Corinthians 12:7-10
Personal Application:
- What "bitter pill" currently exists in your life? How is God using that for His glory and your growth in Him?
- Thank Him right now for that "bitter pill," trusting that He will help you endure.
- Thank Him also for the abundance you enjoy in your life, for it all comes from Him.

Week 2, Day 2: Calling Out Our Men

Recent studies testify that too many men are disengaged with the church, in their faith, and in their families. Nearly two-thirds of people attending our churches are women. Over 60% of the children in America will go to bed this evening without a biological father in the home. It is over 80% in the inner-city.

Too many men believe the Church is no longer relevant. Yet, research shows that men are struggling in many areas of their personal lives with depression, despair, loneliness, aimlessness, unfaithfulness, pornography, deception, debt, and spiritual emptiness. Our culture and lifestyle continue to ask for more from men without regard to a man's dedication to his faith or family.

Many Christian men have become distracted. We've allowed "The worries of this life, the deceitfulness of wealth and the desires for other things to come in and choke the word, making it unfruitful" in our lives (Mark 4:19). We've lost our "first love" for Jesus Christ (Revelation 2:4).

We've forgotten that we're in a spiritual battle. Many Christian men are AWOL, while others lounge around unarmed and unprepared, vulnerable to the enemy's attacks. That's why we're calling out men. Men, we need to wake up!

Nearing the end of his life, King David commissioned his son Solomon with the monumental task to govern the people of Israel. David's words still apply to each of us today:

When the time drew near for David to die, he gave a charge to Solomon his son. "I am about to go the way of all the earth," he said. "So be strong, act like a man, and observe what the Lord your God requires: Walk in obedience to him, and keep his decrees and commands, his laws and regulations, as written in the Law of Moses. Do this so that you may prosper in all you do and wherever you go and that the Lord may keep his promise to me: 'If your descendants watch how they live, and if they walk faithfully before me with all their heart and soul, you will never fail to have a successor on the throne of Israel." (1 Kings 2:1-4)

God wants Christ-loving men to "be strong and act like men" toward our families, our churches, our businesses, our nation, and our world. Whether we like it or not, we serve as examples to those around us what it means to be a godly man in this culture.

Strong men recognize their weaknesses. Strong men surround themselves with other men who can mutually encourage, support, and protect each other.

Scripture Reading: Ephesians 6:10-18

Personal Application:
- What elements of the devotional for today hit you square between the eyes?
- What steps will you take to "be strong and act like a man"?
- What men have you surrounded yourself with? If no one, who could you partner with?

Week 2, Day 3: Are You Known as a Friend of God?

For many years I had the privilege of providing chaplain services for a few college and professional football teams. Many of the superstars and coaches that you've seen and admired on national television have heard me proclaim God's Word.

Some of my friends couldn't understand why I wasn't more awestruck when dealing with so many high-profile personalities. My answer was simple: "I'm too old to be a groupie!" I was and still am committed to helping prominent men become disciples, and I measure a man not by his football expertise or prominence in the business community, but by his commitment to knowing and loving God.

As a model for my approach to these athletes, I looked to Abraham, the Old Testament patriarch. His greatness was found in his hospitality to strangers (Genesis 18:1–8), his obedience to God (Genesis 26:5), and the blessing of the Lord upon his family and his life (Genesis 24:1). In three separate places in God's Word, we see Abraham called a "friend of God." How encouraging! I want to be known as a friend of God.

I encouraged the football players, coaches, and business leaders to develop Christlike character and to pursue a deep relationship with God, so that they too can be called a friend of God. I reminded them that the greatest honor is not playing in a Super Bowl, being inducted in the Hall of Fame, or making another million dollars, but rather in having their name used to describe the attributes of God the Father. Scripture refers to the Lord as "the God of Abraham" (Genesis 26:24). What an honor! Can you imagine someone someday referring to God using your name?

The Apostle Paul urges us, "Follow my example, as I follow the example of Christ." (1 Corinthians 11:1) As Christians, our lives are being watched and examined all the time—we don't have to be sports celebrities or business icons. What reflection of God do we give the world? What legacy of His love are we leaving for others to follow?

Abraham's example of love, respect, obedience, faithfulness, and praise should inspire each of us to become known as a "friend of God" so that we can leave a legacy that truly glorifies our Father and points others to His plan of salvation and hope.

Scripture Reading: Isaiah 41:8-10

Personal Application:

- In John 15:15, Jesus said, "I no longer call you servants, because a servant does not know his master's business. Instead, I have called you friends, for everything that I learned from my Father I have made known to you."
- What does it mean to you to be called Jesus' friend?
- In what ways should your friendship with Jesus work itself out in your daily life?

Week 2, Day 4: God's Love Is Greater than Our Sin

Tucked away in the later books of the Old Testament is the small but powerful message from the prophet Hosea. Hosea was the only prophet from the northern kingdom who prophesied over the northern 10 tribes of Israel just before the Assyrian captivity. The sins of the people were blatant. Lying, thievery, bloodshed, oppression, perverted justice, sexual immorality, idolatry, and prostitution were rampant. Adultery and prostitution were incorporated into the worship of Baal, the god of fertility.

Physical adultery does not originate in a vacuum; it begins with spiritual adultery in the heart. The hearts of the 10 northern tribes were unfaithful and corrupt. They had lost their way in their spiritual journey and obedience to God. The covenant God had formed with Israel on Mount Sinai in Exodus 24 and renewed in Joshua 8 was like that of a husband who cherishes his bride. God's deep, intimate love for Israel He often phrased in terms of a husband toward his beloved wife. But they were unfaithful to Him and became like a harlot. Yet, God still loved her.

As a remarkable object lesson of God's unwavering love toward unfaithful Israel, He commanded the prophet Hosea to take the prostitute Gomer as his wife. God knew that Hosea's wife would not remain faithful but instructed his obedient prophet to marry her anyway. Hosea was to love Gomer despite her unfaithfulness. And when she left Gomer for her lovers, God sent him to pursue her, bring her home again and love her. We call this unconditional love.

While it doesn't make sense to us, God used this couple and the healing that took place after Gomer's failures to model what unconditional love looks like. Hosea's love, grace, and mercy redeemed Gomer's spirit and caused her to abandon her evil ways and return to her loving husband.

This story became an example of how our loving God wishes to restore the lost to a loving relationship with Him. The Apostle Paul underscores the power and grace of our loving God: "Where sin increased, God's grace increased all the more." (Romans 5:20)

My friend, no matter what your sin or the sin of those you love, God's grace is more than abundant to forgive, cleanse, and restore. "I am convinced that neither death nor life, neither angels nor demons, neither the present nor the future, nor any powers, neither height nor depth, nor anything else in all creation, will be able to separate us from the love of God that is in Christ Jesus our Lord." (Romans 8:38-39) And, may we, like God, have a forgiving spirit to those who offend us.

Scripture Reading: Hosea 14:1-9

Personal Application:

- To what extent have you perhaps drifted in your affection for Christ?
- What sins do you need to confess before God? (See 1 John 1:9.)
- In what ways can you demonstrate your love for Christ?

Week 2, Day 5: Handcuffed by a Fish!

One of the greatest joys in life is visiting with long-time friends. Bill Dunn was my best friend and fishing partner in college and to this day. He visited us recently which gave us an opportunity to talk about some memories and experiences while enjoying God's great outdoors.

During our time together, we fished one of our local lakes. Bill caught a nice pike. I've never seen Bill so worried about un-hooking a fish as he did that three-pound pike. When asked why he was being so careful with this chore, Bill reflected upon a trip he had taken with his brother to Canada where a pike had ruined his day.

Apparently, Bill and his brother Steve had flown into a remote lodge where they got into separate boats to try to locate the fish. Bill caught a pike and was in the process of taking one of the treble hooks out when the fish jumped. The radical movement embedded a set of treble hooks into each hand. With the subsequent movements of the fish, the barbs of the hooks penetrated to the bone at the base of both thumbs.

Bill was handcuffed by the lure. Every time he would try to make a move to free himself, the fish would jump creating more pain for my friend. After several minutes of agony and no way out of this predicament, Bill began yelling for his brother. Steve politely waved to Bill acknowledging that he could see the nice fish his brother caught. However, Bill's persistent calls, finally registered with Steve that his brother was in trouble.

After applying the recommended American Red Cross first aid treatment for removing hooks, Bill was free from the constraining lure that attached him to the fish. He was grateful for his brother, without whom he could not have gotten out of this awkward and painful situation.

And so, it is with our pain. God intended that we share our concerns, fears, problems, frustrations, and worries with a trusted friend. Even as I write this devotional, a dear friend just called asking for prayer as his pregnant daughter was just rushed to the hospital with complications. Friends have each other's back especially in times of need.

The Apostle Paul reminds us, "He comforts us in all our troubles, so that we can comfort those in any trouble with the comfort we ourselves have received from God." (2 Corinthians 1:4) God designed us and ordained it so that we would stand with each other and help one another.

Scripture Reading: 2 Corinthians 1:3 and Hebrews 10:23-25

Personal Application:
- Proverbs 27:17 says, "As iron sharpens iron, so one man sharpens another." Who do you have in your life to "sharpen" you and spur you on to love and good deeds (Hebrews 10:24)?
- Meet regularly with another man who loves Jesus. Challenge, encourage, and pray for each other, mutually building each other up in the faith.

Week 2, Day 6: Who are You Following? Who is Following You?

"Come, follow me," Jesus said, "and I will make you fishers of men."
– Matthew 4:19

There is nothing more fundamental to being a Christian than discipleship. For forty years I've been captivated with the subject of discipleship or what I call spiritual mentoring. Through speaking, writing, and teaching, I've endeavored to underscore the mission Jesus gave all of us before returning to the Father:

"Then Jesus came to them and said, 'All authority in heaven and on earth has been given to me. Therefore, go and make disciples of all nations, baptizing them in the name of the Father and of the Son and of the Holy Spirit, and teaching them to obey everything I have commanded you. And surely, I am with you always, to the very end of the age." (Matthew 28:18–20)

How did Jesus make disciples? He used a small group approach. He took twelve very common guys and poured His life into them. Christ taught by example and with short stories. He connected with His followers in both attitude and action. Through everyday life situations, Jesus showed them how to relate to each other and with the Father. They also enjoyed deep fellowship together. The entire process was relational and mutually supportive.

A disciple is:

- A person who is following Christ
- One who is endeavoring to become more like Jesus
- One who is committed to the mission of Christ
- A leader in training

A person who disciples using the method Christ used not only shares the Good News, he builds a relationship with the person, walking beside him through thick and thin, and modeling love.

In praying to the Father, Jesus said of us, "As you sent me into the world, I have sent them into the world." (John 17:18)

Sharing our lives with others and encouraging them to grow in relationship with the living God is not an option but a command for anyone who takes God's Word seriously.

Let's devote ourselves to being true disciples—building relationships with others, modeling love, and sharing the Good News.

Scripture Reading: John 1:35-49

Personal Application:

- Reflect over your life. Who were those who invested in you spiritually? How did they do this?
- Each morning asks the Lord to help you live your life in a way that represents Him well to others. Then, with this attitude, look for opportunities to represent Christ with others throughout your day.

Week 2, Day 7: Weekly Recap and Prayer

On the seventh day of each week, use the **ACTS** acronym to spend time with the Lord reviewing and assessing your week and praying to God. (**A**=Adoration; **C**=Confession; **T**=Thanksgiving; **S**=Supplication)

First, look back over the previous six days for this week to remind yourself what you read and agreed to. Then, follow the ACTS pattern for prayer below. Finally, use the space below to journal what God is doing in your life and share this with a trusted spiritual partner.

Adoration: Simply spend time in adoration of the Lord. Praise Him and glorify His name. (See 1 Chronicles 29:10-13; Psalm 100; Romans 11:33-36.)

Confession: Confess your sins and shortcomings before God. ("If we confess our sins, he is faithful and just and will forgive us our sins and purify us from all unrighteousness." – 1 John 1:9) To confess (or agree with God) about your sin, implies that you are repentant and desperately want Him to change you.

Thanksgiving: Thank God for what He has done and is doing in your life and the life of your family. Give Him credit, for everything you have comes from Him. (See Psalm 136.)

Supplication: Supplication is just a fancy word for making your requests known to God. Based on the devotions of this past week and the things going on in your life right now, what do you want to ask Him for? "If you, then, though you are evil, know how to give good gifts to your children, how much more will your Father in heaven give good gifts to those who ask Him!" (Matthew 7:11)

Journal: What is God doing in your life right now?

Week 3, Day 1: Servant Leadership

Leadership can be expressed in many ways. All too often, it seems like those who are most bullish, abrupt, impulsive, dynamic, and charismatic find their way into the news. But as we know there are many kinds of leaders.

One of my favorite leaders in the Old Testament is Joshua. But none of the above characteristics applied to him. Yet, Joshua proved himself a powerful military, political and spiritual leader during a time of tremendous transition for the people of Israel.

The Bible introduces Joshua to us initially as Moses aide or assistant. And we read that Joshua had served Moses in this capacity since he was a youth (Numbers 11:28). In other words, Joshua had to learn to serve before he could become a leader.

Many of us want to bypass the servant phase of leadership development. And it turns out that serving others isn't merely a stepping-stone to becoming a leader. But we learn from Jesus that servanthood is a key characteristic of leadership in Kingdom living.

Jesus explained to His disciples, "You know that those who are regarded as rulers of the Gentiles lord it over them, and their high officials exercise authority over them. Not so with you. Instead, whoever wants to become great among you must be your servant, and whoever wants to be first must be slave of all. For even the Son of Man did not come to be served, but to serve, and to give his life as a ransom for many."

If you follow Joshua's early life, he shadowed Moses and assisted him in every way that Moses needed. In Numbers 12:3 we read, "Now Moses was a very humble man, humbler than anyone else on the face of the earth." In this way, Moses mentored Joshua to be humble as well, another key characteristic of a godly leader.

Both Joshua and Jesus led others by their own example. When Moses sent the 12 spies into the land of Canaan, Joshua was one of those spies. And only Joshua and Caleb gave a good and honest report when they returned. Consequently, only Joshua and Caleb were permitted to enter the land of Canaan 40 years later.

Finally, a godly leader is not only a servant, humble, and leads by example, but he also walks with and trusts the Lord. When Moses died and the Lord appointed Joshua to lead His people, God told Joshua repeatedly, "Be strong and courageous. Do not be afraid; do not be discouraged, for the Lord your God will be with you wherever you go." (Joshua 1:9)

Scripture Reading: Joshua 1:1-9

Personal Application:

- You may or may not see yourself as a leader. Regardless, how can you demonstrate a servant's heart to others?
- In what ways can you honor those who serve you? (E.g., your spouse, your pastor, your government officials, the waiter/waitress at a restaurant, the checker at a store.)

Week 3, Day 2: Perseverance

Recently, I met a young man whose life exemplifies perseverance. Guyvenson Montes was an orphan raised by his grandmother on the island of Haiti. His grandmother saw to it that he got a good education and regularly went to church.

Eventually, Guyvenson married and had two children and enjoyed a good job. Life was going well for Guyvenson and his family until the Category 5 Hurricane Matthew hit the small island in October 2016. The hurricane nearly or completely destroyed 200,000 homes, leaving 1.4 million people in need of aid.

The damage was estimated at $1.9 billion. Nearly all crops were destroyed, and communication systems were wiped out. Their corrupt government grabbed most of the aid and sold it on the black market, leaving little to support those in need like Guyvenson and his family.

After standing in line over 200 consecutive days for a visa, Guyvenson finally received a work permit to find a job in Brazil. There he worked long hours as a waiter in one of the nice hotels. He saved every dollar he could to help bring the rest of his family to join him.

My good friend and businessman, Billy Chapman, spotted this young man and was absolutely amazed at his tenacity and professionalism. My friend enjoyed several meals with Guyvenson as his waiter. The young man anticipated every customer's need before they voiced their request. He moved so fast to respond to every guest that Billy nicknamed him "Flash."

In fact, Billy was so impressed with this young man that he hired him for his amazing Amazon Anglers Inn operation, where he now works.

Guyvenson has worked hard to pull the remainder of his family through the corrupt governmental system in Haiti so they can enjoy the rewards of the life that Guyvenson has made for them in Brazil.

Few of us in America must deal with the extremes that Guyvenson has had to endure. But all of us encounter trials and hurdles that we must overcome. James encourages us, "Blessed is the one who perseveres under trial because, having stood the test, that person will receive the crown of life that the Lord has promised to those who love him." (James 1:12)

Scripture Reading: Hebrews 10:32-38

Personal Application:
- In what aspect of your life are you being challenged to persevere? In the story above, Billy reached out to Guyvenson and helped him persevere. Who can you reach out to for help?
- Who else do you know who might be struggling with perseverance right now? How might you encourage them? Why not send them one of our devotionals?

Week 3, Day 3: Real Security

"I will lie down and sleep in peace, for you alone,
O Lord, make me dwell in safety."
— Psalm 4:8

Many Americans install alarms in their homes and cars to protect their posses-sions against intruders. We purchase firearms and take courses to equip us with the skills necessary for personal protection. We entrust our money to banks and security vaults to protect our finances.

With all our security systems, yearly physicals, savings accounts, and pension plans, the only real peace we can find comes from knowing Christ. Security is im-portant but can only be found in the presence of God.

David, who wrote the Psalm above, understood this. As a boy watching over his flock, he had his sling and a club. As a soldier he carried a sword and a bow. As a General he had his army and companions who surrounded him. As a King he had his guards and servants to protect him. But he knew that the only true security came from trusting God.

Today, despite all our efforts to maintain security, too many people struggle with loneliness and despair. If we know Christ, our security is guaranteed by the presence of the Holy Spirit: "Now it is God who makes both us and you stand firm in Christ. He anointed us and set his seal of ownership on us and put his Spirit in our hearts as a deposit, guaranteeing what is to come." (2 Corinthians 1:21-22)

We are also secure in the fact that Jesus prays for us. Imagine that! Jesus Christ in-tercedes for you and me! "Who is he that condemns? Christ Jesus, who died—more than that, who was raised to life—is at the right hand of God and is also interceding for us." (Romans 8:34)

Our security is also guaranteed by God's power: "To him who is able to keep you from falling and to present you before his glorious presence without fault and with great joy." (Jude 24)

Finally, our security comes from unity and friendships: "In Christ we, though many, form one body, and each member belongs to all the others." (Romans 12:5)

Are you feeling more secure now? Know that God is faithful, and His love is everlasting. In Him and Him alone do we find real security.

Scripture Reading: Romans 8:31-39

Personal Application:

- What keeps you awake at night? What are your major concerns (worries)? List them here.
- Now, take each one of those items you listed and "Cast all your anxiety [cares] on Him because He cares for you." (1 Peter 5:7)
- Finally, embrace the security Christ freely gives you and thank Him for it.

Week 3, Day 4: A Nation Under Attack

"If my people, who are called by my name, will humble themselves and pray and seek my face and turn from their wicked ways,
then will I hear from heaven and will forgive their sin and will heal their land."
– 2 Chronicles 7:14

As we look upon this nation's history and contemplate its spiritual condition–a question comes to mind: Has there ever been a time in the United States when we have been more removed from following the Judeo/Christian values than today? Are we still "one nation under God"?

If you watch the news or even just flip through the listings of television programs, it's obvious that our country is morally and spiritually under attack. The sanctioned killing of babies, the pollution of our young people through a liberal educational system, legalized drugs, and the celebration of sinful practices has never been more rampant.

I'm typically not an alarmist or pessimist. I usually look for positive biblical solutions to the Satanic attacks on our culture. My focus has been on what we can do to help change our godless culture–one person at a time.

While I continue to pray and hope that our nation will experience a spiritual awakening, the signs of our times remind me of the warning the Apostle Paul shared about "End Times":

But mark this: There will be terrible times in the last days. People will be lovers of themselves, lovers of money, boastful, proud, abusive, disobedient to their parents, ungrateful, unholy, without love, unforgiving, slanderous, without self-control, brutal, not lovers of the good, treacherous, rash, conceited, lovers of pleasure rather than lovers of God—having a form of godliness but denying its power. Have nothing to do with them. (2 Timothy 3:1-5)

In 2 Chronicles 32:1-33:13 we see how God wants us to respond when we are attacked by godless individuals. Throughout their history, Israel and Judah faced threats from surrounding nations. The Assyrians posed an especially dangerous threat. King Hezekiah witnessed the Lord's protection against the Assyrian invasion of Judah.

After preparing to defend themselves, Hezekiah encouraged the Israelites, "Be strong and courageous! Don't be afraid or discouraged because of the King of Assyria or his mighty army, for there is a power far greater on our side! He may have a great army, but they are merely men. We have the Lord our God to help us and to fight our battles for us!" (2 Chronicles 32:8)

My friends, when the sins of our culture get you down, remember the words of the King Hezekiah, "Be strong and courageous!" And pray that God will bring spiritual revival to this land!

Scripture Reading: Joshua 24:14-15

Personal Application:
- What signs do you see in our culture that frighten you?
- How can you make a difference in your home, at work, and within your church and community?

Week 3, Day 5: Money: A Tool or a Purpose?

"Whoever loves money never has enough; whoever loves wealth is never satisfied with their income. This too is meaningless."
– Ecclesiastes 5:10

Money is a wonderful tool. With money we can build a house, purchase food, clothing, and other necessities. Money also enables us to buy other more extravagant things to enjoy. With money we can further the work of the Gospel and bless those in need.

Yes, money is a wonderful thing—if we don't have the pursuit of wealth as our primary focus. Someone once said that more people can be trusted with poverty than those who can handle great wealth. I grew up in a lower-middle class area, yet I never felt poor or disadvantaged.

I feel sorry for those who have never known poverty. When money is plentiful, few find reason to look to God for their needs. They have quickly forgotten that everything we have comes from Him.

When the pursuit of wealth is our goal, money becomes a cruel master. It never satisfies. Solomon may have been the richest man to ever live. He denied himself no pleasure. Yet, he found it all meaningless when that was the goal.

Jesus explained, "No one can serve two masters. Either you will hate the one and love the other, or you will be devoted to the one and despise the other. You cannot serve both God and money." (Matthew 6:24) That warning should scare us, but we dismiss it too readily. We either think Jesus was overstating this danger, or that we're somehow immune from it.

Practically speaking, money has no power. Money is an inanimate object that is neither good nor evil. But our affections towards money determines its hold and power over us. Because of this, God often uses the "money test" to define where our hearts are with respect to Him and money.

Paul warned Timothy, "Those who want to get rich fall into temptation and a trap and into many foolish and harmful desires that plunge people into ruin and destruction." (1 Timothy 6:9) Again, we read that and assume it doesn't apply to us. But the misery that lottery winners experience is legendary.

Enjoy what God has given you and share it freely with others. Thank Him for everything and don't let money be your master. Instead, let it serve you. You be its master.

Scripture Reading: 1 Timothy 6:6-10, 17

Personal Application:

- In prayer before the Lord, assess how you're doing regarding the "money test." To what extent are you serving money rather than it serving you?
- Also, consider your money in terms of a "balance sheet," i.e., how well balanced are you in terms of what you spend, save, and give? What those percentages should be is between you and the Lord.
- If you're married, this would be a great conversation to have with your spouse.

Week 3, Day 6: Dealing with Conflict

"Deliver me, O my God, from the hand of the wicked, from the grasp of evil and cruel men."
– Psalm 71:4

It seems like conflict is always with us, especially within unsettled and unforgiving families. Jacob, the son of Isaac and grandson of Abraham, had many conflicts throughout his life; they seemed to follow him wherever he went.

Conflict with his brother Esau motivated Jacob to flee to the land of his forefathers and search for a wife. But as soon as he aligned himself with his uncle Laban, interpersonal conflict began brewing. And the conflict heightened when Jacob married two of Laban's daughters.

After being swindled by Laban for years and quietly enduring it, Jacob finally had enough and left to travel back to the land of Canaan where his parents were.

But Jacob faced two problems on his way home: his father-in-law who was outraged that Jacob had left with his daughters and grandchildren without saying goodbye; and his brother Esau who had been angry that Jacob had stolen both his inheritance and their father's blessing. As God would have it, both men confronted Jacob in the middle of the desert!

Jacob's meeting with Laban went reasonably well despite some tension. But when Jacob learned that Esau was approaching with 400 men, he feared for his life and the lives of his young family. This would be the first time in twenty years the two brothers had seen each other. Jacob had swindled his brother and would now have to face him without their parents' mediation.

As Esau and his war party approached, Jacob was deeply afraid and distressed, so he considered his options, but they were few. Now, instead of trying to weasel his way out of this confrontation, Jacob dealt with this crisis head on by going to the ultimate Problem Solver—the Great I AM—God. In his prayer to the Lord, Jacob humbled himself and clung to the promise God had made to prosper him and multiply his descendants.

God desires such humility from us. He doesn't promise to take away all our conflicts and troubles, but He will see us through them when we choose to follow Him. And when we go to God with our problems, He delights to surprise us with an answer we never could have imagined in our wildest dreams.

Scripture Reading: Genesis 32:9–12; 33:4-5

Personal Application:
- With whom are you in conflict right now?
- Take this conflict to the Lord in prayer much as Jacob did.
- Then, humbly meet with your opponent and seek reconciliation. "Live in harmony with one another. Do not be proud. Do not repay anyone evil for evil." (Romans 12:16-17)

Week 3, Day 7: Weekly Recap and Prayer

On the seventh day of each week, use the **ACTS** acronym to spend time with the Lord reviewing and assessing your week and praying to God. (**A**=Adoration; **C**=Confession; **T**=Thanksgiving; **S**=Supplication)

First, look back over the previous six days for this week to remind yourself what you read and agreed to. Then, follow the ACTS pattern for prayer below. Finally, use the space below to journal what God is doing in your life and share this with a trusted spiritual partner.

Adoration: Simply spend time in adoration of the Lord. Praise Him and glorify His name. (See 1 Chronicles 29:10-13; Psalm 100; Romans 11:33-36.)

Confession: Confess your sins and shortcomings before God. ("If we confess our sins, he is faithful and just and will forgive us our sins and purify us from all unrighteousness." – 1 John 1:9) To confess (or agree with God) about your sin, implies that you are repentant and desperately want Him to change you.

Thanksgiving: Thank God for what He has done and is doing in your life and the life of your family. Give Him credit, for everything you have comes from Him. (See Psalm 136.)

Supplication: Supplication is just a fancy word for making your requests known to God. Based on the devotions of this past week and the things going on in your life right now, what do you want to ask Him for? "If you, then, though you are evil, know how to give good gifts to your children, how much more will your Father in heaven give good gifts to those who ask Him!" (Matthew 7:11)

Journal: What is God doing in your life right now?

Week 4, Day 1: Tragedy

For many, this past year was filled with tragedy. I see it in the front lines of our city as a volunteer chaplain with the fire and police departments. The number of young people dying from opioids and suicide is alarming. Cancer and heart attacks are claiming too many people far too early in life. And so many people are dealing with loneliness, despair, divorce, and anger.

Our nation is still losing too many young men and women who fight daily for freedom in far-away places. Freak storms and natural disasters have also taken lives and destroyed much property this past year. And my heart still aches for those whose lives are taken by terrorists at home and abroad.

Typically, we view tragedy, hardship, and suffering as something out of the ordinary, as unwanted anomalies. But tragedy is a part of life in our fallen world. Peter wrote, "And the God of all grace, who called you to his eternal glory in Christ, after you have suffered a little while, will himself restore you and make you strong, firm and steadfast." (1 Peter 5:10)

Some years ago, we lost some great men and women when the Columbia Space Shuttle vaporized on its reentry from space. One of those individuals was Col. Mike Anderson, the second African American astronaut. He looked at life with a unique spiritual insight. Col. Anderson was from Spokane, Washington and attended a little local Baptist church not far from our home.

Since his death we have heard a great deal about this man's rich spiritual heritage and abiding faith. When his pastor asked him if he was ever frightened about venturing into outer space, Mike said, "If something were to happen in space, I'm just that much closer to God." He went on to say, "Instead of coming down, I'll just be going up to my home in Glory." That is the kind of attitude and assurance that is ours as we trust the Lord with our lives. God has used Mike's story to touch thousands of lives in our region. It is during times of loss that we feel the comfort of prayers and acts of kindness from loving fellow believers.

Scripture reminds us, "Praise be to the God and Father of our Lord Jesus Christ, the Father of compassion and the God of all comfort, who comforts us in all our troubles, so that we can comfort those in any trouble with the comfort we ourselves receive from God." (2 Corinthians 1:3–4)

God allows tragedy to interrupt our lives so He can comfort us. This is part of God's strategy in maturing us. God is in the business of developing comforters. And the best comforter is one who has struggled with pain or sorrow and has emerged from that experience victorious.

Scripture Reading: 2 Corinthians 1:3-11

Personal Application:

- In what ways has God used tragedy in your life to display His glory and mature you?
- Who do you know who is currently suffering tragedy? How might your story comfort them?

Week 4, Day 2: Have We Lost Our Way?

"My people have committed two sins: They have forsaken me, the spring of living water, and have dug their own cisterns, broken cisterns that cannot hold water."
— Jeremiah 2:13

Our culture has all but abandoned God and His Word, the Bible. In its place, they have crafted what they think are new social norms under the guise of being "progressive." In reality, these are old norms that are socially, morally, and spiritually *regressive*.

In keeping with the downward progression of sin and a departure from God, our country is following the pattern described in Romans 1. We've suppressed the truth about God exchanging it for a lie. We worship the creation instead of our Creator. We've chased after our own lustful passions calling what's good evil and what's evil good, and even celebrate our sinfulness. We've become depraved and foolish.

Yet there is still hope. Paul wrote to Timothy, "I urge, then, first of all, that petitions, prayers, intercessions and thanksgiving be made for all people—for kings and all those in authority, that we may live peaceful and quiet lives in all godliness and holiness." (1 Timothy 2:1-2)

Why should we pray for those who would lead us more towards a godless society? Because God is still in the business of doing miracles and changing hearts. In the Scripture, we find a good example of how God can work even in what seems to be a godless environment. After King Hezekiah's death, his son, Manasseh took over as King.

The list of evils perpetrated by Manasseh makes us shudder. Not only did he worship idols and desecrate the Temple, he sacrificed his own children to pagan gods. He led his whole nation astray and paid no attention when God spoke to him. Yet, when Manasseh hit rock bottom, was captured by his enemy, shackled and led around by a ring in his nose, he cried out "in deep distress" to God Almighty and not the pagan gods he had worshipped.

King Manasseh humbled himself in reverence to the "God of his ancestors." And God responded with forgiveness and restored him to his throne. Because Manasseh finally came to honor the Lord as the only true God, Manasseh's life was changed. God extended His grace to this man whose great sins had created negativity for His nation.

Thanks to this example, we know God will forgive any sin if there is heartfelt repentance. And God can even change the heart of a whole nation. What is our part in this? To pray for our leaders and live exemplary lives ourselves instead of being led into the sins of our culture.

Scripture Reading: Matthew 5:13-15

Personal Application:
- In your daily prayer with God, pray for our country's leaders.
- If you have given in to sinful practices, repent from those and pursue Christ.
- Lead your family and those around you by your example of what it means to follow and obey Jesus Christ.

Week 4, Day 3: Great Provisions

"And my God shall supply all your needs according to His glorious riches in
Christ Jesus."
— Philippians 4:19

I just met with a dear friend of mine who does medical missions all over the world. He recently went to war-torn Lebanon to provide medical services to those impacted by the conflict there. My heart aches for the families affected by acts of terrorism or war or natural disasters — especially for the children. Starving for love and affection, they weep and long for the warm embrace of departed family members.

Such was the case after World War II. Hundreds of thousands of orphans were in dire need of shelter, food, medical attention, and love. At the end of the war, the Allies developed special camps for traumatized youth. The children developed and grew with the nutritious meals and good care they received. But in one of the camps, the officials became concerned because the children couldn't sleep. Despite enough food and attention, they lay awake at night, staring at the ceiling.

Mental care professionals were brought in to study the children and determine why they weren't sleeping. Eventually, the doctors came up with an idea. Every night, when the little children were put to bed, someone would come down the row of beds and place a piece of bread in their out-stretched hands. The children would tighten their grip around that bread as if to embrace it for the future.

In a few days the kids were all sleeping through the night! The doctors realized that by giving them hope for tomorrow they were able to sleep in peace.

God has given every believer that same assurance by placing His promises in our hearts and minds. "So do not worry, saying, 'What shall we eat?' or 'What shall we drink?' or 'What shall we wear?' For the pagans run after all these things, and your heavenly Father knows that you need them. But seek first his kingdom and his righteousness, and all these things will be given to you as well." (Matthew 6:31-33)

And David wrote in Psalm 4:8, "In peace I will lie down and sleep, for you alone, Lord, make me dwell in safety."

As we lie down at night, I pray that the hope we cling to is firmly planted in the great provisions of our Heavenly Father and our eternal salvation through Jesus Christ!

Scripture Reading: Matthew 6:25-34

Personal Application:
- What has been weighing heavily on your mind and heart lately?
- In what ways has God faithfully provided for you in the past?
- What specific actions can you take to align your life with Jesus' words in Matthew 6:31-33?

Week 4, Day 4: The Blood of Christ Is Sufficient

The following story suggests some good food for thought when it comes to forgiving and forgetting. Aren't we glad our Heavenly Father has forgotten our transgressions because of the sacrifice Christ made? Praise God!

What an awesome reminder...

One night in a church service, a young woman felt the tug of God at her heart. She responded to God's call and accepted Jesus as her Lord and Savior. The woman had a very rough past, involving alcohol, drugs, and prostitution, but the change in her was evident.

As time went on, she became a faithful member of the church. She eventually became involved in the ministry, teaching young children. It was not very long until this faithful lady had caught the eye and heart of the pastor's son. Their relationship grew and they began to make wedding plans.

This is when the problems began. You see, about one half of the church did not think that a woman with a past such as hers was suitable for a pastor's son. The church began to argue and fight about the matter. So, they decided to have a meeting. As the people made their arguments and tensions increased, the meeting was getting completely out of hand.

The young woman became very upset about all the things being brought up about her past. As she began to cry, the pastor's son stood to speak. He could not bear the pain it was causing his wife-to-be. He said, "My fiancée's past is not what is on trial here. What you are questioning is the ability of the blood of Jesus to wash away sin. Today you have put the blood of Jesus on trial. So, does it wash away sin or not?"

The whole church began to weep as they realized that they had been slandering the blood of the Lord Jesus Christ.

Too often, even as Christians, we bring up the past and use it as a weapon against our brothers and sisters. Forgiveness is a very foundational part of the Gospel of our Lord Jesus Christ. If the blood of Jesus does not cleanse the other person completely, then it cannot cleanse us completely. If that is the case, then we are all doomed! Let's remember the old song, "What can wash way my sins? Nothing but the blood of Jesus!"

"We have been made holy through the sacrificed of the body of Jesus Christ once for all." (Hebrews 10:10)

Scripture Reading: 1 Corinthians 6:7-11

Personal Application:
- How does it make you feel knowing that the blood of Jesus Christ has cleansed you from all sin?
- Spend time thanking the Lord for His gracious and complete forgiveness.
- Who else could you encourage with the message of today's devotional? Pass it along.

Week 4, Day 5: The Faith of Todd Beamer

"I don't think we're going to get out of this thing. I'm going to have to go out on faith." This was the voice of Todd Beamer, the passenger who led the charge against the terrorists who hijacked United Flight 93, that crashed in the Pennsylvania countryside on September 11, 2001.

The whole world knows how brave Beamer and his fellow passengers that day were. But not everyone knows what buttressed that bravery: his faith in Jesus Christ.

Todd died as he lived, a faithful follower of Jesus. In an article titled "The Real Story of Flight 93," Newsweek reveals gripping new details from the actual transcripts of the now-recovered cockpit voice recorder. "Todd had been afraid," Newsweek relates. "More than once, he cried out for his Savior." After passengers were herded to the back of the jet, Beamer called the GTE Customer Center in Oakbrook, Illinois. He told supervisor Lisa Jefferson about the hijacking. The passengers were planning to jump the terrorists, he said. And then he asked her to pray with him.

As Newsweek relates, "Beamer kept a Lord's Prayer bookmark in his Tom Clancy novel, but he didn't need any prompting. He began to recite the ancient litany, and Jefferson joined him: "Our Father which art in heaven, hallowed be Thy name..."

As they finished, Beamer added, "Jesus, help me." And then, Beamer and his fellow passenger prayed a prayer that has comforted millions down through the centuries. The prayer that David wrote in a time of great anguish: "The Lord is my shepherd, I shall not want... Yea, though I walk through the valley of the shadow of death, I will fear no evil..."

And then Todd's famous last words: "Are you guys ready? Let's roll."

We now know from the cockpit voice recorder that Beamer and other passengers wrestled with the hijackers and forced the plane to crash into the ground, killing themselves, but foiling what was believed to have been the hijackers' plan to fly Flight 93 into the Capitol or the White House.

As Christians, we know that God can bring good out of evil. In Todd Beamer, the world witnesses a faith that held up in extreme fear. A faith that is even now comforting his widow and two sons. God answered Todd's prayer and delivered him safely home... to Heaven.

Most of us will never have to demonstrate the type of courage Todd did in overcoming the terrorists on Flight 93. But hopefully all of us will cry out to Jesus for help when any need arises.

Scripture Reading: Psalm 91

Personal Application:
- Todd Beamer didn't act alone. Although unarmed, through his faith and his leadership he rallied the people on Flight 93 to fight. You may not find yourself in such an awful situation, but in what ways are you leading others to follow you as you follow Christ?
- Courage is contagious. "Be strong and very courageous." (Joshua 1:7) Trust God in all things.

Week 4, Day 6: A Covey of Quail

"Be kind and compassionate to one another, forgiving each other,
just as in Christ God forgave you."
— Ephesians 4:32

I have the privilege of traveling around the country and working with numerous congregations. There are many folks working with a harmonious spirit to reach others for God's Kingdom. It's exciting and rewarding to work with such groups.

Unfortunately, some churches are known for their bickering and argumentative nature. The people within these churches tend to focus on each other's faults rather than building a loving environment to reach their communities.

Whether it's a church, a work environment, a sports team, or a family, we can labor more effectively with unity, concentrating on building up, rather than tearing down each other. With that thought in mind, I'm reminded of an old legend about a covey of quail.

The quail would have been happy except for their enemy. The hunter imitated a quail call and gathered the covey together. As they loitered about, he threw his net over them. The birds struggled but to no avail. The hunter placed them into his hunting basket and carried them off to market.

One wise quail who had watched all this offered, "Brothers, I have a plan. If the hunter casts his net over us, we should each put our head into a section of net and begin to flap our wings. Together we can lift the net and fly away with it." All the birds agreed. When the fowler threw his net over the covey, they organized their efforts and flew off with his net.

Several months later the hunter decided to again try his luck at capturing some game to sell at the market. After the luring call was given, the birds came together. This time the birds quarreled with one another over who was lifting the most and which bird would be in the middle of the net. The fowler took advantage of their distraction and quickly gathered up his net, capturing all the birds.

At times all our finger-pointing and bickering ends up doing us all in and nothing is accomplished. If we find ourselves constantly amidst controversy and strife, we need to take a good hard look at ourselves. What are we really fighting over? How is God being glorified?

Jesus sent us on a mission to seek and save the lost. Let's work together in unity, through Christ's love and grace… especially in the church.

Scripture Reading: Ephesians 4:25-32

Personal Application:
- Think about your relationships. Is there anyone with whom you've had an unresolved disagreement? If so, pray for them and go to them to make things right.
- In what situation right now could you proactively cultivate unity, peace, and kindness?

Week 4, Day 7: Weekly Recap and Prayer

On the seventh day of each week, use the **ACTS** acronym to spend time with the Lord reviewing and assessing your week and praying to God. (**A**=Adoration; **C**=Confession; **T**=Thanksgiving; **S**=Supplication)

First, look back over the previous six days for this week to remind yourself what you read and agreed to. Then, follow the ACTS pattern for prayer below. Finally, use the space below to journal what God is doing in your life and share this with a trusted spiritual partner.

Adoration: Simply spend time in adoration of the Lord. Praise Him and glorify His name. (See 1 Chronicles 29:10-13; Psalm 100; Romans 11:33-36.)

Confession: Confess your sins and shortcomings before God. ("If we confess our sins, he is faithful and just and will forgive us our sins and purify us from all unrighteousness." – 1 John 1:9) To confess (or agree with God) about your sin, implies that you are repentant and desperately want Him to change you.

Thanksgiving: Thank God for what He has done and is doing in your life and the life of your family. Give Him credit, for everything you have comes from Him. (See Psalm 136.)

Supplication: Supplication is just a fancy word for making your requests known to God. Based on the devotions of this past week and the things going on in your life right now, what do you want to ask Him for? "If you, then, though you are evil, know how to give good gifts to your children, how much more will your Father in heaven give good gifts to those who ask Him!" (Matthew 7:11)

Journal: What is God doing in your life right now?

Week 5, Day 1: The Pike & Perseverance

"The testing of your faith develops perseverance." – James 1:3

I love the spring season. Our weather in the Northwest doesn't permit much fishing in the winter. On a recent trip I landed one of the biggest pike I've ever caught. It weighed about 15 pounds and put up a good fight as it straightened the hooks on my small bass lure.

The pike is a unique predator. It has a prodigious appetite for live bait and is especially fond of minnows. Its snake-like body and razor-sharp teeth allow it to slither through shallow water scooping up anything in its path.

While conducting some research on this species, I found an interesting story. A person had a large aquarium that served as a home for an adult pike. The researcher noticed that every time he put minnows in the tank the pike would quickly gobble them up. As part of an experiment, the investigator decided to slip a plate of glass into the tank separating the pike from the area where he would introduce the baitfish. He then placed some minnows on the side away from the pike.

The pike immediately swam into the glass in a desperate attempt to capture the minnows. Time after time the pike hit the glass until he finally gave up. The fish apparently concluded that the minnows were unattainable. A few days later the researcher removed the glass from the tank and allowed the minnows to freely swim about. Amazingly the pike did not molest them. The investigator realized that the pike could starve to death while being surrounded by abundant amounts of food.

This illustration reminds me of a few folks I know who give up on their goals and dreams too quickly. They quit the fight because they feel that their vision is unattainable. Dear friend, don't give up! The writer of Hebrews reminds us to run the race with perseverance (Hebrews 12:1). We are encouraged to "Watch your life and doctrine closely. Persevere in them, because if you do, you will save both yourself and others." (1 Timothy 4:16)

Finally, Scripture tells us that if we are in the will of God and persevere, we will receive the reward (Hebrews 10:36). Sometimes the reward is tangible and measurable. There are many incidents where the prize is more related to building great character in others and ourselves. Today, I encourage you to keep on keepin' on and don't give up.

Scripture Reading: Hebrews 10:32-39

Personal Application:
- What are the challenges you are currently facing? Is God telling you not to quit? When the going gets tough what can you do to better persevere?
- Are there situations when it is appropriate to quit? How do you determine that?
- Besides the Word and prayer, in what other ways can you find the encouragement to persevere?

Week 5, Day 2: Consoling those Who Grieve

One of the many privileges we have as followers of Christ is to help those going through difficulties by standing with them. When the best friend of one of my board members died, I consoled him. And after sharing my condolences, this man asked for any thoughts I could give him regarding the address he was preparing for the funeral.

I suggested that he might describe the promises Jesus gave His disciples before His crucifixion (John 14). For those who grieve and feel the sting of death Christ reminds us:

- The Peace that He Provides: "Let not your heart be troubled"
- The Place He Prepares: "I go and prepare a place for you, I will come again, and receive you to Myself."
- The Path He Prescribes: "I am the way, the truth and the life, no one comes to the Father except through me."

I've also learned that sometimes in the face of extreme grief, especially with the loss of a loved one, there are no words to comfort. Instead, we need to empathize with the grieving ones and express love to them. Jesus did this when his friend Lazarus died.

In their grief, both Lazarus' sisters agonized over the fact that Jesus had not been there to heal him. "Lord, if You had been here, my brother would not have died." (John 11:21 & 32) One can't help but sense a hint of blame, or at least an unspoken question, "Why, Lord?"

But notice Jesus' response, "When Jesus saw her weeping, and the Jews who had come along with her also weeping, He was deeply moved in spirit and troubled. 'Where have you laid him?' he asked. 'Come and see, Lord,' they replied. Jesus wept." (John 11:33-35)

The fact that Jesus was deeply moved in spirit and troubled and then wept is even more amazing because He knew He would raise Lazarus from the dead in the next few moments. This incident shows how deeply Jesus identifies with us and our sorrow and grief. He knows how to comfort us, and we need to learn from Him in comforting others in their grief.

We also see the depth of Jesus' compassion and empathy for those who were sick in that He often touched them. He even touched a leprous man. When and with whom it's appropriate, putting your arm around someone, taking their hand, or placing your hand on their shoulder can express more compassion than many words.

Scripture Reading: John 11:1-44

Personal Application:
- Who has comforted you through grief or sorrow in the past? What can you learn from them?
- Who do you know right now that is grieving or suffering and in need of compassion?
- Pray for that person and look for an opportunity to comfort them in their grief or hurt.

Week 5, Day 3: Do You Believe in Miracles?

"Through faith in the name of Jesus, this man was healed—and you know how crippled he was before. Faith in Jesus' name has healed him before your very eyes."
— Acts 3:16 (NLT)

In this fast-paced, high-tech world some people have forgotten that God is in the business of making miracles. Mankind has explored the far reaches of the universe and the depths of the seas. We have modified DNA and created artificial parts for the human body. Through technology, we can supply an endless stream of information and artificial intelligence. We've become self-reliant.

But the reality is, we still can't create miracles. We still get into situations where we're just stuck. God, who created all the physical systems in the universe, is not bound by them. What man sees as impossible; God sees as possible. Before we come to a relationship with the living God, we describe unplanned situations as "chance" or "coincidence." As believers, we should look for God's hand in the unbelievable, impossible, and unimaginable.

Too often we let our own logic, rather than God's Spirit, take control of our lives. How many times do we miss the opportunity for a miracle because we're determined to "fix it"? The prophet Isaiah had a reply for people who thought they could work their own miracles:

"Therefore once more I will astound these people with wonder upon wonder; the wisdom of the wise will perish, the intelligence of the intelligent will vanishes." (Isaiah 29:14) God is amazingly creative! He works outside the realm of normal reasoning. There's no boundary to His love, His power, or His ability.

Still, during our personal storms, it is sometimes difficult to remember that God can handle it. We too often let fear take a foothold in our thinking. The opposite of fear is faith—the faith that ultimately builds courage.

Ask those who have been miraculously healed of cancer, those who have conquered their fears, addictions, and emotional issues, or farmers and ranchers who continually see God's miracles from the soil. Ask moms and dads who have witnessed the miracle of birth.

Remember the miracles in your own life…and those reported to us in the Bible. "Remember the wonders he has done, his miracles, and the judgments he pronounced." (Psalm 105:5)

Today, through the power of the Holy Spirit, Jesus continues to heal people. He heals bodies, marriages, broken hearts, financial messes… you name it! He is still performing miracles.

Scripture Reading: Ephesians 3:14-21

Personal Application:
- When and where have you experienced a miracle of God in your life? Who might be encouraged by hearing about it? Thank God again for that miracle and share it with someone.
- Jesus warned us not to seek miracles but to seek Him. At the same time, we trust God for too little. What would you like to trust Him for right now?

Week 5, Day 4: Can You Hear God?

"Be still and know that I am God."
— Psalm 46:10a

Why do people like the outdoors so much? What is the lure of hunting, fishing, and hiking? For many of us, the serenity of an outdoor experience offers precious, and mostly uninterrupted, time to think through our problems, let our minds unwind, get caught up on prayers, and simply listen to God.

The distractions of our busy lives that are often filled with chaos seem to vanish in the calmness of an outdoor environment. Scripture tells us that Christ spent many hours in quietness. His meditation time was special and allowed Him opportunity to commune with His Heavenly Father. "Jesus often withdrew to lonely places and prayed." (Luke 5:16)

To hear God, we must be quiet and let Him do the talking. Prayer is not simply reading off a list of requests. Calm and quietness are essential to listening. If I'm too busy, I won't hear. If I spend night after night watching television, and then try to listen, I find my mind jammed with carnal interference and His voice is buried under an avalanche of clamor.

The necessary calm and silence can be found in our great outdoors, on a living-room sofa late at night, or at the kitchen table early in the morning. The place isn't important; the decibel scale is.

The fact that you're going through this devotional tells me that solitude and spending time with the Lord is already very important to you. I commend you for it! Keep it up.

In my own life, I find that I need a combination of disciplined routine and spontaneous variety. What I mean by that is that I need the disciplined routine to make my quiet times with the Lord a priority habit in my life.

However, I find that a routine can sometimes become mindless. E.g., my eyes are reading God's Word, but my mind isn't engaged. Or perhaps I've fallen into praying the same things every day, so that I find myself praying mindlessly. Shaking up my schedule or routine a bit from time to time adds freshness and vitality to the time I spend with the Lord.

Also, depending on what stage of life you're in, taking time to be "still" before the Lord can be a challenge. But it's a discipline worth pursuing. I encourage you to make time to be quiet in the presence of the Lord. Enjoy His company. Listen to Him and share your innermost thoughts, desires, and requests with Him.

Scripture Reading: Mark 1:35; 9:2-7; Luke 6:12-13

Personal Application:

- As I mentioned above, the fact that you're reading this devotional indicates that you keep a quiet time with God. Let me encourage you to always observe your time with the Lord clear-headed and with the intent to meet with God and listen to His voice.
- What has God been showing you lately from His Word? Share this with your spouse or a trusted friend.

Week 5, Day 5: No Greater Love

A friend of mine shared the following story about sacrifice—a sacrifice of love.

After a forest fire in Yellowstone National Park, forest rangers began their trek up a mountain to assess the inferno's damage. One ranger found a bird literally petrified in ashes, perched statuesquely on the ground at the base of a tree.

Somewhat sickened by this eerie sight, he knocked over the bird with a stick. But when the bird toppled over, three tiny chicks scurried from under their dead mother's wings.

The loving mother, keenly aware of impending disaster, had carried her offspring to the base of the tree and gathered them under her wings. Perhaps she instinctively knew that the toxic smoke would rise.

She could have flown to safety herself but had refused to abandon her babies. When the blaze arrived and the heat singed her small body, she remained steadfast. And because she had been willing to die, those under the cover of her wings had lived.

Of course, the supreme act of love in the universe is when Jesus Christ willingly gave His life so that we might live. Paul puts it like this: "You see, at just the right time, when we were still powerless, Christ died for the ungodly. Very rarely will anyone die for a righteous person, though for a good person someone might possibly dare to die. But God demonstrates his own love for us in this: While we were still sinners, Christ died for us." (Romans 5:6-8)

By God's grace we are recipients of Christ's sacrificial love. And by trusting in Him, He washes us from all our sin, makes us righteous and reconciles us to the Father. But His work in us doesn't end there.

Jesus said, "My command is this: Love each other as I have loved you. Greater love has no one than this: to lay down one's life for ones' friends." (John 15:12-13)

We are to love each other with the same sacrificial love Jesus demonstrated for us. And if you're married, Christ's command especially extends to us regarding our wives. "Husbands, love your wives, just as Christ loved the church and gave Himself up for her." (Ephesians 5:25)

Truthfully, it's one thing to ponder the possibility of laying down one's life for a loved one. For most of us, we'll never be called upon to sacrifice our lives in death. But it's a totally different thing to *live* sacrificially for others right now. Yet, Jesus says, "Love each other as I have loved you."

Scripture Reading: 1 John 4:7-12

Personal Application:

- To whom and in what ways do you need to demonstrate sacrificial love?
- Love is more than an emotion; it expresses itself in actions. What actions will you take today to love others sacrificially?

Week 5, Day 6: Unashamed of the Gospel

"If anyone is ashamed of Me and My words in this adulterous and sinful generation, the Son of Man will be ashamed of him when he comes in his Father's glory with the holy angels."
— Mark 8:38

Most of us are neither ashamed nor embarrassed to be called Americans. Many of us proudly display flags or other symbols, proclaiming our allegiance to this fine nation. We wear hats that advertise our favorite places and jerseys that tout our favorite teams. Our coffee mugs advertise favorite haunts and our car bumpers often tell all who follow about our hobbies, foods, and political views.

Oh, we're proud to "love chocolate," vote for so and so, and have a kid at such and such school. We're proud of visiting Alaska, eating at Clyde's Steakhouse, and driving a vehicle. But are we proud to be Christians? Now, I'm not promoting Christian bumper stickers, hats, mugs, flags, shirts, or pens. But really, how do you identify with the cause of serving Christ?

Years ago, I received an email from a friend that reminds me of how we should identify with Christ:

The Apostle Paul was converted to Christianity when he met Jesus on the road to Damascus. As a result of becoming a devoted follower of Christ and a passionate proclaimer of the gospel, he suffered innumerable trials including prison.

In spite of all that happened to him, he was so convinced of the reality of Jesus Christ and the gospel message that he boldly said, "I am not ashamed of the gospel (God's good news of salvation) because it is the power of God for the salvation of everyone who believes." (Romans 1:16)

Sadly, today there are many folks in places who are being terribly persecuted and even killed for their faith in Jesus Christ. May those of us in the free world continually remember those who are suffering for Jesus today.

I wish to stand tall when confronted by others for my faith. Scripture reminds us that we have a responsibility to identify with Him whom we love and serve…not in the clothes we wear or slogans we carry, but in the words we speak and in our actions. Jesus Christ humbly died for us so that we can proudly follow Him.

Scripture Reading: Philippians 1:27-30

Personal Application:

- Paul urges us, "So do not be ashamed of the testimony about our Lord or of me his prisoner. Rather, join with me in suffering for the gospel, by the power of God." (2 Timothy 1:8)
- In what ways and under what circumstances can you take a bold stand for Jesus Christ today?

Week 5, Day 7: Weekly Recap and Prayer

On the seventh day of each week, use the **ACTS** acronym to spend time with the Lord reviewing and assessing your week and praying to God. (**A**=Adoration; **C**=Confession; **T**=Thanksgiving; **S**=Supplication)

First, look back over the previous six days for this week to remind yourself what you read and agreed to. Then, follow the ACTS pattern for prayer below. Finally, use the space below to journal what God is doing in your life and share this with a trusted spiritual partner.

Adoration: Simply spend time in adoration of the Lord. Praise Him and glorify His name. (See 1 Chronicles 29:10-13; Psalm 100; Romans 11:33-36.)

Confession: Confess your sins and shortcomings before God. ("If we confess our sins, he is faithful and just and will forgive us our sins and purify us from all unrighteousness." – 1 John 1:9) To confess (or agree with God) about your sin, implies that you are repentant and desperately want Him to change you.

Thanksgiving: Thank God for what He has done and is doing in your life and the life of your family. Give Him credit, for everything you have comes from Him. (See Psalm 136.)

Supplication: Supplication is just a fancy word for making your requests known to God. Based on the devotions of this past week and the things going on in your life right now, what do you want to ask Him for? "If you, then, though you are evil, know how to give good gifts to your children, how much more will your Father in heaven give good gifts to those who ask Him!" (Matthew 7:11)

Journal: What is God doing in your life right now?

Week 6, Day 1: Six-Inch Christians

"And we know that in all things God works for the good of those who love him, who have been called according to his purpose." – Romans 8:28

Did you know that if you catch a small shark and confine it, it will remain a size proportionate to the aquarium? Sharks can be six inches long yet fully matured! But if you turn them loose in the ocean, they grow to their normal length of many feet.

We find the same phenomenon with Christians. Many believers remain six-inch Christians confined by the limits of their small thinking and small faith. Too often we underestimate God and the purpose and power with which He has bestowed upon us. We limit our involvement in God's work and shrink behind disappointment and discouragement. We forget God's promises, His faithfulness, and simply who we are! We forget that He lives within us by His Spirit.

The truth is, we are God's children: "See what great love the Father has lavished on us, that we should be called children of God! And that is what we are!" (1 John 3:1) Think about it, we are children of Almighty God! But sometimes we act like we're powerless and without God's presence and promises.

We are also His servants: "Whatever you do, work at it with all your heart, as working for the Lord, not for human masters, since you know that you will receive an inheritance from the Lord as a reward. It is the Lord Christ you are serving." (Colossians 3:23-24)

I don't know about you, but some of the most important words I could ever hear from my Lord are, "Well done, good and faithful servant! You have been faithful with a few things; I will put you in charge of many things. Come and share your master's happiness!'" (Matthew 25:21)

We are also His soldiers: "You then, my son, be strong in the grace that is in Christ Jesus. And the things you have heard me say in the presence of many witnesses entrust to reliable men who will also be qualified to teach others. Endure hardship with us like a good soldier of Christ Jesus." (2 Timothy 2:1-3) Let's put on the armor of God (Ephesians 6:10-17) and fight the good fight. If ever there was a time to stand up for our faith and values, it is now.

If you have been a "six-inch Christian," bust out! Don't be afraid to be bold in your faith. God has big plans for you. He created you for a great purpose. Be curious and courageous about all God has in store for you and expect great things!

Scripture Reading: Ephesians 3:14-21

Personal Application:
- To what extent have you limited your growth as a follower of Jesus by small thinking and little faith? Memorize Ephesians 3:21 or Jeremiah 29:11 and take them as personal promises to you.
- After committing your verse to memory, spend time alone with God meditating on the truths in that verse and thanking God for His work in and through you.

Week 6, Day 2: The Secret to Happiness

Jesus told His disciples, "If any of you wants to be my follower, you must turn from your selfish ways, take up your cross, and follow me. If you try to hang on to your life, you will lose it. But if you give up your life for my sake, you will save it. And what do you benefit if you gain the whole world but lose your own soul? Is anything worth more than your soul?"
– Matthew 16:24-26 (NLT)

Many people are on a quest to find what the world defines as "success" and "personal happiness." Our culture provides countless models of wealthy, famous, well-dressed people who project that if we can just become like them, we'll be happy.

But what Hollywood and professional sports often project as "winners" are often unhappy and unfulfilled people. Look at the suicide rate, drug abuse, and divorce rate among the rich and famous. It exceeds that of the general population.

The Bible has a different message. It says that we find happiness by following Christ into the life He has planned for us. The way to be happy is really to be joy-filled. Happiness is a fickle emotion that comes and goes with our circumstances. Joy is a character trait we acquire by living in the Holy Spirit (Galatians 5:22-25).

The way to be a joy-filled person is found in the above Bible verses. Jesus gets right to the point by saying to us, "If you give up your life for My sake, you will save it." He wasn't talking only about physical death, (although in some parts of the world, that is a reality for believers); He was telling us that we must submit to God our will, our plans, and our future.

The all-knowing, all-powerful God has a special plan for each of us. When we gratefully walk in the direction He has planned, we will find fulfillment, joy, and true happiness. That doesn't mean that we can't set goals and work toward attaining them. Instead, we make our plans and set our goals always seeking God's guidance and walking obediently as each step becomes clear.

Let's seek a life that models joy by remembering what the Psalmist told us, "Light shines on the godly, and joy on those whose hearts are right." (Psalm 97:11 NLT) And, "Take delight in the Lord, and He will give you your heart's desires." (Psalm 37:4 NLT)

Scripture Reading: Philippians 4:4-7

Personal Application:
- What are the things in your life that bring true joy? A joyful heart is focused upon things like family, friends, and things with eternal value. In what ways do those things bring you joy?
- When you are struggling to find joy in your life, remember that your past doesn't define your future – through the grace and direction of God you define it.
- Christ reminds us to meditate upon His Word: "The joy of the Lord is your strength." (Nehemiah 8:10) "I have told you this so that my joy may be in you and that your joy may be complete." (John 15:11) "May the God of hope fill you with all joy and peace in believing." (Romans 15:13)

Week 6, Day 3: The Lure

Among my many outdoor pursuits is fly fishing. Northern Idaho has numerous Blue-Ribbon streams that cover the area like a large spider web. Fly fishing is considered by most anglers as the ultimate experience in luring a fish to take your bait.

Angling is as old as mankind. We even find several places in the Bible that speak about angling. One time, Jesus asked Peter to go to the lake and cast his line into the water. Jesus told him that the first fish he caught would have a four-drachma coin in its mouth. Peter was to take the coin and pay the annual temple tax for both Jesus and himself (Matthew 17:24-27).

In the second-century AD, the Greek writer Aelian wrote about a way to catch fish. "Between Boroca and Thessalonica runs a river called the Astraeus, and in it, there are fish with spotted skins" (most likely trout). He described a lure to fishermen of that day "to help snare the fish, by which we get the better of them."

Aelian fastened a piece of red wool around a hook and attached two small feathers to it. Apparently, the fish were very attracted to the color and movement believing it was a tasty insect. (From *On the Nature of Animals*.)

Today, nearly 2,000 years later, fishermen are still using this lure (fly). It is called the Red Hackle. The fly continues to fool fish into believing they are swallowing a meal, when it's just a pretty imitation.

In this world, the devil is the great imitator. He constantly tries to lure people away from God and true sustenance by offering a cheap counterfeit. His fake lures come in the form of false religions or false doctrine. And like the fisherman, he often combines a bit of real bait with the phony to make it more alluring.

Some of Satan's bait is blatantly false: pornography, sex, alcohol, drugs, fleshly lusts, etc. He uses anything to lure people away from the safety of God's care (Matthew 13:22).

Pursuit of riches is another of the devil's ploys. "Those who want to get rich fall into temptation and a trap and into many foolish and harmful desires that plunge people into ruin and destruction. For the love of money is a root of all kinds of evil. Some people, eager for money, have wandered from the faith and pierced themselves with many griefs." (1 Timothy 6:9-10)

Paul warns us "Do not give the devil a foothold," and, "Put on the full armor of God, so that you can take your stand against the devil's schemes." (Ephesians 4:27 & 6:11)

Scripture Reading: 1 Peter 5:6-9

Personal Application:
- One of the best ways to identify the counterfeit is to be thoroughly intimate with the real thing. Spend time in God's Word regularly alone and with other followers of Christ.
- In what areas of your life is Satan most likely to try to lure you away from the Lord? Share this with a trusted confidant and ask him to pray for you.

Week 6, Day 4: Why Men Go to Church

Some years ago, my friend David Murrow published the book, *Why Men Hate Going to Church.** In his book David explained:

The modern church is having trouble reaching men. Women comprise more than 60 percent of the typical adult congregation on any given Sunday. At least one-fifth of married women regularly worship without their husbands. There are quite a few single women but hardly any single men in church.

Tough, earthy, working guys rarely come to church. High achievers, alpha males, risk takers, and visionaries are in short supply. Fun-lovers and adventurers are also underrepresented in church.

The good news is that men desperately need what only a loving, nurturing, Christ-centered church can offer. Through the ministry of the church, the following needs of a man can be met:

- To know God and really feel His unconditional love (Romans 1:20)
- To find rest for his weary soul (Matthew 11:28-29)
- To fellowship with other men who face similar issues (2 Corinthians 1:4)
- To hear God's Word proclaimed in both practical and personal ways (Psalm 23:4)
- To feel inspired, encouraged, empowered, and understood (1 Thessalonians 4:18)
- To seek refuge from the world's problems (Psalm 46:1)
- To find ways to deal with the daily issues he faces (James 1:2)
- To find appropriate ways to model Christ's love to his family (Matthew 19:19)
- To receive moral and religious instruction (Psalm 32:8)
- To learn how to be a strong spiritual leader (Ephesians 4:11-13)
- To find godly mentors and role models (Titus 2:1-7)
- To exercise their spiritual gifts (1 Corinthians 12:7)
- To lead his wife and children in following Jesus (1 Timothy 4:12)
- To worship God with other followers of Christ (Ephesians 2:21-22)

Fortunately, pioneering churches and parachurch organizations are enjoying remarkable success in reaching men for Christ. New forms of worship and ministry tailored to the needs of men are springing up in the unlikeliest places. Some of the fastest-growing churches in America are also those most successful in reaching men.

Scripture Reading: Hebrews 11:19-25

Personal Application:
- Look through the bulleted list above and check the top five or six reasons that especially draw you to church.
- In what ways is God speaking to you personally through today's devotional?

*[David Murrow, *Why Men Hate Going to Church* (Nashville: Thomas Nelson, 2005), 5-8]

Week 6, Day 5: Keep Your Eye on the Ball

Many of us are captivated by watching sports. Count the number of channels and programs that feature the actions and performance of athletes. Slow-motion replays and exceptional commentators explore every nuance of a play and point out distractions that cause a player to miss a catch or error in some way.

Frequently, we hear a football commentator or coach talk about a player missing a catch or handoff because he took his eyes off the ball. A good receiver "looks the ball" into his hands—his gaze is so fixed on the spiraling leather that he's oblivious to the possibility of a defender hitting him.

With a similar focus, the running back charges to the line of scrimmage, relying upon the quarterback's eyes and timing to carefully spot the ball into the pocket created with the runner's arms or hands. If for a split second he allows the movements or motions of the defender to distract him the ball could be dropped.

It is critical to the ultimate success of a football player to have excellent hand-eye coordination. Even defensive linemen have special eyes-on-the-ball drills to help them become better focused. This split-second difference in a lineman picking up the snap can make the difference in delivering the attack or waiting for it to come to him. A lineman's catlike quickness can be a positive factor only when he fixes his gaze on the ball.

In short, every player must put himself on high alert, keep his eyes on the ball, and anticipate what will happen next. In the same way, when it comes to Jesus' return, we too are in danger of "missing the ball."

In Mark 13, Jesus spoke to His disciples about His return and the events surrounding it. By way of analogy, we might say that He lectured His disciples (us) much like a football coach would before a Superbowl game. Here are some of the warnings Jesus gave us:

"But about that day or hour no one knows, not even the angels in heaven, nor the Son, but only the Father. Be on guard! Be alert! You do not know when that time will come. Therefore keep watch… If he comes suddenly, do not let him find you sleeping. What I say to you, I say to everyone: 'Watch!'" (Mark 32-33, 35, 37)

Repeatedly, Jesus urges us to "keep watch," "be on guard," "be alert," and "be ready" for His return. Regarding Christ's second coming, we definitely want to "keep our eye on the ball" by anticipating and looking for His coming, living holy lives, and sharing the Gospel with others.

Scripture Reading: 2 Peter 3:10-14

Personal Application:

- In 2 Timothy 4:8, Paul refers to those who long for Christ's return. To what extent does that apply to you? Why or why not?
- How is the Holy Spirit speaking to you right now about being alert, watchful and ready for Jesus' return?

Week 6, Day 6: The Glory of God

As we seek to have more boldness in our faith and live for Jesus daily, let's consider the glory of God.

We find God's glory in various representations throughout Scripture. After leading the Children of Israel out of Egypt, God met them at Mount Sinai:

On the morning of the third day there was thunder and lightning, with a thick cloud over the mountain, and a very loud trumpet blast. Everyone in the camp trembled. Then Moses led the people out of the camp to meet with God, and they stood at the foot of the mountain. Mount Sinai was covered with smoke because the Lord descended on it in fire. The smoke billowed up from it like smoke from a furnace, and the whole mountain trembled violently. (Exodus 19:16-18)

As the Israelites wandered in the desert, they witnessed the glory of God displayed in a great cloud during the day and a pillar of fire at night. And at one point, Moses begged God, "Please, show me Your glory" (Exodus 33:18). God responded, "You cannot see my face, for no one can see me and live" (vs. 20). But God permitted Moses to see His back, the "afterglow" of His glory as He passed by.

When King Solomon dedicated the new temple in Jerusalem, we read, "Then the temple of the Lord was filled with the cloud, and the priests could not perform their service because of the cloud, for the glory of the Lord filled the temple of God." (2 Chronicles 5:13-14)

Christ is "the radiance of God's glory and the exact representation of His being." (Hebrews 1:3). And John records, "The Word [Jesus] became flesh and made his dwelling among us. We have seen His glory, the glory of the one and only Son, who came from the Father, full of grace and truth." (John 1:14).

As a mirror reflects lights, we are to reflect Christ's glory to a sinful world, imitating His character. "And we all, who with unveiled faces contemplate the Lord's glory, are being transformed into His image with ever-increasing glory, which comes from the Lord, who is the Spirit." (2 Corinthians 3:18)

When we live a life that represents Christ's character and when we give God the credit for the blessings and achievements in our life, God is glorified. Others see the "afterglow" of His glory in us.

Scripture Reading: 2 Corinthians 4:4-7

Personal Application:

- Take time to evaluate your life. To what extent do you reflect God's glory? What aspects of His nature do people see in you?
- Pray the following passages of praise to the Lord: Revelation 4:11; 5:9-10, 12-13.

Week 6, Day 7: Weekly Recap and Prayer

On the seventh day of each week, use the **ACTS** acronym to spend time with the Lord reviewing and assessing your week and praying to God. (**A**=Adoration; **C**=Confession; **T**=Thanksgiving; **S**=Supplication)

First, look back over the previous six days for this week to remind yourself what you read and agreed to. Then, follow the ACTS pattern for prayer below. Finally, use the space below to journal what God is doing in your life and share this with a trusted spiritual partner.

Adoration: Simply spend time in adoration of the Lord. Praise Him and glorify His name. (See 1 Chronicles 29:10-13; Psalm 100; Romans 11:33-36.)

Confession: Confess your sins and shortcomings before God. ("If we confess our sins, he is faithful and just and will forgive us our sins and purify us from all unrighteousness." – 1 John 1:9) To confess (or agree with God) about your sin, implies that you are repentant and desperately want Him to change you.

Thanksgiving: Thank God for what He has done and is doing in your life and the life of your family. Give Him credit, for everything you have comes from Him. (See Psalm 136.)

Supplication: Supplication is just a fancy word for making your requests known to God. Based on the devotions of this past week and the things going on in your life right now, what do you want to ask Him for? "If you, then, though you are evil, know how to give good gifts to your children, how much more will your Father in heaven give good gifts to those who ask Him!" (Matthew 7:11)

Journal: What is God doing in your life right now?

Week 7, Day 1: Why, God?

I can't remember a time when so many friends were under such physical, mental, and/or spiritual attack. Maybe it's a sign of my age. Maybe it's the result of the chaos in our sin-filled world. I don't know. I do know that there are many people suffering and being challenged.

The Psalmist cried out, "Why, Lord, do you stand far off? Why do you hide yourself in times of trouble?" (Psalm 10:1) It's human to ask, "Why, Lord? Why is this happening to me?" In George MacDonald's book *Donal Grant,* the character Arctura says to Donal, "You speak always like someone who has suffered." To which Donal replies, "Who has not suffered that lives at all?"

Someone has said, "Indeed, life is suffering: contradiction, misfortune, disappointment, and heartbreak surround us." And Paul and Barnabas strengthened and encouraged new followers of Jesus by telling them, "We must go through many hardships to enter the kingdom of God." (Acts 14:22) *Why must we go through many hardships to enter the Kingdom of God?*

I used to believe I knew the answers to those questions, but life – now that I'm much closer to its end than to its beginning – has knocked most of them right out of my head. God rebuked Job and his friends, as Jesus did when His disciples drew unwarranted conclusions from suffering. In the face of affliction, I'm learning now to be more silent. When my friends tell me their lives are difficult, I answer, "I understand and will pray for you." When they ask me why they're suffering, I tell them, "I really don't know, but my God knows your suffering intimately and loves you dearly."

Why life should be this way, I cannot say, but I do know this: It will not always be this way; there will be an end. Eternal glory lies ahead, as Peter promised, "The God of all grace, who called us to His eternal glory by Christ Jesus, after you have suffered a while, will perfect, establish, strengthen, and settle you." (1 Peter 5:10)

And Paul adds, "For our light and momentary troubles are achieving for us an eternal glory that far outweighs them all. So we fix our eyes not on what is seen, but on what is unseen, since what is seen is temporary, but what is unseen is eternal." (2 Corinthians 4:17-18)

There in that "eternal school room" our Lord will explain "each separate anguish," but I doubt we will care then. Instead, we will bask in the awesome flood of His presence. "He will wipe every tear from their eyes. There will be no more death or mourning or crying or pain." (Revelation 21:4) My friends, it's a matter of perspective; God's perspective.

Scripture Reading: Lamentations 3:19-26, 31-33

Personal Application:
- If you are enduring something difficult right now, instead of asking "Why, Lord?" tell the Lord that you trust Him. Praise Him and thank Him that He loves you and is in control.
- Which of the passages above speaks to you most right now and why?

Week 7, Day 2: Who's in Control?

A friend of mine was experiencing difficulties in his marriage and his career. He was going through the motions of trusting the Lord for all that was happening in his life, but he felt defeated and abandoned.

During this particularly dark time in his life, he was visiting his daughter who lived near Chicago. She picked him up at the airport and then drove him downtown to see the sites. That afternoon they stopped at a coffee shop in downtown Chicago before driving home to one of the suburbs.

They had just reached his daughter's home when my friend realized that he had forgotten his laptop at the coffee shop in Chicago! He was beside himself with worry and fret. Added to everything else he was struggling with, this did him in. He admits that he had already resigned himself to the probability that his laptop was gone.

Frantically, he called the coffee shop, and to his amazement, a barista said she had his laptop and would hold it for him until he arrived. Somewhat relieved, but still feeling sorry for himself, he and his daughter made their way back to Chicago and to the coffee shop.

When they arrived, my friend burst through the door, ran to the counter, and told the barista that he was the guy who had forgotten his laptop. The barista asked him to wait while she retrieved it from the back office.

When she returned, she began to hand the laptop to him over the counter as he eagerly reached for it. But then she held it back, looked him in the eye and said, "God is very merciful to you!" Stunned, my friend just looked at her for a moment. Then he reached once again for his laptop. But again, she pulled it back and said loudly, "No, listen! God is very merciful to you!" And then she handed him his laptop.

At that, my friend broke down and sobbed. If you had asked him before this incident whether he was surrendered to Christ, he would have said, "Yes, of course." But in this divine moment, he realized the extent to which he had pushed God away, had been sulking in self-pity and was trying to make it on his own.

"Therefore, I urge you, brothers and sisters, in view of God's mercy, to offer your bodies as a living sacrifice, holy and pleasing to God – this is your true and proper worship. Do not conform to the pattern of this world, but be transformed by the renewing of your mind. Then you will be able to test a approve what God's will is – his good, pleasing and perfect will." (Romans 12:1-2)

Scripture Reading: Isaiah 41:10

Personal Application:

- We tend to hang on to things with a grip of uncertainty and fear. But God wants us to trust Him with every aspect of our lives, our loved ones, and our possessions.
- Meditate on Proverbs 3:5-6, "Trust in the LORD with all your heart and lean not on your own understanding; in all your ways acknowledge Him, and He shall direct your paths."

Week 7, Day 3: The Message of the Cross

"For the message of the cross is foolishness to those who are perishing, but to us who are being saved it is the power of God." – 1 Corinthians 1:18

I'm reminded of a story that helps put the cross of Christ into perspective. In 1967 a young student from the University of Cincinnati was working through the issues of his faith. Charles Murray was an Olympic prospect as a very skilled high diver. He was not raised in a Christian home. But his roommate had talked to him about the forgiveness of sin and the saving power of the Cross of Christ. And now, Charles was struggling with God over those issues.

Charles began reading the New Testament and continued to debate spiritual issues with his roommate. For some reason, the clarity of God's message did not reach Charles' heart. He became frustrated with his confusion and declined any further discussions on this topic.

Because he was training for the Olympics, Charles had special privileges at the University pool facilities. One evening he became restless and confused with his spiritual struggle and decided to spend some additional time practicing dives. Sometime between 10:30 and 11:00 PM he went to the pool. It was a clear night in October and the moon was big and bright.

The University pool was housed under a glass ceiling. The moon shone brightly across the top of the wall in the pool area. Charles came through the back door, put down his gear, and immediately climbed the tall ladder leading to the highest platform. He didn't turn on the pool lights because the glow of the moon filtered enough light into the building.

At that moment the Spirit of God began to convict Charles of his sins. All the Scripture he had read, and all the occasions others witnessed to him about Christ flooded his mind. He stood on the platform backwards to make his dive, spread his arms to gather his balance, looked up to the wall, and saw his own shadow on the side of the pool building. The moonlight silhouetted his body projecting the shape of a cross on the stark, white wall.

When he saw the cross, Charles could bear the burden of his sin no longer. His heart broke as he sat down on the platform and asked God to forgive him and save him. He trusted Jesus Christ on a twenty-foot platform with only the walls of the building to hear his confession.

Suddenly, a door opened, and the pool lights came on. One of the maintenance workers had come to check some work he had been doing on the pool. As Charles looked down from his platform, he was shocked to see an empty pool. It had been drained for repairs. He had almost plummeted to his death, but the cross had kept him from disaster.

Scripture Reading: Colossians 2:13-15

Personal Application:
- When did you embrace Christ's death for you on the cross? What difference has Christ made in your life? Share your story with someone today.
- Meditate on 1 Peter 2:24.

Week 7, Day 4: Trekking through Life

Most guys I know enjoy a hike in the woods. There is something about trekking in the forest and getting away from all the synthetic stuff and paved roads that breathes life back into a man's spirit.

On a hike, especially if it's a challenging one, men bond with each other in camaraderie, having experienced the same grueling climb together. There's something very fulfilling about summiting a mountain, forging a glacial river, or braving the elements.

The hiking experience also offers a great opportunity for men to disciple each other. Jesus did this with His disciples. Several times a year, Jesus would make the trek between Capernaum and Jerusalem with His disciples to attend the various Jewish feasts. One way that's 75 miles as the crow flies, and significantly farther by road.

It was on these long treks that Jesus often taught and mentored His disciples. Many other times, we find Jesus and His disciples climbing a mountain, traversing a field, in a boat on the lake, or somewhere else outdoors. Frequently, He used items along the trail as props for the life lessons He was imparting to the twelve. In His teachings He refers to the birds of the air, the flowers of the field, the rocks, the grass, and the trees.

Often, out in nature, men are more open and willing to share what's going on in their lives. In our day-to-day routines, it's easy to compartmentalize our lives, separating our "spiritual" activities from all other activities. But out in nature, when we pray, discuss the Word, and talk about our joys and struggles, we demonstrate how natural and integrated these practices can be in real life.

Finally, hiking can serve as a great metaphor for life. Consider the following:

- Sometimes the trail is hard and sometimes it's easy.
- Some hikes are uphill all the way in and downhill all the way out.
- Sometimes the trail is strewn with hazards, rocks, holes, mud, ice, and roots.
- Sometimes there are other dangers along the way: cougars, bears, and moose.
- Sometimes it's so foggy you can't see where you're going.
- Sometimes the weather is your friend and at other times it's your enemy.

When hiking in remote areas, there's a cardinal rule: never hike alone. While many men don't realize this, the same holds true trekking through life. We need other men in our lives. We need a confidant. Someone who has our back. Someone whom we can trust and in whom we can confide. "As iron sharpens iron, so one man sharpens another." (Proverbs 27:17)

Scripture Reading: Psalm 23

Personal Application:

- Who is the man in your life that you trust to "sharpen" you?
  Spend time regularly meeting with him. Pray together, discuss the
  Word, and share your joys and challenges with each other.

Week 7, Day 5: Deferring to Others

I fondly recall a hunting trip to High Point Buck Ranch, near Moose Jaw, in the center of Saskatchewan Canada. High atop this plateau, where rolling hills give way to naturally forested valleys, I joined a small group of friends, hunting for world-class elk, buffalo, and fallow deer. But God chose this place to teach us more about His great creation… and godly friendships.

There were eight hunters in our party; most were archers. During our four-day stay, we harvested eleven animals: six trophy elk, three giant buffalo, and two beautiful fallow deer. All the trophy whitetails scampering about were left for another trip. Many stories have come out of that trip, but my favorite is about an ornery buffalo named "Nasty," and his trusty pal.

For months Rick and Michele Nestman, the owners, and operators of this unique guest ranch, had told me about a defiant herd buffalo they called "Nasty." The bull had a difficult disposition, regularly knocking over fences and chasing hunters off the property. I had secretly dreamed many times about bringing down Nasty with my 60-pound Mathews Bow and 100 grain Muzzy Broadheads. I could hardly wait.

A few in the group arrived a day earlier than the rest of us. My long-time friend, Greg, had a chance to size up Nasty before I got there. When I arrived my feet hardly hit the ground before he approached with a Cheshire-cat grin and said, "Well Jim, I saw Nasty…and I just have to have him!" I felt a pang in my chest and swallowed hard. Immediately recalling Greg's generous heart, I conceded, "Nasty is all yours! I'll even back you up with the cameras."

The next morning, it was on! Greg was the first up to greet the day, preparing himself for his great buffalo hunt. Leaving my bow behind, I loaded the cameras, gulped down a cup of coffee with Rick and Greg, and headed off to the lower pasture to meet up with the 2000-pound bull.

After a short stalk, Greg lowered himself into a prone position for his shot. I focused the video camera on Greg and easily observed just how important this animal was to my good friend. Looking through his scope, Greg carefully adjusted himself for the best 100-yard shot he could muster. With the squeeze of the trigger, his 30-06 rifle barked out, and ol' Nasty tumbled over without a twitch.

We were so excited! But then, we noticed that all the other buffalo were surrounding Nasty…and were not pleased. Rick's son, Craig, grabbed the 4x4 quad and attempted to chase off the remaining angry buffaloes. Despite his extraordinary efforts, one large devoted bull remained with Nasty… (Continued tomorrow!)

Scripture Reading: Mark 9:30-37

Personal Application:

- In the flesh, we all want to be first. In the flesh, it's all about us. But Jesus calls us to higher ground—deferring to others—thinking of others first.
- During the day today, look for opportunities to defer to others.
  Let them go first. Humble yourself to serve them. At the end of
  the day, ask yourself what you learned from this exercise.

Week 7, Day 6: Loyalty

In yesterday's devotional, I told how my friend Greg had just dropped a 2000-pound bull buffalo called Nasty. But one large devoted bull refused to leave Nasty's side after he was down. Realizing this animal could be quite a challenge, I decided I'd get my bow and take care of him. I sprinted to the cabin, grabbed my bow, some arrows, and broadheads, and began stalking the buffalo I'd decided to call Nasty II! This guy must have been a relative of Nasty's; he wasn't about to let me within bow range. I positioned my friend Bill, an excellent marksman with his 300 Win. mag., about 125 yards out and told him to take the powerful buffalo down if he started to charge.

I carefully moved in and waited for the bull to turn and look back to his fallen comrade. When he did, I pulled back my bow and aimed. The arrow's forty-yard flight was true and hit exactly where I had aimed... sort of. Unfortunately, Nasty II had lifted his front leg just as I released. The arrow struck just above his elbow and he took off, retreating. Bill, a bit anxious, fired but missed.

I knew the arrow wasn't lethal and that I would have plenty of time to hunt him down. I started walking back when I noticed the bull reappearing from the thick brush. He was not going to leave his friend. Talk about loyalty! Nasty II was committed to protecting his fallen friend.

I moved in for another shot. He spotted me and got really agitated, snorting and stomping the ground. This 1300-pound, freight-train-like beast raised his tail, signaling for attack. I moved closer. When I got about 45 yards from him, he changed position, attempting to move to higher ground. I placed a shot through his lungs. He ran for about 120 yards and fell over dead. What courage! What a fighter! We all cheered and triumphantly moved in to harvest both kills.

Nasty II had shown the kind of dedication, courage, and devotion we all look for in a godly friendship. I want to be that kind of friend, too! It challenges me to look a little closer at myself:

- Do I come alongside my friends when life brings them down, or do I slink away, waiting till the "coast is clear"?
- Do I persevere with them, or do I just make a quick show of loyalty and then retreat?
- Is my commitment more important than my comfort?
- Can my friends really count on me?

The truth is, I'd like to say yes to all of those, but I don't always do it perfectly. In fact, there's only one Friend I know who does: Jesus. What devotion! What commitment! What perseverance and sacrifice! What a Friend we have in Jesus!

Scripture Reading: Romans 8:31-39

Personal Application:
- To what extent do you turn to Jesus for the kind of loyalty and support we all long for?
- Look over the bulleted list above. What can you do to be the kind of friend to others described here? Who in your life needs this kind of courage and commitment right now?

Week 7, Day 7: Weekly Recap and Prayer

On the seventh day of each week, use the **ACTS** acronym to spend time with the Lord reviewing and assessing your week and praying to God. (**A**=Adoration; **C**=Confession; **T**=Thanksgiving; **S**=Supplication)

First, look back over the previous six days for this week to remind yourself what you read and agreed to. Then, follow the ACTS pattern for prayer below. Finally, use the space below to journal what God is doing in your life and share this with a trusted spiritual partner.

Adoration: Simply spend time in adoration of the Lord. Praise Him and glorify His name. (See 1 Chronicles 29:10-13; Psalm 100; Romans 11:33-36.)

Confession: Confess your sins and shortcomings before God. ("If we confess our sins, he is faithful and just and will forgive us our sins and purify us from all unrighteousness." – 1 John 1:9) To confess (or agree with God) about your sin, implies that you are repentant and desperately want Him to change you.

Thanksgiving: Thank God for what He has done and is doing in your life and the life of your family. Give Him credit, for everything you have comes from Him. (See Psalm 136.)

Supplication: Supplication is just a fancy word for making your requests known to God. Based on the devotions of this past week and the things going on in your life right now, what do you want to ask Him for? "If you, then, though you are evil, know how to give good gifts to your children, how much more will your Father in heaven give good gifts to those who ask Him!" (Matthew 7:11)

Journal: What is God doing in your life right now?

Week 8, Day 1: Godly Friendship

"A friend loves at all times..."
– Proverbs 17:17a

Godly friendship is so rewarding. One of my favorite examples of godly friendship is in 1 Samuel 23. There we find the unique fellowship Jonathan and David shared. They were total opposites: Jonathan was the well-educated, multi-talented, and privileged son of King Saul, while David was a poor shepherd boy, mocked by his brothers, and discouraged by his father.

But God saw David's heart and passion and declared him a man after His heart. So, when Saul rejected God, the Lord anointed David to succeed him as king. Therefore, Jonathan's father, Saul, was envious of David and plotted to kill him, but Jonathan knew of his father's evil intent and decided to protect and defend his friend. Jonathan did this even though David, and not he would be the next king.

In Jonathan's example, I find five traits of a godly friendship:

1. A godly friend moves us closer to the Lord. "And Saul's son Jonathan went to David at Horesh and helped him find strength in God." (1 Samuel 23:16) Jonathan knew David needed to be encouraged in his faith.
2. A godly friend seeks what's best for us. "You will be king," Jonathan declared. He expressed his loyalty with a covenant before God. He loved and supported David placing himself in mortal danger.
3. A godly friend reinforces God's truth, purpose, and plan for our lives. Jonathan knew of God's ultimate plan for David and chose to support that vision over his father's cruel intentions.
4. A godly friend follows through with his commitments. Jonathan modeled unconditional acceptance, absolute loyalty, and unquestionable commitment. He did this despite strong pressure from his father and others to betray David. "'Don't be afraid,' he said. 'My father Saul will not lay a hand on you. You will be king over Israel, and I will be second to you.'" (vs. 17)
5. A godly friend is willing to give grace and forgive. Jonathan was willing to forget the past and focus upon David's future. He chose not to remember David's shortcomings but elected to think about his strengths. Good friends are not without conflict; they are friends who value the relationship enough to work through it, give grace when needed, and forgive always.

Jonathan was a true friend. If you want godly friendships in your life, you must be a true friend.

Scripture Reading: 1 Samuel 23:14-18

Personal Application:

- Seek God first in your life. As you do, you become more like Him and His unconditional love can flow through you.
- To whom do you need to be a godly friend? How will you cultivate such a friendship?

Week 8, Day 2: Out of Control

"A fool gives full vent to his anger, but a wise man keeps himself under control."
– Proverbs 29:11

Outdoorsmen are known to be passionate about their sport. For an angler, there are at least 7 Warning Signs that your passion for fishing is out of control:

1. Your refrigerator drawer is full of night crawlers.
2. You carry pictures of your favorite lures in your wallet.
3. You named your kids Gill, Rod, and Stinkbait.
4. Cats follow you everywhere you go.
5. You practice casting in the bathtub.
6. Selling your gear could put the kids through medical school.
7. You leave your hotspot to someone in your will.

Seriously though, some individuals spend more time, effort, and resources trying to perfect the ballistics of their ammunition or tying a fly than improving relationships in their family. I've seen professional bass fishermen sacrifice everything in their quest to attain success. At one time or another we have all suffered from addiction to our passions.

God has a lot to say about self-control. Throughout the New Testament, the Apostle Paul reminds us that we should have authority over our bodies, including our tongues. "It is God's will that you should be sanctified…that each of you should learn to control his own body in a way that is holy and honorable." (1 Thessalonians 4:3-4)

And, "If anyone considers himself religious and yet does not keep a tight rein on his tongue, he deceives himself and his religion is worthless." (James 1:26)

A person who does not keep his tongue or passions in check is an embarrassment to God and his family. Self-control is a chief ingredient to spiritual maturity and effectiveness in the kingdom. "Like a city whose walls are broken down is a man who lacks self-control." (Proverbs 25:28)

Whether it's an out-of-control passion or addiction, a quick temper, the loose lips of gossip, crude joking, or an undisciplined mind that allows improper thoughts to roam freely, let's confess our weaknesses and allow the Holy Spirit to "add self-control to our knowledge" of truth.

Scripture Reading: 2 Peter 1:5-9

Personal Application:

- What would your wife, children, or others close to you say about your self-control?
- Is there someone from whom you need to ask forgiveness for your lack of self-control?
- What specific areas of your life do you need to surrender to Christ's control? Share those with a trusted friend who will pray for you, encourage you, and help hold you accountable.

Week 8, Day 3: Remember Who You Are

"To God's holy people in Colossae, the faithful brothers and sisters in Christ."
– Colossians 1:2

A friend of mine often reminds his children, "You are my children. I have given you my name. Honor it…and me. When you leave this house, you carry it with you. When you return, bring it back as good as it was when you left."

When our twins entered their teenage years, Louise and I really tried to impress on them the importance of developing godly character. We found a plaque that emphasized developing a legacy and protecting the family name. We bought two and hung one in each boy's room. Much like a Jewish boy would honor a Mezuzah when leaving his home, we prayed the boys would note this reminder when leaving their rooms.

A Christian man I know used to address me with the words, "Greetings, you holy man of God!" At first, this made me feel very uncomfortable. I thought, *I'm not fit or worthy to be called holy.* But then I realized, that's what God calls us. And it's not because we're fit or worthy, but because Jesus Christ is.

When we accept Christ as Savior, we become part of God's family. We are God's children. We receive Christ's righteousness. He makes us holy.

In 1 Corinthians 6:9-10, the Apostle Paul lists many of the sins which the Corinthians previously practiced. Then, in verse 11 he states, "And that is what some of you were. But you were washed, you were sanctified, you were justified in the name of the Lord Jesus Christ and by the Spirit of our God."

The Apostle Paul often spoke about the importance of developing godly character. When addressing the believers in Colossae he reminded them that (we) are God's chosen, holy, and beloved. He surely knew that our behavior only changes for the good when we are first conscious of our identity.

Let's remember who we are and Whose name we bear!

"You are a chosen people, a royal priesthood, a holy nation, God's special possession, that you may declare the praises of Him who called you out of darkness into His wonderful light. Once you were not a people, but now you are the people of God." 1 Peter 2:9-10a

Scripture Reading: Ephesians 5:1-10

Personal Application:
- In what ways does your identity in Christ affect the way you think about yourself?
- In what ways does knowing that you are a child of God affect your behavior?
- As you begin each day, pray that God would use you today to represent Him well to others through your life and words.

Week 8, Day 4: Christ's Sufferings Predicted

For about 13 years, David fled from King Saul who was trying to kill him. At some point during his severe trials, David wrote Psalm 22. In this Psalm he poured out his heart to God. At times in the Psalm, you can feel the depths of his agony.

But what is truly amazing about this Psalm is its prophetic nature, for it describes in detail what Jesus endured on the cross. Jesus even quoted from this Psalm during His crucifixion. Below is a portion of this Psalm that demonstrates this:

My God, my God, why have you forsaken me? Why are you so far from saving me, so far from my cries of anguish? (See Matthew 27:46; Mark 15:34)

But I am a worm and not a man, scorned by everyone, despised by the people. All who see me mock me; they hurl insults, shaking their heads. "He trusts in the Lord," they say, "let the Lord rescue him. Let him deliver him, since he delights in him." (See Matthew 27:42-43; Mark 15:29-32)

I am poured out like water, and all my bones are out of joint. My heart has turned to wax; it has melted within me. My mouth is dried up like a potsherd, and my tongue sticks to the roof of my mouth; you lay me in the dust of death. (See John 19:28-29)

Dogs surround me, a pack of villains encircles me; they pierce my hands and my feet. All my bones are on display; people stare and gloat over me. They divide my clothes among them and cast lots for my garment. (See John 19:23-24, 36-37)

Those prophecies were made approximately 1,000 years before Jesus was crucified. God foresaw it all. He knew exactly what Jesus' executioners would say and do. He knew what Jesus would experience on the cross—physically, emotionally, and spiritually.

All this stirs in me a great sense of awe for God regarding His sovereign plan, and His great love for mankind (you and me). I am amazed that God sent His Son to die for us knowing exactly how it would play out. And I'm in awe over God's Word—it's accuracy and reliability.

"Thanks be to God for his indescribable gift!" (2 Corinthians 9:15)

Scripture Reading: John 19:23-37

Personal Application:

- The prophecies that Jesus fulfilled from Psalm 22 represent a tiny portion of the Old Testament prophecies concerning Jesus' birth, life, ministry, death, burial, resurrection, and return. What is your personal response knowing all this?
- Spend time worshiping and thanking God for what He did for you through His Son Jesus Christ.
- Share this devotional today with someone who doesn't know Christ.

Week 8, Day 5: Unexpected Difficulties

The renowned editor of Buckmaster Magazine, Russell Thornberry, once made his living as an outfitter and guide in the Canadian province of Alberta. His recollections of the various difficulties he experienced are worth repeating.

In late September of 1974, Russell was with a client, hunting for an elusive bull moose. As they made their way through the black spruce muskeg, they started calling for the big bull. Suddenly a hush fell over the area and a strange feeling settled in on the hunters.

With rising intensity, a strange beating sound began to fill the woods. Looking up, Russell saw some movement in the distance. Within minutes the brush around the two woodsmen began to stir. "Before I could comment," remembers Russ, "a pack of wolves was standing in a semi-circle around us. It all happened so quickly that it seemed almost imaginary."

Once the wolves realized the hunters were not a moose, they fled as quickly as they had appeared. While Russ brushed it off as an unusual encounter with nature, his client was not so sure.

Two days later at dusk, the two were hiding in a pile of dead trees, calling for their moose, when a twig behind the two hunters snapped. Bull moose sometimes tip toe in on an unsuspecting hunter who is calling. Expecting a big moose, they slowly turned to get a better look at the intruder.

But they were shocked to see a huge black bear rearing up on its hind legs just six feet from them. The men screamed in horror, firing a warning shot in the air. The bear instantly vanished, and the hunters danced a jig of relief and uncontrollable nervous tension—half crying and half laughing.

The client just couldn't believe that these events were exceptional occurrences and decided he most likely would never hunt again. In fact, his confidence in becoming an outdoorsman was so shaken that he probably never left the comfort of his penthouse apartment again.

Unexpected difficulties—we all experience them. How do you handle them? Many people believe that once you become a Christian, all your troubles go away. This is simply not biblical. What we can count on with absolute confidence is that God is in control, and He is with us during times of trouble. We can draw strength, wisdom, and endurance, and even joy from Jesus Christ!

Scripture Reading: Psalm 34

Personal Application:
- What unexpected difficulties are you experiencing right now?
- Meditate on James 1:2, "Consider it pure joy, my brothers, whenever you face trials of many kinds." What is the Lord saying to you from this passage?

Week 8, Day 6: Use Your Story as a Bridge to Share the Gospel

I had the opportunity to excel in fishing and hunting. As a Hall-of-Fame fisherman and record-book archer, I've been around the world on various fishing and hunting excursions. Over forty years ago, through the encouragement of one of my mentors, I began using my passion for the outdoors as a bridge to connect with men.

At that time, there were over forty million fishermen and almost thirteen million hunters over the age of sixteen. I also figured that over half of these populations were male. So, there is no shortage of unsaved guys to communicate God's truth to through outdoor adventure stories.

For instance, I remember during one trip several things had gone wrong and we were trying to keep warm so we wouldn't freeze to death. I had an opportunity to share with my companion the faithfulness and protection God provides, and I did so through my personal stories. Our conversation over that campfire changed the heart of this man toward things of the Lord.

People have a way of remembering something if it's in the context of a good adventure story. I think Jesus knew this and often hid transforming truths within His stories (See Matthew 13:11-13). His stories not only impacted His twelve disciples but have resonated with followers for over two thousand years.

I'm always amazed how I can remember details of those things that interest me. Batting averages of key baseball players, quarterback ratings, and the speed of the latest Corvette are easy things for me to remember because they connect with information that have stories behind the statistics.

Often men see themselves as independent self-starters, and maybe even a little bit prideful or hard-hearted. Storytelling has a way of breaking through barriers and softening hearts so they can hear and feel emotion. When transformation takes place, men are more willing to share their experiences at a deeper level than we might expect.

It's interesting that when the Apostle Paul had opportunity to share the Gospel with Roman officials and kings, he often did so by telling his own conversion story. He could have gone into a lengthy discourse citing the Law and the Prophets. Instead, he simply told his story. I love that because it means that anyone who has a conversion story can share the Gospel with others.

Scripture Reading: Acts 26:9-32

Personal Application:

- Spend time thinking about your story—how you came to Christ. Arrange in terms of: 1) here's what I was like before Christ; 2) here's how I met Christ; and 3) here's what Christ has done in my life since I've trusted Him.
- Share your story with someone who may not know the Lord. Just tell them, "I'm working through a daily devotional for men. One of my assignments is to share my story with someone. Would you be willing to hear my story?" (Pray that God will empower you and use your story either to bring them to Christ or play a role in doing so.)

Week 8, Day 7: Weekly Recap and Prayer

On the seventh day of each week, use the **ACTS** acronym to spend time with the Lord reviewing and assessing your week and praying to God. (**A**=Adoration; **C**=Confession; **T**=Thanksgiving; **S**=Supplication)

First, look back over the previous six days for this week to remind yourself what you read and agreed to. Then, follow the ACTS pattern for prayer below. Finally, use the space below to journal what God is doing in your life and share this with a trusted spiritual partner.

Adoration: Simply spend time in adoration of the Lord. Praise Him and glorify His name. (See 1 Chronicles 29:10-13; Psalm 100; Romans 11:33-36.)

Confession: Confess your sins and shortcomings before God. ("If we confess our sins, he is faithful and just and will forgive us our sins and purify us from all unrighteousness." – 1 John 1:9) To confess (or agree with God) about your sin, implies that you are repentant and desperately want Him to change you.

Thanksgiving: Thank God for what He has done and is doing in your life and the life of your family. Give Him credit, for everything you have comes from Him. (See Psalm 136.)

Supplication: Supplication is just a fancy word for making your requests known to God. Based on the devotions of this past week and the things going on in your life right now, what do you want to ask Him for? "If you, then, though you are evil, know how to give good gifts to your children, how much more will your Father in heaven give good gifts to those who ask Him!" (Matthew 7:11)

Journal: What is God doing in your life right now?

Week 9, Day 1: Simple Obedience

I heard a story about a lady who cashed a couple of checks and received $500 more than she deserved. The lady didn't realize the error until she had left the bank and was recounting her bills. The following business day she returned to the bank and gave the money back to the manager. The manager said, "The teller would have lost her job over this." It might have been easy for some folks to have kept the extra money. One could rationalize, "Hey, I didn't steal it! It's not my fault that the teller gave me too much money." But a true believer seeks to obey God, even when it means losing something. This lady was an obedient disciple; she honored God with her actions.

Following Jesus means living as Jesus did. He called us to be imitators of His life. How do we do that? For the Apostle John, it came down to obedience. If we love God, then we obey Him. While that can sound a little simplistic, there is something wonderful in knowing that each act of obedience has meaning. Even the most unnoticed act – the honest claim on our tax return, the extra twenty dollars (or $500 dollars) we return to the bank teller who mistakenly gave us too much cash, the act of kindness that no one saw, the forgiveness we find in our heart for someone who inadvertently wounded us – can all be meaningful expressions of our love for God and obedience to Him.

Obeying God isn't about keeping rules; it's about honoring your relationship with Him. It's about understanding that God is the source of any light and life in your existence. When you obey God's teachings, you show your love, your devotion, and your commitment to God.

The Apostle John summed it up pretty well when writing, "We know that we have come to know Him if we obey His commands. The man who says, 'I know Him,' but does not do what He commands is a liar, and the truth is not in him. But if anyone obeys His word, God's love is truly made complete in him. This is how we know we are in Him." (1 John 2:3-5)

The great preacher Dwight L. Moody regularly took a bus to the seminary where he taught. As was his custom, he would hand the bus driver a dollar and receive back the change. Once, when he sat down in the bus and looked at his change, he realized that the driver had given him back too much money. When departing, Moody told the driver, "You gave me too much change back." The driver said, "I know. I visited your church last Sunday when you spoke about honesty and obedience. I just wanted to see if you really practiced what you preached."

Like D. L. Moody, let's practice what we preach...

Scripture Reading: 1 John 2:1-11

Personal Application:

- In what way is God speaking to you personally from today's devotional?
- We sometimes limit our view of obedience merely to avoiding a violation of God's law. But obedience to Him also means doing those things that please Him. What specific acts of obedience to the Lord will you engage in today?

Week 9, Day 2: Manly Men Emote

So often, conversations between males center around non-threatening topics like sports, weather, cars, hobbies, and so forth. Men typically are protective of their feelings and emotions. They believe that if they let someone see their "underside," they will be judged as weak or insecure. So, the usual response to "How are you doing?" is "I'm fine, how are you?"

Jesus was compassionate, understanding, communicative, and loving. Scripture portrays Jesus as strong, bold, masculine, and fearless. He stood up to the religious leaders of the day calling them out on their hypocrisy. He threw over the tables of the money changers in the temple and drove them out with a whip. He rebuked storms and faced Satan head-on.

Jesus fasted forty days in the wilderness, to which Mark's Gospel adds, "He was with the wild animals." I did some checking and there were wolves, bears, lions, and hyenas in that region at the time. And by the way, Jesus was a carpenter till He began His ministry at about 30 years old.

David is another great example of a courageous man who was unafraid to reveal his emotions. Consider the fact that as a youth tending his father's sheep, David killed a lion and a bear with nothing but a club and his bare hands! Then, he stood alone against Goliath and took him down with a sling and a stone.

David was by no means perfect, but he loved the Lord with all his heart. When he brought the Ark of the Covenant to Jerusalem, "David danced before the Lord with all his might." (1 Samuel 6:14) David boldly worshiped and praised the Lord in public. He also vented his emotions freely before the Lord, writing those expressions down for our benefit. (See Psalms 51; 70; and 139.)

I could go on and on, citing Moses, Daniel, Jeremiah, Peter, John, and Paul. All these men were manly men, passionate about the Lord and unafraid to express their deepest feelings.

One of the best ways I've found to help men open up is to ask "tough" questions. These are always open-ended questions. Here are some examples:

- What has God been doing in your life lately?
- What one thing would you like to see Christ change in your life?
- In what ways are you leading your wife and family into deeper relationship with Christ?
- What has God been showing you from His Word lately?

We need men in our lives with whom we can challenge each other in these ways.

Scripture Reading: Titus 2:6-8

Personal Application:
- Ask the Lord to provide a comrade-in-arms brother in Christ—someone you can mutually spur on in your relationships with Christ.
- Meet with this man this week and introduce him to the above questions. Agree to ask each other one or two of them each time you meet.

Week 9, Day 3: Trust and Obey

"Sometime later God tested Abraham. He said to him, 'Abraham!' 'Here I am,' he replied. Then God said, 'Take your son, your only son, whom you love—Isaac—and go to the region of Moriah. Sacrifice him there as a burnt offering on a mountain I will show you.' When they reached the place God had told him about, Abraham built an altar there and arranged the wood on it. He bound his son Isaac and laid him on the altar, on top of the wood."

– Genesis 22:1-2, 9

The text says, "God tested Abraham." Typically, we focus on Abraham's obedience in connection with this testing, and surely that was a significant element of this testing (Genesis 22:18). However, I think there are two other things going on here as well.

Before the birth of Isaac, God had promised Abraham, "Your wife Sarah will bear you a son, and you will call him Isaac. I will establish my covenant with him as an everlasting covenant for his descendants after him." (Genesis 17:19)

God's promise to Abraham is very specific: 1) his wife, Sarah, would bear a son. 2) His name would be Isaac. 3) God would establish an everlasting covenant with Isaac. 4) Isaac would have descendants who would inherit this everlasting covenant.

Based on the above promise, God was now testing Abraham's trust in the promise God had given him. Surely, Abraham must have been conflicted inside because God's testing ran counter to His promise. Hebrews 11:17 tells us, "By faith Abraham, when God tested him, offered Isaac as a sacrifice. He who had embraced the promises was about to sacrifice his one and only son."

So, when Isaac asked his father, "The fire and wood are here, but where is the lamb for the burnt offering?" Abraham told his son, "God himself will provide the lamb for the burnt offering, my son." (Genesis 22:7-8) Abraham's response to Isaac represents a tremendous expression of faith in God's former promise (Genesis 17:19) and God's ability to provide. (See Hebrews 11:19.)

But I believe there's one more issue at play here. In Joshua 24:2 we read, "Long ago your ancestors, including Terah the father of Abraham and Nahor, lived beyond the Euphrates River and worshiped other gods."

Abraham grew up worshiping other gods and many of those pagan gods required human sacrifice. I believe God was graphically demonstrating for Abraham that He is not like the pagan gods and would never require human sacrifice. Instead, God, and God alone, would provide the necessary sacrifice—for Abraham that day it was a ram, and ultimately, God provided His own Son, Jesus Christ (Romans 3:25-26).

Scripture Reading: Genesis 22:1-18

Personal Application:

- Review some of God's promises to us: Matthew 6:33; 7:11; John 3:16; 14:27; Romans 8:38-39; Ephesians 3:20; Philippians 4:19; Revelation 22:20; and believe God for what He has promised.
- What do need to trust God for right now? To what extent might He be testing you in some way at this time? Follow Abraham's example and trust and obey the Lord.

Week 9, Day 4: High Wire

Keeping focused can be a challenge. It's easy to get distracted if we start looking around at other things. Whether it's studying for a big test, taking mental notes during a key meeting, giving your wife your full attention, or following through on some plan of action, maintaining focus is essential.

I remember an interview I once heard from a member of a successful international circus act. This young man made his living by walking a high wire near the top of the circus tent—a feat that required a lot of focus. The interviewer asked him how he developed his skill and overcame the dangers of his profession.

The young man explained, "My grandpa started me out on a wire suspended just two feet above the ground. After falling off several times, he had me concentrate on the end of the wire rather than on my feet. By looking forward to my goal, I was able to keep good balance and eliminate my falls."

As believers, we too can be distracted by fear and doubt, measuring every step with uncertainty. When we keep our eyes on Christ, on His strength and faithfulness, like Peter, we can "walk on water." But the minute we become distracted by the affairs of life, we will sink…or fall.

Solomon charged his son, "Above all else, guard your heart, for everything you do flows from it. Keep your mouth free of perversity; keep corrupt talk far from your lips. Let your eyes look straight ahead; fix your gaze directly before you. Give careful thought to the paths for your feet and be steadfast in all your ways. Do not turn to the right or the left: keep your foot from evil." (Proverbs 4:23-27)

The author of Hebrews adds, "Therefore, since we are surrounded by such a great cloud of witnesses, let us throw off everything that hinders and the sin that so easily entangles. And let us run with perseverance the race marked out for us, fixing our eyes on Jesus, the pioneer and perfecter of faith." (Hebrews 12:1-2a)

How easily we get off track when our focus strays from Christ. The Christian life is pictured as a marathon, not a sprint. Our goal is to be consistent and diligent in our faith and daily walk. Endurance is that steady determination that keeps us going, regardless of the temptations to slow down or give up.

Scripture Reading: 1 Timothy 4:15-16

Personal Application:
- As you face each day, consider how to keep your focus on Jesus and the goal set before you of knowing Him better and making Him known. How do you personally do this?
- What specific actions will you take today to keep your focus on Jesus?
- Who else can you encourage and prompt in this regard?

Week 9, Day 5: Men and Our Stuff

There is something about men and their stuff. It might be a classic car, a beautiful home, a special set of tools, a fast boat, fishing and hunting gear, or some other type of precious possession. Whatever it is, we don't typically part with our stuff too easily. Most garage sales I've been to have household items and some women's clothing. The guy's stuff is usually carefully stored on shelves out of sight from potential buyers.

It's interesting to realize, we really don't possess what we have in this life: our homes, our jobs, our toys, our automobiles, or even our families. They are simply entrusted to us for a time by a loving God. After all, He is the Author of life, death, prosperity, success, and promise. It is all His. He gives us the ability and relationships to acquire things, but ultimately, our stuff is just on loan to us.

Many of us have accumulated so much stuff that we've expanded our already-crowded space by renting a storage unit. And we've become so "toy" oriented, that on a weekend we're left with the dilemma whether to take the boat out, go camping in the RV, or go on a joy ride with the motorcycle. And if we can afford it, we've bought a rig that allows us to take it all with us!

There's nothing wrong with having any or all that stuff, but it can easily get the best of us. I'll never forget conversations I had with two men in church the same Sunday. Both men were ecstatically happy—one because he had just spent a relaxing week on his sailboat—the other because he had just sold his sailboat that he said had been a millstone around his neck!

Perhaps the basic question here is: *Do you own your stuff, or does it own you?* Letting our stuff own us can sneak up on us. Even that guy who finally shed the burden of that sailboat probably thought he was buying himself lots of joy and fun back when he bought it.

What are some warning signs that our stuff owns us?

- We spend more time and money serving our toys than they serve us.
- Our toys come between us and our relationships—especially our relationship with God.
- We become very proud and possessive of our stuff.
- Our possessions dictate how we live our lives.
- They bring stress and worry to our lives.

King Solomon, one of the wealthiest men who ever lived, warned, "Whoever loves money never has enough; whoever loves wealth is never satisfied with their income. This too is meaningless." (Ecclesiastes 5:10)

Scripture Reading: Ecclesiastes 2:1-11

Personal Application:

- Take time to thoughtfully consider your relationship to your belongings. How tight is your grip on them? What does this tell you?
- What is the Lord saying to you through todays devotional? How will you follow through?

Week 9, Day 6: Fatherhood

On Father's Day and on my dad's birthday, I especially miss my dad. As we grow older, our appreciation for our dads seems to increase. But I know that some reading this either never knew their father, he was never around, or their memories of their father are unpleasant.

Our concept of God as our heavenly Father is molded to a great extent by the actions of our dads. Therefore, as a father and grandfather, it's sobering to consider how well I'm representing to my children and grandchildren what our heavenly Father is like.

The word "Father" is mentioned 245 times in the New Testament. Jesus referred to His Father 14 times in the Sermon on the Mount alone. Jesus revealed to us that God is not merely a transcendent force somewhere in the universe, but rather a loving, personal, heavenly Father who is profoundly interested in the details of His Creation, and of our lives.

When the Lord Jesus gave His disciples a pattern for prayer, He addressed His words to "Our Father who is in heaven." And in Galatians, the Apostle Paul explains, "Because you are His sons, God sent the Spirit of His Son into our hearts, the Spirit who calls out, '*Abba*, Father.'" (Galatians 4:6)

I've had the privilege of visiting Israel. Our tour guide was as Israeli whose daughter tagged along with us. Whenever he spoke to our group, he spoke English. But when he and his daughter conversed, they spoke in Hebrew. A couple times, I picked up on the fact that his daughter called him "*Abba*" (Papa, or Daddy). The name *Abba* expressed her deep love, respect, and relationship with her dad.

This experience made Galatians 4:6 come alive in a way I had not yet known. God invites us to call Him "Daddy." The tenderness of this brings tears to my eyes as I write it. For it demonstrates again the depth of God's love for us and the extent to which He has not only forgiven us in Christ but declares us His beloved children.

These truths have a profound impact both on how we view our heavenly Father and how we view our role as fathers. God, our *Abba*, Father, seeks intimacy in our relationship with Him. He wants to commune with us. He loves us unconditionally. He is patient, forgiving, and gracious. He disciplines us justly and for our good. He teaches us what is right.

These are all characteristics of fatherhood that we should mimic. "Follow God's example, therefore, as dearly loved children." (Ephesians 5:1)

Scripture Reading: Romans 8:12-17

Personal Application:
- Take time in prayer to your heavenly Father thanking Him for who He is and what He has done for you.
- What are some of the character traits of your heavenly Father that you wish to model for your children and/or grandchildren?

Week 9, Day 7: Weekly Recap and Prayer

On the seventh day of each week, use the **ACTS** acronym to spend time with the Lord reviewing and assessing your week and praying to God. (**A**=Adoration; **C**=Confession; **T**=Thanksgiving; **S**=Supplication)

First, look back over the previous six days for this week to remind yourself what you read and agreed to. Then, follow the ACTS pattern for prayer below. Finally, use the space below to journal what God is doing in your life and share this with a trusted spiritual partner.

Adoration: Simply spend time in adoration of the Lord. Praise Him and glorify His name. (See 1 Chronicles 29:10-13; Psalm 100; Romans 11:33-36.)

Confession: Confess your sins and shortcomings before God. ("If we confess our sins, he is faithful and just and will forgive us our sins and purify us from all unrighteousness." – 1 John 1:9) To confess (or agree with God) about your sin, implies that you are repentant and desperately want Him to change you.

Thanksgiving: Thank God for what He has done and is doing in your life and the life of your family. Give Him credit, for everything you have comes from Him. (See Psalm 136.)

Supplication: Supplication is just a fancy word for making your requests known to God. Based on the devotions of this past week and the things going on in your life right now, what do you want to ask Him for? "If you, then, though you are evil, know how to give good gifts to your children, how much more will your Father in heaven give good gifts to those who ask Him!" (Matthew 7:11)

Journal: What is God doing in your life right now?

Week 10, Day 1: On What Do You Base Your Fear?

Fear can absolutely extinguish the joy in life. It can make the healthiest person sick to their stomach. It can paralyze our ability to think clearly. Fear can drive us to do foolish things we wouldn't otherwise do. And fear promotes doubt and discouragement.

Today, many people focus on their fears instead of the rich promises of God. We fear financial ruin because of recession. We fear the loss of our jobs because of a declining economy and devaluation of U.S. currency. As I write this, the whole nation and world is fearful of the coronavirus and its global impact.

Some fear nuclear war with countries like Iran, North Korea, or terrorist groups. Both conservatives and so-called progressives fear each other. And many of us fear what will happen to America due to the decline of the moral and social values we once cherished.

Fear is nearly always based on conjecture. Fear is letting negative imaginations run rampant. Fear is an inordinate response to what *might happen*. This is one reason fear is so dangerous. When we allow fear to dictate our thoughts and actions, the hypothetical runs our lives.

Often, if we stop and logically consider what we really know, we can halt fear in its tracks. But sometimes, there seems to be strong evidence that our fears will be realized. This may come in the form of a doctor's prognosis, past experiences, or the common cry of the media and people around us.

But whatever the "evidence," we must find certainty in God. After leaving Egypt, the Children of Israel were in the wilderness. They feared for their lives: "How will we find water? Where will we find food for this great company of people? What will we do if enemies attack us along the way?"

The "evidence" at hand led them to doubt, discouragement, and fear. And their fear led them to sin through their grumbling, complaining, and even rebellion. But in every single case, they had failed to take one crucial, game-changing factor into account: Almighty God of the Universe was present with them and would provide for them and protect them.

Standing with their little ones, their backs against the Red Sea and the mighty Egyptian army bearing down on them, Moses encouraged them: "Do not be afraid. Stand firm and you will see the deliverance the Lord will bring you today. The Egyptians you see today you will never see again. The Lord will fight for you; you need only to be still." (Exodus 14:13-14)

Scripture Reading: Exodus 14:10-31

Personal Application:

- What are you fearing right now? On what are those fears based? What happens to your fear when you consider God's presence, protection, and care for you? Meditate on Isaiah 41:10.

Week 10, Day 2: Boast in the Lord

"Therefore, as it is written: 'Let the one who boasts boast in the Lord.'"
— 1 Corinthians 1:31

Someone once asked me if I was proud of my accomplishments. I had just released another book and was getting some positive feedback. Plus, my dear friend and outdoor writer, Stan Fagerstrom along with some other national pros, had placed my name for consideration with the National Freshwater Fishing Hall of Fame. I was later inducted into that prestigious organization. Great joy...sure, it felt good, but "proud"?

Several verses about pride raced through my mind, reminding me that whatever my perceived successes—I owed it all to God. Moses instructed the Israelites before they entered the Promised Land: "You may say in your heart, 'My power and the strength of my hand made me this wealth.' But you shall remember the Lord your God, for it is He who is giving you power to make wealth." (Deuteronomy 8:17-18a)

I know that everything I have or have accomplished is because of God's grace and strength in my life. Satan may tempt us to be prideful and haughty in spirit because of our abilities or success, but we must remember that every good thing we have comes from God.

I believe God wants us to have a "healthy pride" in whatever we do, but not to be prideful. He wishes to have us do our very best—to work in our jobs, develop relationships, and encourage our families as if we were serving Him: "Whatever you do, work at it with all your heart, as working for the Lord, not for men." (Colossians 3:23)

Healthy pride is satisfaction in a job well done. It's taking joy in what God has enabled us to do, not gloating over how good we are, or how much better we are than others. God's Word speaks against a prideful spirit and a heart that boasts in vanity, conceit, egoism, narcissism, self-love, and self-glorification.

When we're excited, thinking, "Wow! Look at what God has done in my life, with my hands, with His love, and strength running through me and by His mercy," it is a healthy pride that glorifies God. But if we gloat and say, "Wow! Look what I was able to do...look at me...look how great I am! Our arrogance disgraces our Heavenly Father, friends, and family. James warns, "All such boasting is evil." (James 4:16)

I love the Message's rendering of Proverbs 16:18, "First pride, then the crash—the bigger the ego, the harder the fall."

Scripture Reading: Proverbs 6:16-19

Personal Application:

- In what areas of your life are you most prone to pride?
- The antidote for pride is humility and gratefulness. Look for ways today to conduct yourself humbly, giving thanks to God and others for everything.

Week 10, Day 3: Deflecting Praise

"Love is patient, love is kind. It does not envy, it does not boast, it is not proud."
– 1 Corinthians 13:4

Yesterday, we looked at the sin of pride. Pride caused Satan to rebel against God. And Satan enticed Adam and Eve to eat the forbidden fruit from a sense of pride and entitlement. The Scripture says that sin is rebellion against God. That puts pride and boasting at the core of all sin.

From time to time, people congratulate us on a job well done. If we're sensitive to avoid pride and boasting, how do we deal with such attention? We don't want it to reject their compliment, and we also don't want to dishonor or discredit the person who is recognizing our accomplishment. In fact, we too should be generous with our compliments to others.

Humility and gratefulness are the antidotes for pride. Humility is seeing ourselves as God sees us. Here's what Jesus had to say about pride and humility:

To some who were confident of their own righteousness and looked down on everyone else, Jesus told this parable: "Two men went up to the temple to pray, one a Pharisee and the other a tax collector. The Pharisee stood by himself and prayed: 'God, I thank you that I am not like other people—robbers, evildoers, adulterers—or even like this tax collector. I fast twice a week and give a tenth of all I get.'

"But the tax collector stood at a distance. He would not even look up to heaven, but beat his breast and said, 'God, have mercy on me, a sinner.' "I tell you that this man, rather than the other, went home justified before God. For all those who exalt themselves will be humbled, and those who humble themselves will be exalted." (Luke 18:9-14)

Like this tax collector, we must see ourselves as God sees us: utterly needy before Him. Everything we have comes from Him. We are dependent on Him for all things.

So, what if someone had come up to the tax collector after hearing his prayer and commended him for it. How should he (we) respond? We do so by deflecting praise, honor, and glory to God.

We can sincerely thank the person for their kind words and express our gratefulness to God for what He is doing in and through us. When someone compliments a friend of mine, he humbly replies, "Thank you! Isn't God good!?" In this way, we humbly acknowledge the person's compliment, and we also sincerely give glory to God.

Scripture Reading: 1 Corinthians 1:26-31

Personal Application:
- Talk to God in prayer and tell Him about your neediness and dependence on Him.
- Determine to deflect pride when someone compliments you by sincerely thanking them and giving glory to God.

Week 10, Day 4: The Joy of Giving

One Christmas I was doing some last-minute shopping in a toy store. I noticed a nicely dressed little girl enthusiastically browsing—a roll of money clamped tightly in her little hand. Whenever she spied a Barbie she liked, she'd turn and ask her father if she had enough money to buy it. He usually said "yes," but she kept looking, repeating the ritual over and over, searching for the perfect treasure.

A little boy wandered in across the aisle and started sorting through the Pokémon toys. He was dressed neatly but wore a jacket that looked to be a couple of sizes too small and well worn. He, too, had money in his hand, but it looked to be no more than five dollars or so. He and his father had a similar ritual, his father faintly shaking his head as the young lad touched various video games and searched his father's eyes.

The little girl chose a beautifully dressed, glamorous doll—sure to be the envy of every little girl on the block. She suddenly stopped, watching the interchange between the little boy and his father. The boy reluctantly gave up on the video games and chose a book of stickers instead. He and his father started walking through another aisle and disappeared. The little girl paused, smiled, and put her Barbie back on the shelf. She spoke with her father and dashed over to the Pokémon games, picking up one lying on top and racing toward the registers.

I picked out my own purchases and got in line behind the little girl and her father. Then, much to the little girl's delight, the little boy and his father got in line behind me. After the toy was paid for and bagged, the little girl handed it back to the cashier and whispered something in her ear. The cashier smiled, putting the package under the counter.

I paid for my purchases and lingered, watching the little boy come up to the cashier. She rang up his purchases and then exclaimed, "Congratulations, you are my hundredth customer today, and you win a prize!" With that, she handed the little boy the Pokémon game. He stared in disbelief—it was just what he'd wanted.

The little girl and her father were standing at the doorway watching. I saw the biggest, prettiest grin on that little girl that I've ever seen in my life. As she walked out the door, I followed close enough behind to hear her talk to her father. Amazed and delighted at what I'd just witnessed, I heard the father ask his daughter why she had done that. I'll never forget what she said to him. "Nana and Papa wanted me to buy something that would make me happy…and I just did." Then she giggled and skipped off toward their car…and I smiled deep inside.

Scripture Reading: Luke 6:38

Personal Application:

- Jesus said, "It is more blessed to give than to receive." (Acts 20:35) Brainstorm ways that you can bless others today with your time, attention, service, or funds.
- At the end of the day, record ways you were able to give to others. In what ways did your acts of giving affect them? How did these acts affect you?

Week 10, Day 5: Confidence Is Contagious!

"I thank my God every time I remember you… being confident of this, that he who began a good work in you will carry it on to completion until the day of Christ Jesus." – Philippians 1:3, 6

I truly enjoy watching various NFL playoff teams compete for the coveted prize of their division's championship. After watching my friend and All-Pro quarterback Rich Gannon perform years ago for the Oakland Raiders, I was convinced, and still am, that the confidence of the quarterback is a key factor for the success of any team.

When a quarterback passes the ball, there are basically four possibilities for an outcome: a completion, an incompletion, a penalty, or an interception. With only fifty percent odds that the outcome will be good, a quarterback needs a great deal of confidence. If a quarterback loses confidence in himself, his line, or his receivers, he runs the risk of being intercepted or having an incompletion. Gannon exuded confidence in his team, his coaches, his play-calling abilities, and his God-given skills.

In his book, *Play Football the NFL Way*, Tom Bass states, "Height and weight may vary considerably from one quarterback to another, but all successful quarterbacks have an inner strength and belief in themselves." They bring an air of confidence to the field and the huddle that is quickly transmitted to the players.

We too can be confident when we "enter the field." If our confidence is in the truth of salvation and the person of Jesus Christ, our hope is eternal. We must also display confidence in Christ and the ultimate outcome of the game of life. We may experience temporary setbacks and losses, but we know that in Christ we are on the winning team. Therefore, we can exude confidence in Christ and His game plan to those around us.

When the Apostle Paul was facing the executioner's sword, he did so with an assurance that had sustained him through other trying times. His ministry was full of danger, and yet he wouldn't have had it any other way. He was serving his Lord. Paul knew that through his belief and trust in God, he would eventually find perfect peace. He had confidence and assurance in his Savior and his salvation. This determined optimism is more than "positive thinking." It's grounded in truth.

May the truth of the gospel give us all confidence and may our confidence in Jesus Christ glorify God…and be contagious!

Scripture Reading: 2 Corinthians 5:1-10

Personal Application:
- Concerning your life right now, what truths and assurances are you confident of in Christ?
- List the people in your life whom you could greatly influence by your confidence in the Lord.
- In what specific ways can you model your confidence in Christ and in those around you?

Week 10, Day 6: The Lure of Sin

Lowell Lundstrom, Bible teacher and evangelist, and his son L.J. had a rare opportunity to get away and experience the great outdoors. On their way to Lake Winnipeg River in Canada, the two outdoorsmen stopped at a local tackle shop to check out the fishing reports.

L.J. spotted a large minnow-shaped, shallow running lure that was decked out in all kinds of colors. Lowell remembered the old saying, "More lures are designed to catch fishermen than fish." But the persistence of a young boy and the curiosity of an old fisherman provoked a sale.

After several days of difficult fishing and a small stringer of fish to show for all their hard work, Lowell snapped on his son's new lure just to show the boy some encouragement. The evening sun was setting on his last cast of the trip when a 23-pound musky grabbed the lure. The unique qualities of this bait were more than the big fish could resist, and the two elated fishermen netted the monster, taking it to the dock with their newfound love of a very tempting lure.

The world is full of fancy lures. I'm sure we can all remember times when we have been tempted. Biblically speaking, to be "tempted" means to be lured or enticed. The word temptation *(peirasmos)* held great meaning for the first century disciples. It meant "to catch in a snare or trap" or "to lure a fish from his hiding place."

Temptation comes in many forms. The media is full of temptation. Some folks are obsessed with trying to obtain more, better, bigger, and newer. The exploitation of sex has driven many men and women into the dark closets of pornography. The culture tells us to "Look out for number one," "If you don't get caught, it's okay," and "Do whatever it takes to get what you want." The lure of riches tempts people to steal, cheat, or simply take advantage of someone else's accounting mistake.

Our flesh may be tempted by food or sexual fantasies, our mind by fantasies of power, fame, and fortune. But our spirit can also be tempted, as Satan wages war on our very souls. The author of Hebrews comforts us: "For we do not have a high priest who is unable to empathize with our weaknesses, but we have one who has been tempted in every way, just as we are—yet he did not sin." (Hebrews 4:15)

Jesus urges us, "Watch and pray so that you will not fall into temptation. The spirit is willing, but the flesh is weak." (Matthew 26:41) Stay alert and protect yourself from the things you know could tempt you. Make yourself accountable to another man, pray, and fill your heart with God's Word. These are keys in dealing with temptation.

Scripture Reading: 1 Corinthians 10:6-13

Personal Application:

- In what areas are you most likely to be tempted? Order your life such that you avoid those areas and situations like the plague! Instead, satisfy your cravings by feasting on God's Word.
- Meet regularly with a spiritual confidant—another man who is following Jesus.Be totally open with him about your struggles. Pray for each other and encourage one another.

Week 10, Day 7: Weekly Recap and Prayer

On the seventh day of each week, use the **ACTS** acronym to spend time with the Lord reviewing and assessing your week and praying to God. (**A**=Adoration; **C**=Confession; **T**=Thanksgiving; **S**=Supplication)

First, look back over the previous six days for this week to remind yourself what you read and agreed to. Then, follow the ACTS pattern for prayer below. Finally, use the space below to journal what God is doing in your life and share this with a trusted spiritual partner.

Adoration: Simply spend time in adoration of the Lord. Praise Him and glorify His name. (See 1 Chronicles 29:10-13; Psalm 100; Romans 11:33-36.)

Confession: Confess your sins and shortcomings before God. ("If we confess our sins, he is faithful and just and will forgive us our sins and purify us from all unrighteousness." – 1 John 1:9) To confess (or agree with God) about your sin, implies that you are repentant and desperately want Him to change you.

Thanksgiving: Thank God for what He has done and is doing in your life and the life of your family. Give Him credit, for everything you have comes from Him. (See Psalm 136.)

Supplication: Supplication is just a fancy word for making your requests known to God. Based on the devotions of this past week and the things going on in your life right now, what do you want to ask Him for? "If you, then, though you are evil, know how to give good gifts to your children, how much more will your Father in heaven give good gifts to those who ask Him!" (Matthew 7:11)

Journal: What is God doing in your life right now?

Week 11, Day 1: The Easy Way or the Hard Way?

"Wisdom is more precious than rubies,
and nothing you desire can compare with her." – Proverbs 8:11

A smart man learns from his own mistakes, but a wise man learns from the mistakes of others. I've learned many lessons the hard way, but I prefer learning like the wise man.

Wisdom is the proper application of the learning that we've collected along the way. It's the good sense we've gained through experience, teaching and observation. Wisdom guides us, protects us, and shapes us. No wonder it is written, "How much better to get wisdom than gold, to choose understanding rather than silver!" (Proverbs 16:16)

The following poem is a collection of wisdom—a testimony to the writer's life experiences and desire for truth.

As I've walked through life, I've learned:

- *You can do something in an instant that will give you heartache for life.*
- *It takes a long time to become the person you want to be.*
- *Always leave loved ones with loving words. It may be the last time you see them.*
- *You can keep going long after you think you can't.*
- *Either you control your attitude, or it controls you.*
- *No matter how hot and steamy a relationship is at first, the passion fades and there had better be something deeper to take its place.*
- *Heroes do what must be done when it needs to be done, regardless of the cost.*
- *Money is a lousy way of keeping score.*
- *I may be right to be angry but being angry doesn't give me the right to be cruel.*
- *Both love and true friendship continue to grow, even over long distance.*
- *Maturity has little to do with age and more to do with how you treat others.*
- *Even your best friend is going to hurt you occasionally and you must forgive them.*
- *It's good to be forgiven by others, but sometimes you must learn to forgive yourself.*
- *Even when you feel spent, when a friend cries out, you'll find the strength to help.*
- *Credentials on the wall do not make you a decent human being.*
- *Your background and circumstances may have influenced who you are, but you are responsible for who you become.*
  – Author unknown (abbreviated)

Scripture Reading: Proverbs 2:1-17

Personal Application:

- Reflect on your life. In what areas of your life would you like more wisdom?
  1. Search the Scriptures for wisdom in those areas.
  2. Seek out another man who is wise in those areas and ask his counsel.

Week 11, Day 2: Bitterness

The writer of Hebrews warns, "See to it that no one falls short of the grace of God and that no bitter root grows up to cause trouble and defile many."
— Hebrews 12:15

Recently, I was repairing a fence. The post had rotted at its cement base, so I had to dig out the old cement footing to pour a new one. But when I began digging around the old footing, I found that a large tree nearby had spread its roots out and they had encircled this footing.

There was no way to extract the footing without first cutting away the roots that were wrapped around it holding it in place. And one of those roots was as big as my arm!

When someone offends us in some way and we harbor bitterness against them, we're in danger of letting that bitterness take root in our lives. And when it does, it will consume us. Bitterness wraps itself around our hearts like those tree roots around that footing. Bitterness fills our minds and thoughts with malice and ill-will toward that person.

But as the passage in Hebrews warns, bitterness doesn't confine itself to the person it focuses on. Instead, bitterness spreads, permeating and spoiling our relationships with others around us as well.

In Genesis 27, Jacob cheated his brother Esau out of the blessing that was due him as the first-born son. As a result, verse 41 of that chapter says, "Esau held a grudge against Jacob because of the blessing his father had given him. He said to himself, 'The days of mourning for my father are near; then I will kill my brother Jacob.'"

This incident shows how quickly and thoroughly bitterness can grow in a person's life. Bitterness seeks revenge. Bitterness wishes harm to come to the person, even to the point of wanting them dead. In this case, Esau was so angry at his brother Jacob that he planned to kill him.

Perhaps few of us have let bitterness go to that extreme. Regardless, bitterness toward someone causes us to think ungodly things and act foolishly. We must recognize that bitterness not only affects others, but it eats away at us as well.

Once bitterness has taken root, the remedy is forgiveness. We must extend forgiveness to the person who offended us. But better yet, by bearing with one another and being patient with each other we can avoid becoming bitter at all. As the Hebrews passage suggests, God's grace is available to us if we'll ask Him for it.

Scripture Reading: Colossians 3:12-14

Personal Application:

- Is there someone in your life who has offended you in some way? If so, guard your heart. If you're already holding a grudge, forgive that person and let Christ fill you with compassion for them instead.
- Meditate on the Scripture reading for today. Let God's Word permeate your heart. If you are prone to holding grudges, ask Christ to transform you in this regard.

Week 11, Day 3: Reconciling Suffering with a Loving God

"What then shall we say? Is God unjust? Not at all!"
– Romans 9:14)

Perhaps one of the toughest questions we Christians are asked is how a loving God can allow so much suffering. Suffering and pain seem hard to reconcile with a loving God unless a person knows Christ and trusts in His goodness. We try to explain our faith and use all sorts of analogies, but this issue can be a tough one to navigate. But it's an important question. Too often it's the excuse people give for not believing in God.

The following story is one of the best explanations of why God allows pain and suffering that I have seen:

A man went to a barbershop to have his hair cut and his beard trimmed. As the barber began to work, they got into a good conversation. They talked about many things and various subjects. Eventually, they touched about God and the barber said, "I don't believe that God exists."

"Why do you say that?" asked the customer.

"Well, you just have to go out in the street to realize that God doesn't exist. Tell me, if God exists, would there be so many sick people? Would there be abandoned children? If God existed, there would be neither suffering nor pain. I can't imagine a loving a God who would allow all of these things." The customer thought for a moment but didn't respond because he didn't want to start an argument. The barber finished his job and the customer left the shop.

Just after he left the barbershop, he saw a man in the street with long, stringy, dirty hair and an untrimmed beard. He looked dirty and unkempt. The customer turned back and entered the barber shop again and he said to the barber, "You know what? Barbers do not exist."

"How can you say that?" asked the surprised barber. "I am here, and I am a barber. And I just cut your hair!"

"No!" the customer exclaimed. "Barbers don't exist because if they did, there would be no people with long, dirty hair and untrimmed beards, like that man outside."

"Ah, but barbers DO exist! What happens is, people do not come to me."

"Exactly!" affirmed the customer. "That's the point! God exists too! But people don't go to Him and do not look for Him. That's why there's so much pain and suffering in the world."

Scripture Reading: Romans 10:13; 2 Peter 3:9

Personal Application:
- One of the greatest arguments for the existence of God is the evidence of a transformed life. Live in such a way that people see God's love, mercy, and grace in your life.
- Look for an opportunity to share today's devotional with someone and see what God does!

Week 11, Day 4: Living with Eager Expectation

I don't know about you, but I'm tired of the doom and gloom stories that characterize the media nowadays. Even comedians and talk-show hosts who are supposed to cheer us up are in a real funk. The late-night shows intended to entertain us and make us laugh are filled with discontent, cynicism, and pessimism.

Sure, the economy may be in despair. Yes, we wish the wars were over so our brave troops could come home. True, we're dealing with new and deadly viruses. And yes, our politicians have let us down. And each of us may be working through more personal challenges.

But despite all this there is so much to be thankful for. Knowing Christ and simply being alive has so many benefits. Instead of tracking with the pessimists, let's remind ourselves that our ultimate hope is in Christ Jesus. "May the God of hope fill you with all joy and peace as you trust in him, so that you may overflow with hope by the power of the Holy Spirit." (Romans 15:13)

If you are living a paltry life, resolve to stop it today. Expect great things to happen. Confidently receive God's abundant blessings. Do not think *lack*. Instead, think *prosperity*, *abundance*, and *the best of everything*. God wants to give us, His children, every good thing (Matthew 7:11).

This doesn't mean we won't experience pain and suffering. But don't hinder His blessings with negative thinking. Instead, boldly walk through life with a sense of hope, joy, curiosity, and expectation. God wants us to discover His abundant and eternal love and peace.

The prophet Isaiah urges us to pursue a peaceful mind and spirit by trusting in the Lord. "You will keep in perfect peace all who trust in you, all whose thoughts are fixed on you!" (Isaiah 26:3 NLT) If our minds are filled with negative thoughts and an attitude of defeat, we will be in a state of mental unrest and turmoil, and there will be no inner peace.

Let's fix our thoughts and gaze upon the One who died on Calvary's cross so that we might experience His great peace and grace. "Now to him who is able to do immeasurably more than all we ask or imagine, according to his power that is at work within us." (Ephesians 3:20)

From a Roman prison cell, Paul wrote, " I eagerly expect and hope that I will in no way be ashamed, but will have sufficient courage so that now as always Christ will be exalted in my body, whether by life or by death. For to me, to live is Christ and to die is gain." (Philippians 1:20-21)

Scripture Reading: 1 Corinthians 2:9-10

Personal Application:

- Assess your state of mind right now. Are your thoughts characterized by hope, joy, and peace, or are you living in dread and defeat?
- Find strength and purpose in Christ. Feed on His Word.
  Enjoy the company of other Christ followers.
  Count your blessings and be thankful. Worship the Lord.

Week 11, Day 5: Who Is Jesus to You?

If you hang around folks who like football it won't be long before they mention the nicknames of their favorite stars, plays and positions. To those less passionate about the game, it's as if some weird charismatic spirit took over the animated fans. Their language becomes coded and mixed with abbreviations and non-sensible words: blitz, red-dog, cover-man, T.D., red zone, rollout, under center, screen, and wide-out.

Nicknames for some of the players have included names like The Gipper, Papa Bear, Slingin' Sammy, Golden Boy, Mercury Morris, Bum Phillips, Boomer Esiason, The Snake, Mr. Hollywood, Neon Dion, Hacksaw Reynolds, Ickey Woods, Deacon Jones, The Galloping Ghost, Broadway Joe Namath, Billy Whiteshoes Johnson, The Zonk, The Fridge, Mean Joe Green, and Dandy Don Meredith.

Each of these names means something to pundits of the game. Most often it's local sportswriters or teammates that give a person his nickname. Some nicknames are earned while others reflect an athlete's playing style or persona. If you listen to ESPN's Chris Berman describing clips from various games, you could almost fill a notebook with such monikers. His enthusiastic style helps fans identify the person or experience with unusual adjectives and graphic terms.

God's Word is also full of nicknames. A nickname in Scripture often signifies the special relationship someone had with God. When God established His covenant with Abram, He changed his name to "Abraham," meaning, *a leader and father to many nations.* God renamed Jacob "Israel," meaning, *the one who has overcome.* And Jesus changed Simon's name to "Peter," which means *rock.* But we also find Doubting Thomas, and Judas, the Betrayer.

Following is what the Scriptures say about Jesus' name: "Therefore God exalted him to the highest place and gave him the name that is above every name, that at the name of Jesus every knee should bow, in heaven and on earth and under the earth, and every tongue acknowledge that Jesus Christ is Lord, to the glory of God the Father." (Philippians 2:9-11)

After spending considerable time with His disciples, Jesus asked them one day, "Who do people say that I am?" "They replied, 'Some say John the Baptist; others say Elijah; and still others, Jeremiah or one of the prophets.' 'But what about you,' he asked, 'Who do you say I am?' Simon Peter answered, 'You are the Messiah, the Son of the living God.'" (Matthew 16:13-16)

How about you? Who do you say that Jesus is?

Scripture Reading: John 1 (pay special attention to all the names of Jesus)

Personal Application:
- What names for Jesus do you find in John chapter one?
- When you pray, integrate some of the names of Jesus into your prayers to Him.
- If Jesus were to give you a nickname to describe you, what do you think it would be?

Week 11, Day 6: Look to the Interests of Others

"Carry each other's burdens, and in this way you will fulfill the law of Christ."
– Galatians 6:2

For over three decades we've had the privilege of providing a unique outreach event to disabled youth: Special Kids Day (SKD). These are always extraordinary times for the participants, their parents, the staff, and the helpful volunteers. It is a time of serving and assisting those who have special needs.

Most of the kids have additional issues to cope with beyond their physical disabilities. Many are from single-parent homes, and most desperately desire attention and affection. As the young people experience our program and the loving people who assist them, they become very excited and joyful. Throughout the morning, the love of God is demonstrated in some very tangible ways. I have a special fondness for children with disabilities and always look forward to these events.

So, I was especially touched when I heard a story several years ago from the Seattle Special Olympics. Nine contestants, all physically or mentally disabled, assembled at the starting line for the 100-yard dash. At the gun, they all started out, not exactly in a dash but with a relish to run the race to the finish…and win! All, that is, except one little boy who stumbled on the asphalt, tumbled over a couple of times, and began to cry.

The other eight heard the boy cry. They slowed down and looked back. Amazingly, they all turned around and went back—every one of them! One girl with Down's Syndrome bent down and kissed him on the forehead, saying, "This will make it better." Then, all nine linked arms and walked together to the finish line. Everyone in the stadium stood, and the cheering went on for several minutes.

People who were there still tell the story today. Why? I think it's because deep down inside, they knew that what matters in this life is more than winning for ourselves. What matters is helping others win, even if it means slowing down and changing our course. What matters are the lives around us.

The Apostle Paul reminds us, "Each of you should look not only to your own interests, but also to the interests of others." (Philippians 2:4) Every year this verse plays out as we rarely have difficulty getting enough volunteers to help with the SKD programs. I'm so thankful for folks who look to the interests of others, who truly understand the importance of the lives around us.

Scripture Reading: Romans 12:9-13

Personal Application:

• Look for opportunities today to "look not only to your own interests, but also to the interests of others."
• At the end of the day, come back and celebrate what God did through you in the lives of others today.

Week 11, Day 7: Weekly Recap and Prayer

On the seventh day of each week, use the **ACTS** acronym to spend time with the Lord reviewing and assessing your week and praying to God. (**A**=Adoration; **C**=Confession; **T**=Thanksgiving; **S**=Supplication)

First, look back over the previous six days for this week to remind yourself what you read and agreed to. Then, follow the ACTS pattern for prayer below. Finally, use the space below to journal what God is doing in your life and share this with a trusted spiritual partner.

Adoration: Simply spend time in adoration of the Lord. Praise Him and glorify His name. (See 1 Chronicles 29:10-13; Psalm 100; Romans 11:33-36.)

Confession: Confess your sins and shortcomings before God. ("If we confess our sins, he is faithful and just and will forgive us our sins and purify us from all unrighteousness." – 1 John 1:9) To confess (or agree with God) about your sin, implies that you are repentant and desperately want Him to change you.

Thanksgiving: Thank God for what He has done and is doing in your life and the life of your family. Give Him credit, for everything you have comes from Him. (See Psalm 136.)

Supplication: Supplication is just a fancy word for making your requests known to God. Based on the devotions of this past week and the things going on in your life right now, what do you want to ask Him for? "If you, then, though you are evil, know how to give good gifts to your children, how much more will your Father in heaven give good gifts to those who ask Him!" (Matthew 7:11)

Journal: What is God doing in your life right now?

Week 12, Day 1: You Are a Child of God

A seminary professor was vacationing with his wife in Gatlinburg, Tennessee. One morning, they went to a little restaurant, hoping to enjoy a quiet meal. While waiting for their food, they noticed a distinguished looking, white haired man moving from table to table visiting with the guests. The professor rolled his eyes and whispered, "I hope he doesn't come over here." But sure enough, the man did come over to their table. "Where are you folks from?" he asked in a friendly voice. "Oklahoma," they answered. "Great to have you here in Tennessee," the stranger said. "What do you do for a living?" "I teach at a seminary," the professor replied. "Oh, so you teach preachers how to preach, do you? Well, I've got a really good story for you." And with that, the gentleman pulled up a chair and sat down at the table with them. The professor groaned and thought to himself, "Great. Just what I need–another preacher story!"

The man pointed out the window and said, "Not far from the base of that mountain over there, a boy was born to an unwed mother. He had a hard time growing up, because wherever he went, everyone asked him the same question, 'Hey boy, who's your daddy?' At school, he would hide at recess and lunchtime from other students. He would even avoid going anywhere in public because the question, 'Hey boy, who's your daddy?' hurt him so badly.

When he was about twelve years old, a new preacher came to his church. The little boy would always go in late and slip out early to avoid the question, 'Who's your daddy?' But one day, the new preacher caught him, and not knowing anything about the boy, put his hand on his shoulder and asked him, 'Son, who's your daddy?' The whole church got deathly quiet. The boy could feel every eye on him. The new preacher sensed the awkward silence and said, 'Wait a minute! I know who you are. I see the family resemblance. You are a child of God. Son, you've got a great inheritance. Go and claim it.'

With that, the boy beamed and walked out the door a changed person. Since then, whenever anybody asked him, 'Who's your Daddy?' he'd just tell them, 'I'm a child of God.'" The distinguished gentleman got up and asked, "Isn't that a great story? You know, if that new preacher hadn't told me I was one of God's children, I probably would never have amounted to anything!" And he walked away.

The seminary professor and his wife were stunned. He called the waitress over and asked her, "Who was that gentleman?" The waitress grinned and said, "That's Ben Hooper. He's the former governor of Tennessee!"

Scripture Reading: John 1:10-13

Personal Application:

- What does it mean to you to know that you are a child of God?
- Someone you know may need to be reminded that they too are a child of God. Keep your eyes and ears open for an opportunity to remind them today who their Daddy is.

Week 12, Day 2: Through It All

Life has taught me that God can't use us greatly until we've experienced some suffering. Suffering has a way of refining our faith. And despite our circumstances, God also desires us to be filled with joy.

One of our sons introduced me to a man, who despite his blindness, is one of the most joy-filled individuals I've ever met. His name is Gordon Mote. Besides being one of my favorite contemporary Christian artists, he is one of the most sought-after musicians in Nashville.

If you look at the credits on an album from Brad Paisley, Alan Jackson, or Martina McBride, the name Gordon Mote, accomplished musician, master prankster, and devoted follower of Jesus will appear on the album jacket.

For Gordon, music became a way to transcend the challenges associated with his disability and deepen his relationship with God. And if there was an award on Nashville's famed Music Row for Mr. Congeniality, Gordon would be the recipient. The likes of Rascal Flatts, Randy Travis, The Martins, Mark Lowry, Trace Adkins, The Gaither Vocal Band, Kenny Chesney, and many others have all experienced his charm, wit, and talents.

Joy is an attribute that exudes from every pore of Gordon's body. He has a contagious positive spirit that delights audiences and other musicians. Gordon is one of the most remarkable people I've ever met. The music and warmth of this man are so special.

What is joy? Joy is a character trait of our loving heavenly Father. Joy is the fruit from living in surrender to the Holy Spirit. Joy is a deep inner peace that projects a sense of well-being and satisfaction. Therefore, joy is a net of love, a strong attractant by which you can catch souls.

Gordon has learned that the best way to show his gratitude to God and people is to accept life situations with joy. A joyful heart is the inevitable result of a heart burning with love.

Joy-filled people, like Gordon, underscore their belief that one should never let anything so fill you with sorrow as to make you forget the joy we possess in knowing Christ.

As the Book of James reminds us, "Consider it all joy, my brethren, when you encounter various trials." (James 1:2) Despite his blindness and many other trials in Gordon's life, he decided to be a joy-filled person and use his amazing talents for God's glory. When Andre Crouch and Gordon Mote wrote and performed the inspirational song, "Through It All," they got it right.

"Through it all, through it all, (Oh,) I've learned to trust in Jesus; I've learned to trust in God. Through it all, through it all, I've learned to depend upon His Word."

Scripture Reading: Nehemiah 8:8-12

Personal Application:

- What is the source of your joy?
- How will you joyfully overcome the hardships and trials you're bound to experience?

Week 12, Day 3: Discovering God's Will for Your Life

A question I often hear from men who want to know and do God's will is "How can I seek and know God's will in a situation?" According to Scripture we can do the following:

- Pray and ask God for clear direction.
- Seek the wise counsel and support of other believers.
- Evaluate the circumstances: Is God making certain things obvious?
- Trust in God who wants us to know and do His will.
- Focus on the universal purposes God has given all of us.
- Keep an eternal perspective.

God's plan for our lives will ALWAYS agree with Scripture. We must use God's Word like a filter to sift out nonsense and fleshly desires and use it like a compass to keep us on course. And the better we know God, the easier it is to discern His voice and His ways.

As a young man, I was struggling to know God's will in an important situation. I asked Him to reveal His will to me through His Word. He very clearly showed me Ephesians 5:17, "Therefore do not be foolish, but understand what the Lord's will is." Initially, I was angry at Him for giving me this verse. I thought sarcastically, "Thanks, that helps a lot! NOT!"

But when I calmed down, I realized three things: First, God loves me. Second, He has a sense of humor. And third, most of His will is laid out for us in Scripture already and some of the other stuff we worry about is petty and not worth the effort of worry we put into it.

But knowing God's will for our lives is just the beginning. Truly seeking His will also involves accepting God's will and obeying Him. This is not always easy. Sometimes it's costly.

Before His crucifixion, as a man, Jesus agonized over what He was about to experience. In Mark 14:35-36 we read, "Going a little farther, He fell to the ground and prayed that if possible the hour might pass from Him. 'Abba, Father,' He said, 'everything is possible for You. Take this cup from Me. Yet not what I will, but what You will.'"

Jesus wasn't trying to get out of going to the Cross, but he was expressing his human emotions – his aversion to the pain, torture, and suffering He would experience in obeying God's will. We thank and praise Jesus that He obeyed God's will.

Accepting God's will isn't always easy, but it's always the right and good thing to do.

Scripture Reading: Psalm 32:8-11

Personal Application:
- To what extent do you seek God's will in your important decisions?
- In what ways have you struggled with knowing His will in the past?
- What strategies will you use moving forward for knowing and doing His will?

Week 12, Day 4: Need a Vacation?

"It is useless for you to work so hard from early morning until late at night, anxiously working for food to eat; for God gives rest to his loved ones."
– Psalm 127:2 (NLT)

Over the years, I've enjoyed traveling to various parts of this beautiful country. There is so much to see, and some of the best times have been on very simple vacations with my family. We visited and enjoyed places like Lake Camanche, Lake Berryessa, and Lake Shasta in California. As a family we built great memories around fishing and water-skiing activities.

I'm reminded of how important it is to spend quality time with those we love. In an interview for *Today's Christian Woman*, writer and speaker Carol Kent told this story:

One day when my son Jason was young, we were eating breakfast together. I had on an old pair of slacks and a fuzzy old sweater. He flashed his baby blues at me over his cereal bowl and said, "Mommy, you look so pretty today."

I didn't even have makeup on! So, I said, "Honey, why would you say I look pretty today? Normally I'm dressed up in a suit and high heels."

And he said, "When you look like that, I know you're going someplace; but when you look like this, I know you're all mine."

There is a lot of pressure these days to go on expensive trips with the family—exotic locations, all-inclusive packages, luxury condos, and once-in-a-lifetime opportunities. While these vacations may very well be fun, the extravagance is not the point. The point is to get away from distractions and the hustle and bustle of our daily lives so we can focus on "us"—the family.

Some people decide to forego time with the family for years so they can save up for that perfect vacation. Don't let glitzy sales gimmicks or "keeping up with the Jones's" keep your family from experiencing some powerful bonding time. Our kids don't need fancy; they need us!

We don't have to spend a fortune, or even a bunch, to create lasting memories. Sharing time and s'mores around a campfire is priceless! And if circumstances won't allow us to leave home, we can find ways in our own town—in our own backyards—to make special family vacation memories. After all, vacation is merely an intermission from our regular life. All we really need to do is set aside time.

Nothing can replace the beauty of being together with those we love. How long has it been since you had an intermission? If "rest" is not a part of your vocabulary, it's time to reevaluate. Enjoy each moment you can with your loved ones. Life is precious…and often too short!

Scripture Reading: Mark 6:30-32

Personal Application:

- What would a very relaxing and bonding vacation look like for you and your family?
- Share the ideas in this devotional with your family and come up with a family vacation plan.

Week 12, Day 5: The Holiness of God

"Holy, Holy, Holy, is the Lord God, the Almighty, who was, and is, and is to come."
– Revelation 4:8b

God is holy. He is completely righteous and totally separated from evil. He transcends everything else. The word "holy" has its roots in the Greek and means "separated from sin." Because God is not subject to the frailties and limitations of His creation, He excels any standard of excellence and purity we might invent. He is the standard for holiness.

The Apostle Peter urges every follower of Jesus to be holy: "But like the Holy One who called you, be holy yourselves also in all your behavior; because it is written, 'You shall be holy, for I am holy.'" (1 Peter 1:15-16 NASB). I don't know about you, but in my own strength I cannot be totally holy and pure day in and day out. How then can I reconcile my inappropriate thoughts and actions with my desire to follow Christ and be like Him? How can anyone be holy?

According to Scripture there is only one way we can be holy. "But now God has reconciled you by Christ's physical body through death to present you holy in his sight, without blemish and free from accusation." (Colossians 1:22)

Positionally, through Christ, God sees us as holy before Him. But in *practice*, I'm afraid, all too often we're not living the holy lives that God has called us to. Unfortunately, we are too often unholy in our thoughts, attitudes, and behaviors.

We know that it's only in Christ that we are declared holy before God. And it's also only through the power of Christ that we can live holy lives in practice. We cannot "beat" the flesh, by relying on our own strength in the flesh! We need to rely on the Holy Spirit's power, but that doesn't mean we're passive onlookers either.

Scripture instructs us, "Everyone who confesses the name of the Lord must turn away from wickedness." (2 Timothy 2:19b) And, "Walk by the Spirit, and you will not gratify the desires of the flesh." (Galatians 5:16)

We need to live by the Holy Spirit and separate ourselves from the temptations, sin, and behaviors that drag us down and take away our peace. In fact, we are told to flee from sin (1 Corinthians 6:18; 10:14). Like the angels urged Lot and his family when they led them out of Sodom and Gomorrah, "Flee for your lives! Don't look back, and don't stop anywhere in the plain! Flee...or you will be swept away!" (Genesis 19:17)

May our prayer be, "And lead us not into temptation, but deliver us from evil." (Matthew 6: 13)

Scripture Reading: Galatians 5:16-26

Personal Application:
- What aspects of your life right now conflict with the holiness that the Lord calls us to?
- Flee from those things and replace them with thoughts and actions that come from God.
- Share these things with a spiritual partner who will hold you accountable.

Week 12, Day 6: Be a Team Player

Over the years I've had the privilege of providing chaplain services for basketball, football, and baseball teams. And from what I've observed, successful teams encourage and support one-another. Of course, "support" can be subject to interpretation.

For example, it seems every season, baseball has its fair share of "bean-ball" incidents. This is when a player retaliates against the other team by throwing the ball at a player with the intention of causing harm. The umpires call this "getting after it" and will often throw a player out of the game if the officials believe that such an incident was intentional. Some defend these actions, declaring, "He's supporting his teammates." But I believe that a good team leader will support his team best by encouraging them to excel both professionally and morally.

The Apostle Paul was a great team leader. He challenged his followers to love and serve each other—to be committed to "the team." (Romans 12:10). At times, we either need to lean on others or others need to lean on us. We were not made to live this life alone! The following story demonstrates the importance of teamwork, especially when the going gets tough:

Sadhu Sundar Singh and a companion were traveling through a high pass in the Himalayan Mountains when they came across a man lying in the snow. The man was barely alive. Sadhu told his traveling companion they needed to help the stranger. But his companion felt his best chance of survival was to keep going on his own.

After his friend left, Sundar hefted the poor traveler upon his shoulders and slowly carried the man onward. The high altitude and snowy conditions caused Sundar to fully exert himself. The heat from his body warmed the victim and gradually restored life to him. The two men struggled together and, leaning upon one another, kept each other warm and encouraged.

Tragically, as they neared their destination, they came across the frozen body of Sundar's first companion. His independent struggle for survival had failed, and he died alone.

We must learn to work together through the grace and unconditional love that comes only from the power of the Holy Spirit. Let's re-define "getting after it" to being team players who are committed to the good works that Christ has called us to. Let's serve each other, support each other; and carry each other's burdens (Galatians 6:2).

Scripture Reading: Galatians 6:1-6

Personal Application:
- Think about all the people who are on your "team." This can include your family, small group, church, workplace, etc.
- Now think of some practical ways you can support them, love them, and encourage them.

Week 12, Day 7: Weekly Recap and Prayer

On the seventh day of each week, use the **ACTS** acronym to spend time with the Lord reviewing and assessing your week and praying to God. (**A**=Adoration; **C**=Confession; **T**=Thanksgiving; **S**=Supplication)

First, look back over the previous six days for this week to remind yourself what you read and agreed to. Then, follow the ACTS pattern for prayer below. Finally, use the space below to journal what God is doing in your life and share this with a trusted spiritual partner.

Adoration: Simply spend time in adoration of the Lord. Praise Him and glorify His name. (See 1 Chronicles 29:10-13; Psalm 100; Romans 11:33-36.)

Confession: Confess your sins and shortcomings before God. ("If we confess our sins, he is faithful and just and will forgive us our sins and purify us from all unrighteousness." – 1 John 1:9) To confess (or agree with God) about your sin, implies that you are repentant and desperately want Him to change you.

Thanksgiving: Thank God for what He has done and is doing in your life and the life of your family. Give Him credit, for everything you have comes from Him. (See Psalm 136.)

Supplication: Supplication is just a fancy word for making your requests known to God. Based on the devotions of this past week and the things going on in your life right now, what do you want to ask Him for? "If you, then, though you are evil, know how to give good gifts to your children, how much more will your Father in heaven give good gifts to those who ask Him!" (Matthew 7:11)

Journal: What is God doing in your life right now?

Week 13, Day 1: Good for the Soul

The first miracle Jesus performed in His public ministry was turning water into wine at the wedding in Cana. Of course, the miracle itself demonstrates the creative power of Jesus. But what really amazes me is that He performed this miracle in secret simply for the joy and enjoyment of all at this wedding.

How wonderful it is to experience God's presence in our lives and to know that our loving Father desires to give us good things. The following story reminds us about the goodness of our heavenly Father and the importance of sharing His gifts with others.

Last week I took my children to a restaurant. My six-year-old son asked if he could say grace. As we bowed our heads he said, "God is good, God is great. Thank you for the food, and I will even thank you more if Dad gets us ice cream for dessert. And liberty and justice for all! Amen!"

Along with the laughter from the other customers nearby I heard a woman remark, "That's what's wrong with this country. Kids today don't even know how to pray… asking God for ice cream! Why, I never!"

Hearing this, my son burst into tears and asked me, "Did I do it wrong? Is God mad at me?" As I held him and assured him that he had done a terrific job and God was certainly not mad at him, an elderly gentleman approached the table.

He winked at my son and said, "I happen to know that God thought that was a great prayer." "Really?" my son asked. "Cross my heart," the man replied. Then in a theatrical whisper he added (indicating the woman whose remark had started this whole thing), "Too bad she never asks God for ice cream. A little ice cream is good for the soul sometimes."

Naturally, I bought my kids ice cream at the end of the meal. My son stared at his for a moment and then did something I will remember the rest of my life. He picked up his sundae and without a word, walked over and placed it in front of the woman.

With a big smile he told her, "Here, this is for you. Ice cream is good for the soul sometimes, and my soul is good already."

I love this story! I hope God sends you some "ice cream" this week.

Scripture Reading: Psalm 16:11

Personal Application:
- Reflect on the above story and perform a heart check. With whom do you most identify in the story and why?
- Why do you think we so often struggle with the fact that our heavenly Father wants to give us good things? Spend time thanking Him for all the "ice cream" He has given you.

Week 13, Day 2: 4 Strategies for Putting Down Pride

Proverbs 6:16 warns us, "There are six things the Lord hates, seven that are detestable to him," and the first thing on the list is "haughty eyes" or "pride." You might wonder, "Why does God hate pride so much?"

Pride was what prompted Satan to rebel against God. Speaking of Satan, the Lord says, "Your heart became proud on account of your beauty, and you corrupted your wisdom because of your splendor." (Ezekiel 28:17)

Then, the evil one used pride, the desire to "be like God," to entice Adam and Eve to sin. Pride is at the heart of all sin. For this reason, when pride rears its ugly head, we should shudder!

Here are four strategies for putting down pride:

1. Humble yourself. Humility breaks the back of pride. The self-worth and prominence that we errantly hope to gain through pride is only attained through humble submission to Jesus Christ. "Humble yourselves, therefore, under God's mighty hand, that He may life you up in due time." (1 Peter 5:6)

2. Seek God's wisdom. In God's economy, wisdom and humility are closely linked. James asks, "Who is wise and understanding among you? Let them show it by their good life, by deeds done in the humility that comes from wisdom." (James 3:13) And this wisdom comes from God (James 3:17).

3. Cast all your cares on God. This strategy may seem strange too, but catch this, "Therefore humble yourselves under the right hand of God, that He may exalt you in due time." And how do we humble ourselves? By "Casting all your care upon Him, for He cares for you." (1 Peter 5:6-7) In our pride we boast, "I got this. I can handle it." No, give it to God and rely on Him.

4. Love others well. In 1 Corinthians 13, the love chapter, we read, "Love... does not boast, it is not proud... it is not self-seeking." (1 Corinthians 13:4-5) Expressing godly love is all about others. When we humbly focus on the needs of others, pride is put down.

The Apostle Peter warns us, "God opposes the proud but shows favor to the humble." (1 Peter 5:5) We can either humble ourselves or God will do it for us!

Scripture Reading: Philippians 2:5-11

Personal Application:

- Under what circumstances are you most prone to be prideful?
- From Philippians 2:5-11, we could add a fifth strategy for putting down pride—to worship God. We can only worship, praise, and exalt Him from a place of humility.
- Spend time in prayer confessing your sins and worshiping the Lord. Ask Him for His humility.

Week 13, Day 3: What's Your Life Investment?

"By this all men will know that you are my disciples, if you love one another."
– John 13:35

Chuck Swindoll has been a long-time friend and mentor. Chuck is such an encourager; he loves to uplift others. His keen insights on life and people have encouraged many folks, including me, to become more Christlike in our character. I recall a story he tells about a man he greatly admired, Dawson Trotman (fondly known as Daws), founder of the organization, Navigators.

Daws wasn't a great orator. He wasn't a gifted artist or poet. He never scored a touchdown in the Super Bowl, but he launched a disciple-making movement and died saving another. Chuck's story:

When Dawson Trotman passed away, he probably left a legacy of discipleship on this earth equaled only by the Apostle Paul himself. Daws is known for his disciple-making methods. Besides leading countless others to Christ and nurturing them in their walk with Christ, Daws profoundly impacted the ministries of Billy Graham and Bill Bright (founder of Campus Crusade for Christ—now CRU).

Daws died in Schroon Lake, New York, doing something he was expert in. He drowned, although he was an expert swimmer.

Daws was speaking at a camp. One afternoon, he and some campers were riding in a boat when they hit some choppy water, throwing him and a girl out of the boat. Daws lifted the girl out of the water, saving her life. Then, exhausted from the effort, he slipped below the surface of the water. He was not found until Search and Rescue located him a few hours later... Billy Graham spoke at Daws' funeral saying, "Daws died the same way he lived—holding others up." In one sentence, that was Trotman's life-investment in people...holding them up. What a legacy!

At the end of our journey through this life, how will we be remembered? What will others say about us? Will we be known for our encouragement, our grace, our forgiveness, mercy, and love? Will others have seen Jesus in us? What will they say was our life-investment? How many will have come to know Jesus Christ because we lived out our faith day by day?

It is my prayer that by God's grace, we each might leave a legacy that points people to Jesus.

Scripture Reading: 2 Timothy 4:6-8

Personal Application:

- Few of us will die like Daws did, giving his life for another.
  But how are we living?
- May I challenge you to pray daily, "Lord, help me to represent You well to others though my life and words."

Week 13, Day 4: The Name of Jesus

While in the Army, a friend of mine attended mandatory "Sensitivity Training," the Army's attempt to curb racial prejudice. During the training, the facilitator asked for solutions. After a lengthy pause, my friend boldly spoke up and said, "I believe that Jesus Christ is the answer to racial prejudice and all our social ills." Hearing the name of Jesus, the facilitator exploded with profanity, angrily yelling that the name of Jesus was not to be spoken of again!

Why does the name "Jesus" cause such an emotional stir? Mention Brahma, Buddha, Gandhi, or Mohammad and you may even be considered politically correct. The word "God" usually doesn't offend people. But if we bring up the name "Jesus Christ" in public, there's almost always some kind of emotional if not physical reaction. Why? Why does this name strike a nerve more than any other name?

I believe the controversy surrounding Jesus comes because of who He is and His words. He rocked the ancient world and continues to rock the modern world. Jesus interrupts our view of God in a way that no spiritual guru can or ever will. Christ's assertions cause us to pick a side. He claimed to be God in the flesh!

Early in His ministry, Jesus took His disciples to Nazareth where He had grown up. One Sabbath, Jesus read from the book of Isaiah in the local synagogue:

The scroll of the prophet Isaiah was handed to Him. Unrolling it, He found the place where it is written: "The Spirit of the Lord is on me, because He has anointed Me to preach good news to the poor. He has sent Me to proclaim freedom for the prisoners and recovery of sight for the blind, to release the oppressed, to proclaim the year of the Lord's favor." Then He rolled up the scroll, gave it back to the attendant and sat down. The eyes of everyone in the synagogue were fastened on Him, and He began by saying to them, "Today this scripture is fulfilled in your hearing." (Luke 4:17-21)

As He continued speaking to them, they became furious with Him. They drove Him from the synagogue, out of town to a cliff intending to throw Him off, but He eluded them. (Luke 4:28-30)

Josh McDowell in his book, *More Than A Carpenter,* explains, "When we think of Jesus, we must eventually come to one of three decisions. Either He is a lunatic, a liar, or Lord."

After declaring Jesus innocent three times, the Governor Pilate asked the crowd, "What now shall I do, with the man called Jesus?" (Matthew 27:22a) That question still rings in our ears and everyone must decide what to do with the man called Jesus.

Scripture Reading: Colossians 1:15-20

Personal Application:
- Meditate on Colossians 1:15-20 and worship Jesus Christ affirming who He is.
- Share this devotional with someone who doesn't yet know the Lord.

Week 13, Day 5: Extraordinary Love

Kurtis, the stock boy, was busy working when an unfamiliar voice came over the intercom, asking for a carry-out at register four. He was almost finished and wanted to get some fresh air, so he answered the call. As he approached the check-out stand a smile caught his eye; the new check-out girl was beautiful! She was older than he—maybe 26 (he was 22). He fell in love.

Later that day, after his shift was over, he waited by the timeclock to learn her name. Entering the break room, she smiled at him, took her card, punched out, and left. Her card said, Brenda.

Running outside, he just caught sight of her as she walked up the road. The next day he waited outside after work, and he offered her a ride home. He looked harmless, so she accepted.

When he dropped her off, he asked if maybe he could see her again, outside of work. She said it simply wasn't possible. He pressed, and she explained she had two children and couldn't afford a babysitter. He offered to pay for the babysitter. Reluctantly she accepted his offer for a date the following Saturday.

But when he arrived that Saturday night, she explained that her babysitter had canceled, so she was unable to go with him. Kurtis didn't miss a beat. He simply replied, "Well, let's take the kids with us." She protested; taking the children was not an option. Again, he pressed.

Finally, Brenda brought him inside to meet her children. She had a daughter just as cute as a bug. Then, Brenda brought out her son...in a wheelchair. He was born a paraplegic with Down's Syndrome. Kurtis asked Brenda, "I still don't understand why the kids can't come with us?" Brenda was amazed. Most men would run away from a woman with two kids, especially if one had disabilities. Just like her ex-husband, the father of her children had done.

That evening Kurtis and Brenda loaded up the kids and went to dinner and the movies. When her son needed anything, Kurtis took care of him. The kids loved Kurtis.

At the end of the evening, Brenda knew this was the man she wanted to marry and spend the rest of her life with! A year later, they were married, and Kurtis adopted both of her children. Since then, they have added two more kids.

So, what happened to the stock boy and check-out girl? Well, Mr. & Mrs. Kurt Warner moved to St. Louis. There, he got picked up by the St. Louis Rams—as their quarterback!

You see there really are heroes in this world. There really are men and women with true character—selfless, loving, and dependable. Sometimes they're famous; sometimes they're just everyday guys or gals making good decisions, putting others first...showing the world extraordinary love.

Scripture Reading: John 15:9-13

Personal Application:

- For whom in your life right now could you demonstrate extraordinary love? Look for opportunities today and carry through with a plan.

Week 13, Day 6: What Do You Do with Your Pain?

I suppose everyone develops aches and pains as they get older. My lower back is what troubles me. I've tried all sorts of ways to strengthen my back and manage the pain. My physical therapist told me that the small muscles along the spinal column needed to be stretched. He said there was a machine that would assist me with that. I knew I needed aggressive therapy, but even the name of that contraption sounded painful: Absolute Isometric Torque.

God has taught me a lot about pain through the years. Pain is not always physical but presents itself in many ways. There's emotional pain when others accuse us wrongly, breach our trust, or reject us. There's the soul ache of grief when we lose someone close to us or when we watch someone we love fall into addiction or walk away from God. The pain of financial struggles, public humiliation, or personal failure are no less real.

How we handle our pain says a lot about what we really believe. Do we hide our pain? Do we search desperately for ways to "cope"—sometimes adding trouble to our troubles? Does pain strengthen us or make us bitter? Do we try to handle it all on our own? Do we turn to God or away from Him? Do we really believe God loves us, wants what's best for us, and has it all under control?

Fortunately, God's Word has much to say about pain. The Apostle Peter tells us, "For it is commendable if someone bears up under the pain of unjust suffering because they are conscious of God." (1 Peter 2:19)

During a particularly difficult and painful time in David's life he wrote Psalm 38. There, David agonized, "My guilt has overwhelmed me like a burden too heavy to bear. My wounds fester and are loathsome because of my sinful folly. I am bowed down and brought very low; all day long I go about mourning. My back is filled with searing pain; there is no health in my body. I am feeble and utterly crushed; I groan in anguish of heart." (Psalm 38:4-8)

We can almost feel the agony of David's heart! But the short portion I included from that Psalm only scratches the surface of David's troubles.

But here's the key: What did David do with this pain? He cried out, "Lord, I wait for you; you will answer, Lord my God." And, "Come quickly to help me, my Lord and my Savior." (vs. 15 & 22)

The Psalmist confesses, "Before I was afflicted, I went astray, but now I obey your word." And, "It was good for me to be afflicted so that I might learn your decrees." (Psalm 119:67 & 71) I believe the secret of "pain management" is being in the presence of Jesus Christ and trusting Him. In your pain, draw near to God and cast your cares on Him.

Scripture Reading: Revelation 21:4

Personal Application:

- How do you typically handle pain? How would your loved one's answer that on your behalf?
- When you're in pain, press into the Lord for insight, comfort and a right response.

Week 13, Day 7: Weekly Recap and Prayer

On the seventh day of each week, use the **ACTS** acronym to spend time with the Lord reviewing and assessing your week and praying to God. (**A**=Adoration; **C**=Confession; **T**=Thanksgiving; **S**=Supplication)

First, look back over the previous six days for this week to remind yourself what you read and agreed to. Then, follow the ACTS pattern for prayer below. Finally, use the space below to journal what God is doing in your life and share this with a trusted spiritual partner.

Adoration: Simply spend time in adoration of the Lord. Praise Him and glorify His name. (See 1 Chronicles 29:10-13; Psalm 100; Romans 11:33-36.)

Confession: Confess your sins and shortcomings before God. ("If we confess our sins, he is faithful and just and will forgive us our sins and purify us from all unrighteousness." – 1 John 1:9) To confess (or agree with God) about your sin, implies that you are repentant and desperately want Him to change you.

Thanksgiving: Thank God for what He has done and is doing in your life and the life of your family. Give Him credit, for everything you have comes from Him. (See Psalm 136.)

Supplication: Supplication is just a fancy word for making your requests known to God. Based on the devotions of this past week and the things going on in your life right now, what do you want to ask Him for? "If you, then, though you are evil, know how to give good gifts to your children, how much more will your Father in heaven give good gifts to those who ask Him!" (Matthew 7:11)

Journal: What is God doing in your life right now?

Week 14, Day 1: Where is Your Hope?

Sometimes we face the unpleasant, the impossible or the unthinkable, and we lose hope. All we see is the suffering, the immense task, or the loss. Any way out seems impossible. The following historical account in 2 Kings 18-19 reminds us that the Lord is both merciful and all-powerful.

At the time, Hezekiah was king of Judah (the southern two tribes of Israel). The Assyrians had already conquered Israel (the northern ten tribes) and carried the people off to Assyria. Then, the mighty Assyrian army had attacked all the fortified cities of Judah and captured them. Only Jerusalem was left and now the Assyrian army had it surrounded. We're told that "This happened because they had not obeyed the Lord their God but had violated His covenant—all that Moses the servant of the Lord commanded. They neither listened to the commands nor carried them out." (2 Kings 18:12)

Within earshot of those on the city wall, the Assyrian field commander taunted King Hezekiah and he especially taunted God: "Do not listen to Hezekiah, for he is misleading you when he says, 'The Lord will deliver us.' Has the god of any nation ever delivered his land from the hand of the king of Assyria?" (2 Kings 18:32-33) But King Hezekiah humbled himself before the Lord and prayed, "Lord, the God of Israel, enthroned between the cherubim, you alone are God over all the kingdoms of the earth. Give ear, Lord, and hear; open your eyes, Lord, and see; listen to the words Sennacherib has sent to ridicule the living God. Now, Lord our God, deliver us from his hand, so that all the kingdoms of the earth may know that you alone, Lord, are God." (2 Kings 19:15-16, 19)

So, God sent Isaiah the prophet to Hezekiah and told him, "I have heard your prayer concerning Sennacherib king of Assyria. He will not enter this city or shoot an arrow here. I will defend this city and save it, for my sake and for the sake of David my servant." (2 Kings 19:32, 34)

"That night the angel of the Lord went out and put to death a hundred and eighty-five thousand in the Assyrian camp. So, Sennacherib king of Assyria broke camp and withdrew and returned to Nineveh." (2 Kings 19:35-36) And there Sennacherib's two sons murdered him while he was worshiping in the temple of his god Nisrok. (2 Kings 19:37)

God is bigger than any trial or situation. He cares for you and He is in control. He is powerful and mighty and merciful. He will carry you through the trials you face or bring you home to be with Him. Either way, you have nothing to fear. Simply trust the Lord!

Scripture Reading: Psalm 65
Personal Application:
- What difficult situation are you facing right now? Lay it out before the Lord and ask Him for His wisdom, guidance, and help.
- Did you know that all the treasures of wisdom and knowledge are hidden in Christ? (Colossians 2:3) Whatever your area of expertise, Jesus is your Consultant, your subject matter expert!

Week 14, Day 2: Acts of Kindness

*"So in everything, do to others what you would have them do to you,
for this sums up the Law and the Prophets."*
– Matthew 7:12

A poor Scottish farmer named Fleming was trying to eke out a living for his family. One day, while hard at work, he heard a cry for help coming from a nearby bog.

Dropping his tools, he ran to the bog. There, mired to his waist in black muck, was a terrified boy, screaming and struggling to free himself. But for all his efforts, the boy was sinking deeper. Mr. Fleming was able to save the lad from what could have been a slow and terrifying death.

The next day, a fancy carriage pulled up to the Scotsman's humble farm. An elegantly dressed nobleman stepped out and introduced himself as the father of the boy Mr. Fleming had saved.

"I want to repay you," said the nobleman. "You saved my son's life."

But the Scottish farmer waved off the offer saying, "Thank you, but I can't accept payment for what I did." At that moment, the farmer's own son came out the door of the family hovel.

"Is that your son?" the nobleman asked.

"Yes, it is," the farmer replied proudly.

"I'll make you a deal," said the nobleman. "Let me take your son and give him a good education. If the lad is anything like his father, he'll grow to become a man you can be proud of." And so, it was.

In time, Farmer Fleming's son graduated from St. Mary's Hospital Medical School in London. Eventually, he became known throughout the world as the noted Sir Alexander Fleming, who discovered Penicillin.

Years later, the nobleman's son was stricken with pneumonia, only to be saved by Penicillin. The name of the nobleman was Lord Randolph Churchill. His son was none other than Sir Winston Churchill.

We just never know when God may use a single act of kindness to change the world! Let's take the time to notice the needs of others, to consider how we would want to be treated, and to serve one another with love. The impact of our actions may have eternal repercussions for those we are serving!

Scripture Reading: Matthew 25:34-36

Personal Application:

- Today, and every day, keep your eyes open for opportunities to perform acts of kindness for those around you. And don't forget to do so especially with those closest to you.
- Meditate on the above Scripture reading from Matthew's Gospel. What do you take away from that passage that you can apply to your life?

Week 14, Day 3: Obedience Training

My wife, Louise, and I are dog lovers. We have owned eleven Labrador retrievers who have produced seven litters of pups. And those puppies have gone all over the world—including one that served in Vietnam.

Dogs are like people in many ways. Most basically, they need to learn who their master is and to obey. And in this sense, aren't we all in obedience training?

For a dog, the "listening position" is sitting. Everything depends on the dog's ability to sit and focus on its master. To a puppy, the command, "Sit," means more than just, "Don't move." It means, "Freeze, now. Look at me—then wait, and wait, and wait…," until we tell it to move.

If the dog can't learn to obey the command to sit, it will have problems obeying every other command. In Psalm 46:10, the Lord tells us, "Be still, and know that I am God." In other words, God tells us to sit and wait. As followers of Christ, learning to be still before the Lord is crucial for learning to obey Him in every other respect.

But dogs are easily distracted by other things and sometimes we must get their attention before they obey the command to sit. We are like that too. There are so many distractions out there that it's sometimes difficult for us to just sit and wait on God. Instead, we behave like a new puppy, running around doing our own thing, naively oblivious to God's directions.

On YouTube, we often see videos of dogs doing crazy things at their master's bidding. Many of these stunts are designed to impress us or make us laugh. In this respect we are not like dogs. God does not ask us to obey Him for frivolous reasons, or simply to impress others. He loves us and wants to give us a more abundant life. Through obedience to Him we bless others and glorify Him.

Jesus urges us, "But seek first the kingdom of God and His righteousness, and all these things shall be added to you." (Matthew 6:33 NKJV) Seeking God and being still before Him is our "sit" command. Having done that, we're ready to obey. In this regard, Jesus said, "You are my friends if you do what I command. This is my command: Love each other." (John 15:14 & 17)

Our Master Trainer, God, has His perfect plan for our lives if we would just stop, listen, and obey. Next time you find yourself running things your own way, try "sitting."

Scripture Reading: Luke 5:16

Personal Application:
- We all seem to struggle with finding time to just sit before the Lord and wait on Him. To what extent do you struggle with "sitting" and "waiting" on God? Why do you think this is so?
- When we go to meet with the Lord, we often think we've got to fill the silence with our prayers and petitions. But we need to learn to listen in prayer as well, just sitting still before the Lord.
- Spend time before the Lord simply being quiet before Him and listening to Him. Make this a regular practice in your quiet time with the Lord.

Week 14, Day 4: Do You Have What It Takes to Be an MVP?

Every year a few dozen professional football players from each conference are selected to compete in the Pro Bowl Game held the first week in February. The starting AFC Quarterback for the 2000 Season Pro Bowl was thirteen-year veteran Rich Gannon of the Oakland Raiders.

By the end of the first quarter, Gannon had thrown for 164 yards, including two touchdowns. His performance testifies to his strong character, deep commitment, and God-given abilities. He was unanimously selected as the Pro Bowl Most Valuable Player (MVP).

As we look through the Bible there are several MVP's that stand out for their godly character and great accomplishments.

During the Babylonian captivity, Daniel and his three friends, Shadrach, Meshach, and Abednego, kept their faith and their integrity. As exiles in a foreign land, they trusted God and obeyed His commands. Amidst adversity, they developed godly character that impressed all who observed them. Their priority was to serve God with humility, honor, and integrity.

King Nebuchadnezzar conscripted these exiled Jews into service. During their training he prescribed a specific diet that included foods and wine that had been offered to idols. Partaking in this food would have gone against God's laws. So, they drew the line and took a stand on biblical principles, and they did so tactfully and respectfully (Daniel 1).

That is godly character! Daniel and his pals knew that standing on principle would sometimes put them at odds with those in authority. But they were so committed to being obedient to God's Word, that they suggested a creative alternative to the king's order. In this way, they were able to honor both God and the king.

It's one thing to take a bold stand against evil or something we have strong convictions about. But it's another thing to do so in a tactful and discrete way that honors those with whom we disagree. Of course, there are some situations in which we must choose to either obey God or man. Daniel had to make such a decision when he chose to continue praying to God even when the king forbade it by decree (Daniel 6).

The Apostle Peter gives us a great plan for achieving MVP status in this world, "Dear friends, I urge you, as foreigners and exiles, to abstain from sinful desires, which wage war against your soul. Live such good lives among the pagans that, though they accuse you of doing wrong, they may see your good deeds and glorify God on the day he visits us. Show proper respect to everyone, love the family of believers, fear God, honor the emperor." (1 Peter 2:11-12 & 17)

Scripture Reading: 1 Peter 3:15-17

Personal Application:

- Based on God's Word, what issues do you take exception to right now at work or in our culture?
- In what creative ways could you oppose this practice or philosophical view that honor both God and people around you?

Week 14, Day 5: Spinning Plates

I don't know about you, but sometimes I get myself in way over my head. Sometimes it's hard to remember my priorities—God's priorities. A dear friend of mine once provided some timely advice that helped me reorder my private world.

How Many Plates Should You Spin?

One of the most important and difficult decisions in life is deciding how many responsibilities to accept. It's difficult to know when to say "no," but it can be even more difficult when we say "yes" too many times. Invitations to "worthwhile" endeavors seem unending, and as long as there's a shortage of "spinners," "plates" will come begging to be "spun." But how many should we "spin"? Perhaps the following questions can help you determine whether to say "yes" or "no."

1. Is this the right thing to do? Does this responsibility fit into my values; is it worth the investment of my time? Bottom line: Is this an ego thing, fun thing, feel-pressured-into thing, busy thing, or the right thing to do? Read Psalms 23. Am I at rest and peace with God if accept this thing?

2. Am I qualified to accept this responsibility? Do I have both the ability and capacity to do this job well? God's Word says that satisfaction in what we do is derived from how well we "spin," not how many we spin (Galatians 6:4).

3. Can I handle this responsibility without jeopardizing any other? Do my current "plates" benefit from additional "spinning," or does this place a liability on the other "plates"? Do those with whom we're already involved approve of my "spinning" more? We can test this from time to time by asking our loved ones if they're happy with our relationship with God, attitudes, behavior, and priorities.

4. Am I physically and mentally up to the task right now? Do I have enough time for personal exercise and relaxation? Am I feeling good, thinking clearly, and acting rightly—not reacting in a negative and bitter fashion?

Others will continue to ask good leaders to help them with their "spinning." And if we're not careful, we can spend our entire life helping others keep their pottery together while our fine china lies in ruins! Let's be honest with ourselves and graciously say "no" when we need to—when it's what's best!

Scripture Reading: Proverbs 3:1-12

Personal Application:

- Think of a situation in the past (or present) when you took on too much. Is there a pattern or repeating theme when you take on too much?
- What were your motivations for saying "yes" to those things? In hindsight, in what ways do you wish you had responded differently?
- What guidelines will you use to determine whether to take on a new task or responsibility in the future?

Week 14, Day 6: Where Is Your Treasure?

"Wealth is worthless in the day of wrath, but righteousness delivers from death."
– Proverbs 11:4

I've always enjoyed reading about John Wesley, itinerant evangelist and founder of the Methodist Church. I especially admire his dedication, perseverance, and generosity. Pastor Wesley's sacrificial life has helped me better understand how to honor God, particularly in my finances.

Wesley devoted his life to serving and assisting others while riding thousands of miles on horseback and preaching in hundreds of churches. What is not as well known is that he earned considerable funds from the royalties off his books and hymns.

Although a very wealthy man, he had a godly perspective of his resources. At one time, he gave away 40,000 pounds of sterling from his fortune to promote God's work; he died with only twenty-eight pounds in his estate!

When told that his house had burned down, he simply replied, "I don't own a house. The one I have been living in belongs to the Lord, and if it has burned down, that is one less responsibility for me to worry about." This is exactly how God wishes us to view our earthly resources…as temporary! True wealth is stored up in heaven and is eternal.

Many of us wouldn't consider ourselves to be wealthy, but compared to most folks in the world, most Americans are extremely wealthy. The trouble is we compare ourselves to the people next door, the guys at work, or the kids at school. Somebody always has newer, better, faster, and more. And advertising seeks to capitalize on these desires.

God's Word reminds us, "Do not store up for yourselves treasures upon earth…. But store up for yourselves treasures in heaven…. For where your treasure is, there will your heart be also." (Matthew 6:19-21)

God gives us the ability and resources to obtain any earthly wealth we have. While it is good to support our families, make reasonable plans and sound investments for the future, keep a business running, and give to the Lord's work, we should not hoard or be selfish with earthly possessions.

Jesus warns us about greed, "Watch out! Be on your guard against all kinds of greed; a man's life does not consist in the abundance of his possessions." (Luke 12:15) Let's keep our resources in proper perspective and honor God with them, remembering our true wealth is in heaven!

Scripture Reading: Luke 12:13-21

Personal Application:
- Take stock of the possessions and wealth you own. What is your relationship and attitude toward them? Where is your treasure?
- Spend time with the Lord asking Him to reveal any improper attitudes you might have toward money and possessions. Worship Him as your Treasure.

Week 14, Day 7: Weekly Recap and Prayer

On the seventh day of each week, use the **ACTS** acronym to spend time with the Lord reviewing and assessing your week and praying to God. (**A**=Adoration; **C**=Confession; **T**=Thanksgiving; **S**=Supplication)

First, look back over the previous six days for this week to remind yourself what you read and agreed to. Then, follow the ACTS pattern for prayer below. Finally, use the space below to journal what God is doing in your life and share this with a trusted spiritual partner.

Adoration: Simply spend time in adoration of the Lord. Praise Him and glorify His name. (See 1 Chronicles 29:10-13; Psalm 100; Romans 11:33-36.)

Confession: Confess your sins and shortcomings before God. ("If we confess our sins, he is faithful and just and will forgive us our sins and purify us from all unrighteousness." – 1 John 1:9) To confess (or agree with God) about your sin, implies that you are repentant and desperately want Him to change you.

Thanksgiving: Thank God for what He has done and is doing in your life and the life of your family. Give Him credit, for everything you have comes from Him. (See Psalm 136.)

Supplication: Supplication is just a fancy word for making your requests known to God. Based on the devotions of this past week and the things going on in your life right now, what do you want to ask Him for? "If you, then, though you are evil, know how to give good gifts to your children, how much more will your Father in heaven give good gifts to those who ask Him!" (Matthew 7:11)

Journal: What is God doing in your life right now?

Week 15, Day 1: Not Easily Angered

We're probably familiar with two types of anger: reactive and passive-aggressive. Think of a recent incident in which you got angry. What prompted your anger and how did you respond? How did you feel after you cooled off? Here's an example of a reactive response: An old man in a new pickup was searching for a parking spot, but the lot was crowded. Finally, he found a spot and was preparing to back in when a Porsche appeared out of nowhere and whipped into the spot he had claimed.

The driver of the Porsche got out of his car and walked away. But the old man yelled at him, "I found that spot first! What give you the right to butt in and take it?" The brash young man laughed and said, "Because I'm young and quick!" And he kept walking. But after a few steps, he heard the terrible sound of metal smashing. He turned around to see the old man in the pickup repeatedly ramming his big truck into the Porsche. The old man coolly looked the young man in the eye and said, "That's because I'm old and rich!"

Here's a passive-aggressive response: A businessman at the airport was in a hurry to get to his gate and was getting frustrated with the young man checking his bags. The businessman liberally berated and belittled the customer service agent. But the young man kept his cool and continued doing his job. After the businessman left, a woman who had witnessed the whole interchange asked the young man how he put up with such awful treatment. The young man replied, "Easy! That man is going to New York, but I sent his luggage to Brazil!"

Although we may smile at these made-up stories, anger is usually no laughing matter. And passive-aggressive response is no better, it's just not as explosive. Anger works like a weapon destroying relationships and the abuser's integrity.

Typically, we become angry when things don't go our way. When someone violates what we perceive to be our right, we tend to get angry. Also, one sharp word (whether intended or just perceived) often triggers an angry response. When it comes down to it, anger is all about self. We get angry because we see ourselves and our issues as more important than others.

The Scriptures remind us that "love…is not easily angered;" and gentleness and self-control, rather than anger, rule when we're walking in the Spirit (1 Corinthians 13:5; Galatians 5:23). We need Christ's indwelling power to overcome fits of rage and anger.

Scripture Reading: Proverbs 14:3, 17, 29; 15:1

Personal Application:

- To what extent have you let anger become your go-to response? Neither reactive nor passive-aggressive anger is better than the other. Both are destructive. Which type do you default to?
- To battle anger, fill your mind with Scripture, walk in the Spirit, and seek help from a spiritual partner who can help hold you accountable. Seek forgiveness from those you have hurt.

Week 15, Day 2: Humility, Justice & Mercy

The gradual moral decline we've witnessed in our country is nothing new. But what scares me is how insidious it is. What was considered wrong and unthinkable just a few years ago is now flaunted and even celebrated. And the media and special interest groups have every intention of changing our moral standards, often without our even being aware of it, like the frog-in-the-kettle metaphor.

Such was the case in Micah's day. The nation of Israel had gradually turned away from the Lord until they had become as pagan as the peoples God had driven out of the land. God sent the prophet Micah to Israel about 700 years before Christ. Micah's calling was to help the nation of Israel turn its affections back to God.

The leaders of Israel had abandoned justice, loving evil, and hating good. Thus, their treatment of their people was so cruel that the Lord used this graphic metaphor to shock them into reality, "You...eat my people's flesh, strip off their skin and break their bones in pieces; and chop them up like meat for the pan, like flesh for the pot." (Micah 3:3)

Their sins were not isolated instances but permeated the culture, spoiling its economy, living conditions, and the moral tenor of the whole nation. Things had gotten bad, and now the whole nation was suffering the consequences of their sins. But Micah told the nation of Israel exactly what God desired from them.

God was not looking for more sacrifices and religious observances. He wasn't satisfied with a mere ritualistic relationship. God wanted a genuine relationship with them. He wanted them to obey Him out of desire and devotion to Him rather than obligation. Obedience was never meant to be a burden.

The prophet Micah stated God's expectations clearly and concisely in Micah 6:8, "He has showed you, O man, what is good. And what does the LORD require of you? To act justly and to love mercy and to walk humbly with your God."

God saw their suffering and gave them instructions, explaining how to make things "good" again. He called them "To act justly and to love mercy and to walk humbly with your God." While God was speaking to their circumstances and current behavior, these words apply to us today. God is not interested in our religious observance. He wants us to imitate Him as His children. He wants us to be fair in our dealings with others, carry through on our commitments to meet others' needs, and pursue Him humbly.

Scripture Reading: Matthew 22:34-40

Personal Application:
- To what extent have you allowed the culture to mold your moral standards?
- How would you describe your relationship with the Lord? What part of Micah 6:8 speaks most personally to you? Spend time in prayer over what you have read today in this devotional.

Week 15, Day 3: When You Hurt Someone

Have you ever spoken a harsh word to your spouse, to your child, or to someone else close to you? Of course, we all have, and we've done this all too frequently we must admit. But we must not find comfort in our solidarity as offenders.

Because we are sinners, it's inevitable that we will offend or hurt others. There are all sorts of reasons behind why we do so. Someone violates our rights and we get angry. Someone offended us and we retaliate. Maybe we've been storing up offenses of another person. Sometimes, we're just having a bad day and we lash out in our frustration. And sometimes, we hurt someone unintentionally and may not even be sure what we did!

But did you know that God cares more about our relationships than anything else? We know this from Matthew 22:34-40. When asked what the most important commandment is, Jesus responded with two: "Love God, and love others." Period.

Loving others and maintaining healthy relationships translates into two basic strategies. First, we must live in a loving way. This involves putting others before ourselves and really caring for others and demonstrating that through our words, actions, and attitudes.

Second, when we offend or hurt someone, we are responsible to make it right as quickly as possible. To emphasize the urgency of this, Jesus told a short parable in Matthew 5:23-24, "Therefore, if you are offering your gift at the altar and there remember that your brother or sister has something against you, leave your gift there in front of the altar. First go and be reconciled to them; then come and offer your gift."

We see from that passage that God cares more about our relationships with each other than any service we might offer Him. Also, Jesus underscores the fact that it is our responsibility to initiate. Don't wait for the other person to initiate. You take the initiative!

We reconcile with others by asking forgiveness. This takes humility and it's hard for a lot of us men to humble ourselves in this way. It's difficult to sincerely say, "I'm sorry. I was wrong. Will you forgive me?"

Some guys think they're giving up too much ground by asking forgiveness, or that they'll be perceived as weaklings. But the opposite is true. A man who can admit his errors and ask forgiveness stands out as strong and full of integrity. So, when you offend or hurt someone, take the initiative, ask forgiveness, and be reconciled.

Scripture Reading: Romans 12:17-21

Personal Application:

- Perhaps while reading this devotional you were reminded of someone you've hurt or offended. Or maybe you're aware of a relationship that needs repair.
- Take initiative to go to that person and ask forgiveness. Trust God in this and watch what He does on your behalf when you obey Him.

Week 15, Day 4: When Someone Hurts You

Yesterday, we talked about asking forgiveness to restore a relationship when we've hurt someone. Today, we want to look at extending forgiveness to others when they hurt us.

Holding a grudge is horribly destructive. Holding a grudge and withholding forgiveness eats away at us. It consumes us and makes us bitter, cynical, and untrusting. This attitude oozes out of us affecting even those we love. Jesus said, "If you do not forgive others their sins, your Father will not forgive your sins." (Matthew 6:15) So, this is serious business!

For this reason, forgiving someone is incredibly restorative, both for them and us. Extending and receiving forgiveness offers a cleansing, renewed emotional outlook, and can restore broken relationships.

Sometimes we erroneously think that we're giving up ground by extending forgiveness. But from an emotional and spiritual standpoint, extending forgiveness is something we do from a position of power and authority. Seeing ourselves as victims, leaves us powerless and imprisoned by that mentality. But when we extend forgiveness, we break free from whatever held us captive.

Forgiveness is something we must give freely. No one can demand or pry forgiveness from us. We can't extend forgiveness grudgingly. For forgiveness to be genuine, it must be given willingly. When we forgive our offender, we do so by exercising our will with grace and mercy. The Lord's Prayer says we ask God to forgive us our sins, as we forgive those who sinned against us (Matthew 6:12).

When we talk about forgiving a person who hurt us, we're not in any way minimizing what they did to us. Nor are we dismissing it. On the contrary, forgiveness is only required where sins and offenses exist.

If the person who offended you asks forgiveness, God is giving you an opportunity to forgive them as God has forgiven you. If the person who hurt you does not ask you to forgive them, you may simply need to forgive them in your heart rather than say, "I forgive you."

Also, pray and tell God that you forgive that person and ask Him to help you love them as He does. This too is very freeing. Extend forgiveness to others as freely as Christ has forgiven you.

Scripture Reading: Matthew 18:21-35

Personal Application:

- To what extent are you stewing over an incident in which someone offended or hurt you? What is it doing to you to dwell on that situation?
- Extend forgiveness to that person and experience the freedom and peace that will bring you.
- Spend time in prayer thanking God for His forgiveness and tell Him you forgive this other person as well.

Week 15, Day 5: Fishing for Men

"Then Jesus said to Simon,
'Don't be afraid; from now on you will fish for people.'"
— Luke 5:10

The three most important qualities a fishing guide can bring his clients are: tips on the best tackle to use, knowing where to find the "hot spots," and an encouraging spirit.

Once the fish are located, it's important for the guide to encourage the anglers so they fish with confidence. A good guide inspires people. An expectant cast will have a much greater chance of landing a fish than one that is simply dunked into the water. If we believe we are going to catch a fish, we stand ready to work the lure in a tempting manner. And so, it is with "fishing for men."

I have fished with many professional fishing guides over the last several decades. But believe me, as good as some of them are, no one can compete with the success of Jesus, the Master Guide. Whether His disciples were pursuing fish or people, Jesus was (and still is) truly the Lord of the harvest.

Peter, Andrew, James, and John are among the eight fishermen-disciples that are identified in Scripture. Even with their professional expertise, they needed the Master Guide's help to catch a fish on more than one occasion.

In Matthew 17, Jesus told Peter where to go and what to use to catch a fish that would have a coin in its mouth. In Luke 5, the disciples had fished all night without a catch. Jesus told them where to cast their nets, and they caught so many fish that they filled two boats

But Jesus' primary objective wasn't catching fish, it was to show them the way to the Father and train them how to lead others to God. He used fishing illustrations to help these common men recognize the importance of "catching" men for Christ. He left them (and us) with a command, the authority to carry it out, and a promise of His presence with us.

All followers of Jesus have the assignment to "fish" for men and women in the name of Jesus Christ. I'm so glad we're on a guided trip. Let's spend time with our Master Guide, learning His ways, catching His passion and purpose, and gaining our confidence from Him. Surely there will be no greater reward and honor than to stand with the Master Guide on the grandstand of Heaven to welcome those who were lured by our testimonies and landed by His Spirit.

Scripture Reading: Matthew 4:19; 28:18-20

Personal Application:
- Think back on how who led you to Christ. What individuals impacted you? What was it they did and said that enticed you to consider Christ? What can you learn from their example?
- What's the number one thing preventing you from freely sharing the Gospel with others? What steps do you need to take to move that obstacle out of the way?
- Take that first step today and pray every day that the Lord would use you to represent Him well to others through your life and words.

Week 15, Day 6: God Is in the Details (A true story submitted by Pastor Rob Reid)

A new pastor and his wife took their first assignment to reopen a church in Brooklyn. They arrived early October, excited about the opportunity. The church building was very run down, so they set a goal to have everything done in time to have their first service on Christmas Eve.

They worked hard, repairing pews, plastering walls, painting, etc., and on December 18th they were nearly finished. But on December 19th a terrific rainstorm hit lasting two days. On the 21st, the pastor went to the church, only to find that the roof had leaked, causing a large section of plaster to fall off the front wall just behind the pulpit.

The pastor cleaned up the mess and headed home expecting to postpone the Christmas Eve service. On the way, he noticed a flea market sale for charity, so he stopped in. There he saw a beautiful handmade, crocheted tablecloth with a cross embroidered in the center. It was just the right size to cover up the hole in the front wall, so he bought it and went back to the church.

Meanwhile, it had begun to snow. In front of the church, he met an older woman who had just missed her bus. So, he invited her to wait in the warm church for the next bus 45 minutes later. She sat in a pew while he got a ladder to hang the tablecloth on the wall. The pastor could hardly believe how beautiful it looked and how it neatly covered the hole.

Then he noticed the woman gazing at the tablecloth. "Pastor, where did you get that tablecloth?" So, he explained it to her. The woman asked him to check the lower right corner to see if the initials, EBG were crocheted into the tablecloth. They were. This very woman had made this tablecloth 35 years before in Austria.

She could hardly believe it and explained that before the war she and her husband had lived in Austria. When the Nazis came, she was forced to leave and her husband was sent to prison, and she never saw him or her home again. The pastor wanted to give her the tablecloth; but she insisted the church keep it. So, the pastor offered her a ride home.

On Christmas Eve the church had a wonderful service! Afterward, the pastor and his wife greeted an older man, whom the pastor recognized from the neighborhood. The man was mesmerized by the tablecloth and asked how the church came by it. He recognized it as one his wife had made before the war in Austria. He had been arrested and never saw his wife again.

The tearful pastor asked the man if he would allow him to take him for a little ride. They drove to the same house where the pastor had taken the woman three days earlier. He helped the man climb the stairs to the woman's apartment, knocked on the door, and he saw the greatest Christmas reunion he could ever imagine, a reunion only God could have orchestrated!

Scripture Reading: Proverbs 3:5-6

Personal Application:
- God is in the details of your life as well. Consider your life right now and what's going on.
- Tell the Lord you trust Him and live your life accordingly today.

Week 15, Day 7: Weekly Recap and Prayer

On the seventh day of each week, use the **ACTS** acronym to spend time with the Lord reviewing and assessing your week and praying to God. (**A**=Adoration; **C**=Confession; **T**=Thanksgiving; **S**=Supplication)

First, look back over the previous six days for this week to remind yourself what you read and agreed to. Then, follow the ACTS pattern for prayer below. Finally, use the space below to journal what God is doing in your life and share this with a trusted spiritual partner.

Adoration: Simply spend time in adoration of the Lord. Praise Him and glorify His name. (See 1 Chronicles 29:10-13; Psalm 100; Romans 11:33-36.)

Confession: Confess your sins and shortcomings before God. ("If we confess our sins, he is faithful and just and will forgive us our sins and purify us from all unrighteousness." – 1 John 1:9) To confess (or agree with God) about your sin, implies that you are repentant and desperately want Him to change you.

Thanksgiving: Thank God for what He has done and is doing in your life and the life of your family. Give Him credit, for everything you have comes from Him. (See Psalm 136.)

Supplication: Supplication is just a fancy word for making your requests known to God. Based on the devotions of this past week and the things going on in your life right now, what do you want to ask Him for? "If you, then, though you are evil, know how to give good gifts to your children, how much more will your Father in heaven give good gifts to those who ask Him!" (Matthew 7:11)

Journal: What is God doing in your life right now?

Week 16, Day 1: Can You Spot a Fake?

"Do your best to present yourself to God as one approved, a worker who does not need to be ashamed and who correctly handles the word of truth."
– 2 Timothy 2:15

Deception and trickery are not always bad. A couple of my favorite receivers were unbelievably deceptive on the field. Former All-Pro Hall-of-Famers Fred Biletnikoff and Ed McCaffrey were great fakes. They not only had a tremendous work ethic, great hands, ran precise patterns, and a desire to perfect their position, but they used all sorts of trickery to fool the cornerbacks covering them, routinely eluding their adversaries into thinking they were heading one direction, only to move the other. A fake could be as simple as a head bob, a short-cut in the opposite direction, or faking a catch. Anything that throws off the pace and speed of the defender helps the receiver get some separation from his opponent. Quarterbacks often use fake hand-offs to fool their opponents.

The world is full of fakes, too. If we're not careful, we can easily be fooled. Fakes can be quick to win our confidence and even quicker to take advantage of our neediness, cravings, kindness, and wallets. Whether it's the latest laundry softener, exercise machine, or technical device, we are bombarded with advertisements making outlandish claims. Fakes exploit causes as well. We want to help the hurting and the less fortunate, but sometimes it's hard to know who we can trust. While it's important to do our own research as consumers and givers, the real danger is when we buy into spiritual phonies who attempt to separate us from God's Word.

Tragically, many turn to an assortment of psychics, astrologers, and spiritualists instead of relying on Christ. Some deceivers pose as church leaders too. We need to be especially cautious of religious leaders who take Scripture out of context and lead their unwitting followers into believing they have a special revelation, that truth is relative, or there are other ways to God. The Bible warns us that these "false prophets" are demonic and full of trickery. "Do not be carried away by all kinds of strange teachings." (Hebrews 13:9a) Spiritual fakes, and their messed-up teachings, distort truth, pull our focus off the One True God, and can ultimately lead us astray.

The best way I know to protect oneself and others from deception is to know God's Word and obey it. "Do not merely listen to the word and so deceive yourselves. Do what it says." (James 1:22) "I have hidden Your Word in my heart that I might not sin against You." (Psalm 119:11)

Scripture Reading: 2 Peter 2:1-3

Personal Application:
• Based on a previous week's devotion, you may now be meeting with a spiritual partner. Consider challenging each other to read through the New Testament or the whole Bible. Hold each other accountable and discuss what God shows you through His Word.

Week 16, Day 2: Waiting on the Lord

As difficult as we men find it to admit, there are times in which we find ourselves helpless. We don't like to ask for directions, much less help. But when it comes to our relationship with God, we need to humbly wait on Him as the following incident in my life demonstrates.

It was a beautiful scene on this tributary of the Motu River in New Zealand. We'd been airlifted to a very remote area. As the morning light dawned, Gary, Mark and I prepared for an exciting day of hiking and fishing. I couldn't wait to fish this pristine stream; a stream I'd had the privilege of fishing on my last visit.

During a two-day whitewater rafting adventure, we had stopped to fish this same creek. Within a dozen casts I had caught and released a beautiful nine-pound German Brown trout. I was hoping we'd run into some of his cousins, introducing them to my favorite flies.

The dry algae and moss on the rocks was a sign that the creek had been dropping fast in the previous weeks. With each cast into the crystal-clear water our disappointment grew. We had only landed a couple fish the day before, which should have been an indicator of things to come.

We walked miles downstream, hopping from rock to rock and fishing the larger pools. I made a sneak move on the next pool, when my foot slipped, throwing my body forward. Despite a wading staff and good shoes, I fell. When my knee hit a jagged rock, I knew I was in trouble. Piercing pain shot up my leg. Only later did I notice that my hand, wrist, and equipment were also damaged.

Mark and Gary were at my side immediately. "That was an ugly fall! Are you going to make it?" I couldn't answer or even begin to move my leg for quite a while. The swollen knee and pain convinced me I was finished for the day. Mark and Gary built a fire and left me some granola bars, then hiked back to camp to wait for the helicopter that was due later in the day. I knew it would be 6-7 hours before any help would arrive. All I could do was wait.

My only comfort was knowing that God was still in control. I recalled Scriptures like, "Wait on the Lord: be of good courage, and He shall strengthen your heart; wait, I say, on the Lord!" (Psalm 27:14 NKJV). Waiting is difficult, and yet that is the very thing God tells us to do. Praying is part of waiting. I prayed for strength and found strength in God's presence and His Word.

In the quietness of that day, I remembered the importance of being still and listening to God. In the listening, I received comfort and strength. By the time the helicopter arrived, I had a great peace about my circumstance.

Scripture Reading: Isaiah 40:27-31

Personal Application:

- What do you personally find most difficult about waiting on the Lord? Why do you think this is?
- What passages of Scripture can you secure your faith to in times when you must wait on the Lord?

Week 16, Day 3: Are You on God's Team?

Football has been in my blood since the early 1950s. The excitement, passion, pageantry, and strategic planning associated with this great sport all seem to resonate with my character.

As a young person I would come home from Sunday church and immediately put on my football helmet and prepare for the television game of the week. But it was rare for me to sit through an entire game. My excitement spilled over to our long front yard where I lived out all my fantasies about someday being an NFL player. Our neighborhood lacked other boys, so I played a one-man football game.

I pretended to be an NFL quarterback, snatching the ball from center, then racing back to chuck a pass as far and high as I could throw. This gave me time to race down to the end of the lawn to make a diving catch—sometimes landing on the lawn and sometimes on the walkways. To play the quarterback and receiver was not enough for me though. I was the announcer too! I called out the play-by-play action with all the enthusiasm, sounds, and football jargon I could muster at eleven years old.

My passion carried over into high school where the coach told me I was too scrawny to play (5'11" and 135lbs). Without even checking out my skills, he told me to go out for golf instead. Perhaps he was right. Most football players in my school were guys who had flunked a grade or two and had the physical maturity of a man. They were big, strong, and intimidating. And when I finally got to college, and could fill out a large jersey, the only option left was to play intramural sports…and frankly, that just wasn't that satisfying.

I may have missed the opportunity to become a professional football player, but I didn't miss the draft for the most important team—a team with a mission far greater than any NFL game or championship: God's Team of disciple-makers.

When Jesus gave the command to make disciples, He challenged us all to join Him on the battle for souls. This wasn't a call to professional ministry. This was a call to every able-bodied follower of Christ. You won't find "benches" when playing on God's Team either. Benches are for folks who don't play. God is serious about His Team! Jesus calls us to follow Him. He drafts us just like we are and asks us to submit to His coaching and leadership.

As we spend time with Him, He heals our hearts and builds character in us that brings Him glory. We join Him in His mission rather than chasing after our own ambitions. When we pursue Jesus with passion and devotion, we discover a deep and satisfying relationship with Him!

Scripture Reading: Matthew 28:18-20

Personal Application:
- God has given you unique abilities and a unique collection of people whom you influence. Ponder those two ideas and thank God for them.
- Pray each day for the Lord to use you to represent Him well to others through your life and words. Then look for opportunities to share Christ with others and follow through.

Week 16, Day 4: A Wonderful Choice

All my life, I've had a tender spot in my heart for people with disabilities. This no doubt came from watching my mom and dad take care of my disabled grandma and participating in her care myself. Eventually my mother also became disabled and I helped care for her.

Then, many years ago, I was rendered disabled for a time, while recovering from brain surgery. All these experiences have given me a tremendous compassion for those with disabilities. And I've found I don't have to look very far to find people who need a little extra help.

Jesus tells us, "Whatever you did for one of the least of these brothers of mine, you did for me." (Matthew 25:40) Whether it's opening the door for someone in a wheelchair, taking a meal to a shut-in, helping an older person with his groceries, or even fetching a ball for a small child, there are so many opportunities to help "the least of these."

Every day we make choices of whether we will show compassion or walk on by. Every day we make choices of whether we'll encourage someone or put them down. Every day we make choices of who we'll serve and how we'll serve them.

I honestly can't remember where I heard the following story, but I've tried to retell it as best I can. I think it beautifully demonstrates the power of choices we make every day.

At a fundraising dinner for a school that serves learning-disabled children, the father of one of the school's students delivered a speech that would never be forgotten by all who attended. After extolling the school and its dedicated staff, he offered a question. "Everything God does is done with perfection. Yet, my son, Shay, cannot learn things as other children do. He cannot understand things as other children do. How is God's plan reflected in my son?" The audience was stilled by the query. The father continued. "I believe," the father answered, "that when God brings a childlike Shay into the world, an opportunity to realize the Divine Plan presents itself. And it comes in the way we treat that child."

Then, he told the following story: Shay and his father were walking past a park where some boys Shay knew were playing baseball. Shay asked, "Do you think they will let me play?" Shay's father knew that most boys would not want him on their team. But he understood that if his son could play it would give him a much-needed sense of belonging. So, Shay's dad approached one of the boys and asked if Shay could play.

(To be continued...)

Scripture Reading: Matthew 19:13-14

Personal Application:

- Picture yourself in the above story. If you were one of the boys playing ball, would you let Shay play? What criteria would you use to make your decision?
- Keep your eyes open today for opportunities to serve others with Jesus' love.

Week 16, Day 5: God's Divine Plan (Continued from Day 4:)

Shay's father approached one of the boys on the field and asked if his disabled son Shay could play. The boy looked around for guidance from his teammates. Getting none, he took matters into his own hands and said, "We are losing by six runs, and the game is in the eighth inning. Sure, he can be on our team and we'll put him up to bat in the ninth inning."

In the bottom of the eighth inning, Shay's team scored a few runs but was still behind by three. At the top of the ninth inning, Shay put on a glove and played in the outfield. Although no hits came his way, he was obviously ecstatic just to be on the field, grinning from ear to ear.

In the bottom of the ninth inning, Shay's team scored again. Now, with two outs and bases loaded, the potential winning run was on base. Shay was scheduled to be the next at bat. Would the team let Shay bat at this juncture and give away their chance to win the game?

Surprisingly, they let Shay bat. Everyone knew that a hit was all but impossible because Shay didn't even know how to hold the bat, much less connect with the ball. However, as Shay stepped up to the plate, the pitcher moved closer to lob the ball in softly so Shay could at least make contact. The first pitch came, and Shay swung clumsily and missed.

The pitcher again took a few steps forward to toss the ball softly toward Shay. As the pitch came in, Shay swung at the ball and hit a slow ground ball to the pitcher. The pitcher picked up the soft grounder and could easily have thrown Shay out at first base, ending the game.

Instead, the pitcher threw the ball on a high arc to right field. Everyone started yelling, "Shay, run to first. Run to first." He scampered down the baseline, wide-eyed and startled.

Then, everyone yelled, "Run to second, run to second!" The right fielder had the ball now and could have thrown the ball to the second baseman for a tag. But the right fielder understood what the pitcher's intentions, so he threw the ball high and far over the third baseman's head.

As Shay reached second base, the opposing shortstop ran to him, turned him in the direction of third base, and shouted, "Run to third!" As Shay rounded third, the boys from both teams were screaming, "Shay! Run home!" Shay ran home, stepped on home plate, and was cheered as the hero, for hitting a "grand slam" and winning the game for his team.

With tears rolling down his cheeks, Shay's dad explained, "That day, the boys from both teams helped bring a piece of the Divine Plan into this world."

Scripture Reading: Matthew 25:34-40

Personal Application:

- I believe we're given powerful choices every day. Sometimes we're just so busy, so focused, or so wrapped up in our own stuff, that we just miss them. How often do we miss the opportunity to bring a piece of the "Divine Plan" into this world?
- Let's approach today and each day with expectancy and a commitment to show compassion to "the least of these."

Week 16, Day 6: The Deadly Side of Perfectionism

As the first-born male born to parents who both came from dysfunctional homes, my idea about what makes a good family were distorted. As I matured into adulthood, I thought about what a "good life" should look like: a good marriage, a good family, a good home, a good job, and some nice toys. I believed this is what I had to do to make it good…or perfect is more like it.

It makes me shudder to think back on all that. For too much of my life I was a slave to perfectionism, to idealism, to lists, and to my desperate search for what the world defined as success. I found safety in following rules and holding others to them. I found comfort in being the best, the top dog, and the high achiever.

I needed more education and degrees, a position of responsibility and authority, more recognition and awards, and more and bigger fish and game. I thought my picture of *perfect* guaranteed peace, comfort, and acceptance.

I was punctual, pleasant, and prepared. I was a good husband, a good father, a dedicated friend, and a son who honored his parents. I remembered birthdays and anniversaries. I paid all the bills on time, didn't cheat on my taxes, voted Republican, let others go first, and tried to live by the golden rule. I was very critical of myself, wanting to be a "billboard for Jesus." I worked so hard to have it all together that I completely burned myself out.

The stress of trying to pull off "the picture of life" I'd imagined was more than my body and mind could handle. I battled depression, sudden bouts of anxiety, and eventually even panic attacks. I was a mess…and I knew it. I was exhausted and disgusted with everyone in the picture…especially myself. I gave up.

I walked into a counselor's office and said, "I give up." I had no plan, no strategy, no formula, no hope. I had been a Christian since I was thirteen, but somehow, I had missed a big chunk of the Good News – it was called GRACE. Jesus came to give us life more abundant (John 10:10). I knew how to live obediently, but abundantly? I didn't even know what that word meant.

I viewed salvation as something for the hereafter, not for this present life. I was so busy trying to create my own "heaven on earth," that I hadn't taken time to get to know Jesus. I knew all about Him, had lots of biblical knowledge, even went to seminary, but I didn't really know Him.

As I pursued a real relationship with Him, His love overwhelmed me. I began to let go and truly live. I stopped trying to fix things and let Jesus fix my heart. I learned that there are many ways to do things, that efficiency never supersedes love and patience, and people are more important than tasks. I mean I learned it deep down in my heart where it counts. Jesus changed my life!

Scripture Reading: 1 Corinthians 13:1-3
Personal Application:
- To what extent does my story describe your own? If so, how is that working for you?
- Yield your whole life to Christ. Pursue the Perfect One instead of perfection.

Week 16, Day 7: Weekly Recap and Prayer

On the seventh day of each week, use the **ACTS** acronym to spend time with the Lord reviewing and assessing your week and praying to God. (**A**=Adoration; **C**=Confession; **T**=Thanksgiving; **S**=Supplication)

First, look back over the previous six days for this week to remind yourself what you read and agreed to. Then, follow the ACTS pattern for prayer below. Finally, use the space below to journal what God is doing in your life and share this with a trusted spiritual partner.

Adoration: Simply spend time in adoration of the Lord. Praise Him and glorify His name. (See 1 Chronicles 29:10-13; Psalm 100; Romans 11:33-36.)

Confession: Confess your sins and shortcomings before God. ("If we confess our sins, he is faithful and just and will forgive us our sins and purify us from all unrighteousness." – 1 John 1:9) To confess (or agree with God) about your sin, implies that you are repentant and desperately want Him to change you.

Thanksgiving: Thank God for what He has done and is doing in your life and the life of your family. Give Him credit, for everything you have comes from Him. (See Psalm 136.)

Supplication: Supplication is just a fancy word for making your requests known to God. Based on the devotions of this past week and the things going on in your life right now, what do you want to ask Him for? "If you, then, though you are evil, know how to give good gifts to your children, how much more will your Father in heaven give good gifts to those who ask Him!" (Matthew 7:11)

Journal: What is God doing in your life right now?

Week 17, Day 1: Change for the Better

I marvel at my grandparents who, in their lifetime, witnessed the transition from horse and buggy to landing a man on the moon! And yet, we're told that the changes we're experiencing today even eclipse those! Indeed, we could say that life is defined by perpetual change.

We seem to have developed a love-hate relationship with change. We may say we like change, but not too much, or not in that direction, or not for those reasons, or why change now? Change can be good, and I usually embrace it. I like living on the edge of innovation and creativity. But sometimes it seems like I've just learned a new software application when it's time to learn a new one. Change is inevitable, and it's also necessary.

But not all change is good. Sin is a change of heart. It is rebellion or turning away from God. Even as Christians, if we let our love for Christ grow cold, we change for the worse. We begin taking on the character of the world and adopting its vices. "Do not conform to the pattern of this world but be transformed by the renewing of your mind." (Romans 12:2)

I think of two kinds of change that are both pleasing to God and beneficial to us: repentance and transformation. To repent means to make a 180-degree change from pursuing our own way to pursuing God's way. We repent from evil and turn to God (Acts 3:19). And when we turn to God by receiving Jesus Christ, He begins a transformation (or change) process in us that continues our whole life. These are good changes that make us more like Christ in our character. Finally, when Christ returns, we shall all be changed and put on immortality (1 Corinthians 15:52).

There are also some things that never change. God's love for mankind and His Word, the Gospel, never change. "For you have been born again, not of perishable seed, but of imperishable, through the living and enduring word of God. For, 'All people are like grass, and all their glory is like the flowers of the field; the grass withers and the flowers fall, but the word of the Lord endures forever.'" (1 Peter 1:23-25)

We can be flexible and change the methods by which we share the Gospel, but we must be careful not to change the Gospel message. "Jesus Christ is the same yesterday and today and forever." (Hebrews 13:8) I am so thankful that no matter how the times change, God and His truths remain the same.

Scripture Reading: Hebrews 1:10-12

Personal Application:

- What is one thing you'd like to see Christ change in you? What has been preventing you from letting Him change you in this area?
- What changes do you need to make to see that desired change come about? Share these things with your spiritual partner and let him help keep you accountable.

Week 17, Day 2: Safe and Sound

"I will lie down and sleep in peace,
for you alone, O Lord, make me dwell in safety."
— Psalm 4:8

Americans really value safety and security. We install alarms, dead-bolt locks on our doors, and get dogs to protect our homes. We purchase firearms and take courses in self-defense to protect ourselves. We save our money in FDIC insured accounts or safes, so it can't be taken or lost. We may consult financial advisors to make sure our limited funds are wisely invested, and to ensure our future financial well-being.

We load up on insurance: life, accident, disability, homeowner's, flood, dental, health, liability, auto, traveler's—and even pet insurance. We do everything we can think of and afford to put safety nets around ourselves and our loved ones and ourselves. We seek to avoid catastrophe, misfortune, and ruin at all cost...but we can't.

We simply can't cover all the bases. Life is unpredictable, full of sin, and misfortune. So much of life is out of our control. At 60 mph, we couldn't see that nail in the road that caused a flat tire. There was no way to prevent that loved one from getting cancer. There's no insurance against a broken heart caused by the cruelty of others.

There's just no way we can completely protect ourselves from pain and suffering. The truth is there are a lot of people who spend their whole lives trying to feel "safe," only to end up lonely and depressed.

The Good News is that God cares; He offers us joy and salvation. He offers us security today and for all eternity...and it's free! When we put our trust in Him, we find "the peace that passes understanding." We find joy amidst the struggle. We find hope and strength when even the worst in this life happens. When we know Jesus, we are never alone. God's offer is real security.

Our security is guaranteed by the presence of the Holy Spirit: "Now it is God who makes both us and you stand firm in Christ. He anointed us and set his seal of ownership on us and put his Spirit in our hearts as a deposit, guaranteeing what is to come." (2 Corinthians 1:21-22.)

Our security is guaranteed by Christ's intercession for us: "Therefore He is able to save completely those who come to God through Him, because H always lives to intercede for them." (Hebrews 7:25).

Finally, our security is guaranteed by God's power: "To him who is able to keep you from falling and to present you before his glorious presence without fault and with great joy..." (Jude 1:24)

Scripture Reading: Romans 8:31-39

Personal Application:

- Your security is not dependent on your faithfulness or precautions, but on God Himself. Thank Him for the safety and security that you and your family enjoy in Him. Knowing that you're safe and secure, how should that impact the way you live?

Week 17, Day 3: The Weeds of Life

When I was very young, my punishment—or chores, depending on how you viewed the task—was to pull weeds in our large yard. I hated it! It seemed a waste of time and pointless because every week there would be a new crop. If you have any kind of landscaping or garden yourself, you know the challenge of keeping up with the weeds.

Maybe you've experienced the hope of planting a new garden or lawn. You had a picture in your mind of what it would look like—high expectations of vegetable-laden plants or of your neighbor looking enviously at your lush, green lawn. But you discovered good gardens and thick, carpet-like lawns don't grow naturally. Weeds do.

Through my adult years, working in my yard has taken on new meaning and has given me some spiritual insights. Pulling weeds and planting seeds is the story of life. We are each like plots of ground on which either weeds of bitterness and selfishness grow, or the fruits of the Holy Spirit grow and flourish. The soil of our hearts is the most valuable acreage on planet earth.

In Mark 4, Jesus taught the parable of the soils to His disciples. He said that spiritual fruitfulness or barrenness depends upon the type of soil that receives the seed of God's Word. He warned of rocky ground, shallow soil, and choking thorns that squeeze the life out of otherwise fruitful plants.

Later in that chapter Jesus explained what He meant by thorns, "The worries of this life, the deceitfulness of wealth and the desires for other things come in and choke the word, making it unfruitful." (Mark 4:19)

Busyness is also a dangerous weed. Even a full schedule of good things can crowd out what's best—like time in the morning with God. I can easily be distracted by urgent things that could be put off for just a few minutes, or even a few days.

Some people are preoccupied with pleasing others and gaining their approval. Still others are pulled by their insecurities, trying to find significance in achievements or performance. And Scripture warns against allowing bitterness to take root in our lives. In short, any sin or distraction signals us that we've got "weeds" in our life and our "garden" needs tending.

A deep relationship with God doesn't grow all on its own. Good marriages and families don't grow naturally. Meaningful relationships with other believers don't sprout up on their own—weeds and thorns do. Let's allow the Holy Spirit to weed out the things in our lives that take away from what really matters—that keep us from experiencing His joy and transformation.

Scripture Reading: Mark 4:13-20

Personal Application:
- What things or practices in your life would you consider to be weeds?
- As you know, it's no good to just mow down weeds, you must pull out their entire root, so they don't grow back. What might that look like for you spiritually?

Week 17, Day 4: Sexual Purity

Sex is a beautiful gift of God for a husband and wife to enjoy. But I don't know of a man alive who hasn't struggled with lust toward another woman. And the availability of porn and nudity in movies and advertising has only made it harder to keep one's thoughts and sexual life pure.

When Jesus was here on earth, the Scribes and Pharisees had so twisted God's law that they had devised ways to keep the outward form of the law, while flagrantly breaking its intent. In His Sermon on the Mount, Jesus sought to correct their warped thinking and part of it had to do with sexual purity. Jesus explained:

"You have heard that it was said, 'You shall not commit adultery.' But I tell you that anyone who looks at a woman lustfully has already committed adultery with her in his heart. If your right eye causes you to stumble, gouge it out and throw it away. It is better for you to lose one part of your body than for your whole body to be thrown into hell. And if your right hand causes you to stumble, cut it off and throw it away. It is better for you to lose one part of your body than for your whole body to go into hell." (Matthew 5:27-30)

The first thing we notice about what Jesus said here is that God cares about our thoughts as well as our actions. Men who indulge in pornography are committing adultery. Not only that, but they are exploiting women, supporting human trafficking, and destroying their own lives and their marriages. And pornography can be a form of addiction that leads to other unhealthy practices.

Also, when Jesus talks about gouging out one's eye, this is hyperbole. He doesn't mean this literally. He's using exaggerated speech to emphasize that *we must do whatever it takes to remain sexually pure*. Maintaining sexual purity is a big deal in God's eyes.

In the context of maintaining sexual purity, King Solomon warned his son, "Why, my son, be intoxicated with another man's wife? Why embrace the bosom of a wayward woman? For your ways are in full view of the Lord, and he examines all your paths." (Proverbs 5:20-21) God sees and knows all. Do we really think what we do or think in secret goes unnoticed by Him?

Here's God's remedy for sexual purity. He's using some figurative language here, so use your imagination. "Drink water from your own cistern, running water from your own well. Should your springs overflow in the streets, your streams of water in the public squares? Let them be yours alone, never to be shared with strangers. May your fountain be blessed, and may you rejoice in the wife of your youth. A loving doe, a graceful deer—may her breasts satisfy you always, may you ever be intoxicated with her love." (Proverbs 5:15-19)

Scripture Reading: Ephesians 5:1-7

Personal Application:

- Sexual sins have deep roots and are difficult to extract, so use every spiritual discipline available to uproot them. Rely on the power of the Holy Spirit and engage the help of a spiritual partner if you struggle with sexual sin.

Week 17, Day 5: Can You Sleep While the Wind Blows?

People often ask me "How is your ministry doing, given this economy?" During four decades of ministry we have been through several economic downturns. During these tough times many are realizing that the truth is they have little control over their own destinies. They see the need to surrender their circumstances to God Almighty and let Him direct their paths, their decisions, and their attitudes.

If you're shaken and find yourself racing around trying to fight off the storms of life, maybe the following story will help you see the importance of preparing yourself…and then letting go.

Years ago, a farmer owned land along the Atlantic seacoast. He constantly advertised for hired hands, but most were reluctant to work on farms along the Atlantic. They dreaded the awful storms that raged, wreaking havoc on the buildings and crops. As the farmer interviewed applicants for the job, he received a steady stream of refusals.

Finally, a small, thin man, well past middle age, applied for the job. "Are you a good farm hand?" the farmer asked him. "Well, I can sleep when the wind blows," answered the little man. Although puzzled by this answer, the farmer, desperate for help, hired him. The little man worked well around the farm, busy from dawn to dusk, and the farmer was satisfied with the man's work.

Then one night the wind howled loudly from offshore. Jumping out of bed, the farmer grabbed a lantern and rushed next door to the hired hand's sleeping quarters. He shook the little man and yelled, "Get up! A storm is coming! Tie things down before they blow away!" The little man rolled over in bed and said firmly, "No sir. I told you, I can sleep when the wind blows."

Enraged by the response, the farmer was tempted to fire him on the spot. Instead, he hurried outside to prepare for the storm. But to his amazement, he discovered that all the haystacks had been covered with tarpaulins. The cows were in the barn, the chickens were in the coops, and the doors were barred. The shutters were tightly secured. Everything was tied down. Nothing could blow away.

Now the farmer understood what his hired hand meant, so he went back to bed to sleep…while the wind blew.

Grounding ourselves in the Word of God prepares us for the storms of life. Surrendering to God's control brings us peace. We don't need to understand all the circumstances, and we don't need to make it all better. We just need to hold His hand, accept His peace, and let Him guide us through. I don't know about you, but I want to be able to "sleep when the wind blows."

Scripture Reading: Psalm 4:1-8

Personal Application:

- Read and meditate on Psalm 4. What is the Lord saying to you personally through that Psalm and this devotional? What will you do because of what He has shown you from His Word?

Week 17, Day 6: Are You Ready for a Thrill?

Anyone who has enjoyed the adventure of dipping a line into the water knows that some strange things can happen on a fishing trip. With all our technology and expertise, we like to think that we have mastered this unique sport. That's about the time when some seven-year-old kid, fishing with a piece of corn from shore, catches a lake-record-breaking bass as the professional bass fishermen look on.

Perhaps the greatest fishing story of all time came from a unique experience the Apostle Peter had during his time with Jesus. It appears that Jesus was often his house guest during His three-and-a-half-year ministry. During this time, Jesus continued to disciple His twelve chosen students, eight of whom were fishermen.

Peter, Andrew, James, and John were partners in a community fishing venture located in Capernaum, on the Northwest side of the Sea of Galilee. Scripture suggests that Peter was most likely the top fisherman in the area. But like any fisherman, he also had his tough days when the fish were not to be found.

This unusual fish story started when tax collectors showed up in Capernaum and asked Peter, "Doesn't your teacher pay the temple tax?" Peter replied, "Yes, He does." When Peter came into the house, Jesus asked him about his conversation with the tax collectors. Jesus seems to argue that under the circumstances He and His disciples should be exempt from paying the tax.

However, in order to avoid offending others, Jesus told Peter to go to the Sea of Galilee, cast a line, and the first fish he caught would have a four-drachma coin (or *stater*) in its mouth. Peter was to pay the tax for both with the coin. Imagine how strange these instructions must have seemed to Peter, a man who earned his living from fishing, and primarily with a net!

I see three strong lessons in this story. First, Jesus set aside His rights to avoid offending others or being misunderstood. Second, He asked Peter to do something that made no logical sense, yet Peter believed Jesus and did what He had asked. Third, everything happened exactly as Jesus told Peter it would. Peter went the lake, cast a line in the water, caught a fish, opened its mouth and there was the four-drachma coin!

Sometimes God asks us to do strange things…things that are out of our comfort zone, or simply don't make sense to us. How is your faith? Are you willing to be an obedient disciple and follow Jesus? Take the rod of obedience, the line of faith, and the hook of perseverance, and follow the Lord's leading in your life. The catch of a lifetime awaits you.

Scripture Reading: Matthew 17:24-27

Personal Application:

- How receptive are you to the leading of the Lord in your life? Rarely does God ask anyone to do something as unusual as what He asked Peter to do. Nevertheless, He may ask you to do something that seems crazy at the time, or due to the circumstances.
- Purpose to obey the Lord when He clearly leads or prompts you to do something.

Week 17, Day 7: Weekly Recap and Prayer

On the seventh day of each week, use the **ACTS** acronym to spend time with the Lord reviewing and assessing your week and praying to God. (**A**=Adoration; **C**=Confession; **T**=Thanksgiving; **S**=Supplication)

First, look back over the previous six days for this week to remind yourself what you read and agreed to. Then, follow the ACTS pattern for prayer below. Finally, use the space below to journal what God is doing in your life and share this with a trusted spiritual partner.

Adoration: Simply spend time in adoration of the Lord. Praise Him and glorify His name. (See 1 Chronicles 29:10-13; Psalm 100; Romans 11:33-36.)

Confession: Confess your sins and shortcomings before God. ("If we confess our sins, he is faithful and just and will forgive us our sins and purify us from all unrighteousness." – 1 John 1:9) To confess (or agree with God) about your sin, implies that you are repentant and desperately want Him to change you.

Thanksgiving: Thank God for what He has done and is doing in your life and the life of your family. Give Him credit, for everything you have comes from Him. (See Psalm 136.)

Supplication: Supplication is just a fancy word for making your requests known to God. Based on the devotions of this past week and the things going on in your life right now, what do you want to ask Him for? "If you, then, though you are evil, know how to give good gifts to your children, how much more will your Father in heaven give good gifts to those who ask Him!" (Matthew 7:11)

Journal: What is God doing in your life right now?

Week 18, Day 1: Knowing God

God is so good. He is holy and righteous and worthy of all praise… and He invites us to know Him in a very personal way. With our finite minds we cannot begin to comprehend how awesome He is. Scripture tells us, "Great is the LORD and most worthy of praise; His greatness no one can fathom." (Psalm 145:3) Yet, despite our limited capabilities, God seeks us out and wants us to know Him. He does this in numerous ways.

First, God reveals Himself to us through His creation. "For since the creation of the world God's invisible qualities—His eternal power and divine nature—have been clearly seen, being understood from what has been made." (Romans 1:20) And, "The heavens declare the glory of God; the skies proclaim the work of His hands." (Psalm 19:1)

I live in a part of the country where it snows in winter. Snow, in and of itself, is a wonder of God. Sometimes mounds of snow cover the grass and other plants in a cold, white blanket all winter long. And when spring comes, it always reminds me of the faithfulness of God. The snow is hardly gone before the crocus, daffodils, and tulips are blooming!

Speaking of flowers, here's what Jesus said, "Why do you worry about clothes? See how the flowers of the field grow. They do not labor or spin. Yet I tell you that not even Solomon in all his splendor was dressed like one of these. If that is how God clothes the grass of the field…will He not much more clothe you?" (Matthew 6:28-30) Yes, in the flowers we see the amazing handiwork of God and His great love and care for our needs.

God reveals Himself to us in innumerable other ways through nature, but He also gave us His Word. In God's Word, the Bible, He shows us His character and nature and we read about God's dealings with mankind through the ages. The Apostle Paul explains, "All Scripture is God-breathed and is useful for teaching, rebuking, correcting and training in righteousness, so that the servant of God may be thoroughly equipped for every good work." (2 Timothy 3:16-17)

God reveals Himself through Jesus: "No one has ever seen God, but the one and only Son, who is Himself God and is in closest relationship with the Father, has made Him known." (John 1:18) Jesus "is the radiance of God's glory and the exact representation of His being, sustaining all things by His powerful word." (Hebrews 1:3) And Jesus said, "Anyone who has seen Me has seen the Father." (John 14:9)

And the Lord continues to reveal Himself to us through His Spirit. Jesus said, "The Spirit will receive from Me what He will make known to you." (John 16:15) In all these ways, God seeks us out so that we might know Him.

Scripture Reading: Colossians 1:15-20

Personal Application:
• Beware of merely knowing *about* God instead of really knowing Him. Always go to the Word with the intent to meet with God and approach prayer in the same way.

Week 18, Day 2: Hang in There!

When times are tough, I often picture a cat hanging for dear life onto a high tree limb by its front paws. The expression on the cat's face says it all. Just like the cat, sometimes all we can do is hang on. The COVID-19 pandemic of 2020 and all the challenges it brought is a good example. Perseverance is that steadfastness and persistence we all admire but don't really like to experience, because of what it requires to obtain.

Bob Schmitt, of Wenatchee, WA, tells a great story about "hanging on." When he was a teenager in Southern Utah, he and some of his friends decided to do their first big game hunting trip together. These determined lads packed a lunch, loaded up their guns, and headed to the nearby woods. They split up and Bob went uphill, and his two friends went downhill to scope out the lower forest. Within an hour Bob spotted a small herd of five deer about 250 yards from his position. He brought up his Remington 30.06 with a five-power scope and began checking out the deer.

He quickly sighted in on a nice 4x4, husky mule deer. Bob peered through the lens and squeezed off a round. The deer appeared to be hit but didn't go down. Bob and his friends headed up the hill to see if they could track the animal. Soon, Bob saw the wounded deer staggering towards him. He fired another round and the old buck hit the ground.

With shouts of joy Bob ran up to the buck, placed his gun against a nearby tree, and pulled out his knife to bleed out the deer. But just as Bob mounted the deer and raised its head to expose its neck, the dazed buck stood up and began to run downhill with Bob on its back! The deer raced past his two astonished friends, who immediately busted out laughing. All Bob could do was hang on to the antlers and ride it out. Once the deer slowed down a bit he jumped off, ran back to his gun, and finally brought the deer down…for good. What an adventure!

Today, many families are coping with difficult issues. All they can do is pray and "hang on." I know a middle-aged man who is fighting cancer as his young family wonders about the future. Some dear friends of ours are juggling the concerns and responsibilities of an older mother who is very sick. Other friends have a daughter with a difficult pregnancy. And others contend with the unknowns associated with a new business venture.

What can we tell folks who are struggling with what seem to be insurmountable circumstances? Sometimes we just don't even know what to say. The writer of Hebrews offers encouragement for times like these, "Let us hold unswervingly to the hope we profess, for He who promised is faithful." (Hebrews 10:23) In other words, "Hang in there!"

Scripture Reading: James 1:2-4

Personal Application:

- What's going on in your life and the lives of those around you right now?
- Perseverance is a godly character trait we all desire. But the only way to obtain perseverance is through trials and the "testing of our faith" (James 1:2). Take courage and hang in there! The Lord is with you.

Week 18, Day 3: No One Can Tame the Tongue

Sometimes we're our own worst enemy, and our troubles often begin and end with our tongue. In fact, James says, "We all make many mistakes. For if we could control our tongues, we would be perfect and could also control ourselves in every other way." (James 3:2 NLT)

James goes on to explain the power of the tongue using a couple of analogies. For instance, we can control a huge horse just with a bit and a lead. Or we can steer a huge ship with its small rudder. In the same way, the tongue, though just a small part of the body, can wield tremendous damage (or good) (James 3:3-6).

Then, James says something astounding, "People can tame all kinds of animals, birds, reptiles, and fish, but no one can tame the tongue. It is restless and evil, full of deadly poison." (James 3:7-8 NLT) Out of the same mouth we praise God and curse our fellow man. We speak a kind word to our wife and children in one moment and in the next we cut them to shreds.

Jesus had some strong and sobering words for the Pharisees, "The mouth speaks what the heart is full of. A good man brings good things out of the good stored up in him, and an evil man brings evil things out of the evil stored up in him. But I tell you that everyone will have to give account on the day of judgment for every empty word they have spoken. For by your words you will be acquitted, and by your words you will be condemned." (Matthew 12:34-37)

What we say, and sometimes what we don't say, carries huge weight and serious consequences. As James said, "No one can tame the tongue." So, what are we to do?

No man can tame the tongue, but Christ can! David recognized this fact when he wrote Psalm 19. He talks about all of nature declaring the glory of God according to God's design. Then he transitions to God's Word and shows how it is perfect, trustworthy, and full of wisdom.

But then David recognizes and confesses his errors, his faults and sins and his inability to control those apart from God's help. Finally, David ends this Psalm with the prayer, "May the words of my mouth and the meditation of my heart be pleasing to you, O Lord, my rock and my redeemer." (Psalm 19:14)

We must continually come humbly before the Lord asking Him to give us a pure heart and giving Him control over our tongues. "Do not let any unwholesome talk come out of your mouths, but only what is helpful for building others up according to their needs, that it may benefit those who listen." (Ephesians 4:29)

Scripture Reading: Psalm 19:1-14

Personal Application:
- In what regard do you personally struggle most with your tongue?
- In Proverbs, chapters 13-16, you'll find many references to the tongue and our words. Highlight those verses and let God's Word replace any idle, hurtful, or foolish words in your life.

Week 18, Day 4: Be an "O" Man for God

Without much fame or fortune the offensive line does their job. While quarterbacks, running backs, and receivers get all the attention from the media, the quarterback wouldn't have time to complete many passes, nor would the running back find the holes to dart through without a great offensive line.

Former Super Bowl coach of the Oakland Raiders and television commentator John Madden says, "You can design the best offensive plays in football, but if your blockers don't do their job, those plays are worthless." Coach Madden and many other coaches believe that assembling the right the "O" line could be a team's most important task.

When the Dallas Cowboys won Super Bowl XXX, their big and powerful offensive line seemed to set the standard for their league. The average weight of the starting five was 324 pounds. All Pro Nate Newton said, "What people don't realize is that we're in shape; in the fourth quarter we've still got our stamina." If a team plays well on offense, it's usually because the offensive line is having a "good day" against an inferior defensive line.

Unlike defensive linemen that usually have nicknames and receive the high-fives coming off the field, the offensive linemen are usually the quiet warriors of the game. Statistics indicate that these humble but powerful players are usually the brightest men on the field. Those same stats also show that most finish college with good grades. They usually take on leadership roles within the team and become mentors to the younger players.

Great "O" men like legendary Steve "Wiz" Wizniewski, set the standard. Coaches want great strength and stamina, compacted in a powerful body that doesn't weigh much over 300 pounds. With the speed of today's players and an increased emphasis in the "west-coast style of offense," more power and speed is needed over the bulk-frame seen in the huge linemen of decades past.

From a spiritual standpoint, others depend on us in all facets of life to serve as "O" men. To be sure, we may serve in other capacities too, but using this metaphor, others count on us to block for them and prevent the evil one from getting around or through us to them.

How do we do this? We do this chiefly by living for Christ and setting the example for others. We also pray "offensively" for our families and others in our lives. We workout, building godly character in our lives and bulk up on God's Word (1 Timothy 4:6-8). We're to "be strong in the Lord and in His mighty power." (Ephesians 6:10) And clothed with God's armor, we can "stand our ground," and "stand firm" against the enemy (Ephesians 6:13-14).

Scripture Reading: Ephesians 6:10-18

Personal Application:
- Who in your life is depending on you as an "O" man?
- What can you do today to stand in the gap for them to block the advances of the evil one?

Week 18, Day 5: Are You Living with God's Wealth?

Some years ago, I heard the following tragic story:

Mrs. Bertha Adams, 71 years old, died alone in West Palm Beach, Florida, on Easter Sunday. The coroner's report read: "Cause of death: malnutrition." She had wasted away to fifty pounds.

When the state authorities made their preliminary investigation of Mrs. Adams' home, they found a veritable "pigpen...the biggest mess you can imagine." The woman had begged food from neighbors' back doors and gotten what clothing she had from the Salvation Army. From all outward appearances, she was a penniless recluse. But such was not the case.

Amid the jumble of her unclean, disheveled belongings, the officials found two keys to safety deposit boxes at two different local banks. In the first box were over 700 AT&T stock certificates, plus hundreds of other valuable certificates, bonds, and solid financial securities, not to mention a stack of cash amounting to nearly $200,000. The second box contained $600,000. Adding the net worth of both boxes, they found well over a million dollars.

As I ponder Mrs. Adams' story, I think of three possible scenarios regarding her untapped resources: either she had forgotten about them; or if left by her deceased husband, she may not have known about them; or she was a hoarder and couldn't bear the thought of using them. In any case, hers is a sad story of one who lived and died in poverty even though she was rich.

We may shake our heads at Mrs. Adams and her plight, but in my experience many of us live just like she did in terms of our spiritual wealth. We have untold resources at our disposal, yet we live as though we were destitute.

I think Paul saw this tendency in the believers in Ephesus and so he prayed the following prayer for them. "I pray that the eyes of your heart may be enlightened in order that you may know the hope to which He has called you, the riches of His glorious inheritance in His holy people, and His incomparably great power for us who believe." (Ephesians 1:18-19)

May we apply that prayer to ourselves as well! "The riches of His glorious inheritance...and His incomparably great power" are ours, yet we often live our lives spiritual bankrupt or penniless. I'm not talking about some "prosperity gospel" here, but the true riches and power that are ours through Christ. And the fun part is, we get to pass along these riches to others!

Scripture Reading: Psalm 36:5-9

Personal Application:
- How would you typify your life? Are you living according to Paul's prayer in Ephesians, or does your spiritual life look more like that of Mrs. Adams?
- Claim your wealth and power in Christ as you live and walk with Him by faith.

Week 18, Day 6: God and Priorities

Have you ever heard the Christian mantra, "God wants to be our number one priority"? Perhaps you've heard it in this format: "God first, family second..." and so on. Depending on how you take that, there may be a kernel of truth in it, but for the most part I want to debunk it. Does that shock you?

Let me pose it to you as a question. Do you really think God wants to be a priority among priorities in your life? Now we're starting to get to the heart of the matter. You see, God doesn't want to be your highest priority, He wants to be your greatest love (Matthew 22:36-40).

Why am I making this distinction? Does it matter? Yes, it does. I'm not just "splitting hairs!"

Perhaps the following scenario will help. If you're married, let's say your anniversary is coming up and it's a big one, so you go out and spend a wad on your bride. But just before you give her your anniversary gift you divulge to a friend that your primary motive in buying the gift is merely out of a sense of duty or obligation to her and this event—because it's expected.

Unfortunately, your wife overheard your conversation. How do you think she would feel? Chances are your wife wouldn't even want your lousy gift now. She wants your love and affection, not obligatory duty. And so, it is with God.

When commitment, priority, duty, or obligation are the primary drivers in our relationship with God, we draw attention to *ourselves* rather than to God. Remember the prayer of the proud Pharisee? "I thank you, God, that I am not like other people—cheaters, sinners, adulterers. I'm certainly not like that tax collector! I fast twice a week, and I give you a tenth of my income." (Luke 18:11-12 NLT) His prayer reeks of duty, obligation—and of self-praise.

But when we make God our greatest love, we express to Him His great worth to us. We live our lives selflessly to Him purely out of love for Him. We make much of Him. We boast about Him before others. We praise Him, adore Him, and worship Him. We love Him.

I love what John Piper says, "God is most glorified in us, when we are most satisfied in Him." When we start living for God out of pure love and affection for Him, we draw attention to Him. We also experience extreme joy in serving Him because we simply want to please Him. William George Jordan observed, "Duty is a hard, mechanical process for making men do things that love would make easy."

In Psalm 37:4 it says, "Delight yourself also in the Lord, and He shall give you the desires of your heart." (NKJV) For years, I wondered what that really meant. Now I know. You see, when we "delight ourselves" or deeply desire the Lord, He satisfies that desire! He gives us Himself.

Scripture Reading: Psalm 73:25

Personal Application:

- Memorize Psalm 73:25 and meditate on it.
  Make God your greatest love.

Week 18, Day 7: Weekly Recap and Prayer

On the seventh day of each week, use the **ACTS** acronym to spend time with the Lord reviewing and assessing your week and praying to God. (**A**=Adoration; **C**=Confession; **T**=Thanksgiving; **S**=Supplication)

First, look back over the previous six days for this week to remind yourself what you read and agreed to. Then, follow the ACTS pattern for prayer below. Finally, use the space below to journal what God is doing in your life and share this with a trusted spiritual partner.

Adoration: Simply spend time in adoration of the Lord. Praise Him and glorify His name. (See 1 Chronicles 29:10-13; Psalm 100; Romans 11:33-36.)

Confession: Confess your sins and shortcomings before God. ("If we confess our sins, he is faithful and just and will forgive us our sins and purify us from all unrighteousness." – 1 John 1:9) To confess (or agree with God) about your sin, implies that you are repentant and desperately want Him to change you.

Thanksgiving: Thank God for what He has done and is doing in your life and the life of your family. Give Him credit, for everything you have comes from Him. (See Psalm 136.)

Supplication: Supplication is just a fancy word for making your requests known to God. Based on the devotions of this past week and the things going on in your life right now, what do you want to ask Him for? "If you, then, though you are evil, know how to give good gifts to your children, how much more will your Father in heaven give good gifts to those who ask Him!" (Matthew 7:11)

Journal: What is God doing in your life right now?

Week 19, Day 1: Give Thanks to the Lord!

Have you ever pondered the words, "Thank you"? The one who utters these words expresses gratefulness to someone else for some act of kindness. Saying "thank you" is polite. It requires a measure of humbleness on the part of the one who gives it and ascribes worth to the one who receives it. Also, giving thanks must be a voluntary action. We cannot demand thanks from someone who fails to give it or doesn't wish to. Giving thanks must come from the heart.

In Luke's Gospel, he records an incident in which Jesus healed ten leprous men who come to Him for healing. He healed them, but of the ten, only one man returned to thank Him. To be healed from leprosy was a big deal, not only affecting their physical wellbeing, but their social, economic, and spiritual health as well. In short, Jesus gave these ten men a new life.

Why did only one return to give thanks? Perhaps the other nine were simply so excited that giving thanks slipped their minds. Hopefully, it wasn't an entitlement mentality that prevented them from giving thanks because they thought they deserved to be healed.

In the case of the healed man who returned, the passage says, "One of them, when he saw he was healed, came back, praising God in a loud voice. He threw himself at Jesus' feet and thanked Him." (Luke 17:15-16) This man felt an overwhelming compulsion to praise and worship God, giving thanks to Jesus for what He had done. Whenever we become aware of who God is and what He has done for us, we too are compelled to thank and praise Him.

Thanking God is an act of worship. We can thank Him *for who He is:* "Give thanks to the Lord, for He is good; His love endures forever." (1 Chronicles 16:34) And, "I will give thanks to the Lord because of his righteousness; I will sing the praises of the name of the Lord Most High." (Psalm 7:17)

And we can thank Him *for what He has done:* "I will give thanks to you, Lord, with all my heart; I will tell of all your wonderful deeds." (Psalm 9:1) And, "Thanks be to God! He gives us the victory through our Lord Jesus Christ." (1 Corinthians 15:57)

The Apostle Paul urges us to, "Sing and make music from your heart to the Lord, always giving thanks to God the Father for everything, in the name of our Lord Jesus Christ." (Ephesians 5:19-20) May all our prayers and thoughts toward God be filled with thanksgiving!

Scripture Reading: Psalm 136

Personal Application:

- Each week on day seven of this devotional, we ask you to spend time thanking God. Thanksgiving should come naturally to us when we contemplate who God is and all He has done for us!
- Why is it appropriate to thank God in every circumstance?
  (See 1 Thessalonians 5:18.)
- What would you like to especially thank Him for right now?

Week 19, Day 2: Dance of Danger

Robert Lewis's book, *The Church of Irresistible Influence*, is filled with great principles on how to create an effective church. Throughout his book, Lewis uses bridge metaphors. The following is my attempt to paraphrase a favorite of his bridge stories.

Newspapers called it the "Dance of Danger" – bridge construction on top of swaying catwalks and high towers, sometimes hundreds of feet in the air, blown by ill winds. This dance had even yielded a calculated fatality rate: For each one million dollars spent, one life would be lost. That was what one could expect.

However, engineers of the Golden Gate Bridge believed the risks could be lowered. In 1932, when construction began, numerous safety measures were put into place and strictly enforced. These required mandatory use of hard hats, prescription eyeglasses, no showing off (cause for immediate dismissal), tie-off lines, and an on-site hospital. All these measures helped to greatly reduce the casualty rate. After all, only one worker died during nearly four years of construction and after $20 million spent!

The most effective safety device, without question, was as new to bridge-building as it was old to the circus: the use of a trapeze net. Costing $130,000, this large net draped sixty feet below the bridge under construction and extended ten feet beyond each side.

The safety net was so effective that the newspapers began running a score chart: "Score on the Gate Bridge Safety Net to Date: eight Lives Saved!" Those men whose lives were saved by the net were said to have joined the "Halfway-to-Hell Club."

The net had another benefit, though perhaps less publicized, but still very significant: It freed many of the workers from an often-paralyzing sense of fear. And many said that helped them work more productively and with more enjoyment.

The Lord and His great care for us is our safety net. Here's what King David wrote, "The Lord makes firm the steps of the one who delights in Him; through he may stumble, he will not fall, for the Lord upholds him with His hand." (Psalm 37:23-24)

And Jesus said, "Are not two sparrows sold for a penny? Yet not one of them will fall to the ground outside your Father's care. So don't be afraid; you are worth more than many sparrows." (Matthew 10:29-31)

Scripture Reading: Psalm 37

Personal Application:
- What "dance of danger" do you feel like you're currently dancing?
- In what ways does it comfort you to know that God will uphold you with His hand?
- Be alert today to share the message of this devotional with someone else who needs it.

Week 19, Day 3: A Quarrelsome Person

*"A quarrelsome person starts fights as easily as
hot embers light charcoal or fire lights wood."*
– Proverbs 26:21 (NLT)

Quarrelsome or contentious people like to argue, quarrel, and disagree—sometimes just for the heck of it! Some are downright mean, while others apparently think that they must challenge or correct everything that anyone says. They nitpick. But whichever the case, the contentious person is difficult to live with and difficult to love.

Solomon commented, "A nagging spouse is like the drip, drip, drip of a leaky faucet; you can't turn it off, and you can't get away from it." (Proverbs 27:15-16 MSG) I worked with a quarrelsome person once and dreaded going to work if he was going to be there. I could never understand why he took such pleasure in arguing, mocking, and fighting.

Paul described such people in this way: "They have an unhealthy interest in controversies and quarrels about words that result in envy, strife, malicious talk, evil suspicions and constant friction between people of corrupt mind, who have been robbed of the truth...." (1 Timothy 6:4-5)

As we read the above passages, the first thing that should come to our minds is, "Am I ever like that? Do I come across to others as contentious?" It's important to stop and assess ourselves from time to time. And if we're unsure of how we come across to others, we can ask our wife or a spiritual partner. At any rate, we want to know if we are contentious so we can seek help to weed this pattern out of our lives.

Also, don't fall into the trap of saying, "That's just the way I am." If that's truly the way you are, then Christ wants to change you! Such behavior is of the flesh, not of the Spirit (Galatians 5:19-26).

Second, if you live or work with a contentious person, there are several strategies you can work through to interact with this person graciously:

1. Love them and seek to live at peace with them. (1 Thessalonians 3:12; 5:13)
2. Don't argue or quarrel with them. (2 Timothy 2:24)
3. "Let your conversation be always full of grace...." (Colossians 4:6)
4. Confront and seek to restore this person to fellowship. (Galatians 6:1-2)
5. Shun them if nothing else works. (2 Thessalonians 3:14)

The Lord has called us to love and live peaceably among each other. "If it is possible, as far as it depends on you, live at peace with everyone." (Romans 12:18)

Scripture Reading: Galatians 5:19-26
Personal Application:
• Whether you struggle with being quarrelsome, or you live or work with a quarrelsome person, rely on the Holy Spirit to help you, and employ one or more of the above strategies.

Week 19, Day 4: Never Quit!

Do you ever feel like quitting? Maybe it's your boss, your company, your marriage, or just your circumstances in life. For some, all it takes is watching the news, and the seeds of despair take root. Terrorism, violence on our streets, the drug epidemic, the decline of the traditional family, the coronavirus pandemic! Sometimes it's just too much.

Despite his great wisdom, Solomon was a quitter. His dad was David, a man after God's heart. Solomon started out so well, building the temple and enjoying peace in his kingdom. Instead of asking for riches, Solomon asked God for wisdom and God blessed him with wisdom *and* wealth. All these factors played in his favor, yet he turned away from the Lord and followed other gods.

God told him, "Since this is your attitude and you have not kept my covenant and my decrees, which I commanded you, I will most certainly tear the kingdom away from you and give it to one of your subordinates." (1 Kings 11:11)

Later in the chapter we read of God's intention to divide Solomon's kingdom, and establish a northern headquarters in Samaria. In the 200-plus years of the northern kingdom's existence, not one of its 19 monarchs was godly. Instead, they led Israel into deep sin and idolatry. And in the 340-plus years of the southern kingdom's existence, only a handful of their kings walked with God—some of those inconsistently. Some legacy Solomon left!

Why do some men quit, and others don't? Men like Abraham Lincoln and Thomas Edison come to mind as men who persevered amid terrible defeat and disappointment, yet they persevered and became renowned for their achievements.

Paul explains that "suffering produces perseverance." (Romans 5:3) But that's only if we endure. If we give up under suffering, we lose perseverance. The next verse goes on to say that "perseverance produces character." (Romans 5:4) Men like Lincoln and Edison developed strong character because they persevered under suffering. Men who continually quit develop character flaws.

None of us likes suffering. But it's interesting that Solomon failed to persevere when everything was going well! He had it all—wine, women, wealth, and wisdom. Perhaps he needed some suffering!

Whatever your situation, whether you're suffering, or just bored because everything is going well for you, don't quit! "You need to persevere so that when you have done the will of God, you will receive what He has promised." (Hebrews 10:36)

Scripture Reading: Galatians 6:9

Personal Application:
- What safeguards can you place in your life to prevent you from ever quitting your relationship with God?
- To whom do you look in your life for encouragement and accountability?

Week 19, Day 5: Can You Dance?

Now, I'm not claiming to be a good dancer. Many men I know are not. But awhile back, I discovered a funny thing while meditating on the word "guidance." I kept seeing "dance" as the last five letters of that word.

Then, I remembered reading once that following God is a lot like dancing. When two people try to lead in a dance, nothing feels right. Their movements don't flow with the music, and everything is uncomfortable and jerky. But when one person lets the other lead, both individuals begin to flow with the music.

One gives gentle cues, perhaps with a nudge to the back or by pressing lightly in one direction or another. It's as if two become one, moving beautifully. The dance takes surrender, willingness, and attentiveness from one person and gentle guidance and skill from the other. Knowing and following God's leading is much like a dance.

Life is full of options, choices, and decisions. But our first decision answers the question, "Who is going to lead in our lives?" We men struggle with this. We talk about "being our own man," being decisive, and being in control. But learning how to *follow* is part of growing in our relationship with Christ. It's noteworthy that Joshua merely served as Moses' aide or assistant for 40 years before God elevated him to Commander and Chief of the whole Israeli nation.

So, how does God guide and lead us? How do we engage in this "dance"? Here are four ways:

1. Most often, He will speak through His Word. "Your Word is a lamp for my feet, a light on my path." (Psalm 119:105)

2. God often speaks through others in our lives. "Instruct a wise man and he will be wiser still; teach a righteous man and he will add to his learning." (Proverbs 9:9)

3. He may also speak through circumstances—making it rather obvious that it is He who is opening (or closing) doors of opportunity. When Paul went to Troas to preach the gospel of Christ, he found that the Lord had opened a door for him there. (See 2 Corinthians 2:12.)

4. Also, the Holy Spirit may simply prompt us, like in Acts 13:1-3. While the leaders in the church at Antioch were "worshiping the Lord and fasting, the Holy Spirit said, 'Set apart for me Barnabas and Saul for the work to which I have called them.' So after they had fasted and prayed, they placed their hands on them and sent them off."

We need to learn the "dance" of letting the Lord lead in our lives.

Scripture Reading: Galatians 5:16-26

Personal Application:

- In what ways do you struggle most in following the Lord's leading in your life?
- From what we shared in today's devotion, what steps will you take to ensure you're in step with God's Spirit and God's direction for your life?

Week 19, Day 6: A Nation in Crisis

The great statesman Edmund Burke said, "The only thing necessary for the triumph of evil is for good men to do nothing."

Throughout Scripture we read about various civilizations crumbling and being judged for their sin. Today, our country is heading down a slippery moral and spiritual slope. Our foundations have already begun to crumble.

We've polluted our land with the innocent blood of millions of unborn children. We've sacrificed babies on the altar of the god of convenience and choice.

Our nation's teen suicide rate is soaring at an alarming rate. More and more youth are falling prey to the insidious meth epidemic, often leading to addiction and ultimately death. Our children, from the primary years through high school, are being taught in public schools that "alternative lifestyles" are socially acceptable, encouraged, and even celebrated.

Over 60 percent of our young people grow up in a single-parent home. And according to a recent survey, over 60 percent of men engage in pornography. Our nation is in crisis!

The media perpetuates the problem, with fake news and sensationalism. Many of today's television programs present men as foolish, inept clowns. Unfortunately, many churches have even begun to compromise their stance on Scripture and what is good and right and proper. We are in a battle!

The Lord warned: "But mark this: There will be terrible times in the last days. People will be lovers of themselves, lovers of money, boastful, proud, abusive, disobedient to their parents, ungrateful, unholy, without love, unforgiving, slanderous, without self-control, brutal, not lovers of the good, treacherous, rash, conceited, lovers of pleasure rather than lovers of God—having a form of godliness but denying its power." (2 Timothy 3:1-5)

So, what are we to do? Should we just give in and give up? No! "Evildoers and impostors will go from bad to worse, deceiving and being deceived. But as for you, continue in what you have learned and have become convinced of." (2 Timothy 3:13-14)

Let's take back our homes, churches, communities, and nation from those who seek to destroy it from within. Let's elect leaders who share our values and concerns. Let's live for Christ and demonstrate to our culture by our example what's good and right.

Scripture Reading: 2 Thessalonians 2:15-17

Personal Application:

- Prayerfully reflect on your own life. Where have you inadvertently succumbed to the evil influences of our culture?
- What steps can you take to graciously lead your family toward godliness? In what ways can you lead them and others through your example?

Week 19, Day 7: Weekly Recap and Prayer

On the seventh day of each week, use the **ACTS** acronym to spend time with the Lord reviewing and assessing your week and praying to God. (**A**=Adoration; **C**=Confession; **T**=Thanksgiving; **S**=Supplication)

First, look back over the previous six days for this week to remind yourself what you read and agreed to. Then, follow the ACTS pattern for prayer below. Finally, use the space below to journal what God is doing in your life and share this with a trusted spiritual partner.

Adoration: Simply spend time in adoration of the Lord. Praise Him and glorify His name. (See 1 Chronicles 29:10-13; Psalm 100; Romans 11:33-36.)

Confession: Confess your sins and shortcomings before God. ("If we confess our sins, he is faithful and just and will forgive us our sins and purify us from all unrighteousness." – 1 John 1:9) To confess (or agree with God) about your sin, implies that you are repentant and desperately want Him to change you.

Thanksgiving: Thank God for what He has done and is doing in your life and the life of your family. Give Him credit, for everything you have comes from Him. (See Psalm 136.)

Supplication: Supplication is just a fancy word for making your requests known to God. Based on the devotions of this past week and the things going on in your life right now, what do you want to ask Him for? "If you, then, though you are evil, know how to give good gifts to your children, how much more will your Father in heaven give good gifts to those who ask Him!" (Matthew 7:11)

Journal: What is God doing in your life right now?

Week 20, Day 1: Are You Ready?

In Matthew's Gospel we read about the Magi who came to King Herod in Jerusalem from the east. They asked, "Where is the one who has been born king of the Jews? We saw His star when it rose and have come to worship Him." (Matthew 2:2) This news greatly troubled Herod and all Jerusalem. So, Herod called the chief priests and teachers of the law and asked them where the Messiah was to be born. "In Bethlehem in Judea," they replied, for they knew the Old Testament prophecies. But what astounds me is that knowing this crucial, life-changing information, none of the priests or teachers of the law accompanied the Magi to Bethlehem! They had awaited the coming of the Messiah for centuries. Now, He had been born. They knew when and where to look for Him, but they were merely content to continue going about their business. How sad this is!

But what about us? Jesus, our Messiah, is coming back. He promised He would. And like the star of Bethlehem that led the Magi to Jesus, the Lord has given us signs of His return.

I don't know whether Jesus will return in our lifetime. I desperately hope He does! But what I do know is that He told us to "keep watch," and "be ready" (Matthew 24:42 & 44) We must live each day as though He were coming today, for He may return today. Are you ready?

Peter warned, "that in the last days scoffers will come…they will say, 'Where is the promise of His coming? For since the fathers fell asleep, all things continue as they were from the beginning of creation.'" (2 Peter 3:3-4 NKJV) Peter goes on to explain, "the Lord is not slow in keeping His promise, as some understand slowness. Instead He is patient with you, not wanting anyone to perish, but everyone to come to repentance." (2 Peter 3:9)

So, how should we live right now in view of Christ's return? "You ought to live holy and godly lives as you look forward to the day of God and speed its coming." (2 Peter 3:11-12) You might wonder, "How can we speed the coming of the Lord?" I think He gives us two primary ways.

First, we already saw the hint in 2 Peter 3 that the Lord is not willing that anyone should perish. Jesus said, "The Good News about the Kingdom will be preached throughout the whole world, so that all nations will hear it; and then the end will come." (Matthew 24:14 NLT) This first way is to share the Good News of salvation with others. Share Christ with those around you.

The second way to speed His coming is simply to pray for it. We see this in Revelation 22:20, "He who testifies to these things says, 'Yes, I am coming soon.' Amen. Come Lord Jesus." Lord, we long for Your coming!

Scripture Reading: 1 Thessalonians 5:1-11

Personal Application:
- To what extent are you watching for and longing for the Lord's return?
- To what extent are you ready for His return and seek to speed it coming?

Week 20, Day 2: How Do You Want to Be Remembered?

After you have finished your career, raised your children, and left your earthy existence, what legacy do you hope to leave? What would be a fitting eulogy at your funeral?

While working many years ago as a chaplain and character coach for three NFL teams, I stressed the importance of building a positive legacy and developing good character. I explained that character is the moral, ethical, and spiritual undergirding that rests on truth, reinforces a life, and helps us resist the temptation to compromise. It is doing the right thing on purpose, regardless of the consequences, and even when nobody is looking. Character ultimately defines your legacy.

During my meetings with the young players and coaches, I challenged them to focus on the image they would leave when retiring from football. Proverbs 22:1 instructs us that "A good name is more desirable than great riches."

I knew that most people wouldn't remember the ranking of a player as much as they'd recall his attitude, comments in front of a camera, or how he lived his personal life. After all, disgrace and scandals fill the headlines of the news. Reporters seem to revel in broadcasting the moral failures of prominent people, especially those connected with politics, professional sports, and ministry. Hypocrisy prevails as people adopt an attitude of prideful arrogance.

So how do we develop godly character? Godly character is more caught than taught. We especially "catch" godly character by spending time with godly people. If you've read any of my books, you know the importance I place on godly mentorship. We all need mentors in our lives, especially those who model for us what it means to follow Jesus.

Paul repeatedly told those he had led to Christ, "Follow my example, as I follow the example of Christ." (1 Corinthians 11:1) When I read that passage as a young man, I thought I'd never be able to say that. I had put Paul on a pedestal and assumed it was his over-the-top piety that enabled him to say that. But now I know that any follower of Jesus should be able to say that. "Follow my example, as I follow the example of Christ."

After all, what greater legacy to leave than to be known as one who truly followed Jesus? And don't think you have to have grey hair to be able to claim such a legacy. Paul told Timothy, "Don't let anyone look down on you because you are young, but set an example for the believes in speech, in conduct, in love, in faith and in purity." (1 Timothy 4:12) So, "Follow my example, as I follow the example of Christ."

Scripture Reading: 2 Peter 1:3-9

Personal Application:

- How would those closest to you remember you? What would you like to change about how they would remember you?
- Who do you know who could serve as a mentor in your life?
  Take the initiative to ask this man if he'd be willing to serve as a mentor in your life.

Week 20, Day 3: Where Is Your Treasure?

I remember when our water heater broke and flooded the den on the lower level of our home. What a hassle! We had to remove the carpet, cut open walls, and move everything out of the den that we had stored in there. It was like gutting the room. And the den had been the graveyard of countless books, older furniture, pictures of old memories, and all sorts of outdoor gear, "treasures" I'd hung on to.

After the cleanup and repair, I spent about 20 hours moving all my treasures back into the refurbished room. I wondered how I had ever collected so much fishing and hunting gear. The sponsor support I'd received during the forty-five years I was associated with these industries provided many worldly rewards.

I sorted through the items, and at the end of the day, I realized I had two piles: stuff with just temporal value (trophies, plaques, recognitions, game mounts, equipment, etc.) and stuff with eternal value (photographs depicting memories with our family, faith-based tapes, videos, and messages, a few Bibles, and study materials).

It's true, I've enjoyed all the things God has entrusted to me while living my earthly life. Many of these items mean a great deal to me, but I can't take them with me when I die. Come to think of it, with all the funerals I've officiated, I've never seen a hearse with a U-Haul trailer behind it! We can't take our stuff or our money with us. "For we brought nothing into the world, and we can take nothing out of it." (1 Timothy 6:7) But we will not be without wealth!

In Ephesians 1:18-19 we read, "I pray that the eyes of your heart may be enlightened in order that you may know the hope to which He has called you, the riches of His glorious inheritance in His holy people, and His incomparably great power for us who believe."

In the here and now, the most important treasures to me are my relationships with the Lord, my family, and the friendships I experience. None of the other stuff will last. In God, we are rich beyond compare as we share in "His glorious inheritance!"

"Do not store up for yourselves treasures on earth, where moths and vermin destroy, and where thieves break in and steal. But store up for yourselves treasures in heaven, where moths and vermin do not destroy, and where thieves do not break in and steal. For where your treasure is, there your heart will be also." (Matthew 6:19-21)

Scripture Reading: Ecclesiastes 5:8-15
Personal Application:
- Sometimes it's good to stand back and take a good look at our lives and the stuff we've accumulated. How do you react when something bad happens to your stuff and you suffer damage or financial loss? Your reaction gives you insight into what you most value.
- Commit your finances and your belongings to the Lord anew. Ensure that what you treasure most are things that hold eternal value.
  But thank God for all the earthly goods He gives you for your enjoyment, for those come from Him.

Week 20, Day 4: The Majesty of Christ

"O LORD, our Lord, how majestic is your name in all the earth!
You have set your glory above the heavens."
– Psalm 8:1

Rev. Jack Hayford, senior pastor of the Church of The Way in Van Nuys, California, wrote a popular contemporary song that praises the majesty of Christ. Pastor Hayford relates the following account for the writing of "Majesty":

"In 1977, my wife Anna and I spent our vacation in Great Britain, traveling throughout the land from the south country and Wales to the northern parts of Scotland. It was the same year as the 25th Anniversary of Queen Elizabeth's coronation, and symbols of royalty were abundantly present beyond the usual."

While viewing many of the ancient castles throughout the land, he began to reflect on the truth that Christ's provisions for the believer not only include forgiveness for sin but also restoration to a royal relationship with God as His sons and daughters. We've been born into the heavenly family through His Majesty.

Pastor Hayford continues:

"As Anna and I drove along together, at once the opening lyrics and melody of 'Majesty' simply came to my heart, I seemed to feel something new of what it meant to be His—to be raised to a partnership with Him in His throne."

Pastor Jack Hayford provides this interpretation for his song:

"'Majesty' describes the kingly, lordly, gloriously regal nature of our Savior— but not simply as an objective statement in worship of which He is fully worthy. 'Majesty' is also a statement of the fact that our worship, when begotten in spirit and in truth, can align us with His throne in such a way that His Kingdom authority flows to us—to overflow us, to free us and channel through us. We are rescued from death, restored to the inheritance of sons and daughters, qualified for victory in battle against the adversary, and destined for the Throne forever in His presence."

May the lyrics to his song inspire all of us to worship…His Majesty!

"Majesty, worship His majesty—Unto Jesus be all glory, power and praise— Majesty, kingdom authority flow from His throne unto His own, His anthem raise. So, exalt, lift up on high the name of Jesus—Magnify, come glorify Christ Jesus, the King. Majesty, worship His majesty—Jesus who died, now glorified, King of all kings."

Scripture Reading: Revelation 5:11-14

- When you read that Scripture from Revelation, what is the response you feel in your inmost being?
- Incorporate that Scripture reading or the lyrics to the song, "Majesty" into a heartfelt prayer to the Lord and worship Him.

Week 20, Day 5: The Antidote for Fear

Although many men don't like to admit it, at some time or another we all become fearful. Some of the more common types of fear include:

- Fear of failure
- Fear of intimacy with others
- Fear of the unknown
- Fear of physical danger
- Fear for your loved ones
- Fear of financial loss
- Fear of illness or death
- Fear of losing one's job
- Fear of fully trusting God

As I am writing this, we're in the middle of the COVID-19 pandemic, around which numerous fears have spawned and lurk.

While some fear is healthy and warranted, the fear we're talking about here is dangerous and destructive. Most fear is fear of "what might happen." In other words, it's just conjecture. It's hypothetical. It's fantasy, yet we accept it as being very real. This kind of fear paralyzes and cripples, preventing us from moving forward. When we fear something, we give it power and our fears take over, controlling our thoughts, decisions, and actions.

From a spiritual standpoint, we can see from this why the Lord tells us to fear Him only (Deuteronomy 6:13). When we allow fear to control our lives and attitudes, we are giving it authority that is not warranted or deserved. Hence, our fears can become a sort of idolatry.

Paul told Timothy, "God has not given us a spirit of fear, but of power and of love and of a sound mind." (2 Timothy 1:7) The antidote for fear is not the avoidance of risk, but to embrace risk with a sound mind, and with love for the Lord and others through God's power.

Here are three actions for finding strength in the Lord in the face of fear:

1. Pray to the Lord for boldness and strength. Admit your fears to Him and trust Him.

2. Find strength and encouragement in God's Word. Mighty men of valor like Joshua, Gideon, and David all experienced fears. Discover how they overcame their fears.

3. Meet with a spiritual partner or confidant. Tell them about your fears and pray with and for each other.

Scripture Reading: Matthew 10:28-31

Personal Application:
- Where in your life are you prone to fear right now?
- Apply those three actions above to beat your fear.

Week 20, Day 6: "I Will Build My Church"

The Apostle Paul's testimony is an amazing one. He persecuted the church, arresting Christians, dragging them out of their homes, and even putting some of them to death. But when Jesus confronted him on the road to Damascus, Jesus asked him, "Why do you persecute Me?" (Acts 9:4) In other words, Jesus so identifies with His church that to persecute the church is to persecute Jesus.

Why am I sharing this with you? Because there's been a mass exodus from church in recent years. Many are disillusioned and frustrated with the church. Many are content to sit in front of the TV, watch a preacher deliver a sermon and call it church. Others say, "I worship God in the woods, or on the lake. I don't need a building." So, what is church and why is it so important?

In Matthew 16:18, Jesus declared, "I will build My church." The church is God's idea, not man's. In Scripture, the word "church" refers to those who follow Jesus. Sometimes the word is used in a universal sense of His whole family of believers, and sometimes in the sense of a local gathering of believers. Knowing Jesus Christ makes you and me members of His church. To my knowledge, the word "church" never refers to a building in Scripture.

However, a key component of understanding "church" (Grk.: *ekklesia*) is the idea that local followers of Christ *assemble* to worship Him. In fact, the word *ekklesia* is sometimes used in Scripture merely to denote a non-religious assembly (Acts 19:41). But as with many words in any language, the context of a text determines the meaning of the word. Thus, the word "church," in the sense of Christ-followers, occurs well over 100 times in the New Testament (NT).

We see phrases in the NT like, "they gathered the church together;" (Acts 15:30) and, "Greet also the church that meets at their house." (Romans 16:5) The writer of Hebrews urges, "And let us not neglect our meeting together, as some people do, but encourage one another, especially now that the day of his return is drawing near." (Hebrews 10:25)

In building His church, I believe the Lord allows a great deal of creativity and variety. But one thing that is crucial to our being the church is getting together with other followers of Jesus to worship Him, read Scripture, encourage one another, pray, fellowship together, and serve one another. Acts and all the NT epistles bear this out.

Whether you're drawn to a house-church, a church startup in a strip mall, a country church, or a mega church, give yourself to that assembly of believers. You and I need the church to grow in our relationship with Christ and each other, and the church needs you and me as well.

Scripture Reading: 1 Timothy 3:14-15

Personal Application:

• What is your current relationship with a local church? If you are not currently attending a church, I urge you to be a part of what Christ said He would build. Give of yourself, your service, and your offerings to a local assembly of believers and watch what God does in and through you.

Week 20, Day 7: Weekly Recap and Prayer

On the seventh day of each week, use the **ACTS** acronym to spend time with the Lord reviewing and assessing your week and praying to God. (**A**=Adoration; **C**=Confession; **T**=Thanksgiving; **S**=Supplication)

First, look back over the previous six days for this week to remind yourself what you read and agreed to. Then, follow the ACTS pattern for prayer below. Finally, use the space below to journal what God is doing in your life and share this with a trusted spiritual partner.

Adoration: Simply spend time in adoration of the Lord. Praise Him and glorify His name. (See 1 Chronicles 29:10-13; Psalm 100; Romans 11:33-36.)

Confession: Confess your sins and shortcomings before God. ("If we confess our sins, he is faithful and just and will forgive us our sins and purify us from all unrighteousness." – 1 John 1:9) To confess (or agree with God) about your sin, implies that you are repentant and desperately want Him to change you.

Thanksgiving: Thank God for what He has done and is doing in your life and the life of your family. Give Him credit, for everything you have comes from Him. (See Psalm 136.)

Supplication: Supplication is just a fancy word for making your requests known to God. Based on the devotions of this past week and the things going on in your life right now, what do you want to ask Him for? "If you, then, though you are evil, know how to give good gifts to your children, how much more will your Father in heaven give good gifts to those who ask Him!" (Matthew 7:11)

Journal: What is God doing in your life right now?

Week 21, Day 1: Buck Fever

Tom Rakow, the founder and President of The Christian Deer Hunters Association, is an outstanding deer hunter. His leadership and inspiration have encouraged many hunters, improving their hunting skills as well as their spiritual lives.

As a boy, Tom dreamed about becoming distinguished as a great outdoorsman. Some years later, Tom was invited on his first deer hunt. After setting up camp, he and the others spread out for the hunt. Shortly after leaving camp, however, Tom fell victim to a non-fatal disease commonly found among first-time deer hunters. Tom recalls, "I will long remember the opening day of my very first deer season. A member of our hunting party kicked out a nice six-pointer to me that stopped broadside only yards away. You couldn't have asked for an easier shot. Unfortunately, I fell under the power of that dread disease, 'Buck Fever.'"

Buck Fever is famous for making hunters behave in some strange ways. I even read about a hunter who broke two legs when, upon seeing a large deer, he got so excited that he attempted to stand up—forgetting he was in a tree stand more than fifteen feet off the ground!

Having been struck with Buck Fever, Tom's arms felt like lead. He knew what we wanted to do, but oddly, he just couldn't bring the rifle to his shoulder. Instead, he shot four times from the hip hitting dirt and trees just a few feet in front of where he was standing. Tom recalls, "The buck seemed to smile at me, winked, and darted back into the woods without a mark on him."

Buck Fever may be powerful and crippling; however, there is a force far more dangerous and devastating in our daily lives. It's a disease that can injure and damage everyone who is infected with its poison. If left untreated, it not only cripples us, but eternally destroys us. That disease is *Sin*. On our own, we are powerless to fight it.

Jesus is our only remedy. He conquered sin on the cross, not only paying its penalty, but removing its power over us. If we've trusted Jesus Christ as Savior, the Holy Spirit dwells in us, empowering us to live lives pleasing to God. As Paul encourages, "You, however, are not in the flesh but in the Spirit, if in fact the Spirit of God dwells in you. Anyone who does not have the Spirit of Christ does not belong to him." (Romans 8:9 ESV)

Tom may have missed the mark on his first hunt, but he didn't miss the mark on the most important hunt of all—eternal life. We don't have to be overcome by sin, but rather, Christ, who is in us, has overcome sin for us! Let's not let sin cripple us. Trust Him and rely on His power.

Scripture Reading: Romans 6:1-7
Personal Application:
- What sin in your life do you struggle with most?
- Go after that sin with the help of a spiritual partner or mentor. Yield yourself to the Holy Spirit. Take precautions to remove temptation from your life.

Week 21, Day 2: Love God, Love Others

"Dear friends, let us love one another, for love comes from God.
Everyone who loves has been born of God and knows God. Whoever does not love
does not know God, because God is love."

– 1 John 4:7, 8

I've always been competitive. I like challenges. Maybe that's why I still bow hunt, play basketball with my grandson, and occasionally compete in a fishing tournament. But the greatest challenge to me doesn't have anything to do with sports, hunting, or fishing. It has to do with loving people who create stress for me or my family. Sometimes they're direct challenges, but many times these attacks come from people who just don't agree with my spiritual orientation.

Exodus 20 records for us the Ten Commandments and is the clearest explanation in the Bible of God's moral law. From them, we can understand right from wrong. However, the intent God must have had was deeper than what was given to Moses.

Jesus summed up the depth of God's laws with this statement: "'Love the Lord your God with all your heart and with all your soul and with all your mind.' This is the first and greatest commandment. And the second is like it: 'Love your neighbor as yourself.'" (Matthew 22:37-39)

You see, the Pharisees created an elaborate system to distinguish what they deemed the more important laws from the less important ones. Jesus blew their artificial system away when He pointed to the simple way one could fulfill the entire Law—by loving God and loving our neighbor as ourselves.

Jesus made the point that God made us for relationships. He created us in His image so that we could have a relationship with Him (vertical) and model life, truth, love, joy, and peace to all those we know (horizontal).

Unfortunately, human sin fractured that relationship, but God made a way through Jesus Christ, for that relationship to be restored. Love for God is our highest calling and the path to true fulfillment as a human being. Love for God always leads to love for one's neighbors. Although the world says, "Look out for yourself," true happiness is found when we put the needs of our family, friends, neighbors, and even total strangers before our own.

As difficult as it may be, we need to learn to love the unlovely. We don't have to love their sin, their behavior, their appearance, or their attitudes, but we need to learn to love the individual. When we learn to really love God, loving others—even the difficult ones—doesn't seem so challenging. And eventually, our lives feel happier and less negative!

Scripture Reading: Romans 12:9-16

Personal Application:
- Spend time alone with the Lord basking in His great love.
- Considering God's great love for you, how does it make you feel
- toward others?
- Look for ways to demonstrate your love for God and others throughout the day.

Week 21, Day 3: Faith through Trials

In 1981, I was diagnosed with a benign, but highly dangerous brain tumor. Because of where the tumor was and its aggressive growth, surgery was imperative. But the surgeon warned that this surgery could be life-threatening, and he urged me to put my affairs in order and say goodbye to my family in case I didn't survive.

My goodbyes to my beloved wife and twin, eleven-year-old boys was the most painful and tearful experience I've ever endured. I was far more fearful of their welfare than of my own.

During this ordeal, I chose to meditate on the Lord and His promises. Trust in God won out, not because I survived the surgery, but because God was glorified through our response to it. In the midst of it, He gave us tremendous peace. We knew He would take care of us no matter the outcome.

When we experience difficult challenges like that, we often equate success, healing, or deliverance from the trial as the chief benefit. But God is much bigger than that. Others have gone through similar situations trusting the Lord but did not survive the surgery. Was the Lord still present and loving in their trials? Absolutely!

Hebrews 11 is the great faith chapter of the Bible. The first thirty-five verses of that chapter regale the amazing faith feats of those who have gone before us. Those accounts all represent huge victories, miracles, and God-sized accomplishments. But in verse 36 a shift occurs:

There were others who were tortured, refusing to be released so that they might gain an even better resurrection. Some faced jeers and flogging, and even chains and imprisonment. They were put to death by stoning; they were sawed in two; they were killed by the sword. They went about in sheepskins and goatskins, destitute, persecuted, and mistreated—the world was not worthy of them. They wandered in deserts and mountains, living in caves and in holes in the ground. These were all commended for their faith, yet none of them received what had been promised, since God had planned something better for us so that only together with us would they be made perfect. (Hebrews 11:36

As humans, we go through our life with limited vision. Hebrews 11:1 explains, "Now faith is the substance of things hoped for, the evidence of things not seen." (NKJV) We must put on our eyes of faith to recognize the power and plan of God beyond what we can see or conceive with our minds. He is faithful. He will never leave you or forsake you. (Hebrews 13:5). Believe it!

Scripture Reading: Hebrews 11:1-6

Personal Application:
- What trial or difficulty are you enduring right now?
- Trust God through your ordeal. Pray for His deliverance but accept by faith whatever outcome He provides.

Week 21, Day 4: Needed Inspiration

In 1928, Notre Dame's Head Coach Knute Rockne gave his famous rallying words, "Win one for the Gipper," motivating his players to leave it all on the field. It had its effect. Notre Dame won over a very tough Army team 12-6 in the final minutes on a touchdown pass from Butch Niemiec to Johnny O'Brien.

A few years before, George Gipp had been a very quiet and unassuming player as a triple threat (runner, passer, and kicker) for Notre Dame. He had great confidence and inspired others with his dedicated efforts. Rockne later recalled, "I learned very early to place full confidence in his self-confidence." Had there been a Heisman Trophy that year, most coaches felt George Gipp would have received it.

In 1920 Notre Dame finished its season with a 25-0 victory over Michigan State, but their dedicated Gipp was in the college infirmary at South Bend with a life-threatening infection. Antibiotics had not yet been developed, and Gipp's condition was worsening by the hour. In the last few hours before his passing, Coach Rockne made one of his daily visits to see Gipp. The lanky collegiate All-Star looked into his coach's eyes and said, "Someday in a tough game, ask the players to win one for the Gipper."

For eight years Rockne considered the proper time to encourage his players with the deathbed words of this dedicated athlete. Many on the 1928 Notre Dame team knew of George Gipp and had been in grammar school with the legendary running back. The motivation and inspiration of the famous locker room words helped guide Notre Dame to a victory and into the hearts of millions of future fans.

We all need inspiration like that from time to time. When God commissioned Joshua to take over leadership of Israel in Moses' stead, He told Joshua repeatedly, "Be strong and courageous. Do not be afraid; do not be discouraged, for the Lord your God will be with you wherever you go." (Joshua 1:9)

But those words were not just for Joshua's benefit. Paul explained, "For everything that was written in the past was written to teach us, so that through the endurance taught in the Scriptures and the encouragement they provide we might have hope." (Romans 15:4)

And even beyond that encouragement, the Lord continues to inspire and encourage us: "Be watchful, stand firm in the faith, act like men, be strong." (1 Corinthians 16:13 ESV) "And be sure of this: I am with you always, even to the end of the age." (Matthew 28:20)

Scripture Reading: 1 Timothy 4:11-16

Personal Application:
- In what situation or particular area of your life do you need to be strong right now?
- Receive and act on the assurance and encouragement that the Lord offers you. Be strong and courageous, don't be afraid. The Lord is with you!

Week 21, Day 5: Do You Find It Hard to Rest?

I don't know about you, but I have a hard time sitting still. I'm a very driven individual. I've got a lot going on in my life. I'm goal-oriented and am always striving to better myself and others. In short, I'm a type-A person who, I must confess, finds it difficult to rest. And I don't think I'm alone in this.

I'm glad we're no longer under the Law, because if we were, I'd constantly be an offender in terms of keeping the Sabbath. In my world, there's always more to do: more people to connect with, more books to read, more books to write, more ideas to flesh out. And that doesn't even begin to touch my goals and responsibilities in my personal life! But again, you probably know all too well what I'm talking about.

Why is it we have such a difficult time resting? Of all the spiritual disciplines, resting seems to be one of the most difficult. Those of us who are goal-driven flounder when it comes to rest because we can't quantify or measure it. I can set a goal to read three chapters in the Bible every day. And I can set aside time to pray. But how do I quantify rest?

Here's what I've found. Ironically, rest used to seem burdensome to me. I knew God wanted me to rest, but it was so hard to stop working and rest. There have been times, like after my brain surgery, when God has imposed a period of rest for me. It was during times like that I realized some important things about rest.

First, it occurred to me that God modeled rest before He asked us to rest. The Scripture says, "By the seventh day God had finished the work He had been doing; so on the seventh day He rested from all His work." (Genesis 2:2) But then I thought, *Why did God rest? Certainly, He wasn't tired or needed refreshing.* He didn't *need* to rest, so why did He rest?

I believe the answer to that question is given at the close of each day of creation. For instance, on the evening of the sixth day it says, "God saw all that He had made, and it was very good." (Genesis 1:31) I believe God rested, not because He was tired, but so He could enjoy what He had made. In the same way, a day or period of rest for us serves to enjoy what God has done in and through and for us. We rest because He rested and showed us what rest looks like.

Second, I realized that God gave us rest—not as a burden—but as a gift. He knows much better than we do how much we need rest. Time to reflect. Time to process. Time to enjoy Him. Time to enjoy our loved ones. Time to refresh. Time to recognize how much we need Him. Jesus still beckons us, "Come with me by yourselves to a quiet place and get some rest." (Mark 6:31)

Scripture Reading: Psalm 23; Mark 2:27

Personal Application:

- When was the last time you simply took a day off and set aside time to enjoy your loved ones and all God has given you?
- Take time this week to rest. If you're not clear on what rest looks or feels like, ask God to teach you how to rest.

Week 21, Day 6: Are You Missing All the Action?

Several years ago, legendary basketball coach Bobby Knight was pheasant hunting in Eastern Montana with some friends of mine. While I may not agree with his coaching methods or character all the time, he sure knows his basketball. His college basketball teams won 902 games while playing for "The General."

Well, "The General" had dropped a bit behind the two local boys who were guiding him on the hunt, when they spotted a covey of pheasants in the brush. Within seconds, the pheasants scattered, and the locals began firing and knocked down several nice pheasants.

After the shooting stopped, Bobby ran up to the guides and said, "How come you didn't wait for me?" After quick consideration, one of the guides said, "Bobby it's kind of like basketball. You either get in the game or sit on the bench."

Today, too many Christians are sitting on the bench. They have become complacent about their faith. Christ wants us to be passionate and engaged in what He has given us to do:

"Then Jesus came to them and said, 'All authority in heaven and on earth has been given to me. Therefore go and make disciples of all nations, baptizing them in the name of the Father and of the Son and of the Holy Spirit, and teaching them to obey everything I have commanded you. And surely I am with you always, to the very end of the age.'" (Matthew 28:18-20)

When God's people "get in the game" exciting things happen: people come to Christ, church becomes a "team sport" rather than a show, believers become energized and filled with the Spirit, lives are transformed, families are united, communities come together, reconciliation among races happens, people experience the healing power of a loving Savior, and we experience the thrill of discipling others!

Much like a basketball player, we have choices to make. To become a good player, we must take some chances, step out of our comfort zone, and step up to the challenge before us. It means being willing to "go inside where the big guys are." Occasionally, we get fouled or even knocked down. If we're playing all out, we get sweaty and dirty. We might get a bloody nose, bruises, and negative comments—even from some of our own team members and fans.

Out on "the court" things do get rough sometimes, but like a hard-fought game, we cannot give up. "Pursue righteousness, godliness, faith, love, endurance and gentleness. Fight the good fight of the faith. Take hold of the eternal life to which you were called when you made your good confession in the presence of many witnesses." (1 Timothy 6:11b-12)

Scripture Reading: Hebrews 12:1-3

Personal Application:
- To what extent would you say you are "in the game" as far as making disciples is concerned?
- What can you do today to represent Christ well to others through your life and words?

Week 21, Day 7: Weekly Recap and Prayer

On the seventh day of each week, use the **ACTS** acronym to spend time with the Lord reviewing and assessing your week and praying to God. (**A**=Adoration; **C**=Confession; **T**=Thanksgiving; **S**=Supplication)

First, look back over the previous six days for this week to remind yourself what you read and agreed to. Then, follow the ACTS pattern for prayer below. Finally, use the space below to journal what God is doing in your life and share this with a trusted spiritual partner.

Adoration: Simply spend time in adoration of the Lord. Praise Him and glorify His name. (See 1 Chronicles 29:10-13; Psalm 100; Romans 11:33-36.)

Confession: Confess your sins and shortcomings before God. ("If we confess our sins, he is faithful and just and will forgive us our sins and purify us from all unrighteousness." – 1 John 1:9) To confess (or agree with God) about your sin, implies that you are repentant and desperately want Him to change you.

Thanksgiving: Thank God for what He has done and is doing in your life and the life of your family. Give Him credit, for everything you have comes from Him. (See Psalm 136.)

Supplication: Supplication is just a fancy word for making your requests known to God. Based on the devotions of this past week and the things going on in your life right now, what do you want to ask Him for? "If you, then, though you are evil, know how to give good gifts to your children, how much more will your Father in heaven give good gifts to those who ask Him!" (Matthew 7:11)

Journal: What is God doing in your life right now?

Week 22, Day 1: The Impact of Grandparents

Sometime ago I was asked to deliver a message at a workshop for retirees. My message on "Strategies for Being an Effective Grandparent" suggested different ways we can better connect with our grandchildren. Christian psychologists are touting the importance of the grandparent-grandchild relationships. "The bond between a child and a grandparent is the purest, least psychologically complicated form of human love," says Dr. Arthur Kornhaber. "Grandparents can offer an emotional safety net when parents falter. They pass on traditions in the form of stories, songs, games, skills, and crafts." They also can serve as a model of godly character and can demonstrate the importance of grace.

And grandparents have another magical ingredient that parents often lack – TIME. Kornhaber has found that children who are close to at least one grandparent are more emotionally secure than other children; and they have more positive feelings about older people and about the process of aging.

Another great thing about being a grandparent: you get do-overs! It gives every grandparent a second chance. Perhaps history's most dramatic illustration of that truth is the story of King Manasseh in 2 Chronicles 33. Manasseh has been called the most wicked man who ever lived, but in his old age he repented and turned to God. The son who succeeded him was also evil, but Manasseh's grandson, Josiah, became one of the most godly, beloved kings in Jewish history.

Maybe you're not a grandparent yet. However, I encourage you as a parent to ensure your children can spend quality time with their grandparents. If their grandparents are not around or unable to be with your children, find an older, godly couple close by who might serve as surrogate grandparents. My wife and I serve in this way because our grandchildren live in another state. Truth be told, my wife and I find it difficult doing long-distance grandparenting. It takes extra effort to understand how to engage with them through the phone, texting, and Skyping. But the effort is worth every minute of the investment.

Also, the earlier you can establish a strong relationship with your grandchildren, the better. When they hit their teen years, spending time with them becomes more of a challenge. But if ever there was a time when the younger generation needed the mentoring and wisdom of more experienced people, it is now.

Scripture Reading: Proverbs 17:6; Titus 2:1-8

Personal Application:

- What kinds of challenges do you encounter in communicating with your grandchildren?
- What new ways can you think of to connect with your grandchildren? What stories, including your failures, can you tell your grandchildren from your life that would encourage them to walk with Christ?

Week 22, Day 2: Jesus Showed Us How to Love and Serve

When Jesus washed the feet of His disciples, it was one of the most striking examples of love and service any of us can imagine.

First, the text says, "Jesus knew that the hour had come for Him to leave this world and go to the Father." This incident occurred just hours before Jesus was betrayed and went to the cross and He knew it! If you or I knew we were about to be betrayed and nailed to a cross, what would we be thinking and doing? But the text goes on to explain, "Having loved His own… He loved them to the end." (John 13:1) Jesus wasn't thinking about Himself in this dark hour but about His disciples whom He loved.

Second, we read, "Jesus knew that the Father had put all things under His power, and that He had come from God and was returning to God." (vs. 3) Jesus knew who He was—the very Son of God who was and is sovereign over all! Yet, knowing this, "He got up from the meal, took off His outer clothing, and wrapped a towel around His waist." (vs. 4) Then He began washing His disciples' dirty feet. God stooped to wash the smelly feet of common men!

When He had finished washing their feet, He sat down and said to them, "'Do you understand what I have done for you?' He asked them. 'You call Me "Teacher" and "Lord," and rightly so, for that is what I am. Now that I your Lord and Teacher, have washed your feet, you also should wash one another's feet. I have set you an example that you should do as I have done for you.'" (John 13:12-15)

But if we think Jesus' point was merely about foot-washing, then we've missed the point. Instead, through this menial task, He demonstrated what love and true godly service look like: gracious, compassionate, humble, and selfless. This is how we are to love and serve one another.

In verses 16-17, Jesus continued, "'Very truly I tell you, no servant is greater than his master, nor is a messenger greater than the one who sent him. Now that you know these things, you will be blessed if you do them." Another, not-so-obvious lesson for us here is that the best way to disciple others is by our example.

So often, we're quick to want to teach, counsel, and advise others. And there is a time and place for that. But how much more powerful it is to simply demonstrate by example what it means to follow Jesus and to love and serve others. Later in this chapter, Jesus said, "Love one another; as I have loved you." (vs. 34) Jesus showed us how to love, now we must show each other how to love.

Scripture Reading: Ephesians 4:32-5:2

Personal Application:
- In what ways can you follow Jesus' example in loving and serving others today?
- Pray that the Lord would prompt you to demonstrate His love and service to those around you.

Week 22, Day 3: Loyalty

Louise and I have welcomed at least 14 purebred Labrador retriever dogs into our lives. We enjoyed the fun and work of having seven litters and placing the pups into loving homes. Without a doubt the best dog we ever had was Penny.

Penny was excellent in the field flushing pheasants from tight cover, as well as comforting our home Bible study group as we sat in a circle sharing our fears, tears, and concerns. She was supportive and protective of children, especially when she attended events at our Special Kids Day Programs for the Disabled. She was a devoted, friendly, and loyal dog.

When I wrote this, we had just put old Penny down. We bring our dogs into our lives and homes and love them. We spend hours talking to them like we might to a trusted counselor. We trust them implicitly and they never let us down. What more could we possibly want?

More time with them is the first thing that springs to mind. Our dogs have much shorter life spans than we do, so almost everyone has had to say good-bye to a beloved dog at some point in their lives. And while it's not easy saying good-bye, it is inevitable. And so is the grief that follows.

When God created labs, He went the extra mile to put a willing and loving spirit in them to please their masters. The devotion they show to obeying our commands and serving our needs for companionship and love are uniquely different than most other breeds.

One of the stories that best reminds me of how Penny lived to please her master occurred on a pheasant hunt with a few friends and their bird dogs. Penny was the youngest dog in the group, but she pointed out and retrieved more birds than any other dog. At the end of the hunt, we all gathered in a circle on the lawn to eat our lunch. All the other dogs were kenneled in the trucks except for Penny. She lay obediently beside me.

I could see that Penny was intently looking at the pile of birds stacked up about 30' from our circle. Without any command or reference to the birds she quietly got up and one-by-one went to the pile of birds and brought all the pheasants to my side and then laid back down.

As we read God's word His desire is that, like Penny, we would so love Him that our devotion and obedience would "be pleasing" in every manner. The Apostle Paul summed it up with this note to the Corinthians, "And this I say for your own profit, not that I may put a leash on you, but for what is proper, and that you may serve the Lord without distraction." (1 Corinthians 7:35 NKJV)

Scripture Reading: Romans 6:15-18

Personal Application:

- What's one area of your life where you need to obey the Lord instead of yielding to sin?

Week 22, Day 4: Spiritual Disciplines for Following Jesus

When we receive Christ, we launch into a lifelong quest to become more like Him. But we are totally dependent on Him to bring about His sanctifying work in us. At the same time, we are not passive in this process. To this end, the Lord gave us His Holy Spirit, each other, and what we call "spiritual disciplines."

Spiritual disciplines are simply activities that help us draw closer to Jesus. For it's in His presence that we are changed. Some of the more common spiritual disciplines include reading and studying God's Word, prayer, solitude, fasting, resting, worship, service, etc.

God's Word reveals to us what God is like. We learn about His character and His dealings with mankind. Paul explains, "For everything that was written in the past was written to teach us, so that through the endurance taught in the Scriptures and the encouragement they provide we might have hope." (Romans 15:4) Spending time in God's Word is vital for our growth in Christ.

Prayer, of course, is communing with the Lord. Prayer is not merely a one-way conversation but involves listening as well as talking. The more we grow in our relationship with the Lord, the more natural prayer becomes. Communication like this is vital to any relationship.

Solitude is an important discipline especially in this fast-paced, noisy world. In solitude, we deliberately take time to get alone with God. This can be in the woods, on a lake, or simply in a room at home. We remove ourselves from all other distractions and spend time with our Lord. We can couple solitude with other disciplines like prayer, fasting, and the Word as well.

Those are just a few examples of spiritual disciplines and what they look like. However, I must warn you about a common error we fall into with spiritual disciplines. It's easy to make the discipline as the "ends" instead of the "means" to an end. We must always remind ourselves that the reason we pursue any spiritual discipline is primarily to draw closer to Jesus—for in His presence we are changed.

But many fall into the trap of focusing so intently on the discipline to perfect that discipline that they forget that growing closer to Christ is the goal. Then they become proud of how long or how well they study the Word, or how eloquently they can pray, and that gets ugly.

Like a friend of mine says, "Always go to the Word with the intent to meet with God." The same could be said for prayer, solitude, and any of the other disciplines. Paul urged Timothy, "Train yourself to be godly." (1 Timothy 4:7) And the spiritual disciplines help us do just that by drawing closer to Jesus!

Scripture Reading: 2 Timothy 3:16-17; Luke 11:1-4

Personal Application:
- Experiment with some of the spiritual disciplines that you may not have used before like fasting, solitude, resting, meditation, and simplicity.
- Read the Word daily and always go to the Word expecting to meet with God.

Week 22, Day 5: The Holy Spirit

Have you ever wondered what it would be like to be one of Jesus' inner-circle disciples? How amazing it would be to follow Him around, enjoy His presence, watch Him perform miracles, and hear His profound, life-changing teachings?

Well, you and I can and do experience these things first-hand through the presence of God's Holy Spirit in our lives.

On the night that Jesus was betrayed, He spent considerable time talking with His disciples. He told them He was about to go away, but at the time they didn't understand. But then He told them something quite astonishing:

"Very truly I tell you, it is for your good that I am going away. Unless I go away, the Advocate will not come to you; but if I go, I will send Him to you." (John 16:7) When Jesus was here on earth physically, He subjected Himself to the physical realm so that He could only be in one place at a time. Now that He has sent His Spirit to us, He is present in His followers all over the world all the time.

Here are some other things Jesus told His disciples (us too) about His Spirit:

- He is our Advocate and will be with us forever (John 14:16).
- He will teach us and remind us of what Jesus has said (John 14:26).
- He will convict the world of sin (John 16:8).
- He guides us into truth (John 16:13).
- He always glorifies Jesus (John 16:14).
- He gives us power to testify about Jesus (Acts 1:8).
- He distributes and bestows spiritual gifts for the good of Christ's church (1 Corinthians 12:4-7).
- He helps us get rid of sins in our life (Romans 8:13).
- He testifies with our spirit that we are God's children (Romans 8:16).
- He came into our lives when we believed as a seal that we belong to God (Ephesians 1:13)

We learn in 1 Corinthians 6:19 that our bodies are the temple of the Holy Spirit. He lives within us and we are to honor or glorify God with our bodies (1 Corinthians 6:20). The more we allow the Holy Spirit to guide us and lead us, the more we will be living as the Lord wants us to live.

Scripture Reading: Romans 8:1-17

Personal Application:
- What assurances do you have that the Spirit of God is living within you?
- Thank God for His Spirit living within you and tell Him you want to learn to hear His promptings and obey Him. (Know that God's Spirit never contradicts His Word. He will never prompt you to do something contrary to the Word or God's character.)

Week 22, Day 6: Biblical Irony

Football, like most sports, is full of irony. Often the smallest guy on the field is the last defense against a huge running back headed for the end zone. And even its modest beginnings as a sport are full of irony.

In the late 1890's, Clinton Beckett, a teacher and principal of the small Pine Village School, in Pine Village, Indiana, introduced the sport of football to the townspeople. Two teams formed, one from the high school students and one from former students. This tradition continued for almost 20 years.

Other surrounding towns began forming teams and independent leagues. This was fertile ground for the establishment of coaches, sports facilities, rule books, ticket sales and concessions. How ironic that a small rural community ushered in this new sport that ultimately became the National Football League.

When we read the Bible, we also see how God often uses irony to accomplish His purposes:

- David, a young shepherd boy brings down the fierce giant Goliath with a sling and a stone.
- Hundred-year-old Abraham and his aged wife Sarah give birth to Isaac, the father of a great nation.
- Joseph, sold as a slave by his own brothers, becomes the second most powerful man in Egypt, and fulfills prophecy by bringing Israel to Egypt for 400 years.
- God save Israel from the Midianite army through Gideon and a force of just 300 men who use pots and torches as "weapons."
- The King of Kings was born in a stable in a tiny village. He learned the trade of a carpenter and launched a worldwide movement with 12 ordinary men.
- "If you cling to your life, you will lose it; but if you give it up for me, you will find it." (Matthew 10:39 NLT)

God delights in using ordinary people to accomplish God-sized tasks. He turns misfortune on its head and brings good from it. "God chose the foolish things of the world to shame the wise; God chose the weak things of the world to shame the strong. God chose the lowly things of this world and the despised things—and the things that are not—to nullify the things that are, so that no one may boast before Him." (1 Corinthians 1:27-29)

The primary lesson behind this for us is to recognize our own frailty and neediness before the Lord, to humble ourselves and depend fully on Him to do His work in and through us. "As it is written: 'Let the one who boasts boast in the Lord.'" (1 Corinthians 1:31)

Scripture Reading: 1 Corinthians 1:26-31

Personal Application:

- Humbly submit yourself to the Lord and watch what He does in and through you. If you tend to be proud of your accomplishments, confess that and continually thank God for His grace.

Week 22, Day 7: Weekly Recap and Prayer

On the seventh day of each week, use the **ACTS** acronym to spend time with the Lord reviewing and assessing your week and praying to God. (**A**=Adoration; **C**=Confession; **T**=Thanksgiving; **S**=Supplication)

First, look back over the previous six days for this week to remind yourself what you read and agreed to. Then, follow the ACTS pattern for prayer below. Finally, use the space below to journal what God is doing in your life and share this with a trusted spiritual partner.

Adoration: Simply spend time in adoration of the Lord. Praise Him and glorify His name. (See 1 Chronicles 29:10-13; Psalm 100; Romans 11:33-36.)

Confession: Confess your sins and shortcomings before God. ("If we confess our sins, he is faithful and just and will forgive us our sins and purify us from all unrighteousness." – 1 John 1:9) To confess (or agree with God) about your sin, implies that you are repentant and desperately want Him to change you.

Thanksgiving: Thank God for what He has done and is doing in your life and the life of your family. Give Him credit, for everything you have comes from Him. (See Psalm 136.)

Supplication: Supplication is just a fancy word for making your requests known to God. Based on the devotions of this past week and the things going on in your life right now, what do you want to ask Him for? "If you, then, though you are evil, know how to give good gifts to your children, how much more will your Father in heaven give good gifts to those who ask Him!" (Matthew 7:11)

Journal: What is God doing in your life right now?

Week 23, Day 1: The Remedy for Guilt and Shame

Guilt and shame can be crippling. As I write this, a local organization that ministers to post-abortive men and women reports that a man who agreed to his girlfriend's abortion was so distraught over his role in killing his unborn child that he took his own life. His girlfriend is now struggling both with the guilt and shame over the abortion and the grief of losing her boyfriend in this way.

In 2 Corinthians 11, Paul talks about his "thorn in the flesh, a messenger of Satan, to torment" him. It's possible that he was referring to the weight of guilt and shame he must have carried from the years that he persecuted believers, even consenting to their death. Paul alludes to his shame when he confesses, "I do not deserve to be called an apostle, because I persecuted the church of God." (1 Corinthians 15:9)

For many of us, the guilt and shame we bear may not seem as serious compared with the above two examples. Despite that, we all deeply regret past decisions, actions, or words maliciously spoken. We all know what it feels like to carry that load of guilt and shame and it can be debilitating, affecting our relationships and all areas of our lives.

How do we effectively shed such a burden of guilt and shame? There's only one way—through the forgiveness and cleansing that Jesus Christ offers. The writer of Hebrews urges, "Let us draw near to God with a sincere heart and with the full assurance that faith brings, having our hearts sprinkled to cleanse us from a guilty conscience and having our bodies washed with pure water." (Hebrews 10:22) And John wrote, "If we confess our sins, He is faithful and just and will forgive us our sins and purify us from all unrighteousness." (1 John 1:9)

We see this truth played out in Paul's life. He wrote to Timothy:

Even though I was once a blasphemer and a persecutor and a violent man, I was shown mercy because I acted in ignorance and unbelief. The grace of our Lord was poured out on me abundantly, along with the faith and love that are in Christ Jesus. …Christ Jesus came into the world to save sinners—of whom I am the worst. But for that very reason I was shown mercy so that in me, the worst of sinners, Christ Jesus might display His immense patience as an example for those who would believe in Him and receive eternal life. (1 Timothy 1:13)

Through faith in Jesus, we too enjoy forgiveness and cleansing of sin and the removal of the awful guilt and shame that sin heaps on us. Praise Him for His grace and mercy!

Scripture Reading: Hebrews 9:14; 10:14, 17

Personal Application:

- What are you feeling a weight of guilt and shame over? Confess it to Jesus and let Him cleanse you and remove the guilt and shame. Encourage someone else today with this devotional.

Week 23, Day 2: What It Means to Fast

Fasting, like prayer or reading God's Word, is a spiritual discipline. Like all spiritual disciplines, the chief purpose of fasting is to draw us closer to Christ.

What is fasting? Fasting means to voluntarily abstain from food for a specified period. A fast may be total abstinence from all food except water, or a fast from certain foods and drinks. We don't fast to impress God or others. Nor do we fast as a means of self-punishment.

Fasting is usually associated with humbling oneself before God and coming to Him in complete dependence. In the Bible, fasting often occurred:

- Along with prayer and petition to God. (Daniel 9:3)
- As a form of worship. (Acts 13:2)
- In association with mourning or confession of sin. (Joel 2:12)
- Simply with a desire to draw closer to God. (Psalm 35:13)

In Matthew 4, we read about Jesus being led by the Holy Spirit into the wilderness to be tempted by the devil. During that time of severe temptation when the evil one threw all his evil ploys at Jesus our Lord chose to fast. In this way, fasting can be a means of shutting out all other distractions and desires and drawing near to God.

The evil one also tried to tempt Jesus even regarding His fast. For at the end of those 40 days, Jesus was hungry. We read, "The tempter came to Him and said, 'If You are the Son of God, tell these stones to become bread.' Jesus answered, 'It is written: "Man shall not live on bread alone, but on every word that comes from the mouth of God."'" (Matthew 4:3-4)

Jesus was quoting Deuteronomy 8:3, which refers to the Lord sustaining Israel for 40 years in the wilderness by giving them manna. Jesus was telling the tempter, "I don't need to take matters into my own hands to demonstrate who I am. My trust is in God, the sustainer of My life."

As with other spiritual disciplines, you can couple fasting with prayer, the reading of God's Word, worship, solitude, and other disciplines.

Personally, I've employed fasting at times when I needed to make a major decision and wanted the Lord's leading. I've fasted as a means of humbling myself before the Lord, worshiping Him and expressing my love for Him. Fasting has been called "feasting on God," and I like that description, because that's really what it is.

Scripture Reading: Daniel 9:1-19

Personal Application:

- If you've never fasted, consult a doctor, then set aside a time in which you will fast with the purpose of simply spending time with the Lord and drawing near to Him. You can fast from food for a meal, a day, or even a few days, but be sure to drink plenty of water during your fast.
- In your fast, enjoy the Lord's presence and worship Him. Trust Him and depend on Him for all.

Week 23, Day 3: An Encouraging Word

"The tongue has the power of life and death."
– Proverbs 18:21a

Bart Starr was probably the greatest encourager in NFL history. A Hall-of-Fame quarterback, he used encouraging words to motivate and inspire his team to greatness. Bart realized the importance timely, comforting remarks can have on a person's perspective and performance.

While football was a very important part of Bart's life, his family was his central focus. During the season he'd try to stay updated with the kids' activities by reviewing their homework and tests every week. If a paper was particularly good, he'd tape a dime to the work and write a note: "I Love You, and I'm Proud of You!"

In 1965 Bart had a bad game against the St. Louis Cardinals. Most of America's football audience was glued to their televisions. The Green Bay quarterback fumbled a few times and, in the last minutes, threw an interception that cost his team the victory. That night the team flew back to Green Bay. Bart got home late and found a note stuck on the refrigerator door: "Dad, I saw your game today. I want you to know I love you, and I'm still proud of you—Bart Jr." These words of encouragement had a powerful impact on Bart, his family, and the Green Bay Packers.

No doubt—words are powerful. Jesus used the power of words to spread the Good News. He used parables to convey principles of God's Kingdom. He used words of forgiveness and mercy to heal. He used words to challenge, instruct, and inspire His disciples to miraculous faith. And today His words still give us tremendous hope and comfort.

Encouraging words comfort, inspire, motivate, and give life, but harsh words discourage and destroy. Our tongues, though just a little muscle, have enormous power for both good and evil.

How many children have been shamed and lost hope? How many wives have lost their self-respect and ability to love? How many athletes have lost their "fight" because of constant criticism? "Reckless words pierce like a sword, but the tongue of the wise brings healing." (Proverbs 12:18)

Do our words give life? Do they inspire and challenge others to greatness? Do they bring comfort and healing? Do they lead others to forgiveness and reconciliation with Christ? We either send a message of hope or despair. Let's choose to speak love to a discouraged world.

"Do not let any unwholesome talk come out of your mouths, but only what is helpful for building others up according to their needs, that it may benefit those who listen." (Ephesians 4:29)

Scripture Reading: James 3:5-10

Personal Application:

- In what relationships or areas of your life do you struggle most regarding your tongue? Ask the Lord to help you tame your tongue and let your words be life-giving today and every day.

Week 23, Day 4: Better than Most

*"When they measure themselves by themselves and
compare themselves with themselves, they are not wise."*
– 2 Corinthians 10:12b

Who is your standard of goodness or righteousness? Do you consider yourself "better than most"?

In Luke 18:9-14 Jesus tells the parable of the Pharisee and the Tax Collector:

To some who were confident of their own righteousness and looked down on everybody else, Jesus told this parable: "Two men went up to the temple to pray, one a Pharisee and the other a tax collector. The Pharisee stood up and prayed about himself: 'God, I thank you that I am not like other men—robbers, evildoers, adulterers—or even like this tax collector. I fast twice a week and give a tenth of all I get.' But the tax collector stood at a distance. He would not even look up to heaven, but beat his breast and said, 'God, have mercy on me, a sinner.' I tell you that this man, rather than the other, went home justified before God. For everyone who exalts himself will be humbled, and he who humbles himself will be exalted."

This parable is a study in contrasts. The difference in the posture of these two men reveals plenty. The Pharisee "stood up," and the tax collector "stood at a distance," not even looking up to heaven, humbling himself before God.

The Pharisee compared himself to other men and found himself better than most. He was satisfied with and boastful in his own self-righteousness. The tax collector compared himself to God, thus recognizing his great need for God's mercy and forgiveness.

The Pharisee chose to brag about his works, as if God would be impressed; the tax collector had nothing to offer except to acknowledge that he was sinner.

Whenever I read this parable, I am struck by the audacity of the Pharisee. His attitude suggests that he didn't even think he needed God. I've met a lot of men like that. Their attitude is always, "I got this!" And in their puny self-righteousness they boast, "I'm better than most."

We need to take Jesus' words in this parable to heart. I pray that none of us thinks or acts like that religious Pharisee. May we come humbly before God, confessing our sins, and relying on His strength to be the men He would have us be. Let us not compare ourselves with each other but contrast our lives with the life and character of Jesus. May we aspire to ever be more like Him!

Scripture Reading: Ephesians 4:17-24

Personal Application:

- Spend some time in prayer confessing your sins and need for God's mercy and strength.
- In view of God's love, mercy, and forgiveness for you, how will this impact the way you interact with others today?

Week 23, Day 5: The Sex Talk

Guys, with a title like that, hopefully I've got your attention!

My wife and I have been married to each other for over five decades. In preparing this devotional, I asked her what she thought every man should know about his wife. This is a summary of what she told me. If you're not married, take this advice to heart for the future.

Men can have sex at the drop of a hat. We don't need a lot of coaxing, emotional preparation, or even the right setting. If you're married, hopefully you've noticed that your wife is different.

My wife explained that women generally need to be wooed. They don't want to feel like they're just a sex object, or simply there to satisfy their husbands sexually. They don't want to be your sexual "conquest."

A woman wants to be touched by her man regularly in a non-sexual way. She likes to hold hands, have her hair played with, and to be hugged and kissed affectionately—with no strings attached.

Women respond sexually to their man when they know he loves her sacrificially. He speaks kind words to her. He respects her role in the household. If she's a stay-at-home mom, he knows she has worked at least as hard as he has during the day and he lets her know it.

A godly man is tender with his wife and considerate. If she lets him know that she isn't up for making love today, he doesn't pout and fuss but continues to love and cherish her. And by the way, men, if she's not ready tomorrow or the next day either, it's okay, you will not die for lack of sex.

When denied sex, some men rationalize that as their excuse for viewing pornography. That's bull kaka! Besides, nothing will turn a woman off faster than knowing her husband gets his sexual fulfillment artificially.

Your wife needs to know that she satisfies you sexually. Women want to hear that they're beautiful and desirable, and, men, it's our responsibility to make sure she knows.

Also, in the act of making love, we need to learn to wait for our wives. There's nothing more pleasurable than knowing you have fulfilled your wife's sexual needs while fully enjoying her and having her meet yours. Be all there for her in body, mind, and spirit.

God gave us sex within marriage as the most intimate of all relational interactions. Be courageous and guard it to keep it pure, holy, and beautiful—the one thing that only you and your wife enjoy with each other.

Scripture reading: Proverbs 5:15-21

Personal Application:

- As awkward as it might feel, ask your wife to read this devotional and ask her to comment on its validity for her. Ask her how you can improve your intimacy together, listen to her, and learn.

Week 23, Day 6: Are You Jesus?

I often reflect upon my daily thoughts and attitudes, considering whether they mimic the love of Christ. Do people see Jesus in and through me? Do I take the time to show I care? Jesus tells us, "Do to others as you would have them do to you." (Luke 6:31)

This "Golden Rule" sounds good, but often comes with sacrifice. The following story demonstrates the importance of taking time to love others in a way we would like to be loved.

Some years ago, a group of salesmen went to a regional sales convention in Chicago. They had assured their wives that they would be home in plenty of time for Friday night's dinner. In their rush to their departure gate with tickets and briefcases in hand, one of the salesmen inadvertently kicked over a display table of apples, scattering them everywhere. Without stopping or looking back, they barely managed to reach their gate in time for boarding.

ALL BUT ONE!!! He paused, took a deep breath, got in touch with his feelings, and experienced a twinge of compassion for the girl whose apple stand had been overturned.

He told his buddies to go on without him, waved good-bye, knowing he'd have to take a later flight. Then he returned to where the apples were scattered about. He was glad he did. The 16-year-old girl was blind! She was softly crying, tears running down her cheeks in frustration, as she helplessly groped about for the apples.

The crowd swirled around her, but no one stopped to help her. The salesman knelt on the floor with her, gathered up the apples, put them back on the table and helped organize her display. He noticed that many of them had become battered and bruised; these he set aside in a basket.

When everything was back in order, he pulled out his wallet and said, "Here, please take this $40 for the damage we did. Are you okay?" She nodded through her tears. He left her saying, "I hope we didn't spoil your day too badly."

As the salesman started to walk away, the bewildered girl called out to him, "Mister!" He stopped and turned to look back at her, "Yes?" Then she asked, "Are you Jesus?" He stopped in mid-stride and teared up. Then, he slowly made his way to catch that later flight, humbled by the girl's question.

That's our goal and our charge, is it not? To be so much like Jesus that people see Christ in us. How about you? Are you Jesus to those around you?

Scripture Reading: Matthew 25:34-40

Personal Application:

- Each morning as you rise, ask the Lord to help you represent Him well to others throughout the day that they might see Jesus in you.
- Do you know someone in whose life you see Jesus? Spend time with that person and ask them to help you become more Christlike.

Week 23, Day 7: Weekly Recap and Prayer

On the seventh day of each week, use the **ACTS** acronym to spend time with the Lord reviewing and assessing your week and praying to God. (**A**=Adoration; **C**=Confession; **T**=Thanksgiving; **S**=Supplication)

First, look back over the previous six days for this week to remind yourself what you read and agreed to. Then, follow the ACTS pattern for prayer below. Finally, use the space below to journal what God is doing in your life and share this with a trusted spiritual partner.

Adoration: Simply spend time in adoration of the Lord. Praise Him and glorify His name. (See 1 Chronicles 29:10-13; Psalm 100; Romans 11:33-36.)

Confession: Confess your sins and shortcomings before God. ("If we confess our sins, he is faithful and just and will forgive us our sins and purify us from all unrighteousness." – 1 John 1:9) To confess (or agree with God) about your sin, implies that you are repentant and desperately want Him to change you.

Thanksgiving: Thank God for what He has done and is doing in your life and the life of your family. Give Him credit, for everything you have comes from Him. (See Psalm 136.)

Supplication: Supplication is just a fancy word for making your requests known to God. Based on the devotions of this past week and the things going on in your life right now, what do you want to ask Him for? "If you, then, though you are evil, know how to give good gifts to your children, how much more will your Father in heaven give good gifts to those who ask Him!" (Matthew 7:11)

Journal: What is God doing in your life right now?

Week 24, Day 1: On Being a Father

A close friend of mine is in his 70s and he is still dealing with the wounds his father inflicted on him. Ironically, his father was a pastor and presented himself as a godly man. However, he was controlling, harsh, demanding, rigid, legalistic, and abusive in his discipline.

My friend's dad failed to recognize the love, grace, and mercy of our heavenly Father, but presented God to his children in the same way he treated them. As a result, my friend has struggled his whole life with his view of God as Father.

Before becoming a dad, I doubt that many of us took a course in fatherhood. As the father of two sons, I know how difficult it is being a dad. And if our own dad wasn't the best role model, it makes our job even harder.

Perhaps you grew up in a household in which your dad was either absent or a poor role model. That doesn't excuse us from perpetuating his poor example of fatherhood.

No dad is perfect. Perfection is not in our wheelhouse. But we can imitate our heavenly Father. And when we do blow it with our children, we must humbly tell them so and ask their forgiveness. Doing this communicates that as fathers, we are as needy for God's grace and love as our children are. It's so much easier for a child to respond to such humble, godly behavior.

Ephesians urges us, "Fathers, do not exasperate your children; instead, bring them up in the training and instruction of the Lord." (6:4) That's a short verse with a whole lot of life behind it. We guard against exasperating our children by listening more, being patient, setting reasonable, age-appropriate guidelines, and disciplining fairly. We bring them up in the training and instruction of the Lord primarily by modeling true Christlikeness. In all walks of life, we demonstrate for them what it means to follow, please, and glorify Jesus.

Perhaps you're dealing with a wayward or rebellious child, it's never too late to model Christlikeness for them. If your child is rebelling, know that you are not alone. And regardless of your track record as a dad, your child is ultimately accountable for their own actions.

Pray for your children and seek wise, Christian counsel in raising them. "Train up a child in the way he should go, and when he is old, he will not depart from it." (Proverbs 22:6 NKJV) That is not an ironclad promise but a sound principle to follow.

Being a father is one of the greatest joys in life, but we must treat fatherhood as a precious privilege and responsibility.

Scripture Reading: 1 Thessalonians 2:11-12

Personal Application:

- What was (is) your dad like? To what extent did he model Christlikeness for you? How well do you model Christlikeness to your children? Who do you know you could go to for wise counsel?

Week 24, Day 2: Hardship Is Your Friend

I love reading true, historical accounts of men and women who have overcome great obstacles. So, I thoroughly enjoyed reading *The Boys in the Boat* by Daniel James Brown, the story of the University of Washington rowing team that won the gold medal in the 1936 Olympics.

I especially appreciated the following metaphor spoken by George Yeoman Pocock, "It is hard to make that boat go as fast as you want to. The enemy, of course, is resistance of the water, as you have to displace the amount of water equal to the weight of men and equipment, but that very water is what supports you and that very enemy is your friend. So is life: the very problems you must overcome also support you and make you stronger in overcoming them."[1]

We don't typically think this way, but if you stop to consider your job, the purpose of nearly any job is to solve problems. Without the problems, we wouldn't have a job. In fact, the longer we're in a position and the greater the variety of problems we've solved, the more skilled we become and the more valuable we are to our employer.

It may be more difficult to think this way about our relationships, but I believe it's also true. Within my marriage, my wife and I have faced a wide variety of problems throughout our marriage. While enduring the problems, many of them were anything but pleasant. But those problems strengthened our marriage, bringing us closer together.

In Romans 5:3-4, Paul wrote, "We... glory in our sufferings, because we know that suffering produces perseverance; perseverance, character; and character, hope." Think about that for a moment. We don't want to be quitters; we want perseverance in our lives. And we desire strong, godly character. We want to be positive men full of hope.

Yet all those positive outcomes result from suffering (or problems). Without suffering, we wouldn't experience perseverance, we wouldn't develop strong character, or be filled with hope.

But what's our first response when we experience suffering or hardship? Usually, we seek to remove it from our lives as quickly as possible. Think of this in terms of trying to row that boat on dry land. Sure, you've got the boat out of the water that was causing so much resistance but trying to row on dry land is even worse—impossible even.

Therefore Paul urges us to "glory in" or "rejoice in" our sufferings. "The very problems you must overcome also support you and make you stronger in overcoming them."

Scripture Reading: Romans 4:18-22

Personal Application:

- What struggles or problems are you facing right now?
- In what way can you view those problems as your "friends"?
  Trust God and persevere!

---

1   Daniel James Brown, *The Boys in the Boat* (New York, NY: Penguin Books, 2013) p. 53.

Week 24, Day 3: Virtual Relationships?

Like most of you, I've had a cell phone for years. But I'm old enough to remember rotary dial phones and party lines. Back then, the idea of a wireless phone was pure fantasy, something you'd see on the Jetson's or a Dick Tracy cartoon.

I'm told that the computing power of the average cell phone today far exceeds what NASA had at its disposal to take Apollo 11 to the moon and back! And with that computing power, the cell phone has evolved way past merely serving as a telephone.

We can text, FaceTime, send emails, and hold virtual meetings with people all over the world. The cell phone is truly an amazing device for communicating.

But there is a downside to cell phones. Go to any coffee shop, airport, or transit system and look around at the people there. They all have their eyes glued to a cell phone or other device. And this practice isn't confined to public places. Recently, I was at a family gathering, and looking around, I realized that everyone in the room, representing three generations, was looking down at their cell phones!

Instead of engaging in conversation with each other, everyone in the room was distracted by their phones and hindering real communication. I've even seen people in the same room texting each other instead of talking with each other. I wonder if our cell phones are even getting in the way of spending time with the Lord in prayer.

A little device with so much potential for expanding our ability to communicate may be more of a hindrance than a help to communicating with each other and building meaningful relationships.

I'm not suggesting we get rid of our cell phones, but that we focus on cultivating real, personal communication when we're with other people. An emoji is not the same as a warm smile with eye contact and kind words spoken.

We're several months into the coronavirus stay-at-home order as I write this. We've been "attending" church and our small group virtually and I've got to tell you, virtual is a very poor substitute for the real thing.

Jesus was so intentional about face-to-face human connections that He even broke with the culture and touched those with leprosy and other diseases to express His love. Keep your cell phone, but let's get real with our relationships and communicating with those around us.

Scripture Reading: Colossians 3:12-17

Personal Application:
- Some have found it helpful to place a basket at the door in which people leave their cell phones while getting together. This isn't about rule-setting but about values.
- Take stock of when and where you use your cell phone. Focus on personal, f ace-to-face interaction whenever possible.

Week 24, Day 4: Who Packs Your Parachute?

Charles Plumb was a US Navy jet pilot in Vietnam. After 75 combat missions, his plane was hit by a surface-to-air missile. Plumb ejected and parachuted into enemy hands. He was captured and spent six years in a Vietcong prison. He survived the ordeal and now lectures on lessons learned from his experience.

One day, Plumb and his wife were sitting in a restaurant. A man at another table came up and said, "You're Plumb! You flew jet fighters in Vietnam from the aircraft carrier Kitty Hawk. You were shot down!"

"How in the world did you know that?" asked Plumb.

"I packed your parachute," the man replied. Plumb gasped in surprise and gratitude. The man pumped his hand and said, "I guess it worked!"

Plumb assured him, "It sure did. If your chute hadn't worked, I wouldn't be here today."

Plumb couldn't sleep that night, thinking about that man. Plumb says, "I kept wondering what he had looked like in a Navy uniform: a white hat; a bib in the back; and bell-bottom trousers.

"I wonder how many times I might have seen him and not even said 'Good morning, how are you?' or anything because, you see, I was a fighter pilot and he was just a sailor." Plumb thought of the many hours the sailor must have spent at a long wooden table in the bowels of the ship, carefully folding the silks of each chute, holding in his hands each time the fate of someone he didn't know.

Now, Plumb asks his audiences, "Who's packing your parachute?" Everyone has someone who provides what they need to make it through the day. He also points out that he needed many kinds of parachutes when his plane was shot down over enemy territory — he needed his physical parachute, his mental parachute, his emotional parachute, and his spiritual parachute. He needed all these supports before reaching safety.

Sometimes in the daily challenges that life gives us, we miss what is important. We may fail to say "hello," "please," or "thank you," congratulate someone on something wonderful that has happened to them, give a compliment, or just do something nice for no reason. As you go through this week, this month, this year, recognize people who pack your parachutes and look for opportunities to pack someone else's parachute.

Scripture Reading: 1 Thessalonians 5:11-15

Personal Application:

- Who packs your parachute? Who in your life encourages and equips you? Go out of your way to thank those individuals.
- Whose parachute are you packing? As you go throughout your day, look for individuals whom you can encourage. But don't merely do this today; make it your way of life.

Week 24, Day 5: Contentment

Some years ago, a friend of mine was transferred by his company to Texas. He was married with three school-age children. Being a northern boy, neither he nor his family took well to Texas. He loved his job, but for a variety of reasons, they found it difficult to adapt to Texas.

He explains:

We never really experienced that "Southern hospitality" you hear so much about, so we found it difficult to make friends. Also, our home was perpetually infested with fleas, roaches, and termites. Then, there was the weather! In our five-and-a-half years there, we had four roofs on our home due to hail damage—I'm talking billiard-ball-sized hailstones!

But finally, one day, my wife and I woke up to the fact that we were malcontent. All we did was complain and it was affecting our lives and relationships negatively in a profound way. So, we determined that by God's grace, we'd learn to be content to live in Texas.

We bought a popup camping trailer and started camping as a family. The kids brought their friends with them and we made some great memories! And God helped us learn to be content to live in Texas.

You might be surprised that contentment is a learned quality, but the apostle Paul also indicates this when he wrote, "I have learned to be content whatever the circumstances. I know what it is to be in need, and I know what it is to have plenty. I have learned the secret of being content in any and every situation, whether well fed or hungry, whether living in plenty or in want." (Philippians 4:11-12)

What was Paul's secret? He reveals it in the next verse, "I can do all things through Him [Christ] who gives me strength." (vs. 13) Because of what Paul had written earlier in his letter, I think of contentment as that peaceful state of body, mind, and heart in which we know that in Christ we have everything we need. Therefore, we can be content.

This is also what David meant when he wrote Psalm 23:1, "With the Lord as my Shepherd, I have everything I need." (author's paraphrase) Our Lord does provide us with everything we need!

Paul also urges us to give thanks to God in all circumstances. We must experience times of need to learn contentment. And under those circumstances, when we give thanks for what God has provided, we learn that it's enough.

Scripture Reading: 1 Timothy 6:6-11

Personal Application:
- In what area of your life are you most prone to discontent?
- Ask the Lord to help you learn contentment as you experience times of need in that area.

Week 24, Day 6: Contentment Is Not Complacency

Yesterday, we talked about contentment as a godly response to life situations. But maybe you were wondering, "Does being content mean that I shouldn't try to improve my situation?" No! Contentment is not an excuse for laziness or inactivity, nor does it fly in the face of creativity and industriousness.

In fact, in the same letter to Timothy in which Paul urges contentment (1 Timothy 6:6-8), he also wrote, "Anyone who does not provide for their relatives, and especially for their own household, has denied the faith and is worse than an unbeliever." (1 Timothy 5:8) Paul also wrote to the Thessalonians that if someone wasn't willing to work, they shouldn't eat!

The Scriptures are full of exhortations to work hard and be industrious. Proverbs 10:4-5 says, "Lazy hands make for poverty, but diligent hands bring wealth. He who gathers crops in summer is a prudent son, but he who sleeps during harvest is a disgraceful son." So being content is not to be confused with laziness or idleness.

Perhaps we can say that contentment is the godly response to any situation when we have done everything, we can improve that situation with the skills and resources God has given us. The desire to improve our situation is a noble pursuit and does not run contrary to contentment.

I think many of us men struggle with being content, because we are hard-charging, motivated guys who are constantly pursuing a better existence for our families and ourselves. But we must be careful to submit our drives and ambitions to the Lord as well. Otherwise, a preoccupation with such ambitions can easily degenerate into discontent.

Discontent basically says God is not providing what we need. It also cultivates an inordinate desire for wealth, things, or experiences beyond our means. Discontent or malcontent breeds greed, envy, jealousy, and if we're not careful, even lying, cheating, and stealing. Discontent focuses on self.

Discontent is a corrupt form of ambition and industry with a love for money at its core. And we know that "the love of money is a root of all kinds of evil. Some people eager for money, have wandered from the faith and pierced themselves with many griefs." (1 Timothy 6:10)

This is truly a solemn warning for us. Never think you can dabble in in that kind of corrupt ambition without being burned. All of us are susceptible to its lure.

Scripture Reading: Luke 12:13-21

Personal Application:

• What are your current ambitions? Where do these ambitions come from? What has motivated them?

• Check yourself for discontent, laziness, or idleness. What do you sense the Lord asking you to do?

Week 24, Day 7: Weekly Recap and Prayer

On the seventh day of each week, use the **ACTS** acronym to spend time with the Lord reviewing and assessing your week and praying to God. (**A**=Adoration; **C**=Confession; **T**=Thanksgiving; **S**=Supplication)

First, look back over the previous six days for this week to remind yourself what you read and agreed to. Then, follow the ACTS pattern for prayer below. Finally, use the space below to journal what God is doing in your life and share this with a trusted spiritual partner.

Adoration: Simply spend time in adoration of the Lord. Praise Him and glorify His name. (See 1 Chronicles 29:10-13; Psalm 100; Romans 11:33-36.)

Confession: Confess your sins and shortcomings before God. ("If we confess our sins, he is faithful and just and will forgive us our sins and purify us from all unrighteousness." – 1 John 1:9) To confess (or agree with God) about your sin, implies that you are repentant and desperately want Him to change you.

Thanksgiving: Thank God for what He has done and is doing in your life and the life of your family. Give Him credit, for everything you have comes from Him. (See Psalm 136.)

Supplication: Supplication is just a fancy word for making your requests known to God. Based on the devotions of this past week and the things going on in your life right now, what do you want to ask Him for? "If you, then, though you are evil, know how to give good gifts to your children, how much more will your Father in heaven give good gifts to those who ask Him!" (Matthew 7:11)

Journal: What is God doing in your life right now?

Week 25, Day 1: What Is Truth?

Pilate spoke those words when Jesus stood trial before him. Jesus had just told Pilate that He had come to testify to the truth. That's when Pilate responded, "What is truth?" From the context we know that he was skeptical that truth could even be known.

This same view about truth prevails today. We hear things like, "That's your truth;" or "Truth is what you make it;" or "Truth is relative." This is madness and we must recognize it as such.

We recognize this relative view of truth as coming from the evil one. In the Garden of Eden, the serpent approached Eve and spoke with her: "Did God really say, 'You must not eat from any tree in the garden'?" The woman said to the serpent, "We may eat fruit from the trees in the garden, but God did say, 'You must not eat fruit from the tree that is in the middle of the garden, and you must not touch it, or you will die.'" "You will not certainly die," the serpent said to the woman. "For God knows that when you eat from it your eyes will be opened, and you will be like God, knowing good and evil." (Genesis 3:1-5) God spoke truth to Adam and Eve. But the evil one twisted God's words, manufacturing his own version of the truth. Adam and Eve rejected God's truth and believed the twisted words of Satan, rebelling against God and sinning. Their rejection of the truth spoken by God hurled all of mankind into our sinful state.

Truth is not relative. It is not personal, meaning my truth may not be yours. If there is no truth, then nothing can be known. Jesus had other things to say about truth:

- Jesus said, "I am the way and the truth and the life. No one comes to the Father except through Me." (John 14:6)
- He also said, "Now this is eternal life: that they know You, the only true God, and Jesus Christ, whom You have sent." (John 17:3)
- And Jesus prayed for His disciples (including us), "Sanctify them by the truth; Your word is truth." (John 17:17)

Don't be fooled by the evil one and the deception he promotes in the world today. Truth comes from God. Truth is knowable. It is neither relative nor specific to only some individuals. People "suppress the truth by their wickedness," and "their thinking became futile and their foolish hearts were darkened." (Romans 1:18 & 21) Trust God and His Word. His Word is truth!

Scripture Reading: Romans 1:18-32

Personal Application:

- On what do you base your beliefs about God? We must go to His Word, for His Word is truth.
- This matter impacts how we understand the Scriptures as well. There is one true interpretation but there are many applications of its truth.

Week 25, Day 2: Abiding in Christ

For thousands of years, farmers have created new fruit trees using grafting methods. The fact that a limb from another tree can be grafted into the host tree is an amazing process. Once the branch is properly grafted on the root stock or tree, it will begin to receive nourishment from the host, so that it becomes a permanent part of the host and can bear fruit.

Of course, the branch by itself can do nothing. For a branch to survive, much less produce fruit, it must be grafted into a living, thriving host. Otherwise it will simply dry up, wither, and die.

In John 15, Jesus used this very metaphor to describe our relationship with Him. He explained, "I am the vine; you are the branches. If you remain in Me and I in you, you will bear much fruit; apart from Me you can do nothing." (John 15:5)

Our source of true energy and strength comes from Christ. When we abide in Him, we have life! It is only in Him that we can be fruitful in our lives. Just as a branch is dependent on the vine for its nourishment, so we are dependent on Jesus.

And when we are fruitful, we bring glory to the Father. "This is to My Father's glory, that you bear much fruit, showing yourselves to be My disciples." (John 15:8)

I believe that abiding or remaining in Jesus (like a branch on the Vine) is synonymous with what Paul describes in Galatians 5 as "walking by the Spirit;" being "led by the Spirit;" "living by the Spirit;" and "keeping in step with the Spirit." But what does this look like?

Have you ever noticed that the more you hang around someone, the more you become like them? In everyday terms, we abide in Christ or walk in the Spirit by hanging out with Him. We spend lots of time with Him. We take Him with us wherever we go. We talk with Him throughout the day and we spend time reading His Word to know Him better.

Walking in the Spirit and abiding in Christ is a faith-walk. It's not something we do mechanically. I love the branch-on-the-vine metaphor because it so beautifully describes our relationship with Christ. Think about it, not only are we dependent on His nourishment, but we also inherit His DNA (Galatians 5:22-23). Also, because we are attached to Him, when we experience storms, He experiences them right there with us!

Drink deeply from Him. Depend on Him. Lean into Him. Take on His character. Rely on Him for life and fruitfulness in your life. Obey Him and trust Him. Bear His fruit.

Scripture Reading: Galatians 5:16-26

Personal Application:

- In what situations have you felt the closest to the Lord and most used by Him? What brought such situations on?
- How can you make abiding in Christ and walking in His Spirit a daily occurrence?

Week 25, Day 3: Faith vs. Fear

In November 1970, a chartered flight carrying 71 passengers from the Marshall University football team, its coaching staff, and boosters crashed, killing all aboard.

In 2006, Warner Brothers released the movie *We Are Marshall* starring Matt McConaughey (Coach Jack Lengyel). The movie depicts life for the small West Virginia town trying to recover from this crash. This tragic loss shocked the sports world, and devastated the small town surrounding the campus.

As I write this, we find ourselves in a different type of crisis – the coronavirus pandemic. The despair, fears, discouragement, and apprehension found in almost every town is palpable. Anger burst onto the scene of a simple grocery shopping excursion as people yelled at others to maintain social distance and to share in the purchase of toilet paper.

Craziness and anxiety are redefined with each daily occurrence and news reports. Like the variety of personalities in the movie *We Are Marshall*, we see people demonstrate a range of emotions from great hope and assurance to sheer panic and desperate actions.

The early church was no stranger to plagues, epidemics, and mass hysteria. According to both Christian and non-Christian accounts, one of the main catalysts for the church's explosive growth in its early years was how Christians responded to disease, suffering, and death.

In A.D. 249 to 262, Western civilization was devastated by one of the deadliest pandemics in its history. Though the exact cause of the plague is uncertain, the city of Rome was said to have lost an estimated 5,000 people a day at the height of the outbreak.

One eyewitness, Bishop Dionysius of Alexandria, noted the difference between Christian and non-Christian responses to the plague. He observed that the non-Christians in Alexandria were dismayed and in panic. The non-Christian response to the plague was characterized by self-protection and avoiding the sick at all costs.

By contrast, the Christian response was to minister to the sick, not considering their own personal safety. The early church leaned into God's promises and prayed for their communities. They showed compassion and love to others. They were comforted by the promise of Christ's return (1 Thessalonians 4:18); God's words, "Fear not, for I am with you... I will uphold you with my right hand;" (Isaiah 41:10); and by God's care for His people (1 Peter 5:7).

Fear paralyzes and seeks only one's own wellbeing. Faith releases God's grace, mercy, and love to those around us.

Scripture Reading: Matthew 25:34-40

Personal Application:
- Who do you know who needs encouragement or help today?
- Ask the Lord to show you how you can minister to them most effectively.

Week 25, Day 4: Two Are Better than One

I remember watching the longest game in NFL history on Christmas Day in 1991. It ran for 82 minutes and 40 seconds, finally ending with a field goal by Garo Yepremian that allowed the Dolphins to win 27-24. I couldn't help but think about the pressure Garo must have felt in that final moment. With all the missed opportunities in the game, no one was taking this kick for granted.

Whether it's punting or placekicking, a kicker can quickly become the hero or the scapegoat, depending on where his foot hits the ball. It is mastering that contact that allows a player to extend his time in the NFL. Kickers are a unique breed. Much of what they do is more mental than physical. There's just no room for fickle footwork.

Nothing frustrates coaches more than a kicker who is unpredictable and erratic in his ability to simply kick the pigskin through the uprights. He watches the kicker in practice make 50- and 60-yard field goals. The Head Coach gets his Special Teams Coach to make sure the kicker warms up and has plenty of time kicking into the net on the sidelines before he enters the game. Then, as the kicker enters the game, the coach still holds his breath, hoping that all the jeering opposition and robust fans don't mess with the kicker's mind, distracting him.

Place kickers are especially careful in choosing a holder with good hands and a calm spirit. The holder is to the kicker what a reel is to a fishing rod. They must work in perfect harmony to complete the job. A holder is usually one of the kicker's best and most trusted friends. After taking the snap, a holder must spin the ball perfectly, so the laces face the goal post. If the laces are anywhere but straight forward the ball can wobble, reduce the distance, or lose accuracy. The ball is centered exactly to the kicker's preference. Confidence in the holder is a critical key to the success of every kick.

Opposing teams work extra hard to intimidate the kicker. They realize that if they can "get into the kicker's head" and make him lose confidence, he's likely to rush his kick and the ball will travel askew.

So, it is in life. Others can get into our heads, distracting us, stirring up fear, or drawing out temptation. Surrounding ourselves with friends we can count on, who will encourage us and keep us on track is essential to staying the course. We all need godly friends—men we can be transparent with, sharing our deepest hopes, fears, and secrets.

Scripture Reading: Ecclesiastes 4:9-12

Personal Application:

- What distracts you most from your walk in Christ?
- Who do you know who can be your spiritual "holder"? And in what ways can you serve as his "holder"?
- Meet regularly with this man to encourage and strengthen each other in the Lord.

Week 25, Day 5: Stand Firm!

In Matthew 24, Jesus' disciples asked Him, "What will be the sign of Your coming and of the end of the age?" (vs. 3) Then, throughout the rest of the chapter, Jesus laid out for them what they (we) can expect.

But one of the signs of His coming especially stands out to me. Jesus said, "At that time many will turn away from the faith and will betray and hate each other, and many false prophets will appear and deceive many people. Because of the increase of wickedness, the love of most will grow cold, but the one who stands firm to the end will be saved." (vs. 10-11)

In Revelation, Jesus sent messages to seven churches in Asia Minor that existed at the time. The apostle Paul and his co-workers had established at least one of those churches (in Ephesus). Yet, at the writing of Revelation, a few short decades later, Jesus urged five of those churches to repent of their sin. In so short a time they were already falling into apostasy. We see the same happening with our churches today.

The antidote Jesus gives for this falling away from the faith is to *stand firm*. As men, we need to stand firm in God's Word. His Word, the Bible, is our standard for faith, truth, and living. We must be men of the Word and live as men who believe and obey God's Word.

We must stand firm in our love for Jesus Christ. To the church at Ephesus, Jesus warned, "You don't love Me or each other as you did at first!" (Revelation 2:4 NLT) We must daily cultivate our love for the Lord and each other and demonstrate our love in the way we live.

We must stand firm by holding to the truth of God's Word in the onslaught of deception introduced by false teachers and our culture in general. The Lord continually urges us to be alert and sober-minded. When the tide of cultural views is so strong and prevailing, it's so easy to be swept away by it.

Today, our culture not only chooses to sin but celebrates it and calls us bigots and haters when we call them out on it. We must always love the sinner but call out and stand against their sin.

Finally, be especially vigilant in your church. Many churches are watering down the Gospel and embracing worldly views and sinful practices. In their efforts to be culturally relevant, they take on the sinful mindset and practices of the culture.

You might be wondering to yourself, "Who am I to stand against this torrent of unbelief and apostasy?" Yet, Jesus urges you and me to stand firm, and if we stand firm together, with God's power, we will make a difference.

Scripture Reading: Matthew 24:4-13

Personal Application:

- Where have you perhaps yielded ground to our sinful culture?
- In what specific ways do you need to stand firm in the faith?

Week 25, Day 6: Knowing Christ

As I get older I realize more and more how quickly our days on this earth pass and how important it is that we pause and pray for a heart of wisdom—that we might live each day in a way that brings glory to God.

In Psalm 39:4 we read, "Show me, LORD, my life's end and the number of my days; let me know how fleeting my life is." With age comes new perspective. We must use our time wisely. Scripture is full of passages encouraging us to be intentional in our relationship with God—living with His presence in all facets of our lives.

The Apostle Paul was in prison in Rome when he wrote the letter to the Philippians. And despite his outward circumstances he exhorted them to keep their eyes on Christ. We are not to put too much emphasis on the past or worry about the future, but to "conduct ourselves in a manner worthy of the gospel of Christ." (Philippians 1:27)

Further, Paul reminds us that our primary focus in life is to pursue an ever-deepening relationship with Jesus Christ. And as we grow in our relationship with the Lord, obeying, serving, and loving to become natural by-products. These characteristics become the "fruit" of spending time in His presence.

Knowing Christ refers to an intimate and intentional relationship. It is not about what church or denomination we belong to. Nor is it about our personal spiritual performance. It has nothing to do with how much we contribute in gifts or works. For it is by God's grace alone that we are saved through faith in Christ's death for us. The "fruits" in our lives are a by-product of our relationship with Christ, not a means for obtaining it.

Paul wrote, "I consider everything a loss because of the surpassing worth of knowing Christ Jesus my Lord, for whose sake I have lost all things. I consider them garbage, that I may gain Christ and be found in Him, not having a righteousness of my own that comes from the law, but that which is through faith in Christ—the righteousness that comes from God on the basis of faith. I want to know Christ...." (Philippians 3:8-10)

Paul says of his pursuit of knowing Christ better and better that he "presses on," and "strains toward" Him. Paul urges us, "Join together in following my example, brothers and sisters, and just as you have us as a model, keep your eyes on those who live as we do." (Philippians 3:17)

Knowing Christ ever more deeply should be the goal of us all. He is the pearl of great price, the treasure found in a field worth selling all else to obtain!

Scripture Reading: Matthew 13:44-45

Personal Application:
- How would you describe your relationship with Christ? What would you like it to look like?
- Based on what Paul says in Philippians, what are some ways you can continue to deepen your relationship with Christ?

Week 25, Day 7: Weekly Recap and Prayer

On the seventh day of each week, use the **ACTS** acronym to spend time with the Lord reviewing and assessing your week and praying to God. (**A**=Adoration; **C**=Confession; **T**=Thanksgiving; **S**=Supplication)

First, look back over the previous six days for this week to remind yourself what you read and agreed to. Then, follow the ACTS pattern for prayer below. Finally, use the space below to journal what God is doing in your life and share this with a trusted spiritual partner.

Adoration: Simply spend time in adoration of the Lord. Praise Him and glorify His name. (See 1 Chronicles 29:10-13; Psalm 100; Romans 11:33-36.)

Confession: Confess your sins and shortcomings before God. ("If we confess our sins, he is faithful and just and will forgive us our sins and purify us from all unrighteousness." – 1 John 1:9) To confess (or agree with God) about your sin, implies that you are repentant and desperately want Him to change you.

Thanksgiving: Thank God for what He has done and is doing in your life and the life of your family. Give Him credit, for everything you have comes from Him. (See Psalm 136.)

Supplication: Supplication is just a fancy word for making your requests known to God. Based on the devotions of this past week and the things going on in your life right now, what do you want to ask Him for? "If you, then, though you are evil, know how to give good gifts to your children, how much more will your Father in heaven give good gifts to those who ask Him!" (Matthew 7:11)

Journal: What is God doing in your life right now?

Week 26, Day 1: "Yes, Jesus Loves Me"

I've attended the funerals and memorial services of many friends. I know first-hand that when death visits your personal address book, it makes you really think about what has eternal significance. Faith, family, and character take precedence over fame, power, and fortune. It's also a time to reflect on the lives of those who are no longer with us—what we can learn from them—what message they might have for us.

While catching a little TV one Sunday afternoon, I watched a church in Atlanta honor one of its senior pastors who had been retired many years. He was 92 at that time, and I wondered why the church even bothered to ask the old gentleman to preach at that age.

After a warm welcome, introduction, and enthusiastic applause, the gentleman rose from his high-back chair and walked slowly, with great effort to the podium. Without notes or written material of any kind he placed both hands on the pulpit to steady himself and then quietly and slowly he began to speak:

When I was asked to come here today and talk to you, your pastor asked me to tell you the greatest lesson I ever learned in my fifty-something years of preaching.

I thought about it for a few days and boiled it down to just one thing that made the most difference in my life and sustained me through all my trials. It was the one thing that I could always rely on when tears and heartbreak and pain and fear and sorrow paralyzed me... the only thing that would comfort was the eternal message of this song:

"Jesus loves me this I know.
For the Bible tells me so.
Little ones to Him belong,
we are weak, but He is strong...
Yes, Jesus loves me. Yes, Jesus loves me. Yes, Jesus loves me,
The Bible tells me so."

Tears welled up in my eyes as I heard this old saint recite those familiar truths. May we live our lives on the firm foundation of Jesus' eternal love for us! Those words express the legacy I want to leave for others as well. How about you?

Scripture Reading: 1 John 4:9-11

Personal Application:

- Take time to reflect on the words of that song, "Jesus Loves Me." As childish as those words may seem, let each phrase wash over you as you meditate on it.
- What did you experience in that little exercise? What message do you have to tell others because of pondering this song?

Week 26, Day 2: "He Is Faithful Who Promised"

The world we live in and the trends we're experiencing in our country can be quite unsettling. Mass-shootings, wars in the Middle East, blatant sinful practices now being embraced and even thrust upon us, pandemics, and a host of other things. And the media seems to thrive on broadcasting only doom and gloom, which casts a social landscape filled with potholes and insecurity.

So, what is a person to do? How should we view the future?

We honor and serve a God who is faithful and stays true to His word. As David urged, "Give thanks to the Lord of lords: His love endures forever." (Psalm 136:3) If our security rests firmly in Him, we can be at peace in the midst of the most chaotic circumstances. God has said, "Never will I leave you; never will I forsake you." (Hebrews 13:5) And when He makes a promise, He always keeps it.

In a speech to the Israelites, Moses hammered home this point. The previous generation knew that God had promised to give them the land of Canaan, but they refused to believe He could do it for them. They perceived the giants in the land to be greater than God apparently. So, God put them in a "timeout," wandering in the wilderness for 40 years until that entire unfaithful generation had died out.

As the new generation stood ready to enter the Promised Land, Moses told them, "Know therefore that the LORD your God is God; He is the faithful God, keeping His covenant of love to a thousand generations of those who love Him and keep His commands." (Deuteronomy 7:9)

Dear friends, remember we serve a God who is faithful and who doesn't waver in His commitments. Praise God that His faithfulness does not depend on us or the strength of our faith. Paul reminds us, "What if some did not have faith? Will their lack of faith nullify God's faithfulness? Not at all!" (Romans 3:3-4a) He will keep every promise.

I love the Lord's assurance to us in Isaiah 41:10, "So do not fear, for I am with you; do not be dismayed, for I am your God. I will strengthen you and help you; I will uphold you with my righteous right hand."

So, despite what's going on around you, encourage yourself and others with words of assurance from the Lord.

Scripture Reading: Psalm 20:1-9

Personal Application:

- It's easy to let the media and all the negativity get us down and into that mode. Be sure to stay above it all with God's promises.
- Speak only what will encourage and build up others and refuse to propagate fear and doubt.

Week 26, Day 3: Forgive Others

One of the most challenging things God asks us to do is to forgive others. I don't know about you, but there are certain people in my life who are hard to forgive, because their words and their actions were so hurtful. When people personally attack me or my loved ones, I find it difficult to forgive them. But that is exactly what God asks us to do (Matthew 5:44; 6:12).

During the last day of the American Civil War, Joshua Chamberlain, an officer with the Union army, surrounded a group of Confederate soldiers. Instead of firing upon the humiliated enemy, he allowed them to surrender with dignity. Commander Chamberlain then ordered his men to form a column on both sides of the road that led to the encampment. Then, he told his men to humble themselves and salute their foes as they passed.

It was a moving moment on the battlefield. Union soldiers who were tired, angry, and frustrated suppressed their feelings and honored their enemy by saluting them with their rifles and raised swords. This event was a great example of the mercy God intended us to show our foes.

It is often difficult to show mercy and forgive those who have sinned against us. Peter came to Jesus one time asking Him about forgiveness. Peter asked, "Lord, how many times shall I forgive my brother or sister who sins against me? Up to seven times?" Peter thought he was being gracious and magnanimous with his offer, but Jesus told him a story:

The kingdom of heaven is like a king who wanted to settle accounts with his servants. As he began the settlement, a man who owned him ten thousand bags of gold was brought to him. Since he was not able to pay, the master ordered that he and his wife and his children all that he had be sold to repay the debt.

At this the servant fell on his knees before him. "Be patient with me," he begged, "and I will pay back everything." The servant's master took pity on him, canceled the debt and let him go."

Perhaps you know the rest of the story. This servant went out and found a fellow servant who owed him a hundred silver coins—a pittance compared with what the first servant had owed his master. The first servant showed no mercy but had this man thrown into debtor's prison. But when his master found out, he was furious and handed the first servant over to be tortured.

So, we too are to forgive our brother or sister from the heart, for this is what God desires. The debt God has forgiven us is incalculable, therefore He asks that we do to others as He has done for us—extending mercy and forgiving them.

Scripture Reading: Matthew 6:9-15

Personal Application:
- Who in your life do you need to extend mercy to and forgive?
- Is there someone who needs to forgive you for something you've done? If so, go and apologize sincerely and ask their forgiveness.

Week 26, Day 4: A Man of the Word

I think one of the most jarring stories in Scripture takes place in 2 Chronicles 34. Josiah was a mere eight years old when he became king of Judah. When he was just 16, the text says, "He began to seek the God of his father David." (vs. 3)

But for 57 years prior to Josiah, his father, Amon, and grandfather, Manasseh, were wicked kings who led the people into idolatry and sin. They neglected the worship of God and let the temple fall into disrepair. So, in the 18th year of Josiah's reign he set about to restore the temple and to usher in a revival of the worship of the one true God in Judah.

While the workers were cleaning and repairing the temple, they found the Book of the Law of the Lord. They brought the book to Josiah and read it to him. "When the king heard the words of the Law, he tore his robes." (vs. 19) This was an act of contrition, repentance, and humbling of himself before God.

Then Josiah gave orders to his attendants, "Go and inquire of the Lord for me and for the remnant in Israel and Judah about what is written in this book that has been found. Great is the Lord's anger that is poured out on us because those who have gone before us have not kept the word of the Lord; they have not acted in accordance with all that is written in this book." (vs. 21)

This account is relevant for us today. While there are still people in the world who do not own a Bible and have never heard God's Word, a great number of Americans own several Bibles in various translations. Unlike Josiah's situation in which God's Word had been lost for so many years, we have God's Word at our fingertips, yet it often goes unread.

If we don't read the Bible, we don't know what it says. Many think they know what it says without ever reading it. They let their assumptions about God and the Christian life guide them instead of looking in the Book to see what God really says. As a result, many have horribly flawed views of God and what He requires of us.

I pray that each of us reading this would cultivate a deep hunger for God's Word, because a longing for God's Word is a longing to know God better and to learn to please Him.

Josiah led a spiritual reformation in Judah because God's Word impacted him so profoundly. He "renewed the covenant in the presence of the Lord [and all the people] – to follow the Lord and keep His commands, statutes and decrees with all his heart and all his soul, and to obey the words of the covenant written in the book." (vs. 31)

How about you? Will you stand with me and many others and be a man of the Word?

Scripture Reading: 2 Chronicles 34

Personal Application:

- Renew your commitment to follow the Lord. Set aside a time each day when you spend time in His Word. Be careful not to just read words, but to let God's Word permeate your heart.

Week 26, Day 5: How to Read the Bible

Yesterday, we challenged you to be a man of the Word. Whether you're new in the faith or have known the Lord for some time, being in the Word is crucial to the health and growth of your relationship with Jesus Christ. But many men are at a loss as to how to read and study the Bible.

Our motivations are a good place to start. Why read and study the Bible? Our motivation should be to meet with God. We want to know Him better and learn what it means to live for Him. We don't read the Word merely to accumulate knowledge or facts about God. We want to know Him better. *Always go to the Word with the intent to meet with God.*

Also, the Apostle Paul wrote, "For everything that was written in the past was written to teach us, so that through the endurance taught in the Scriptures and the encouragement they provide we might have hope." (Romans 15:4) When we read about Abraham, Jacob, Joseph, Moses, David, Daniel, and others, we find encouragement and strength from their relationship with God and all they endured.

If you've never read through the New Testament, I suggest you start there. The first four books: Matthew, Mark, Luke, and John are the four Gospels written by four different men about Jesus' birth, life and ministry, death, and resurrection.

Also, you may be wondering about which version to read, for we are truly blessed to have a number to choose from. The New International Version (NIV), The English Standard Version (ESV), The New Living Translation (NLT), and The New King James Version (NKJV) are among the most popular and are all great translations. They vary slightly in style or readability, so try each one until you land on one you like.

Be patient as you read. The Bible is like no other book. "The word of God is alive and active. Sharper than any double-edged sword, it penetrates even to dividing soul and spirit, joints and marrow; it judges the thoughts and attitudes of the heart." (Hebrews 4:12) Let God's Word permeate your heart. If you don't understand something, ask your pastor or another follower of Jesus, or simply keep reading. The Bible is its own best interpreter.

Finally, "Do not merely listen to [or read] the word, and so deceive yourselves. Do what it says." (James 1:22) Couple your reading of God's Word with faith and action. Understanding often follows obedience.

Scripture Reading: James 1:19-25

Personal Application:

- If you're not currently reading the Word daily, choose one of the Bible reading plans available on the internet or recommended by your pastor. Ask your wife or a friend to read the same plan so you can keep each other accountable and discuss what you've read.
- Pray for understanding and faith as you read God's Word and put it into practice in your life.

Week 26, Day 6: Pride: Man's Downfall

"Pride goes before destruction, a haughty spirit before a fall."
– Proverbs 16:18

Daryl Christensen has been a pro walleye-fisherman for many years. Fishing the major walleye-circuit, he has chalked-up many victories. As with all of us, sometimes success can lead to overconfidence. Such was the case for Daryl on an overcast June day several years ago.

Daryl and his amateur fishing partner were fishing a pro-am tournament on Mille Lacs Lake about six miles offshore. After searching all day, they finally found a "honey hole" where the walleyes were stacked up like cordwood.

Unfortunately, a thunderhead was making its way across the lake heading right toward their position. Daryl doubted they could find this specific "hot spot" again and ignored the advice of his partner to head for safety. As the dark clouds rumbled closer, Daryl joked, "I'm ready if God wants to take me." His partner replied, "Well, I'm not!" Trying to encourage the amateur, Daryl confidently assured him, "I've stayed out in similar situations before without a problem."

Then, just as Daryl was about to cast with his 8-½ foot graphite rod, a bolt of lightning hit his rod! The charge knocked Daryl off his feet and rendered him unconscious for a couple of minutes. When he woke up, the amateur urged him to see a doctor immediately. Daryl was in shock, and his pride was wounded. He insisted that they keep on fishing. But within a few hours the shock of the experience settled in and Daryl decided he'd better go to the doctor after all.

Pride is what turned Satan against God. The Lord says of the devil, "Your heart became proud on account of your beauty, and you corrupted your wisdom because of your splendor." (Ezekiel 28:17) It was also the prideful alure of becoming like God with which Satan tempted Adam and Eve. We might even say that pride is the basis of all sin against God and others.

Pride runs counter to God. James warns, "God opposes the proud but shows favor to the humble." (James 4:6) Pride also obscures logic, reason, and good judgment causing one to act foolishly. "Do you see a man wise in his own eyes? There is more hope for a fool than for him." (Proverbs 26:12)

Pride stirs up strife, acts selfishly, and wrecks relationships. Pride and love cannot share the same heart.

Like Daryl's lesson in pride above, lessons on pride are usually hard learned. "Humble yourselves, therefore, under God's mighty hand, that He may life you up in due time." (1 Peter 5:6)

Scripture Reading: Proverbs 6:6-19

Personal Application:

- In what area of your life are you most prone to pride?
  Ask the Lord for victory in that area.
- Specifically look for ways to practice humility today before
  God and others.

Week 26, Day 7: Weekly Recap and Prayer

On the seventh day of each week, use the **ACTS** acronym to spend time with the Lord reviewing and assessing your week and praying to God. (**A**=Adoration; **C**=Confession; **T**=Thanksgiving; **S**=Supplication)

First, look back over the previous six days for this week to remind yourself what you read and agreed to. Then, follow the ACTS pattern for prayer below. Finally, use the space below to journal what God is doing in your life and share this with a trusted spiritual partner.

Adoration: Simply spend time in adoration of the Lord. Praise Him and glorify His name. (See 1 Chronicles 29:10-13; Psalm 100; Romans 11:33-36.)

Confession: Confess your sins and shortcomings before God. ("If we confess our sins, he is faithful and just and will forgive us our sins and purify us from all unrighteousness." – 1 John 1:9) To confess (or agree with God) about your sin, implies that you are repentant and desperately want Him to change you.

Thanksgiving: Thank God for what He has done and is doing in your life and the life of your family. Give Him credit, for everything you have comes from Him. (See Psalm 136.)

Supplication: Supplication is just a fancy word for making your requests known to God. Based on the devotions of this past week and the things going on in your life right now, what do you want to ask Him for? "If you, then, though you are evil, know how to give good gifts to your children, how much more will your Father in heaven give good gifts to those who ask Him!" (Matthew 7:11)

Journal: What is God doing in your life right now?

Week 27, Day 1: What Makes a Great Team?

When the Miami Dolphins beat the Washington Redskins 14-7 in Super Bowl VII, they wrapped up a Perfect Season. No one could believe it! In fact, Miami's domination in the early 1970's was unparalleled in professional football. They were an absolutely amazing team.

Norm Evans, president and founder of the Professional Athletes Outreach, and former All-Pro right tackle, provided me with some great insights into how Miami built such a terrific team. "Our preparation for the Super Bowl run came when Head Coach Shula and Offensive Line Coach Monte Clark came on board in 1970." The six-foot-five-inch-248-pound former linemen told me that Shula knew every aspect of the game and instilled a sound work ethic in the men. He expected greatness and would not settle for mediocrity.

Shula and Clark began an intense program that built a real "esprit d' corps" among the players. Evans recalls, "Coach Clark insisted upon the offense line hanging out together during our off times. He believed that once we got to really know and respect each other we wouldn't want to let the other guy down."

To develop a truly great team, Shula took advantage of this professional pride and encouraged players to help one another become even greater. His definition of team didn't include the personal pronoun "I." He believed the team was never going to be better than its weakest link. Each player was expected to know his responsibilities on each play, but Shula also made them learn each other's assignments as well. He felt this would build accountability and unity.

If you study game films from that Perfect Season, you can see the intensity and pride each player had in his performance. They worked together as a finely tuned machine. The team's cohesiveness and unity allowed them to make the most of each play called.

The foundation had been laid for that Perfect Season. In 1972, the lack of serious injuries to key players, the fact that the team was fundamentally sound, and the excellent physical conditioning just proved too much for all their opponents. They won every game.

Although the Dolphins played what we call a "perfect season," they weren't perfect. Passes were missed, blocks fell short, fumbles were made, and handoffs were missed, yet they still won. We aren't perfect either. There are plenty of times we'll fail, but in Christ and truly working together we will win. We can win over temptation and sin, and we can win the battle for other's souls as we share the Gospel with them. "In Christ, we are more than conquerors."

As followers of Christ, we are God's team and we can learn a lot from that perfect season. And the stakes we're working with are much greater than those of a game of football.

Scripture Reading: Ephesians 4:1-6

Personal Application:

- What can you take away from this devotional in terms of your role as a member of the body of Christ? Who around you needs your "team" support right now?

Week 27, Day 2: Jesus Is Coming!

In Matthew 24 Jesus told His disciples about His great return.
He warned them (and us) to stay vigilant: "Therefore keep watch, because you do
not know on what day your Lord will come."
– Matthew 24:42

The signs of our time sure seem to parallel the many prophecies related to Christ's return. The political climate in the Middle East alone is clearly a pre-cursor to what the Bible calls "the end times." And with the end times comes the opportunity for revival. Ironically, the church in Iran is one of the fastest growing churches in the world, and many Muslims in other countries are coming to Christ as well.

Let's pray for spiritual awakening in our own country. It's been about 50 years since the last revival here (the Jesus People Movement) and we desperately need reviving! The Holy Spirit is at work in the lives of men, women, and evangelical churches around the globe. People are hungry for a relationship with the Lord.

With the coming of the Lord, we also know that He will judge those who have rejected Him. I was encouraged recently in this regard as I read through Ezekiel. In Ezekiel 33:11, we read, "As surely as I live, declares the Sovereign Lord, I take no pleasure in the death of the wicked, but rather that they turn from their ways and live."

Along these lines, in Romans 10:13, it says, "For everyone who calls on the name of the Lord will be saved." But then Paul asks, "How, then, can they call on the One they have not believed in? And how can they believe in the One of whom they have not heard? And how can they hear without someone preaching to them?" (vs. 14)

Those of us who know Christ know the answers to those questions. We are Christ's messengers. We are to broadcast the message of His love, grace, and mercy to the lost. No matter who we are, if we know Jesus, we have a story to tell.

When the apostle Paul had opportunities to speak to top officials in the Roman government, instead of preaching an eloquent sermon, he simply told his story of how Christ saved him. Any follower of Jesus can do that. All over the Gospels we find people that Jesus saved like the woman at the well (John 4) and the man possessed by demons (Mark 5). When they believed on Jesus, they immediately told others about Jesus. And if they could do it, so can we!

In Matthew 24:14, Jesus said, "And this gospel of the kingdom will be preached in the whole world as a testimony to all nations, and then the end will come." Let's speed the day of His return by sharing the message of salvation through Jesus with others.

Scripture Reading: 2 Peter 3:3-14

Personal Application:
- Write out your story how you came to Christ and rehearse it.
- Share your story with someone this week. Simply ask them,
  "Hey, can I tell you my story?"

Week 27, Day 3: Why Is There Suffering?

He who has not suffered has not lived at all.

Job had a season in his life when he suffered devastating loss. When Job asked God why, the Lord revealed to Job His sovereign control over everything. Job responded, "I know that You can do all things; no purpose of Yours can be thwarted. You asked, 'Who is this that obscures My plans without knowledge?' Surely, I spoke of things I did not understand… Therefore… I repent." (Job 42:2-6)

I have heard it said and asked, "Indeed, life is suffering. Contradiction, misfortune, disappointment, and heartbreak surrounded us. Why must we enter the Kingdom of God through many tribulations? Why does God allow suffering?"

I used to think I knew the answers to those questions, but life—now that I'm much closer to its end than to its beginning—has knocked most of them right out of my head. God chided Job and his friends, as Jesus chided His disciples, when they drew wrong conclusions about suffering.

In the face of suffering, I'm learning now to be more or less silent. When my friends tell me their lives are difficult, I answer "Of course." When they ask me why they're suffering, I shrug and tell them, "I don't know."

"I Shall Know Why" by Emily Dickinson

> I shall know why-when Time is over–
> And I have ceased to wonder why–
> Christ will explain each separate anguish
> In the fair schoolroom of the sky–
> He will tell me what "Peter" promised–
> And I – for wonder at his woe–
> I shall forget the drop of Anguish
> That scalds me now – that scalds me now!

Why life should be this way, I cannot say, but I do know this: It will not always be this way; there will be an end. Eternal glory lies ahead, as Peter promised, "after we have suffered for a little while." There, in that "eternal school room," our Lord will explain our every anguish. But I doubt, then, that we will care. In the awesome flood of His wisdom and love, and in the beauty of His presence, we shall forget our "present, light, momentary afflictions and discouraging trials."

Scripture Reading: 2 Corinthians 4:16-18

Personal Application:

- If you or your loved ones are suffering right now, I encourage you to lean into the Lord for strength. Trust Him with the purpose of suffering that may be beyond our grasp now.
- Consider how you may know the Lord even more intimately through your suffering.

Week 27, Day 4: Share with Those in Need

He almost didn't see the elderly woman, stranded on the side of the road in the rain. But even in the twilight, he could see she needed help. So, he pulled up in front of her Mercedes and got out.

Even with the smile on his face, she was scared. No one had stopped to help for the last hour. Was he going to hurt her? He didn't look safe; he looked poor and unkempt. He could see that she was frightened, and he knew how she felt. So, he said, "I'm here to help you, ma'am. Why don't you wait in the car where it's warm? By the way, my name is Bryan Anderson."

All she had was a flat tire, but for her, that was monumental. She popped the trunk and Bryan got the jack and spare. Then, he got down on his knees in the wet gravel feeling for where to place the jack. He skinned his knuckles a time or two.

With the tire changed and everything put away, the woman rolled down the window and told him that she was only passing through and she couldn't thank him enough for coming to her aid. Bryan just smiled. The lady asked how much she owed him. But Bryan declined her offer. This was not a job to him. This was helping someone in need, and God knows there were plenty who had given him a hand in the past. And now he was happy to be able to help her.

Bryan said, "If you really want to pay me back, the next time you see someone in need just help them and think of me." He waited until she started her car and drove off. It had been a cold and depressing day, but he felt good as he headed for home.

A few miles down the road the lady saw a small café and went in to grab a bite to eat. It was a dingy looking restaurant, but a waitress approached with a sweet smile. You'd never know she'd been on her feet all day. The lady noticed the waitress had to be nearly eight months pregnant, and she didn't let the strain and aches sour her attitude. Then the lady thought of Bryan.

When the lady finished her meal, she paid with a hundred-dollar bill. As the waitress went to get change, but the lady quickly slipped out the door and was gone. The waitress wondering where the lady could be, noticed something written on the napkin. Tears welled up in her eyes as she read, "You don't owe me anything. Somebody helped me today, and I am returning the favor by helping you." Under the napkin were four more $100 bills!

That night when the waitress got home and climbed into bed, she thought about the money and the note. How could that lady have known how much she and her husband needed that sum? With the baby due next month, it was going to be hard, but the near $500 gift would make the difference. She knew how worried her husband was as he lay sleeping next to her. She leaned over and gave him a soft kiss, "Everything's going to be all right. I love you, Bryan Anderson."

Scripture Reading: Romans 12:9-13

Personal Application:

- Think of those who have helped you in the past and thank the Lord for them.
- Look for opportunities to help others in need, expecting nothing in return.

Week 27, Day 5: Knowing God

Some years ago, after moving to the Inland Northwest, we settled on a five-acre parcel located next to the beautiful Spokane River. Much of our acreage was flat and was previously used as a horse pasture. To help reduce our property assessment, Louise and I decided to try our hands at ranching.

We purchased eight Barbados Black Belly sheep that eventually grew to adult size. This breed of sheep are exceptionally wary and are prized for their heavy coats and tremendous horns. We had hoped to eventually sell them to an exotic game farm where some hunter could harvest the animal for its meat and trophy horns.

I learned a lot about life—and God—from the upkeep of these critters. I planted seed and irrigated the land, so there was an ample food supply for them. We installed deep troughs that held enormous amounts of water. We fed the animals vitamins and antibiotics and enough enzymes to make even a rock grow.

You would think, in view of all the energy expended on their behalf, that these sheep would be grateful. Not so. Every time I came to the fence they would take off and run to the other side of the pasture. The only emotion they ever showed me was "fear." Even though I feed them twice a day, they respond to each visit as though I were from outer space. I could not convince them of my true care and concern.

To these sheep, I am their deity. I'm too big for them, my actions too incomprehensible, and my boundaries too restricting. They have no courage to trust me. They see my acts of kindness as cruelty. They see my attempts to doctor their wounds as painful and destructive. They see my attempts to keep them safe and warm (building shelters and fences) as obstacles and barriers. Perhaps to give them understanding, I would have to become a sheep!

As ridiculous as that sounds, for a man to become a sheep is nothing compared to the Omnipotent God coming to earth as a helpless baby. The God of all creation humbled himself to become a man so that He could show us what He is like—so that we could know our true need of His salvation. He so loved mankind that despite His power, His presence, His sufficiency, and His divine transcendence, God took on the form of a lowly human being.

Christ came to earth to proclaim God's desire to have intimate fellowship with His creation. It took Christ's death on the cross to provide the sacrifice necessary for us to enjoy direct access to God. He came that we might know Him!

Scripture Reading: Philippians 2:5-8

Personal Application:
- Take time today to simply worship the Lord Jesus. Thank Him for humbling Himself to be born as a baby, and live and die for your sins.
- Also, consider what you now know about God through Jesus Christ that you would not have otherwise known.

Week 27, Day 6: Playing on One String?

As I write this, we're still during the coronavirus lockdown. Almost daily for the past couple of months I've encouraged and counseled many who are struggling with the threat of the virus.

Fear and uncertainty cloud our focus and hope. What seemed so routine only a few months ago would be a welcome experience today. I've had folks come to me wondering if today's shopping, excursion to the post office, or delivering food to an elderly neighbor could thrust them into a life-changing pandemic.

In the midst of all this, I remembered a story that I thought might help us cope with challenges like these that we face. I first heard this story from Chuck Swindoll during a conference at Mt. Hermon in the Santa Cruz Mountains. The story is about the great violinist Niccolo Paganini, who was performing with a full orchestra one evening before a packed concert hall.

As he began the final piece, one of the strings on his violin snapped. In his genius, Paganini was able to continue playing the piece on the remaining three strings.

But a moment later, a second string snapped. Still, Paganini continued playing the concerto on the remaining two strings.

And then, a third string snapped! But still Paganini continued. He finished the piece, note for note, with one string on his violin. When the performance was over, the crowd rose in thunderous applause.

Paganini, ever the humble musician, raised his violin and boldly proclaimed, "Paganini and one string!" He cued the conductor, the orchestra began to play, and he performed his encore, note for note, with one string on his violin.

The time may come when you feel like you're down to one string — when your marriage is down to one string, or your financial future is down to one string, or your hope is down to one string.

Here's the good news. One string is enough. God's grace is that amazing. His mercy is that plentiful, His bounty and provisions that great, His power that invincible, His love, that unstoppable.

If you feel like one string is all you have left — and maybe it's about to snap — it's time to stop and let God do in your life what only He can do.

Scripture Reading: Matthew 11:28-30

Personal Application:

- In what area of your life do you feel like you're "playing on one string" right now?
  Give that area of your life to the Lord and trust Him with the outcome.

Week 27, Day 7: Weekly Recap and Prayer

On the seventh day of each week, use the **ACTS** acronym to spend time with the Lord reviewing and assessing your week and praying to God. (**A**=Adoration; **C**=Confession; **T**=Thanksgiving; **S**=Supplication)

First, look back over the previous six days for this week to remind yourself what you read and agreed to. Then, follow the ACTS pattern for prayer below. Finally, use the space below to journal what God is doing in your life and share this with a trusted spiritual partner.

Adoration: Simply spend time in adoration of the Lord. Praise Him and glorify His name. (See 1 Chronicles 29:10-13; Psalm 100; Romans 11:33-36.)

Confession: Confess your sins and shortcomings before God. ("If we confess our sins, he is faithful and just and will forgive us our sins and purify us from all unrighteousness." – 1 John 1:9) To confess (or agree with God) about your sin, implies that you are repentant and desperately want Him to change you.

Thanksgiving: Thank God for what He has done and is doing in your life and the life of your family. Give Him credit, for everything you have comes from Him. (See Psalm 136.)

Supplication: Supplication is just a fancy word for making your requests known to God. Based on the devotions of this past week and the things going on in your life right now, what do you want to ask Him for? "If you, then, though you are evil, know how to give good gifts to your children, how much more will your Father in heaven give good gifts to those who ask Him!" (Matthew 7:11)

Journal: What is God doing in your life right now?

Week 28, Day 1: The God of Miracles

In this fast-paced, high-tech world some people have forgotten that God is in the business of performing miracles. Mankind has explored the depths of the universe and the bottom of the seas. We have modified DNA and created artificial parts for the human body. Through technology, we can supply an endless stream of information and artificial intelligence. We've become self-sufficient. But the reality is, we still can't create miracles. We still get into situations where we're just stuck.

The recent coronavirus epidemic clearly demonstrated how helpless we really are. This disease has humbled nations and helped people realize that despite all our wisdom and advances in medicine, we desperately need a compassionate and forgiving Divine Healer.

God's name is Miracle. What man sees as impossible; He sees as possible. Before we come to a relationship with the living God, we describe unplanned situations as "chance" or "coincidence." As believers, we should look for God's hand in the unbelievable, impossible, and unimaginable.

Too often we let our own logic rather than God's Spirit take control of our lives. How many times do we miss the opportunity for a miracle because we're determined to "fix it" ourselves?

The prophet Isaiah had a reply for people who thought they could work their own miracles: "Therefore once more I will astound these people with wonder upon wonder; the wisdom of the wise will perish, the intelligence of the intelligent will vanish." (Isaiah 29:14) God is amazingly creative — He works outside the realm of normal reasoning! There are no boundaries to His love, His power, or His ability.

But during our personal storms, we often forget that God can handle them. We let fear take a foothold in our thinking. The opposite of fear is faith — faith that builds courage and hope.

Today, through the power of the Holy Spirit, Jesus continues to heal people. He heals bodies, marriages, broken hearts, financial messes… you name it! He is the ultimate comforter, encourager, healer, and provider. He is our advocate.

Sometimes we "miss the miracle." Too often God's mighty miracles are overshadowed by the boasting of man's accomplishments, flashy technology, or sizzling sideline stories. Don't expect the media to report on miracles. You may have to read between the lines to see them, but you can be sure, God is still in the business of making miracles… everyday!

God's Word gives us so many examples of how our Father works through miracles. We are to "Remember the wonders He has done, His miracles, and the judgments He pronounced." (Psalm 105:5)

Scripture Reading: Ephesians 3:14-21

Personal Application:

- What miracles have you experienced? What have those miracles taught you about God?
- Share those stories with others with the intent to bring glory to God and encourage others.

Week 28, Day 2: Is Your Glass Half Empty?

"Do not conform any longer to the pattern of this world but be transformed by the renewing of your mind. Then you will be able to test and approve what God's will is, his good, pleasing and perfect will." (Romans 12:2)

I'm tired of the doom and gloom stories we get from the media. Even those folks who are supposed to cheer us up are in a real funk. The late-night shows that used to entertain us and make us laugh are filled with discontent, cynicism, and plain old grumpiness.

As I write this, we are trying to cope with the effects of the coronavirus pandemic. And by the time you read this, there will be other issues to be negative about. Yes, the economy is in shambles. Yes, we wish the wars were over so our brave troops could come home. Yes, our leaders have let us down.

But in all this there is so much to be thankful for. Knowing Christ and living in a free America has so many benefits. Instead of tracking with the pessimists, let's remind ourselves that our greatest hope and joy are ours in Christ Jesus.

If you are living a paltry life, resolve to stop it today. Expect great things to happen. Trust God and confidently receive His abundant blessings. Do not think "lack." Instead, think prosperity, abundance, and the best of everything. God wants to give us, His children, every good thing. Don't hinder His blessings with negative thinking. Have a sense of curiosity! God wants us to discover His abundant and eternal love and peace.

The prophet Isaiah reminds us to trust God and fix our thoughts on Him. "You will keep in perfect peace all who trust in you, all whose thoughts are fixed on you!" (Isaiah 26:3 NLT) If our minds are filled with negative thoughts and an outlook of defeat, we are bound to be in a state of mental unrest, even turmoil, and there will be no inner peace.

Let's fix our minds and gaze upon the One who died on Calvary's Cross so that we might be able to experience His great peace and grace. Let's not devalue the suffering He went through by ignoring the peace, love, and calm He offers.

Christ's resurrection, among other things, represents the new life we can experience when He is in control of our lives. He will guide and direct us only when we allow His affirming Spirit to control our lives daily, minute by minute. Remember, Jesus calmed the stormy seas for His 1st-Century disciples, and He can calm the seas of despair for us, His modern-day disciples.

Scripture Reading: Philippians 4:4-9

Personal Application:
- What is stealing your joy and peace right now?
- List all you are thankful for and spend time thanking the Lord for all He has done and is doing in your life and the lives of your loved ones. Purpose to speak only what is fitting for a disciple of Jesus.

Week 28, Day 3: Follow Me!

When Jesus first called His disciples, He asked them to follow Him. And just before He ascended into heaven, He challenged those same disciples to follow Him. As His disciples, we are to follow Him. Following Jesus is a way of life, and not merely a one-time decision.

When we follow Jesus, He leads us in the attack against the temptations and spiritual battles we face. When we are following Him, we become more and more like Him over time. We learn to desire the things He desires and to shun the things He abhors. In fact, in His presence we cannot remain the same! It's impossible to truly follow Jesus and continue in our old sinful patterns.

Here is a snapshot of what it looks like to follow Jesus: "Therefore, I urge you, brothers and sisters, in view of God's mercy, to offer your bodies as a living sacrifice, holy and pleasing to God—this is your true and proper worship. Do not conform to the pattern of this world but be transformed by the renewing of your mind. Then you will be able to test and approve what God's will is—his good, pleasing and perfect will." (Romans 12:1-2)

And as we yield ourselves to Christ and He changes us, He "uses us to spread the aroma of the knowledge of Him everywhere" (2 Corinthians 2:14). We become His ambassadors imploring others to be reconciled to God (2 Corinthians 5:20). This is what it means to make disciples. We simply represent Christ to others through our life and words.

But I'm afraid we often complicate disciple-making. Many think they must attain some level of spiritual maturity or attend classes or even a unique call to ministry in order to make disciples. But all these misconceptions serve as distractions. They're decoys keeping us from sharing Christ with others right now, right where we are.

Consider these examples from Scripture:

When Andrew met Jesus, "The first thing Andrew did was to find his brother Simon (Peter) and tell him, 'We have found the Messiah' (that is, the Christ)" (John 1:41).

When the woman at the well met Jesus, she ran back into town and said to the people, "Come, see a man who told me everything I ever did. Could this be the Messiah?" And many believed in Jesus because of her testimony.

When Jesus healed the man possessed by demons, he begged to go with Jesus. "Jesus did not let him, but said, 'Go home to your own people and tell them how much the Lord has done for you, and how he has had mercy on you.' So the man went away and began to tell… how much Jesus had done for him." (Mark 5:19-20)

If you know Jesus, then you have a story to share with others.

Scripture Reading: John 1:40-45

Personal Application:
- Pray each day that the Lord would use you to represent Him well to others through your life and words. Share your story freely and watch what God does!

Week 28, Day 4: Riding the "Rapids" of Child-Rearing

When my sons were about fourteen, our scout troop decided to take a whitewater rafting trip down the infamous North Fork of the American River. We had never experienced this type of adventure and were looking forward to the outing with great delight. Our troop arrived at the water's edge on a beautiful spring day. The unusually heavy rain and snowfall of the previous winter had really swollen the river.

We slipped our raft into the placid current and slowly drifted downstream. The guide provided instructions and discussed how we might handle various situations. We cheerfully paddled along, enjoying fellowship, and maneuvering through the first several easy rapids. It was about mid-day when we started tackling the class-five rapids with notorious names like "Satan's Cesspool," "Triple Threat," and "Flower's Rock." Despite our great plans and advanced study, once we were in the fray, it was "every man for himself." At times we couldn't even paddle. We just had to hang on!

Similarly, the currents of early childhood years are often relatively calm and enjoyable. Plans are made, books are read, and parenting doesn't seem like it's going to be a big problem. Then, we are thrown into the turbulent teen years. Sometimes it feels like all we can do is hang on. It can be quite scary and discouraging.

It helps to remember that we aren't alone in this parenting job. There are those who have gone before us who can encourage and counsel us. Always there are other parents facing similar challenges. Family, church, and friends can be a great support network. Most importantly we must remember that God is in control.

I have a real passion to encourage others in this area. As I survey Scripture and evaluate strong families in today's culture, I have discovered five important ingredients:

- Appreciation and Encouragement: Encourage one another.
- Communication: Talk about your day, life, and God.
- Time: Share life together; that's how disciples are made.
- Commitment: Be devoted to one another and love unconditionally.
- Spiritual Wellness: Families that have a sense of a greater good or power in life find purpose and have a moral compass.

Above all else, Jesus Christ is the one who "keeps us in the boat" when things get rough. Let's keep Him in the center of everything we do. Let's let Him be our guide. And no matter how rough it gets, let's all hang on!

Scripture Reading: Deuteronomy 6:4-7

Personal Application:

- Many men find it difficult to talk to their children about the Lord. But it's important to be transparent with them about your walk with Jesus. Tell your children your story—how you came to Christ and what He has done and is doing in your life.

Week 28, Day 5: We've a Wall to Build

The life of Nehemiah provides a valuable lesson on how prayer and trust in the sovereign God can heal a nation. Nehemiah was serving as a cupbearer for King Artaxerxes in Babylon when he received news that the Jews who had returned to Jerusalem after their exile were "in great trouble and disgrace." The wall of Jerusalem was also broken down and its gates burned.

Nehemiah says, "When I heard these things, I sat down and wept. For some days I mourned and fasted and prayed before the God of heaven." (Nehemiah 1:4) Instead of complaining or blaming others, he got on his knees and cried out to God. He confessed the sins of his people and pleaded with God to grant him favor in what he was about to ask the king.

One day, the king noticed that Nehemiah was preoccupied and saddened by something. Nehemiah shared the plight of his homeland and the anguish within his heart. God moved in Artaxerxes' spirit and caused him to react favorably toward Nehemiah. Nehemiah found favor with the king and he released him to go and assist the Jews with rebuilding Jerusalem (Nehemiah 2:1-6).

When Nehemiah arrived in Jerusalem, he quickly discovered that the work was by no means limited to building the physical wall. He had to contend with constant interference and harassment from the enemies of the Jews, try to keep up the spirit of the downcast Jews, and remind them of their need to follow and obey God.

Like ancient Israel, America has its share of sins and "broken walls" in need of repair. Divorce, drug abuse, pornography, abortion, homosexuality, and a host of other evils have left us with deep scars and placed our country in great distress. We desperately need a great healing that can only happen if His people humble themselves, repent of their sins, and cry out to Him.

We need to sit down and weep upon hearing these things. We need to mourn and fast and beg God to work in our hearts and those of our nation. We desperately need a spiritual awakening—that's our wall to build. Like Nehemiah, God may call upon many of us to step into the fray and assume a leadership role to help bring about this spiritual awakening.

Having said that, you may or may not consider yourself a leader in this regard. There's still a job for you. Because of the harassment in rebuilding the walls of Jerusalem, Nehemiah had to assign some to build while others guarded the city. He also dealt with social ills by helping the poor and deal with those who were taking advantage of their fellow Jews. There's plenty of work for all.

You and I are workers in "God's field." We have a job to do representing Christ to a fallen world. Will you join me?

Scripture Reading: Matthew 5:13-16

Personal Application:
- Spend time mourning over the sins of our land and asking the Lord what He would have you do.
- Now, follow through with what God has put on your heart.

Week 28, Day 6: Moral Purity

In a very sobering passage in 2 Peter 2, the apostle blasts "those who follow the corrupt desire of the flesh." (vs. 10) Then, Peter goes on to describe their character. Among other things, he says of these people they have "eyes full of adultery." (vs. 14)

This isn't about merely avoiding the act of adultery. Jesus said, "Anyone who looks at a woman lustfully has already committed adultery with her in his heart." (Matthew 5:28)

Men, this is not a character trait we ever want God to attribute to us! In the way we view women, we do not want to have "eyes full of adultery." We don't want to lust after women or look at them in a lewd way. It demeans women and harms us. We want to view women through pure eyes as Christ does, not as a sex object but as individuals whom Christ loves.

You may feel uncomfortable reading today's devotional, but this is a topic that affects nearly all men. Even men whom I esteem as godly followers of Christ have confided in me that they struggle with lust at times. So, if you also wrestle with lust sometimes, you are not alone.

As we discuss this topic, remember that it not a sin to be tempted, but rather to yield to temptation. James wrote, "Each person is tempted when they are dragged away by their own evil desire and enticed. Then, after desire has conceived, it gives birth to sin; and sin, when it is full-grown, gives birth to death." (James 1:14-15)

We can be certain that even Jesus was tempted in this way as well, for the Scripture says, "He was tempted in every way, just as we are—yet He did not sin." (Hebrews 4:15) This fact should encourage us greatly. Christ not only offers grace and mercy to forgive sins, but He also offers us the grace and strength to *avoid* sin and to establish godly patterns of living.

Here are some suggestions that have helped me in this regard:

- When you see a scantily clad, or provocatively dressed woman, avert your eyes and look at her face, or just look away altogether.
- When you are tempted with thoughts or mental images of a sexual nature, reject those thoughts, and direct your mind to the Lord.
- Avoid all pornographic sites and pornographic material completely. Be careful what movies or TV shows you watch. Don't bait your lust or feed your flesh.
- Be careful where you go and what you do. Always set yourself up for a win in this regard. Only a fool puts himself in temptation's way to see if he can resist it.
- Do as Job did, "I made a covenant with my eyes not to look lustfully at a young woman." (Job 31:1)

Keep following Jesus and imitate His life in your thoughts as well as your actions.

Scripture Reading: Galatians 5:19-26

Personal Application:
- Put the above suggestions into practice until they are habitual in your life.

Week 28, Day 7: Weekly Recap and Prayer

On the seventh day of each week, use the **ACTS** acronym to spend time with the Lord reviewing and assessing your week and praying to God. (**A**=Adoration; **C**=Confession; **T**=Thanksgiving; **S**=Supplication)

First, look back over the previous six days for this week to remind yourself what you read and agreed to. Then, follow the ACTS pattern for prayer below. Finally, use the space below to journal what God is doing in your life and share this with a trusted spiritual partner.

Adoration: Simply spend time in adoration of the Lord. Praise Him and glorify His name. (See 1 Chronicles 29:10-13; Psalm 100; Romans 11:33-36.)

Confession: Confess your sins and shortcomings before God. ("If we confess our sins, he is faithful and just and will forgive us our sins and purify us from all unrighteousness." – 1 John 1:9) To confess (or agree with God) about your sin, implies that you are repentant and desperately want Him to change you.

Thanksgiving: Thank God for what He has done and is doing in your life and the life of your family. Give Him credit, for everything you have comes from Him. (See Psalm 136.)

Supplication: Supplication is just a fancy word for making your requests known to God. Based on the devotions of this past week and the things going on in your life right now, what do you want to ask Him for? "If you, then, though you are evil, know how to give good gifts to your children, how much more will your Father in heaven give good gifts to those who ask Him!" (Matthew 7:11)

Journal: What is God doing in your life right now?

Week 29, Day 1: "Bearing" Under Trials

I enjoy the beautiful, award-winning photography of Idaho photographer Tim Christie. He has a way of capturing the outdoors on film that truly honors and glorifies the Creator. Of course, capturing these shots can be quite an adventure… sometimes more than he bargained for.

During one of his spring safaris in Glacier Park, Tim noticed a few whitetail deer casually feeding along the roadway. Grabbing his camera, Tim quietly slid out of his truck. The deer continued to feed into the woods with Tim in gentle pursuit, snapping pictures. Eventually, through his viewfinder, he noticed a deer suddenly startle. As the deer scampered off, Tim heard a branch snap in the woods behind him. He turned to see a large sow black bear, making her way towards him. Considering taking a picture of this bear, he suddenly became aware of two bear cubs to his right.

The situation became clear to him; this mama bear was in no mood for a casual photo shoot. She was doing what comes naturally to any mother, protecting her young. Tim dropped his camera and ran to the nearest tree. As he began to climb the tree the bear came after him, popping its jaws and growling like a wounded hound. Tim and the bear kept climbing higher in the tree, when at last the bear grabbed his foot. Its sharp teeth pierced the sole of Tim's tennis shoe like a hot knife going through butter. The bear pulled and tugged at Tim's foot with no regard for Tim's shouts. "It seemed like we were having a tug of war to see who would end up with my leg," he recalled. Suddenly, the shoe released from his foot, and the bear dropped from the tree, hitting the ground with a thud. Tim continued his climb as the mother bear growled and roared with disdain. After an angry fit, the bear rejoined her cubs and disappeared in the woods. Tim waited in the tree for two hours, climbed down, pulled his sneaker on, snatched up his camera and dashed back to the truck.

Whether we're outdoorsmen or couch-potatoes, everyone faces trials in life. When troubles come our way, the Lord asks us to do two things: trust and endure. Too many times, when we face problems, we scramble, trying every which way we can to fix it. Then, when all else fails, we pray. God asks us to come to Him first. We are to trust in His Word and His promises. Next, we are to endure. When we lean on God through trying times, He will strengthen us. His Word is full of encouragement, reminding us of the hostility Jesus endured so that we would not give up. The next time you're "stuck up a tree," don't give in, don't give up, and don't look down! Cry out to Jesus. God's loving hand will reach down and either remove the trial or carry you through it.

Scripture Reading: Hebrews 12:2-3

Personal Application:
- What trials are you currently facing? What Scriptures encourage you through them?
- Prepare for suffering and trials by continually trusting the Lord and claiming His promises.

Week 29, Day 2: A Model for Christian Living

Ikigai (I-ka-guy) is a Japanese word that translates roughly to "a reason for being, encompassing joy, a sense of purpose and meaning and a feeling of well-being." The *Ikigai* model has been used to teach leadership principles and help direct people into their calling in life. In business, *Ikigai* is thought to yield the highest levels of employee engagement and productivity while also fostering job satisfaction and loyalty to the organization. Many believe if you follow the essence of this model you will have a long and happy life.

Along these same lines, next to Christ, Solomon was the wisest (and one of the richest) men who ever lived. With all that he had at his disposal, he engaged in an outlandish experiment in which he denied himself nothing. He availed himself of every pleasure and entertainment imaginable. He applied himself to learning and all sorts of knowledge. He built incredible structures renowned for their design and beauty. Yet, apart from a relationship with God, he found all those pursuits meaningless (Ecclesiastes 1-2).

Jesus warned us, "Watch out! Be on your guard against all kinds of greed; life does not consist in an abundance of possessions." (Luke 12:15) He also said, "You cannot serve two masters… You cannot serve both God and money." (Matthew 6:24)

In Jesus' day as today, many seek happiness and ultimate meaning in life in numerous ways like those tried by Solomon. In our pursuit of meaning and happiness we've made so much of our careers, our fitness, our possessions, fame, fortune, sex, sports, and entertainments of all kinds. But as with Solomon, we discover in the end that none of that provides ultimate purpose. Purpose, meaning, and lasting happiness comes only through relationship with Jesus Christ. Jesus said, "I have come that [you] may have life, and have it to the full." (John 10:10)

Ikigai may offer a good business model, but like all the other worldly pursuits it cannot provide the purpose and meaning in life for which we all long. I think Dr. Billy Graham had it right when he proposed the following guidelines for maintaining good spiritual health and a happy life.[2]

1. Read your Bible daily.
2. Learn the secret of prayer.
3. Rely constantly on the Holy Spirit.
4. Attend church regularly.
5. Be a witnessing Christian.
6. Be a wholesome Christian.
7. Let love be the ruling principle of your life.
8. Be an obedient Christian.
9. Learn how to meet temptation.
10. Live above your circumstances.

Scripture Reading: Romans 12

Personal Application:
- To what extent are you currently enjoying your life? Which of the above guidelines would help bring you closer in your walk with Christ?

---

2   "Guidelines for Christian Living" is excerpted from *Peace with God* by Billy Graham, published in 1953, revised and expanded in 1984.

Week 29, Day 3: Discouraged and Disappointed

Often when we feel discouragement settling in on our spirit it comes because of disappointment from unmet expectations. Satan's goal is to weaken, dishearten, discourage, and make us lose hope.

Such was the case for the Israelites because of unbelief at Kadesh Barnea. The Lord had led them to this point to enter and take the land He was giving them. But because of their unbelief and disobedience, He sentenced them to wander in the desert for 40 years until that generation died off before He would allow them into the Promised Land.

After those 40 years, as Joshua prepared to occupy the land that God had given them, he carefully took note of God's instructions. God encouraged Joshua and his men to "Be strong and courageous!" (Joshua 1:6,7,9). God repeated this command three times anticipating their fear in meeting the giants, walled cities, and armies of the land.

Forty years earlier, it had been those factors that had discouraged and disheartened Israel from taking the land then. The factors that we face are different, but often no less intimidating. These feelings can demoralize us and keep us from conquering our fears to tackle tough challenges.

Therefore we must remember that our Omnipotent Father reigns and is in control. Even when life seems totally out of control, God has a game plan that will empower and grow us to trust in Him. We need not be discouraged or disheartened like the ten original spies who would not trust God for the results and obey Him. In fact, they were so discouraged that they wanted to choose a new leader to take them back to Egypt!

Instead God wants us to be strong and courageous; to rejoice in knowing that the God of our salvation is our strength and if we lean on Him, He will give us the power to overcome those discouraging times.

Words are easier written or read than applied in our daily living. But our constant battle as believers is to completely trust Him who is able to help us overcome the threats and challenges life brings. D.L. Moody the great evangelist said, "Real true faith is man's weakness leaning on God's strength."

The book of Isaiah is filled with great promises from a man who regularly faced the twins of discouragement and disappointment. Isaiah states: "He gives power to the weak, and to those who have no might He increases strength." (Isaiah 40:29)

Scripture Reading: Habakkuk 3:18-19; Psalm 18:16-36

Personal Application:
- In what area of your life are you currently experiencing disappointment and discouragement?
- Let the promises of God from His Word wash over you and strengthen you.
- Share your struggles with a spiritual confidant and pray together.

Week 29, Day 4: Looking Back

Early in his career (1989) songwriter/singer Garth Brooks wrote a song called "The Dance." In 1991 The Academy of Country Music Awarded him the Song of the Year for this piece. Why was this song such a hit? Even today it is one of his most requested songs to be sung in his concerts. Let us look at some of the lyrics:

Looking back on the memory of
The dance we shared beneath the stars above
For a moment all the world was right
How could I have known you'd ever say goodbye
And now I'm glad I didn't know
The way it all would end the way it all would go
Our lives are better left to chance I could have missed the pain
But I'd have to miss the dance.

America swarmed around the sweet melody and words that stimulated people to reflect upon memories of the past. Unfortunately, theologically, the song lacks in that our lives are not better "left to chance" so we can miss the pain.

Regardless of how old you are, all of us have accumulated a sizable storehouse of memories – some sweet and some you wish you could forget. Memories seem to resurface even without provocation at a moment's notice when we experience a familiar odor, sound, song, picture, or event.

The memories that are sweet often bring a smile to our face. They add a special sense of peace and harmony to life that can lift-up an otherwise bad day. But what about those memories that have been crushing experiences or sour disappointments. The recollections of unfulfilled goals, disappointing conversations, misunderstandings uncorrected, and events that went a different direction than we had hoped. They too can consume our mind if we let them take residence and steal the joy God intended us to have.

Throughout his letters, the apostle Paul reminds us of three powerful thoughts. First, "Forgetting what is behind and straining toward what is ahead, I press on toward the goal to win the prize for which God has called me heavenward in Christ Jesus." (Philippians 3:13-14)

Second, Paul urges us to "Rejoice in the Lord always." (Philippians 4:4) Finally, the apostle reminds us to present all our requests to God and to center our thoughts only on what is "excellent or praiseworthy." (Philippians 4:4-8) These three approaches help us cloud out of our hearts and minds the misfortunes and flops of the past.

Scripture Reading: Philippians 3:1-14

Personal Application:
- As bad memories surface, get in the habit of turning them over to the Lord. Ask Him to take them from you. Pursue Him each day to build new memories characterized by Christlikeness.

Week 29, Day 5: Grandparenting

Based on interviews and studies with children and grandparents it becomes clear that children need their grandparents and vice-versa. The bond between grandparents and grandchildren is second in emotional power and influence only to the relationship between parents and children. Grandparents affect the lives of their grandchildren, for good or ill, simply because they exist. Unfortunately, a lot of grandparents ignore this fact to the emotional deprivation of the young.

One study showed that of the children studied, only five percent reported close, regular contact with at least one grandparent. The vast majority see their grandparents only infrequently, not because they live too far away, but because the grandparents have chosen to remain emotionally distant. These children appear to be hurt, angry, and very perceptive about their grandparents. One child said, "I'm just a charm on grandma's bracelet."

Positive roles that grandparents play include caretaker, storyteller, family historian, mentor, wizard, confidant, negotiator between child and parent, and model for the child's own old age. When a child has a strong emotional tie to a grandparent, he enjoys a kind of immunity—he does not have to perform for grandparents the way he must for his parents, peers, and teachers. The love of grandparents comes with no behavioral strings attached. The emotional conflicts that often occur naturally between children and parents usually do not exist between grandparents and grandchildren.

Ten Insights about Grandparenting

1. Grandparenting comes not from the head but from the heart.
2. Children have more need of models than critics.
3. Perfection is in the eyes of those who wear blinders like a doting grandparent.
4. The joys of a grandparent-grandchild relationship are best seen in the security of the trust and love they bring.
5. Grandparents can regard a child's blunders merely as stepping-stones to success.
6. Grandparents have the magic of putting fun back into life.
7. No family member can encourage, support, and boost a child's self-esteem like a grandparent.
8. Nothing brings greater joy and helps stem the tide of negativism than entering together into a world of fantasy and wonder.
9. Invest in your grandchildren they are a renewal of life, a little bit of us going on into the future.
10. A child's first impressions of who God might be comes from the love they experience from a parent and grandparent.

Scripture Reading: 2 Timothy 1:3-5; 3:14-15

Personal Application:

- If you are a grandfather, what can you do today to cultivate your relationship with your grandchildren? If you're a parent, what can you do to involve your parents in the lives of your children?

Week 29, Day 6: Take a Stand

Nowadays, we face many social and peer pressures to conform and be compliant. People tell us "not to rock the boat," but to trust political leaders and media sources that try to intimidate us. It is noteworthy when someone stands up for their faith and convictions, others gain confidence to join with us, for courage is contagious. Such was the case with Moses in Exodus 31-34. He was a man who took a stand for what God was telling him to do.

During their time in the desert the Israelites had become frustrated, confused, and genuinely angry about their plight of being without many of the comforts they once enjoyed in Egypt. Moses approached God to ask for direction. God was clear and direct – "Stand your ground Moses and follow Me."

When Moses took a stand, he found that he wasn't alone. It's the same today. Standing up for what is right in the world today can be challenging. Yet when we take a stand for what we believe and face the ridicule and conflict directly we will encourage others with the same convictions to speak out and affirm their convictions as well.

Moses took that public stand. His courage moved the Levites, who had not participated in the others' sins but had stood by silently, to join him openly. In this way, he ultimately convinced the wandering nation to seek God and not the idols they worshipped. When conscience convinces us that something is wrong, we need to follow Moses' lead and take a stand for our convictions. And if other committed believers take on the role of Moses, let's be ready, as the levities were, to support them.

We have constant opportunities to influence others at school, in our work, at church, during gatherings with relatives or neighbors, and within our social circles. Some of us, like Moses and Aaron, may have a position of authority, and the best way to influence others is by standing for what God has shown us and following His Word. Moses met with God regularly to receive His counsel and we need to do the same.

Our impact on the lives of others will be directly proportional to the time we spend face-to-face with God. The aura of God's presence and power in our lives will go with us. He is the stronghold of our lives (Psalm 27:1), He intercedes for us (Hebrews 7:25), He is our fortress and shield (Psalm 144:2), He is our refuge (Psalm 91:1-2), and a Wonderful Counselor (Isaiah 9:6).

At the same time, Paul warns, "Don't have anything to do with foolish and stupid arguments, because you know they produce quarrels. And the Lord's servant must not be quarrelsome but must be kind to everyone, able to tech, not resentful." (2 Timothy 2:23-24) It takes much wisdom to know which battles to stand up for and which to ignore. So, pray for God's wisdom and seek counsel from His Word and other godly people.

Scripture Reading: Exodus 31:1-11

Personal Application:

- What is it that you need to take a stand on that will influence an outcome for others?

Week 29, Day 7: Weekly Recap and Prayer

On the seventh day of each week, use the **ACTS** acronym to spend time with the Lord reviewing and assessing your week and praying to God. (**A**=Adoration; **C**=Confession; **T**=Thanksgiving; **S**=Supplication)

First, look back over the previous six days for this week to remind yourself what you read and agreed to. Then, follow the ACTS pattern for prayer below. Finally, use the space below to journal what God is doing in your life and share this with a trusted spiritual partner.

Adoration: Simply spend time in adoration of the Lord. Praise Him and glorify His name. (See 1 Chronicles 29:10-13; Psalm 100; Romans 11:33-36.)

Confession: Confess your sins and shortcomings before God. ("If we confess our sins, he is faithful and just and will forgive us our sins and purify us from all unrighteousness." – 1 John 1:9) To confess (or agree with God) about your sin, implies that you are repentant and desperately want Him to change you.

Thanksgiving: Thank God for what He has done and is doing in your life and the life of your family. Give Him credit, for everything you have comes from Him. (See Psalm 136.)

Supplication: Supplication is just a fancy word for making your requests known to God. Based on the devotions of this past week and the things going on in your life right now, what do you want to ask Him for? "If you, then, though you are evil, know how to give good gifts to your children, how much more will your Father in heaven give good gifts to those who ask Him!" (Matthew 7:11)

Journal: What is God doing in your life right now?

Week 30, Day 1: Age is No Excuse

I have enjoyed the pleasure that came from several friends and mentors in my life who were in their later years. I remember a dear acquaintance that allowed me to do my college internship that turned into a full-time job with the East Bay Regional Park District in California. He also hired me to replace him when I came to Moraga, CA. to serve for ten years as Deputy Town Manager. In his late 70's he went on to be distinguished as the California Director of Parks and then the National Parks Director under President Ronald Reagan.

I had another mentor for over forty-five years who upon retirement served at his church in various capacities until the Lord called him home in his 80s. And I think of another godly man who has impacted my life. At the age of 90, he is still going strong and flies his Citation Jet and heads a large company.

During King David's time there was a great man named Barzillai. Barzillai had provided for David when he fled from his son Absalom. At eighty years of age, he supported David as David returned to Jerusalem after Absalom was killed. David asked Barzillai to return with him to Jerusalem so he could provide for him in his old age, but Barzillai declined David's offer saying that he wished to spend his final days at home. Barzillai serves as a symbol for those many Christian seniors who give generously to God's work. Most churches and Christian ministries today could not continue without the totality of the dedication and determination of these senior committed Christians sharing their gifts and talents.

Many older believers contribute not only with their wealth but with their time. Every year, older adults contribute billions of hours of service in their communities saving many billions of dollars in labor costs. But many churches and Christian enterprises are stalling out. Approximately, 3,700 churches close each year, up to half are failed church-plants. We need those physically capable seniors to become people like Barzillai.

The Bible encourages us in many ways to be servants for the King. "Do not be afraid; do not be discouraged, for the LORD your God will be with you wherever you go." (Joshua 1:9) God will finish what He started, for Scripture says, "Being confident of this, that He who began a good work in you will carry it on to completion until the day of Christ Jesus." (Philippians 1:6) You and I can only do so much, but God can do the impossible, and he is not through with you yet.

Scripture Reading: Joshua 14:6-13; Titus 2:2

Personal Application:
- Who are or have been the older mentors in your life?
- In what ways can you honor the older men who have invested in you?
- What are the spiritual gifts, talents, resources, and desires God has given you that you can use to further His Kingdom?

Week 30, Day 2: The Scapegoat

Have you ever heard someone refer to a person as a scapegoat? A scapegoat is a person blamed for the wrongdoings of others. Maybe it's that weird uncle who seems to mess up all the time, or the athlete who chokes on a critical play, or a person at work who gets the blame for everything that goes wrong.

In the book of Leviticus Chapter 16 we read about the concept of the scapegoat. On the Day of Atonement (Yom Kippur), the Jewish high priest selected two goats. One was sacrificed, the other, the scapegoat, was set free. But before releasing the scapegoat, the high priest symbolically placed the sins of the people on it by laying his hands on its head. This scapegoat would be taken far away from camp and released into the wilderness.

Hebrews tells us that the blood of bulls and goats could never take away sin. Those sacrifices were merely a foreshadow of what God would do through His Son Jesus Christ. Isaiah wrote of Christ, "We all, like sheep, have gone astray, each of us has turned to our own way; and the Lord has laid on Him [Christ] the iniquity of us all." (Isaiah 53:6) And 1 John 2:2 says that Jesus Christ "is the atoning sacrifice for our sins."

Christ's sacrifice on Calvary's Cross pardoned and canceled our debt and sin. God expresses His infinite grace and forgiveness through the sacrifice of Jesus in which He took on the sins of mankind. Only Jesus, the perfect Lamb of God, could take on the sins of all mankind for all time.

If perhaps you think that God cannot possibly forgive you for the kind or scope of sins you've committed, then consider Romans 5:20. That passage tells us that we cannot sin beyond the scope of God's grace, because where sin abounds, grace increases even more to bring eternal life to all who put their faith in Him.

God delights in providing His love and grace to each of us. We are forgiven for every sin – past, present, and future. Grace is simply defined as unmerited favor from a loving God who desires for each of us to know and experience His love and fellowship with Him. Christ bore our sins that we might know the joy and peace that freedom from sin and guilt brings. Where we were once enemies of God, Jesus reconciles us to God and makes us His children.

Let the assurance of your salvation fill your heart with gladness and thanksgiving. May we be filled with reverence and appreciation to our loving Father and to Jesus who gave Himself for us. And since you've experienced the cleansing and forgiveness of Christ's death for you, live for Him in that grace and share that good news freely with others as well.

Scripture Reading: Romans 5:12-21

Personal Application:

- Have you accepted God's grace in your life? If so, you are completely and utterly forgiven.
- Seeing that you are forgiven by God's grace, how does this impact the way you live your life from now on? (See Romans 6:11-4.)

Week 30, Day 3: A Man After God's Heart

I thoroughly enjoyed all my fishing and hunting adventures with my good friend, Jeff Klippenes. Born and raised in the backwoods of Northern Minnesota, he has a wealth of outdoor experience that adds to the excitement of every outing. One of my favorite memories of Jeff begins with his decision to purchase a consignment boat from me.

After experiencing the thrill of fishing out of a bass boat, Jeff asked if he could buy my boat. I was excited to know that this beautiful boat would have a new home in his garage. Shortly after he took delivery, Jeff planned an outing with a mutual friend. I had no idea that Jeff's Viking bloodline would come out the way it did. To him there is no water that cannot be conquered!

He took his low-profile bass boat out in the San Francisco Bay for a sturgeon fishing trip. In the late afternoon, unexpected gale winds came up and swamped the boat. He called me at about 4:00 PM. "Hey Jim, this is Jeff... Uh, you probably can't guess what happened to our boat today. It seems that it really doesn't handle very well in fierce winds and heavy seas."

I pressed him for further explanation. With humor in his voice, he continued, "I'm okay and everything is alright. The boat is full of water and tied up to a dock in a restricted area of the Naval Weapons Station in Antioch."

I could tell by Jeff's attitude that, while he was shaken, he wasn't going to let these circumstances detour his love for fishing or for God. Despite his financial loss and personal embarrassment, Jeff praised the Lord, "God was really good to us Jim. He watched over us and brought us safely back home."

That evening I met Jeff down at the marina. We bailed out his submerged rig and towed it back to his trailer with my new boat. Throughout the evening, Jeff's attitude was positive and encouraging. His heart was right before God as he honored the relationship he had with his Heavenly Father, understanding that his true treasures were stored up in heaven.

There was another man whose deep love of God and willing heart enabled him to be positive in almost every situation. The most notable thing about King David, was God's own declaration regarding him. God said, "I have found David, Son of Jesse, a man after my own heart; he will do everything that I want him to do." (Acts 13:22)

According to the Bible, God remembers David most as Israel's greatest king, the one whose name would be forever linked with the Messiah—the "Son of David" (Matthew 1:1). God chose David because he was a man of integrity and character. Like Jeff, and like King David, our greatest joy will come from knowing our Heavenly Father and the hope that He has given us through His Son, Jesus Christ... even when our boat is sinking!

Scripture Reading: Psalm 78:70-72

Personal Application:
- Consider what it was about David that made him a man after God's heart. In what ways can you imitate David (or Jeff, for that matter)?

Week 30, Day 4: The Conviction of the Holy Spirit

Texas history is full of heroes, but Sam Houston is one of my favorites. At one time, while he was governor of Tennessee, he was known as "The Old Drunk." It wasn't until much later that he became the great hero of the Texas revolution when he routed General Santa Ana's Mexican army. Houston's battle cry, "Remember the Alamo!" helped win independence for Texas. Much later still, he married the daughter of a Baptist preacher and trusted Christ as his Savior. His was a drastic conversion, as he purposed to live a life of righteousness.

Still, like all of us, he battled some of his old-life tendencies. One day, as he rode along a trail, his horse stumbled. Houston spontaneously cursed, reverting to his old habit. Immediately, he was convicted of his sin. He got off his horse, knelt down on the trail, and cried out to God for forgiveness. Houston had already received Christ, but God was teaching him to live in fellowship with Him moment by moment. As soon as the Holy Spirit convicted Sam Houston of his sin, he confessed it, and repented. And this was the way of his new life.

I don't often talk about guilt, shame, or conviction. I believe many of us get enough of that from memories of our past or legalistic Christians around us. But the idea of conviction is a major theme of Scripture, though the word is rarely used. The agent of conviction is the Holy Spirit (John 16:7–11), and the means of conviction is either the Word of God, God's general revelation through nature, or people's inborn sense of right and wrong (Romans 1:18–20; 2:15).

The purpose of conviction is to lead people to repent of their sins (Acts 2:37–38); to turn to God for salvation and eternal life through forgiveness and grace; and to make course corrections in our thinking and behavior. This grace—an unmerited favor—is God's free gift, and it wipes out all condemnation!

True Christianity is a living and growing relationship with Jesus Christ. Our relationship with Jesus defines our new life. If we have a real passion for God's Word and allow the Holy Spirit to embrace our hearts, we will periodically feel the conviction of the Holy Spirit upon our hearts.

The Holy Spirit may convict us to: change our minds, attitudes, and hearts; change our behaviors; or take a certain action. We learn to listen to and hear the conviction of the Holy Spirit as we walk with Him. The more we obey Him, the more sensitive we are to His promptings.

It's comforting to know that God isn't through with any of us yet. We are all in a process of refinement. There is actually life in conviction! And it is a new life, as Sam Houston's drastic conversion demonstrates.

Scripture Reading: Acts 3:19; Philippians 1:6

Personal Application:

- Make it your practice that when you sense the conviction or prompting of the Holy Spirit to obey Him immediately. This will bring you a tremendous sense of peace and joy!

Week 30, Day 5: Stress

Although stress is not new, the fast pace of the technological age has deceived us. We have all these modern gadgets to make life easier, but they combine to inundate us with stressful stimuli 24/7. Additionally, we are often our own worst enemy by packing our lives so full that we have no margin. When something unexpected occurs, we have no reserves with which to deal with it. Imagine, for instance, a day in the life of a father of three children:

He left work early that morning as usual. For 45 minutes he battled rush-hour traffic before even getting to work. There, he found himself five minutes late for a meeting with his boss and an important client. The rest of his day was a blur of activity, leaving no time for lunch. He merely grabbed more coffee and a bag of potato chips on the run.

Late in the day, he glanced at the clock and realized that if he didn't leave right away, he'd be late for his son's baseball game. But while leaving the office, a senior manager detained him for ten minutes. Finally breaking free, he sprinted to the car, contended with the rush-hour crush again and called his wife to tell her he was running late and would have to meet them at the ball field. She was not happy with him.

He arrived at the ball field just in time to see his son go up to bat. He pecked a kiss on his wife's cheek and hugged his two little girls. Finally, in a more relaxed state, his mind drifted back to the unsettling conversation he had with the senior manager just before leaving work. Deep in his thoughts, he missed his son crossing the home plate.

After the game, the family had arranged to meet with a few other families from the team for ice cream. It was 8 O'clock by the time they got home, and he still hadn't eaten supper. He helped his wife put the kids to bed and stood in front of the open refrigerator looking for something to eat. The microwave flashed 8:40pm as he heated some leftover spaghetti and sat down with his wife in front of the TV.

At 10pm, he was exhausted and dragged himself to the bathroom to get ready for bed. He popped a couple of antacids to calm his stomach. He also had a pounding headache and realized that it was probably dehydration as he couldn't remember the last time, he had any water during the day. So, he drank a glass of water.

His head hit the pillow at 10:20pm, but he couldn't fall asleep, as he was frustrated by the lack of time he had spent lately with his wife and kids. He also felt guilty for not exercising and eating right. His weight had been climbing steadily. Finally, he fell into a fitful sleep until his alarm went off at 5am to repeat his daily routine all over again!

Such is the stressful lifestyle for so many Americans, but Jesus offers a more peaceful approach.

Scripture Reading: Luke 10:38-42

Personal Application:

- To what extent does the above scenario describe your life?
  Based on the above passage in Luke, what would it look like for
  you to pare your life down to those few things that really matter?

Week 30, Day 6: Take My Hand, Precious Lord

Thomas Andrew Dorsey was the first African American elected to the Nashville Songwriters Hall of Fame and the Gospel Music Association's Living Hall of Fame. His notoriety and contributions to Christian music are amazing.

In 1932 he was a new husband and soon to be father. Thomas and his wife, Nettie, lived in a little apartment on Chicago's Southside. It was a hot August afternoon when he was supposed to go to St. Louis, where he would be a featured soloist at a large revival meeting. Something did not feel right. He told Nettie that he was not going to the revival. Nettie, who was in the last month of pregnancy with their first child, insisted that he go to the concert and bless those who came to hear him. So, he went.

The concert was so successful that people were screaming for Thomas to keep on singing. He was exhausted when he finally sat down. Out of the corner of his eye he saw a messenger boy running up to him with a Western Union telegram. He ripped open the envelope. Pasted on the yellow sheet were the words: YOUR WIFE JUST DIED.

Thomas confesses, "When I got back, I learned that Nettie had given birth to a boy. I swung between grief and joy. Yet that night, the baby died. I buried Nettie and our little boy together, in the same casket. Then I fell apart. For days I closeted myself. I felt that God had done me an injustice. I did not want to serve Him any longer or write gospel songs. I just wanted to go back to that jazz world I once knew so well."

Yet, Thomas eventually turned back to the Lord for comfort and relief from his deep grief. In the process, Thomas wrote the song, "Take My Hand, Precious Lord."

These stanzas captured the grief not only of Dorsey, but also of any who have suffered significant loss.

> Precious Lord, take my hand,
> lead me on, let me stand,
> I am tired, I am weak, I am worn;
> Through the storm, through the night,
> lead me on to the light:
> Take my hand, precious Lord, lead me home.

The opening line of stanza one, "Precious Lord, take my hand," indicates a suffering soul that is reaching out. The songwriter/singer acknowledges that he is at the end of his rope: "I'm tired, I'm weak, I'm worn." When Dorsey penned, "Through the storm, through the night, lead me on to the light," perhaps he was thinking of Matthew 8:23-27, where Jesus stilled the storm.

Scripture Reading: Psalm 23

Personal Application:

- Many hymns and messages are conceived in the throes of tragedy. What events or circumstances have drawn you closer to our Lord? How have you been able to share your pain?

Week 30, Day 7: Weekly Recap and Prayer

On the seventh day of each week, use the **ACTS** acronym to spend time with the Lord reviewing and assessing your week and praying to God. (**A**=Adoration; **C**=Confession; **T**=Thanksgiving; **S**=Supplication)

First, look back over the previous six days for this week to remind yourself what you read and agreed to. Then, follow the ACTS pattern for prayer below. Finally, use the space below to journal what God is doing in your life and share this with a trusted spiritual partner.

Adoration: Simply spend time in adoration of the Lord. Praise Him and glorify His name. (See 1 Chronicles 29:10-13; Psalm 100; Romans 11:33-36.)

Confession: Confess your sins and shortcomings before God. ("If we confess our sins, he is faithful and just and will forgive us our sins and purify us from all unrighteousness." – 1 John 1:9) To confess (or agree with God) about your sin, implies that you are repentant and desperately want Him to change you.

Thanksgiving: Thank God for what He has done and is doing in your life and the life of your family. Give Him credit, for everything you have comes from Him. (See Psalm 136.)

Supplication: Supplication is just a fancy word for making your requests known to God. Based on the devotions of this past week and the things going on in your life right now, what do you want to ask Him for? "If you, then, though you are evil, know how to give good gifts to your children, how much more will your Father in heaven give good gifts to those who ask Him!" (Matthew 7:11)

Journal: What is God doing in your life right now?

Week 31, Day 1: "I Am a Christian!"

When you tell others that you're a Christian, what do they think you mean? To some it means you're religious or conservative. Some may assume you're self-righteous or judgmental. Hopefully, to many it means you are a follower of Jesus, not perfect, but forgiven. Interestingly, the name "Christians" occurs only a few times in the Bible. In Acts 11:26 we read, "The disciples were called Christians first at Antioch." A Christian is a disciple or a follower of Jesus. Unfortunately, the name "Christian" today means everything and nothing to most people. I'm not suggesting we abandon the term, but we might find more understanding from others if we call ourselves "followers of Jesus."

I came across the following poem that may help clarify what the name "Christian" really means:

When I Say

When I say...I am a Christian I'm not shouting I am saved.
I'm whispering I get lost. That is why I chose this way...

When I Say... I am a Christian I don't speak of this with pride.
I'm confessing that I stumble and need God to be my guide.

When I say... I am a Christian I'm not trying to be strong.
I'm professing that I am weak and pray for strength to carry on.

When I say .... I am a Christian I'm not bragging of success.
I'm admitting I have failed and cannot ever repay the debt.

When I say ...I am a Christian I'm not claiming to be perfect.
My flaws are too visible, but God believes I'm worth it.

When I say... I am a Christian I still feel the sting of pain.
I have my share of heartaches. Which is why I seek His name.

When I say...I am a Christian I do not wish to judge.
I have no authority. I only know I am Loved.
– Author unknown

When we say that we're Christians, let's show the world humility and grace. Let's show them the love of Christ by the way we live and treat others. And above all, let's draw attention to Jesus Christ and not to ourselves.

Scripture Reading: 1 Thessalonians 1:4-10

Personal Application:

- How do people around you know that you are a follower of Jesus? What evidence do they have?
- What adjustments to your life and speech would make it more evident to others that you follow Jesus?

Week 31, Day 2: Creative Provision

Reading through the Bible, one can't help but notice how creative our loving heavenly Father is in providing for His children. I find this extremely encouraging. So often, when we're in need, we imagine how God's provision must come and typically we even pray that way. But I've found over the years that quite often God will provide for us in a way that makes smile and wonder at the amazing God who cares for us. Consider just a few examples from Scripture:

- God provided manna in the wilderness for the Israelites for 40 years.
- He used ravens as couriers to feed Elijah in the wilderness.
- He used a donkey to talk sense into foolish Balaam.
- He used a great fish to swallow Jonah and get him back on track.
- He used seven dips in the Jordan river to heal Naaman of leprosy.
- Jesus used mud and spittle to heal a man's blindness.
- He had Peter catch a fish to find a coin in its mouth to pay their taxes.
- He sent an angel to release Peter from prison and execution.

And we could go on and on about the creative ways in which God provides. But let me share with you one of the most creative provisions of God I've heard of.

A friend of mine served as a missionary in Austria. He and his wife sensed God's call to a town called Wiener Neustadt. The problem was they couldn't find a place to live. After checking with every realtor in town, there was nothing available. They prayed and a co-worker of theirs found an empty house. When they asked about it, they found out it hadn't been lived in for ten years and was unfit for habitation. But there was nothing else available.

The owner of the house was a nine-year-old boy who had inherited it. The boy's parents were willing to let us fix it up and make it livable, but it was in horrible condition. My friend says it looked like Frankenstein's lair! There was no heat, no water, and the place was a mess.

My friend felt guilty about spending the time to fix up the house, but there was no other way. After many weeks of work, however, he and his family were able to move in. And in the process, they discovered that fixing up the house made such a huge impression on their neighbors that they were able to establish relationships in a matter of weeks that would have taken years otherwise. In this way, God accelerated their ministry rather than setting it back.

But that's not all. My friend wanted to attend an Austrian national prayer retreat but couldn't afford to go. However, while working on the house, he found a cup with human teeth in it. And some of the teeth had gold fillings in them! He took the teeth to a goldsmith who gave him cash for the gold—just enough to pay his way to the retreat! That's the God we serve!

Scripture Reading: Ephesians 3:20-21; Philippians 4:19

Personal Application:

- In what way do you need God's provision right now?
  Pray for His provision and trust Him to provide for you in
  creative ways. (Keep your eyes open so you don't miss it!)

Week 31, Day 3: Two Kinds of Faith

In James 2, James introduces us to two kinds of faith. The one faith is a superficial faith. It's the kind of faith to expect when we hear someone say, "I believe there's a God." Or others might say, "I'm a person of faith." And we've all heard the expression, "Just have faith," when the person saying it does not have God in mind at all.

James even takes it a step further. He says, "You believe that there is one God. Good! Even the demons believe that—and shudder." (James 2:19) So, this first kind of faith is really no faith at all, but just words. This brand of faith has no substance. It's of no effect. It's a sterile kind of faith.

The second kind of faith that James talks about is genuine faith. James first offers the example of Abraham to demonstrate the link between faith and action. Here's what James says, "Was not our father Abraham considered righteous for what he did when he offered his son Isaac on the altar? You see that his faith and his actions were working together, and his faith was made complete by what he did. And the scripture was fulfilled that says, 'Abraham believed God, and it was credited to him as righteousness,' and he was called God's friend." (James 2:21-23)

We see from this passage that genuine faith has two primary qualities. First, genuine faith always results in action. It is interesting that the passage James quotes about Abraham believing God and that it was credited to him as righteousness comes from Genesis 15:6. That declaration by God occurred *before* Isaac was even born. But based on Abraham's implicit trust in God, he later obeyed God when God tested him (see Genesis 22).

We must not misunderstand James. He's not saying that salvation is by works or requires works. But in this passage, we also recognize that a superficial faith is not a saving faith either. Saving faith is always accompanied by repentance and actively embracing the grace and mercy that God extends to us through Christ. Active faith results in life change through Christ.

Second, genuine faith is centered in a personal relationship with God. Faith is not some optimistic feeling or positive self-talk directed toward an impersonal deity. Genuine faith knows the character of God intimately, so the natural result of that relationship is to trust Him. And because we trust Him, we obey Him and seek to please Him.

By contrasting these two kinds of faith, James urges us to consider the faith we claim to have in God. Is our faith based in a personal relationship with God? Do we trust Him implicitly because we know Him? And resulting from our faith and trust in Him, do we obey Him? Is our faith active, producing life change in us and working to serve others? Because "faith by itself, if it is not accompanied by action, is dead." (James 2:17)

Scripture Reading: James 2:14-26

Personal Application:

• Consider your own kind of faith. What evidences do you have that your faith is genuine? Consciously go through the day today exhibiting an active faith based on your relationship with Christ.

Week 31, Day 4: God's Amazing Care

Les, a friend of mine, grew up in Kodiak Alaska. Kodiak is known for its enormous brown bears. But the island is also teeming with black tail deer and my friend is an avid hunter.

Some years ago, Les took his 12-year-old grandson on his first deer hunt on Kodiak Island. Having reached an area they were planning to hunt, Les pointed to some trees a few hundred yards away. Then he told his grandson to walk around the trees to the far side. Les explained that once he was over there, he would work his way through the trees hoping to flush out some deer for his grandson. So, his grandson took off and circled the trees disappearing from sight.

But just about the time Les estimated that his grandson had reached the other side of the trees, he looked up and saw a huge Kodiak brown bear at the top of the hill above his grandson on the other side of the trees! The bear had evidently spotted his grandson and took off down the hill toward him. In a split second, the bear was out of sight. In a panic, Les ran for all he was worth to reach his grandson, knowing that he'd never reach him before the bear did.

Then, in the stillness of that vast wilderness a single shot rang out. Clearly it was Les' grandson who fired the shot, and then all grew quiet again.

Les hurried to get to his grandson and found him on the ground on his back, but unhurt. Just a few yards away from him lay the carcass of the huge brown bear. Having feared the worst, Les was beside himself for joy and wonder over finding his grandson alive and unharmed. Les asked the boy what happened.

His grandson explained that he had not seen the bear until it was almost on him. The bear startled him so, that he backed up, tripped over a log, and as he fell, his rifle went off downing the bear with a killing shot! I've heard stories of hunters putting multiple rounds into a brown bear and still not taking it down. For Les' grandson to have taken down the bear with one, random shot was nothing short of a miracle!

We don't walk away from an incident like that without an enormous boost to our faith. In times like that we realize how great God is and how much He loves and cares for us. Our hearts are filled with praise and thanksgiving to Him for His goodness toward us.

In a similar vein, David cried out, "Lord, our Lord, how majestic is your name in all the earth! You have set your glory in the heavens. What is mankind that You are mindful of them, human beings that you care for them?" (Psalm 8:1, 4)

Scripture Reading: Psalm 8

Personal Application:

- Think of a time when you unmistakably witnessed the power of God in your life. What was your response to Him when this event took place? Worship Him as you recall your story.
- Share that story with someone today and give glory to God in the telling of it.

Week 31, Day 5: Do You Have a Receiving Problem?

I love to give… encouraging words, fishing or hunting gear, a special gift, and even my time serving others. I especially love giving anonymously to folks in real need. I've found a lot of joy in giving, but I've struggled with receiving. As you might imagine, it was difficult going into ministry; Louise and I are far more comfortable being "givers" than "receivers." However, we have learned, as the Apostle Paul points out in Philippians 4:17, that ministry is often about receiving so others can be blessed and rewarded as they too learn the joy of giving.

For most of my life I've had a hard time accepting compliments too. Just saying, "Thanks," seemed vain. If a friend paid for lunch, I protested, making a mental note to reciprocate. Plain and simple, I've had a hard time receiving love. I have always been surrounded with loving people, especially a loving wife, but at the same time, felt unworthy, doubting their sincerity, or skeptical of their motives.

I was a lot like "Doubting Thomas." When the disciples brought him the good news about Jesus, he was skeptical. In fact, he was emphatic; he simply would not receive it. Thomas told them, "Unless I see the nail marks in his hands and put my finger where the nails were, and put my hand into his side, I will not believe." (John 20:25)

Like Thomas, I was afraid to trust, afraid to hope, afraid to receive the love that was offered to me. It was easier to doubt the "good news" than accept it and risk finding out that it was conditional or phony. I think maybe that's why a lot of people don't want to accept God's gift of love. We know we're unworthy, so we think there must be a catch. We go about life longing to be loved and to feel special, looking for something or someone to trust. Yet it is there all along. There is a risk in receiving freely—no strings attached, no reciprocating—but it's the only way God will have it. He will not let us earn His gift. By very definition, grace is free and undeserved.

Mercifully, Jesus didn't leave Thomas in his unbelief. A week later Jesus appeared to His disciples and Thomas was with them. Jesus said to Thomas, "Put your finger here; see my hands. Reach out your hand and put it into my side. Stop doubting and believe." (John 20:26-27)

And God has revealed His love to me. I see it all around me…and I welcome it! In fact, ever since I've been "practicing receiving", God has been pouring out His love in extravagant ways. I mean in fantastic, unimaginable ways. It's as if He's saying, "Oh, and you think that's cool, watch this!"

When we think, "We can't possibly accept this. It can't be real…what did we ever do to deserve this?" We can remember, "We did nothing to deserve it. It's from our Heavenly Father who loves us immeasurably!" So just say, "Thank You, praise God!" and worship Him.

Scripture Reading: 2 Corinthians 9:10-15

Personal Application:

- To what extent do you find it difficult to receive from others? Why is that?
- According to the Scripture reading above, in what ways can you bless others as a receiver?

Week 31, Day 6: The Invisible Player

In December 1958, the powerful New York Giants clashed with the Baltimore Colts and a young quarterback, Johnny Unitas, pushing the game into the NFL's first-ever overtime. What a game that was!

Ironically, Johnny U. had been cut from the Steelers in 1955, because he was "too small and too slow." Eventually the Colts offered him a try-out and signed the skinny rookie for a backup quarterback position. When the starting quarterback broke his knee during the fourth game of the 1956 season, the door opened for Johnny to do his thing.

Unitas went on to set many team records in the following years, including throwing at least one touchdown pass in 47 consecutive games, setting a record that held for 52 years! Then, before a roaring crowd of more than 64,000 in Yankee Stadium, on that cold December afternoon, Unitas led the Colts to a thrilling "come from behind" victory —23 to 17. The ebb and flow of the game kept the fans on the edge of their seats the entire game. It seemed like that finicky invisible player called "Big Mo", AKA momentum, couldn't seem to pick a favorite team. It was perhaps the most exciting football game ever played!

Most coaches will tell you that embracing momentum can mean the difference between victory and defeat. Many things build momentum during a game. Whether it's a ball bouncing your way, a marquee player making a spectacular play, or a little-known player stepping up and playing the game of his life, when the spectacular happens play after play, team excitement builds and confidence soars. Hearts pound and players play with more enthusiasm and abandonment.

In a similar manner, the Holy Spirit empowers a Christian. Through the Spirit, God gives believers all the spiritual power they will ever need to live a victorious Christian life. When the Spirit enters the life of a new believer, new strength, courage, and godly wisdom is available, allowing him to serve others, grow in the knowledge of God, and boldly speak truth.

The Apostle Paul encouraged believers to lean on the resources and power of the Holy Spirit. Paul was regularly challenged physically, emotionally, and spiritually, yet he drew strength and momentum, as well as peace and comfort, from this invisible player: "We are afflicted in every way, but not crushed; perplexed, but not despairing; persecuted, but not forsaken; struck down, but not destroyed." (2 Corinthians 4:8-9)

Like the Big Mo, the Holy Spirit can empower us and give us the victory—over fear, frustrations, failures, threats, temptations, or even sickness. Unlike Big Mo—whether you're a super star player or a skinny rookie—God's Comforter remains faithful and constant, true to the end.

Scripture Reading: Romans 15:13

Personal Application:

- How do you know when the Holy Spirit is speaking to you?
  How do you distinguish His voice from someone else's?
  Learn to listen to the Holy Spirit's promptings and obey Him.

Week 31, Day 7: Weekly Recap and Prayer

On the seventh day of each week, use the **ACTS** acronym to spend time with the Lord reviewing and assessing your week and praying to God. (**A**=Adoration; **C**=Confession; **T**=Thanksgiving; **S**=Supplication)

First, look back over the previous six days for this week to remind yourself what you read and agreed to. Then, follow the ACTS pattern for prayer below. Finally, use the space below to journal what God is doing in your life and share this with a trusted spiritual partner.

Adoration: Simply spend time in adoration of the Lord. Praise Him and glorify His name. (See 1 Chronicles 29:10-13; Psalm 100; Romans 11:33-36.)

Confession: Confess your sins and shortcomings before God. ("If we confess our sins, he is faithful and just and will forgive us our sins and purify us from all unrighteousness." – 1 John 1:9) To confess (or agree with God) about your sin, implies that you are repentant and desperately want Him to change you.

Thanksgiving: Thank God for what He has done and is doing in your life and the life of your family. Give Him credit, for everything you have comes from Him. (See Psalm 136.)

Supplication: Supplication is just a fancy word for making your requests known to God. Based on the devotions of this past week and the things going on in your life right now, what do you want to ask Him for? "If you, then, though you are evil, know how to give good gifts to your children, how much more will your Father in heaven give good gifts to those who ask Him!" (Matthew 7:11)

Journal: What is God doing in your life right now?

Week 32, Day 1: Special Moments

A few years ago, I was asked to deliver a message to a retirement financial corporation. My message on "Strategies for Being an Effective Grandparent" suggests different ways we can better connect with our grandchildren. How can grandparents use their "grand positions" to the best advantage? There are five tools my wife and I have found helpful in being grandparents or adopted grandparents to those young ones whose grandparents are absent or not involved.

1. Prudence. It takes time for grandparents to find the right balance, learning to be involved without interfering with the child's parents. Grandparents have a lifetime of wisdom stored up. Sometimes our children can feel threatened by our knowledge and would rather we have kept silent on most matters. That is difficult, given the depth of our love and commitment to helping them become successful. Be gracious and give your children room to make mistakes and learn from them.

2. Presence. Do all you can to be accessible to your grandchildren. Open your home and schedule to create opportunities to read to them, talk with them, share stories, and create adventures. No time is wasted when you spend it with your grandchildren.

3. Provision. Grandparents can provide materially for their grandchildren. A bit here and there will help. Providing for the vacation treats or extra special needs tell a child they are special. Oh, go ahead—spoil them a little, but respect the wishes of their parents.

4. Patience. Have patience with your children. They do not value or realize the significance of the grandparents until later in life. When spending time with your grandchildren model a patient spirit and temper your reactions. They need to know that both quality and quantity time are part the job description of a loving grandparent.

5. Prayer. Samuel said to the Israelites, "As for me, far be it from me that I should sin against the LORD by failing to pray for you." (1 Samuel 12:23a) And often, grandparents have more time for prayer and Bible reading than anyone else. Also, pray with your grandchildren and model for them what talking with God is like.

If you are a grandparent, take advantage of the unique opportunities you have to positively influence your grandchildren. Even if you feel you absolutely blew it as a parent, step up to the plate and embrace this entirely different role before you. If you are not a grandparent, there are always children who need positive role models and adults who believe in them. So, encourage them, and be willing to spend time with them.

Scripture Reading: 1 Timothy 5:4

Personal Application:

• What comes to mind when you think about being a godly grandparent? What of your failures, praises, and successes would help a younger person cope with this crazy world?

Week 32, Day 2: A Place of Rest

There's something about strolling along a quiet beach that brings calm—an escape from the struggles and challenges of life. With a passion for excellence in any career comes the need to keep balanced as well. Christ regularly took time for solitude with His Heavenly Father. Throughout Scripture we see how God meets man in the "quiet places" of His creation.

When God spoke to Moses, on top of a mountain and in the Sinai desert, the hectic pace of the Egyptian palace was far way. God finds Jacob's undivided attention in a wadi somewhere in Mesopotamia. Both Elijah and John the Baptist went to the wilderness to seek counsel with God.

When Jesus sent His disciples out for the first time, they returned to Jesus to report on their work. But the Scripture says, "Because so many people were coming and going that they did not even have a chance to eat, He said to them, 'Come with me by yourselves to a quiet place and get some rest.'" (Mark 6:31)

I confess that I don't always get this right. Although I'm doing better at managing stress and balancing my priorities, I don't schedule enough time to just get away and rest. Ironically, I think for many men, resting may be the most difficult of all disciplines to practice. We all make excuses for not resting. We convince ourselves we don't deserve it, just don't have time, or can't afford it. The reality is we can't afford not to.

While on a respite in Monterey, California, Louise, and I took a short trip to Big Sur and visited a small log house set among the tall redwood trees. We enjoyed an artichoke and glass of iced tea, while taking in the magnificent vista and surf below. As I think back on that experience, we were so relaxed and reflective in that beautiful setting.

You don't have to go far afield to find rest. Although I find getting away for a few days to be especially refreshing. Seek rest in a solitary place in your home. Perhaps you find rest in putting in the garage on your favorite hobby. Spend a quiet evening with your wife Go for a hike or walk. Sit patiently in a boat fishing. Read a book. Take a nap. Simply get away and rest.

If you have children, teach them to rest too. Ask them to set the X-box or other gaming device aside for a day. Do something restful and relaxing with them. Be an example to them of what it means to rest, and to quietly trust God in your resting.

Use the discipline of rest to draw near to Jesus. When we come to Jesus with no agenda, He helps us forget the sorrow, concerns, and frantic schedules in our lives and move us to a place of rest. There we find peace.

Scripture Reading: Matthew 11:28-30

Personal Application:
- Think back on a time when you experienced real rest. What was it about that situation that made it so restful?
- Come up with a time and place where you can find rest daily.

Week 32, Day 3: Three Kinds of People

In the first three chapters of Romans, the apostle Paul names three kinds of people. First, he introduces the ungodly. These people "suppress the truth by their wickedness. And although they knew God, they neither glorified Him as God nor gave thanks to Him." They "claimed to be wise but became fools and exchanged the glory of the immortal God for images" of God's creation. (Romans 1:18, 21-23)

The ungodly are so rebellious and determined to defy God that He has given them over to the sinful desires of their hearts. They not only practice evil continually, inventing new ways to express their sin, but they seek recruits, and celebrate their immorality.

After describing the ungodly, Paul transitions to the next type of person in chapter two: the morally self-righteous. "You, therefore, have no excuse, you who pass judgment on someone else, for at whate4ver point you judge another, you are condemning yourself, because you who pass judgment do the same things." (Romans 2:1)

The morally self-righteous think they will escape God's judgment. They're the people who say things like, "I'm not so bad. I'm basically a good person. I think God will let me into His heaven." But in relying on their own puny estimation what true righteousness is they "show contempt for the riches of God's kindness, forbearance and patience, not realizing that God's kindness is intended to lead them to repentance." (Romans 2:4)

The morally self-righteous are "storing up wrath for themselves" for the day in which God will judge all people. They too will receive punishment for their sin. (Romans 2:5-6)

The third kind of person Paul talks about are the religious. He uses his own people, the Jews as examples of the religious. They rely on the religious relics and practices as a show of their piety, but that's all it is—an outward show lacking any inner substance. In fact, "God's name is blasphemed among the Gentiles because of them." (Romans 2:24) The religious seek praise from men, rather than from God.

Finally, in chapter 3:9-10, Paul concludes his discussion of the ungodly, the morally self-righteous, and the religious: "Jews and Gentiles alike are all under the power of sin. As it is written: 'There is no one righteous, not even one.'" But Paul doesn't leave us in this hopeless, lost condition.

"God presented Christ as a sacrifice of atonement, through the shedding of His blood—to be received by faith." (Romans 3:25) Through faith in Jesus Christ and His atoning sacrifice, God declares us righteous, whether we are ungodly, self-righteous, or religious. We all need Jesus!

Scripture Reading: Romans 1-3

Personal Application:
- Which of the three types of people represented you before you came to Christ?
- Spend time thanking and praising God for His forgiveness and gift of righteousness through Jesus Christ.

Week 32, Day 4: Spiritual Linebacking

Few words can intimidate an NFL quarterback like the word "blitz." Blitzing is a defensive tactic to prevent the offense from passing. During a blitz, there's a higher than usual number of defensive players on the line ready to rush the opposition's quarterback, either to tackle the quarterback or force him to blunder any pass attempts.

The middle linebacker is to the defense what the quarterback is to an offense. The middle linebacker is the playmaker; the one everyone looks to for guidance, inspiration, and advice. He is the coach's eyes and ears on defense. The linebacker must be one of the most gifted athletes on the field.

Whatever the offensive or defensive scheme the linebacker must provide a triple threat. He must be quick, tough, and strong, and have great vision and great intuition. A good linebacker knows that every offensive alignment brings a certain strength and weakness. Depending on the defensive formation they can either over-play the opponent's strength or prey upon their weakness.

The enduring middle linebacker for the Oakland Raiders was one such player—Greg "Beek" Biekert. In 2000 he led his team in tackles for the third straight season, with 126. After playing for four years at Colorado State, he was voted MVP as a senior and received All American Honorable Mention for his insightful playing.

As I have interviewed running backs who've run against "Beek" they testify to his toughness, declaring, "Hitting Greg is like running up against a rock wall! His feet don't move; he's planted!" According to Defensive Line Coach Mike Waufle and Fullback John Ritchie, "Beek can cause you more problems in the preparation of an offensive game plan than almost any other player. A tough, mobile middle linebacker like Beek can produce a lot of sleepless nights for Offensive Coordinators."

One of Biekert's role models both on and off the field was the legendary Mike Singletary. Former Bear coach Mike Ditka, a real believer in tough linebackers, once asked Singletary, "When's the last time you broke a helmet?" When Singletary replied it had been a while, Ditka challenged him, "I want to hear one break." While playing at Baylor University, Singletary broke 16 helmets—all of them his own!

As followers of Christ, we too are to play tough. "Be strong in the Lord and in His mighty power. Put on the full armor of God, so that you can take your stand against the devil's schemes." (Ephesians 6:10-11) The devil schemes to tempt us, deceive us, and accuse us. "Stand firm then!" (Ephesians 6:14)

Scripture Reading: Ephesians 6:10-18

Personal Application:

- Meditate on the above passage and each of the pieces of "armor." Focus on one piece of armor that the Lord impresses you with and take measures to ensure you've got it on.

Week 32, Day 5: Staying Connected

As I write this, the country is rebooting at the tail end of the coronavirus pandemic. For about 10 weeks now, we've been attending church virtually via Zoom. The upside of these Zoom church services is that apparently many more people have been watching than ever attended a church. The downside of the Zoom church services is the absence of face-to-face communication, fellowship, and communal worship. Virtual relationships just don't cut it!

Face-to-face communication is so important to building deep and lasting relationships. So much of communication is non-verbal. A warm handshake, a hand on the shoulder, or a hug say so much more than we can express through words. All these require in-person relationships.

But technology and modern culture seem to elevate efficiency over intimacy. Voicemail, text messages, Facebook, and emails may expedite communications, but in reality they distance us from others. It's almost like we are avoiding personal contact with people.

Sometimes, we'd rather let a call go to voicemail, just so we don't have to deal with the caller right now. A text message may be less invasive, but it is even less personal and sometimes opens the door for misunderstanding.

Let's face it, relationships are messy. We've all had tough interpersonal exchanges and we all know people we'd rather not socialize with. Nevertheless, relationships are vital to our living and growing in Christ. In fact, I would go so far as to say that without relationships, we cannot grow in Christ! Jesus died to reconcile our relationships with the Father. Now that we have been reconciled with Him, He asks us to reconcile with each other.

God designed humans for relationship with Him and with each other. When God created man, He declared, "It is not good for the man to be alone. I will make a helper suitable for Him." (Genesis 2:18) All the Ten Commandments have to do with relationships—toward God and toward other people. And nearly all the fruit of the Spirit are relational. (See Galatians 5:22-23.)

God made us for intimacy, communication, and fellowship. I challenge us to look at our own lives. How have we disconnected? Let's not so isolate ourselves with the latest gadgets that we forget the power of the spoken word, the importance of a hug, a pat on the back, and the value of sharing our stories and testimonies...face-to-face.

The writer of Hebrews urges, "Let us consider how we may spur one another on toward love and good deeds, not giving up meeting together, as some are in the habit of doing, but encouraging one another—and all the more as you see the Day approaching." (Hebrews 10:24-25)

Scripture Reading: Romans 12:3-8

Personal Application:

- Take a few minutes and evaluate how you communicate with people. Do you lean toward efficiency over intimacy? If so, adjust your habits to get real facetime in with people and especially with your loved ones.

Week 32, Day 6: Jesus, the Storm Calmer

The account of Jesus calming the storm in Mark 4:35-41 is one of my favorite incidents in the New Testament. As you read the text below, climb into the boat with Jesus and His disciples. Use your sanctified imagination to feel the wind and spray on your face, hear the creaking of the wooden boat as it twists in the stormy sea. Experience what the disciples are experiencing and imagine what they're thinking and feeling:

That day when evening came, He said to His disciples, "Let us go over to the other side." Leaving the crowd behind, they took Him along, just as He was, in the boat. There were also other boats with Him. A furious squall came up, and the waves broke over the boat, so that it was nearly swamped. Jesus was in the stern, sleeping on a cushion. The disciples woke Him and said to Him, "Teacher, don't You care if we drown?"

He got up, rebuked the wind and said to the waves, "Quiet! Be still!" Then the wind died down and it was completely calm. He said to His disciples, "Why are you so afraid? Do you still have no faith? They were terrified and asked each other, "Who is this? Even the wind and the waves obey him!"

I don't think it's any accident that crossing to the other side of the Sea of Galilee was Jesus' idea. Given the fact that He is all-knowing, we recognize that Jesus led His disciples *into* this storm. Often, when we seek God's will in a situation and pursue it, when we encounter resistance of some kind, we assume we heard wrong, but don't be so quick to think that.

Most of Jesus' disciples were commercial fishermen. This lake was not new to them, yet they were deathly afraid. Meanwhile, Jesus was asleep. When the disciples woke Him saying, "Teacher, don't You care if we drown?" I hear some accusation and anger in their voices.

But Jesus got up and rebuked the wind and the waves and it became still. Then He asked them, "Why are you so afraid? Do you still have no faith?" I must ask, what would a faith response have looked like in this situation? Perhaps a faith response would have looked different for each of them, but if they had thought back: "This was Jesus' suggestion, and if He is content to sleep through this storm, then we should trust Him."

Have you ever been going through one of life's storms and felt like God was silent? Just remember this account. Jesus was silent, but He was present, nonetheless.

Notice that the disciples had been fearful of the storm but became terrified of who Jesus is. He is more fearsome, more terrifying, more awesome than anything else that comes our way. So, trust Him!

Scripture Reading: Psalm 107:23-31

Personal Application:

- Are you experiencing any "storms" in your life right now?
  Is it possible that God wants you right where you are? So, trust Him.
  And if He seems silent, know that He is present, nonetheless.

Week 32, Day 7: Weekly Recap and Prayer

On the seventh day of each week, use the **ACTS** acronym to spend time with the Lord reviewing and assessing your week and praying to God. (**A**=Adoration; **C**=Confession; **T**=Thanksgiving; **S**=Supplication)

First, look back over the previous six days for this week to remind yourself what you read and agreed to. Then, follow the ACTS pattern for prayer below. Finally, use the space below to journal what God is doing in your life and share this with a trusted spiritual partner.

Adoration: Simply spend time in adoration of the Lord. Praise Him and glorify His name. (See 1 Chronicles 29:10-13; Psalm 100; Romans 11:33-36.)

Confession: Confess your sins and shortcomings before God. ("If we confess our sins, he is faithful and just and will forgive us our sins and purify us from all unrighteousness." – 1 John 1:9) To confess (or agree with God) about your sin, implies that you are repentant and desperately want Him to change you.

Thanksgiving: Thank God for what He has done and is doing in your life and the life of your family. Give Him credit, for everything you have comes from Him. (See Psalm 136.)

Supplication: Supplication is just a fancy word for making your requests known to God. Based on the devotions of this past week and the things going on in your life right now, what do you want to ask Him for? "If you, then, though you are evil, know how to give good gifts to your children, how much more will your Father in heaven give good gifts to those who ask Him!" (Matthew 7:11)

Journal: What is God doing in your life right now?

Week 33, Day 1: Beating Discouragement

Discouragement rears its ugly head for many reasons. It is perhaps heaviest when we realize we've failed to properly represent Jesus Christ. Or worse, we may have even made Him look bad! As maturing Christians, we're on a spiritual journey packed full of lessons in humility.

We also get discouraged when we fumble in our closest relationships. At times, we all struggle to communicate effectively with the ones we really love. Because we're all "works in progress" our relationships will naturally go through periods of ups and downs.

This is especially true in marriage. We get angry, lash out with cruel words and we get frustrated, disappointed, and just plain discouraged. It's also easy to get discouraged when we face unfair criticism—even mean personal attacks. These are particularly hurtful when they come from people we're trying to love and serve.

The Apostle Paul wrote, "The fruit of the Spirit is love, joy, peace, patience, kindness, goodness, faithfulness, gentleness, and self-control. Against such things there is no law. Those who belong to Christ Jesus have crucified the sinful nature with its passions and desires. Since we live by the Spirit, let us keep in step with the Spirit." (Galatians 5:22-25)

I believe he wrote that to encourage us, not to send us on a guilt trip. He also tells us, "And I am certain that God, who began the good work within you, will continue his work until it is finally finished on the day when Christ Jesus returns." (Philippians 1:6 NLT)

Satan seeks to destroy and disable. He lies and schemes and sets up obstacles to discourage us, trying in every way he can to make us ineffective for the Kingdom of God. "Be careful! Watch out for attacks from the Devil, your great enemy. He prowls around like a roaring lion, looking for some victim to devour." (1 Peter 5:8 NLT)

Paul faced many challenges in his ministry. He sometimes felt discouraged and disheartened, but he found comfort, peace, and hope in his relationship with Christ. Paul wrote, "We are hard pressed on every side, but not crushed; perplexed, but not in despair; persecuted, but not abandoned; struck down, but not destroyed. We always carry around in our body the death of Jesus, so that the life of Jesus may also be revealed in our body." (2 Corinthians 4:8-10)

Whenever life or relationships present a significant challenge, fight discouragement. Let's step back and catch God's perspective, gain strength from His Word, and put our hope in Him.

Scripture Reading: 2 Corinthians 4:16-18

Personal Application:
- What kinds of things discourage you most? Why do you think that is?
- What is your go-to approach when you feel discouraged? To what extent does your approach either feed or diminish discouragement? Practice the strategy that Paul provides in 2 Corinthians 4:16-18.

Week 33, Day 2: A Trajectory of Life Change

When we first receive Christ, we feel an amazing sense of relief, joy, and gratitude for His abundant forgiveness in our lives. In the light of Christ, we've recognized the awfulness and great extent of our sin, and now having experienced His grace and forgiveness, we are eternally grateful.

But Christ does not leave us in our sinful state, He wants to transform us. In Romans 6-8, Paul explains that we are no longer slaves to sin; we have died to sin; and sin no longer controls us. In contrast, we are now slaves to righteous, eager to serve Christ in newness of life. We are alive to God and submit to His control.

In Romans 12:1-2, "Therefore, I urge you, brothers and sisters, in view of God's mercy, to offer your bodies as a living sacrifice, holy and pleasing to God—this is your true and proper worship. Do not conform to the pattern of this world but be transformed by the renewing of your mind. Then you will be able to test and approve what God's will is—His good, pleasing and perfect will." The Lord wants us to be transformed into His likeness.

In Philippians 3, Paul expresses his desire to know Christ even more deeply and become more like Him. Then, he goes on to say that he has not yet attained all this or arrived at his goal of being more Christlike. Therefore he says, "But one thing I do: Forgetting what is behind and straining toward what is ahead, I press on toward the goal to win the prize for which God has called me heavenward in Christ Jesus." (Philippians 3:13-14)

We are all (or should be) on a trajectory of life change in Jesus Christ. As we mature in our relationship with Him, He continues to reveal areas in our lives that we need to put under His control. 2 Corinthians 3:18 says, "And we all, who with unveiled faces contemplate the Lord's glory, are being transformed into his image with ever-increasing glory, which comes from the Lord, who is the Spirit."

And Peter urges us, "As obedient children, do not conform to the evil desires you had when you lived in ignorance. But just as He who called you is holy, so be holy in all you do; for it is written: 'Be holy, because I am holy.'" (1 Peter 1:14-16)

Having received Christ as Savior, we dare not stand still in our spiritual development with Him. He wants to transform us, making us more like Him. Therefore, we should be on a trajectory of life change, ever becoming more and more like Jesus as we live in Him.

Scripture Reading: 2 Peter 1:3-8

Personal Application:

- What were you like before you came to Christ? In what ways has Christ changed you?
- To what extent would you say you're currently on a trajectory of life change in Christ?
- Think of three things in your life (practices, thought patterns, habits, etc.) that you would like Christ to transform.
  Submit those areas to Christ and seek His help in changing you.

Week 33, Day 3: "Be Transformed..."

Yesterday, we talked about our need to be on a trajectory of life change. That is, we are not to remain static in our relationship with Christ, but to be ever growing and becoming more like Him in His character. We want to put aside sin in our life and take on the character of Christ. The question we want to pose today is, how does this transformation occur?

First, we recognize that we cannot become more Christlike apart from the grace or power of God. We are all needy before Him. We cannot simply decide to stop sinning. We can't beat the flesh in the power of the flesh. But we also recognize that we are not passive in this process either. There is a "dependent/diligence" involved in our spiritual transformation.

What I mean by "dependent/diligence" is that we are totally and utterly dependent on the Lord and His grace to transform us, AND He asks us to be totally engaged in diligently pursuing His grace to transform us. We see this duo, dependent/diligence working together in numerous places in Scripture.

In John 15, for instance, Jesus uses the metaphor of the vine and branches to describe our dependent relationship in Him. Jesus said, "I am the vine; you are the branches. If you remain in Me and I in you, you will bear much fruit; apart from Me you can do nothing." (John 15:5) We see from this that to bear fruit, just like a branch on a vine, we are totally dependent on Christ.

But in that passage, He urges us repeatedly to abide in, or remain in Him. We are to be diligent in our efforts to abide in or live in Christ. And as we draw near to Christ and live in Him, we cannot remain unchanged. In His presence we are transformed!

Another clear passage that demonstrates this dependent/diligence is 2 Peter 1. In verse 3, Peter says, "His divine power has given us everything we need for a godly life...." That's our dependence in God. But then in verse 5, Peter continues, "For this very reason, make every effort...." That's our diligence. We diligently rely on God's grace to become more like Him.

One of the means through which we can diligently grow in our relationship with Christ is through the spiritual disciplines. Some of these include reading and study-ing the Word, prayer, solitude, fasting, resting, worship, simplicity, spiritual partner-ship, and others. The primary purpose of any spiritual discipline is help us deepen our relationship with Christ, and in this way, He transforms us.

Christ transforms us as we spend time with Him. This occurs in real life and not just in so-called spiritual exercises or experiences. In all of life, we need to diligently pursue His grace. Pursue Christ. Abide in Him and watch Him change you!

Scripture Reading: Romans 8:5-13

Personal Application:

- In what ways is Christ changing you right now? In what ways do you need to be more diligent in pursuing your relationship with Him?

Week 33, Day 4: Our True Goal

Two days ago, we discussed the need for life change. Then yesterday, we talked about how this transformation takes place. But I fear that my short devotionals may leave some with the wrong impression. For you see, our spiritual transformation is not our chief goal, but a bi-product of our true goal.

Let me explain. If spiritual transformation is the goal and Christ is the means to that goal, then our relationship with Christ is merely a means to an end. I hope that sounds "off" to you even as you read it, because our relationship with Christ is not merely a means to an end.

In his letter to the Philippians, Paul expressed so well what I'm getting at. Paul wrote:

I consider everything a loss because of the surpassing worth of knowing Christ Jesus my Lord, for whose sake I have lost all things. I consider them garbage, that I may gain Christ and be found in him, not having a righteousness of my own that comes from the law, but that which is through faith in Christ—the righteousness that comes from God on the basis of faith. I want to know Christ—yes, to know the power of his resurrection and participation in his sufferings, becoming like him in his death.

Christ Himself is the goal! What could be greater than intimately knowing the God of the universe? Consider what Jesus said in Matthew 13:44-46, "The kingdom of heaven is like treasure hidden in a field. When a man found it, he hid it again, and then in his joy went and sold all he had and bought that field. Again, the kingdom of heaven is like a merchant looking for fine pearls. When he found one of great value, he went away and sold everything he had and bought it."

Jesus in the "treasure hidden in a field." Jesus is "the pearl of great value." Make Jesus your chief love. Pursue Him with every fiber in your being! Join Paul in admitting that everything is worthless compared with knowing Christ. Worship Him, praise Him, give your life to knowing Him better, long for His soon return.

In Colossians 2:6-7, Paul urged his readers, "So then, just as you received Christ Jesus as Lord, continue to live your lives in Him., rooted and built up in Him, strengthened in the faith as you were taught, and overflowing with thankfulness."

We received Christ by faith because of His great love for us. He has forgiven us, made us clean, holy before God. We are now God's children. Let's continue living in Jesus by faith each day, moment by moment.

Scripture Reading: Colossians 1:15-23

Personal Application:

• Spend time simply thanking and worshiping Jesus Christ. Tell Him you love Him and want to live your life in Him today and each day. If there's anything preventing you from fully enjoying your relationship with Him, confess that to Him and receive His forgiveness and cleansing.

Week 33, Day 5: The Formula Trap

I have a friend who says she loves the predictability and patterns in math. And many guys I know are like her. Chaos and surprises—even good ones—can put her on edge. Schedules, lists, and formulas make her feel safe.

Many like her approach life as a complex series of formulas with God as the key variable. They live by little formulas like: Gratitude + patience = joy; Prayer + faith = healing; and Giving + joy = God's favor. They claim these formulas as ironclad recipes from God Himself on how to be happy, blessed, and free from disaster!

Soon these little formulas carry over into everything, and suddenly we expect life to work like math: Work hard + good job + tithe + God's blessing = financial security; or Prayer + Bible study + obedience = God's protection and blessings. Just discover the right formula for success!

Living life by formula is an easy trap to fall into. When life doesn't turn out like we expect, eventually disappointment and frustration can well up into resentment and disillusionment. What we really create with all our formulas for living is a formula for disaster! And this is exactly where my good friend found herself one day:

Thank goodness I finally came to the end of myself and realized I had made a mess of it all. I needed a Savior. Not a once-when-I-was-a-little-girl or when-I-was-16-and-got-baptized kind of Savior, but a Lover of My Soul—an everyday kind of Savior! I was lost, desperate and broken.

Late in my 30's, as a pastor's wife and working mom, I gave up. I quit trying to make life work, to fix everything. God opened my eyes to my destructive and controlling behaviors, and He set me free. He lifted my burden and used some wonderful people in my life to teach me how to love freely and accept love, how to dream and be adventurous, how to approach each day, not with a steadfast plan for success, but with curiosity and a sense of awe. They taught me how to pursue God and experience His incredible love. And love me He does!

When I quit spending my time doing "Christian things "and started spending time with Christ, He began transforming me, healing me, opening my eyes. I learned that walking with Jesus is not "safe," but I can trust Him. I learned that the unexpected can be wonderful. Chaos can be quite entertaining. This world is messy, with very few guarantees, but I have a Savior who willingly and lovingly works all things for good. I learned that God works "outside the box." His blessings are "just because," His grace is free, His security is eternal, and His peace passes understanding. No formulas just love.

Scripture Reading: Philippians 1:12-14

Personal Application:

- To what extent can you relate to my friend and living by formulas?
- Let's abandon our formulas and live the adventurous life of faith in Jesus Christ!

Week 33, Day 6: The Character of a Man

There have been some precious folks who have impacted my life by demonstrating a genuine and consistent Christlike love through their attitudes and actions. Several years ago, one of my esteemed role models went to be with the Lord. Both in his public and private life, I saw great evidence of his godly character.

After he died, it was interesting to see the numerous reports and commentaries associated with his words and life work. Despite all his accomplishments in football, the media's primary focus was on his outstanding character. Few editorials I read discussed his many worldly accomplishments, but many underscored his courage and integrity. This legendary Hall of Fame coach left a legacy of love and encouragement to his family, players, fans, and the many community organizations he fostered. Tom Landry was a giant of a man whose character and integrity were unquestionable.

Having good character means having sound moral, ethical, and spiritual undergirding that rests in truth, and that resists the temptation to compromise. Coach Landry was surrounded by hypocrisy and confusion, yet he was grounded. His was a life with focus and conviction. When asked why he wasn't in the bidding wars for a certain All-Pro athlete who had stated he wanted to be a Cowboy, his response was predictable: "The man lacks character. I don't want players who are so full of themselves that they can't be a team player!"

In recent years the National Football League has been focusing on improving the character of their coaches and athletes. Several programs have been developed to help the teams cope with improper behavior and destructive personal attitudes that eventually affect the reputation of the team, league, and even the sport.

As Christians, this needs to be our focus, too. We are directed by Scripture to continually look for ways to encourage, assist, inspire, and devote ourselves to others. If we truly love others the way we want to be loved, we are doing the will of our Lord. When we model a Christlike love to others, we testify to the character of God living within us. The old expression of "more is caught than taught" is true.

Discipleship is about presenting a consistent testimony through our actions, attitudes, and words. Remember, our conduct is a direct revelation of our character. Our actions will always speak louder than our words. Like St. Francis of Assisi said, "Preach the Gospel at all times. When necessary, use words." Are you the role model God intends you to be? As for me, I'm daily trying to be a man of greater character.

Scripture Reading: Matthew 5:14-15

Personal Application:
- What do others say about your character? How comfortable are you asking other to follow you as you follow Jesus Christ?
- Keep growing in your relationship with Christ. Hang out with Him to become more like Him.

Week 33, Day 7: Weekly Recap and Prayer

On the seventh day of each week, use the **ACTS** acronym to spend time with the Lord reviewing and assessing your week and praying to God. (**A**=Adoration; **C**=Confession; **T**=Thanksgiving; **S**=Supplication)

First, look back over the previous six days for this week to remind yourself what you read and agreed to. Then, follow the ACTS pattern for prayer below. Finally, use the space below to journal what God is doing in your life and share this with a trusted spiritual partner.

Adoration: Simply spend time in adoration of the Lord. Praise Him and glorify His name. (See 1 Chronicles 29:10-13; Psalm 100; Romans 11:33-36.)

Confession: Confess your sins and shortcomings before God. ("If we confess our sins, he is faithful and just and will forgive us our sins and purify us from all unrighteousness." – 1 John 1:9) To confess (or agree with God) about your sin, implies that you are repentant and desperately want Him to change you.

Thanksgiving: Thank God for what He has done and is doing in your life and the life of your family. Give Him credit, for everything you have comes from Him. (See Psalm 136.)

Supplication: Supplication is just a fancy word for making your requests known to God. Based on the devotions of this past week and the things going on in your life right now, what do you want to ask Him for? "If you, then, though you are evil, know how to give good gifts to your children, how much more will your Father in heaven give good gifts to those who ask Him!" (Matthew 7:11)

Journal: What is God doing in your life right now?

Week 34, Day 1: God Is at the Wheel

A few years ago, my friend Rob took his wife Linda to Hawaii. They had never been to Hawaii before, so this fulfilled a longtime dream of theirs. They were going to house-sit for a couple who lived on Oahu and had the use of both their vehicles. Rob and Linda drove their hosts to the airport to catch a flight to New York then decided to take the other car, a six-series BMW convertible, on a drive up the west coast of the island. They took a picnic lunch and had a wonderful day exploring the island. On their way home, Rob had just accelerated to 60 mph on the freeway when he heard something hit the undercarriage of the car. The car felt odd and he knew something was wrong so Rob exited it and pulled over.

He shut off the car, got out and walked around the vehicle, but not seeing anything wrong, he got back in, started it, and pulled forward very slowly. Then, he felt the right rear end of the car sag and he knew immediately that the wheel had come off! His first reaction was to cry out to God, "Oh, Lord! Why us? Why *this* car? Why now?" All Rob could think of was dollar signs and how he would break the news to the owner!

He used his cell phone to call a towing service but got a dispatcher. They told him it would be a two-hour wait and cost $300 to tow the vehicle 15 miles! Ugh! Rob declined the offer and hung up. Then, he and Linda held hands, bowed their heads, and prayed for God's provision. They said, "Amen," and Rob looked in the rear-view mirror. There was a tow truck behind them! The tow truck driver had been monitoring the dispatch service, heard their call and happened to be approaching their exit. He jacked up the rear of the BMW and the wheel fell away. All five lug bolts had sheared off in the wheel and three of them were rusted, so they had been gone for a while. The last one that broke off was what Rob heard hit the undercarriage of the vehicle.

The driver of the tow truck took them to the BMW dealer where they left the car and they got a lift home. But the whole time, Rob was thinking, "How am I going to tell the owner!" The owner was still on a long flight to New York. The following day, Rob finally got through to the owner who was extremely grateful for the way Rob handled the situation. The owner explained that the BMW was his wife's car and had she been driving it at the time, she would not have had the presence of mind to do what Rob had done. A wheel coming off the car at 60 mph could have killed someone. The owner was so grateful that he insisted on paying for the towing as well!

This story demonstrates God's sovereign care even in situations that seem against us at the time. Isn't our God awesome!? What Rob saw as calamity was a blessing in disguise.

Scripture Reading: Matthew 6:25-30

Personal Application:

- Think of a time in your life when God turned disaster or misfortune into a blessing. Glorify God by sharing your story with someone today.

Week 34, Day 2: A Bad Rap

We hunters often get a "bad rap" because of our hobby. Many naively believe that the hunter is to blame for the dwindling populations of many threatened species in our world. On the surface, this may sound logical, but the truth is that the sportsmen have done a great deal to preserve and enhance fish and wildlife resources.

Today's regulated sports hunting has never brought a single species close to extinction. The American buffalo (bison) is a good example of how true sportsmen saved a species.

Buffalo numbered between 60-80 million animals when the Europeans first arrived in North America. By the time sportsmen were able to persuade the U.S. Congress to act toward the protection of the species, their numbers had been reduced to about 600 animals.

Those "buffalo hunters" in the 1800's who reduced the great herds to so few, were not sportsmen but actually market hunters. Today over 130,000 head of buffalo roam freely on parks and bison ranges for everyone to enjoy.

A similar argument can be made for the wild turkey, elk, and duck populations. Without the assistance of sportsmen's organizations these species would be threatened.

We can thank the sportsmen's associations who have fostered ethical hunting and conservation. They have helped promote God's command found in Genesis 1:28, "God blessed them and said to them, 'Be fruitful and increase in number; fill the earth and subdue it. Rule over the fish of the sea and the birds of the air and over every living creature that moves on the ground."

In a similar way, followers of Christ get a bad rap today for our stance against abortion, homosexuality, and other moral issues. People dub us as bigoted, unprogressive, uncaring, intolerant, and even unloving. Remember, we should hate sin, but love the sinner. We have all sinned and fall short of God's glory. We are not to judge others but encourage them.

The truth is that through Christ we love all—even the abortionists and those who promote and celebrate homosexuality. And in our love for them, we long to see them repent of their sin, receive Jesus Christ, and be reconciled with God.

In Jesus' day, he battled the religious elite who saw themselves as being above the moral code of God. Hence, they put a bad rap on anyone who didn't agree with them, including Jesus and all His followers.

We must not give ground to those who despise the truth, suppress it, oppose it, or twist it to their own liking. Be courageous and stand up for what is right. Stand for truth!

Scripture Reading: Matthew 23

Personal Application:

- How do you respond when someone gives you a bad rap?
- What was the attitude Christ had when the Pharisees and Sadducees challenged Him?

Week 34, Day 3: Bad Water

In recent years we have heard much about the problems associated with the improper storage of water. Giardia is a common microorganism associated with contaminated water.

One of my fishing partners had taken his motor home to a state bass fishing competition. In his haste to get some pre-fishing completed, he failed to check the water in his motor home. The half-tank of drinking water had set for many weeks. Giardia had built up in the tank and quickly infected him.

The intestinal affliction ravaged my friend's body for months. Dealing with the lasting effects of this condition challenged his faith and stamina. In a similar way, sin is like a spiritual giardia that contaminates our soul and depletes our faith. Instead, we need to drink daily from the well of God's Word.

God often uses trials, loss, sickness, and adversity to help us trust Him more deeply. When Paul and Barnabas traveled back to all the churches they had established, they strengthened the disciples and encouraged them "to remain true to the faith. 'We must go through many hardships to enter the kingdom of God,' they said." (Acts 14:22)

We all long for and pray for prosperity and good health. I'm reminded of the scene in *Fiddler on the Roof* where Tevya's friend tells him that "Money is the world's curse." To which Tevya replies, "May the Lord strike me with it. And may I never recover!" At least secretly, we have all longed-for riches.

But so many times I've seen Christians grow wealthy and gain all this world calls success and prosperity. Yet, in the lap of luxury these Christians often grow cold to Christ. They have everything they need, so they no longer need God. They become boastful, arrogant, and spiritually weak.

David captured this mindset when he said, "When I was prosperous, I said, 'Nothing can stop me now!' Your favor, O Lord, made me as secure as a mountain. Then You turned away from me, and I was shattered." (Psalm 30:6-7 NLT)

Honestly, the good and prosperous times are wonderful, and we should thank God for them. But they will not be our lot all the time, and we recognize that it's during the hard times of testing that our character is reshaped, refined, and our faith strengthened.

When hard times occur, one after another, it is a blessed sign of a divine life in a Christian's experience. "Endure hardship as discipline; God is treating you as His children. Therefore, strengthen your feeble arms and weak knees." (Hebrews 12:7 & 12)

Scripture Reading: Hebrews 12:7-13

Personal Application:
- What current trials or hardships are you encountering? Trust Him and thank Him in all things. True wealth is knowing Christ (Colossians 2:2-3).

Week 34, Day 4: Fair and Equal

Some of the most joyous times for our family were the many houseboat vacations we enjoyed with our young sons at Lake Shasta near the California/Oregon border. The memories that were built while fishing, boating, and water skiing are priceless treasures in our hearts.

We were blessed with twin sons, Dan and Tom, who enjoy God's creation with a passion. From the age of three they caught the fishing bug. They were equally gifted in talent and ability and quickly became proficient in the sport.

By the age of eleven they were using bait casting reels with complete dexterity. My hardest job was to find fish that bit with fair and equal treatment for both sons. There were many days when we stayed out several extra hours to try to even the score between these competitive boys.

I remember when one of the boys was having a tough day and looked up at me with tears in his eyes. He asked, "Daddy, when is it going to be my turn?"

Life sometimes has a way of dealing out circumstances unevenly. Dads and moms often try to balance praise and reward so that each child can feel fulfilled and encouraged. While discovering the distinct gifts and talents of each child, we endeavor to motivate them to explore and develop those precious abilities. As encouragers we try to be even-handed and fair with our appreciation in order that each child feels equally blessed and loved.

In the twentieth chapter of Matthew we find a wonderful parable given to the disciples by our Lord. This lesson taught them about the even-handedness and equally of God's love and grace.

As the parable develops, the landowner hired people throughout the day with the last man only working one hour. But at the end of the day, the landowner paid them all equally, regardless of how long they had worked. Many of the workers grumbled to the landowner because they felt he was being unfair.

Aren't you glad that we have a loving Savior who doesn't measure our success on how long we have been a Christian, or how often we go to church, or how many prayers we offer up to God, or how many good deeds we have done. While these things are important to our spiritual development, Jesus tells us in this parable that we all equally forgiven because of His generosity. The charity of His shed blood on Calvary's cross allows everyone the same opportunity to be forgiven of their sins and to enter Heaven as equal partners in Christ.

Scripture Reading: Matthew 20:1-16
Personal Application:
- Think of a time when you thought life was unfair. How does that situation line up with this devotional?
- Consider God's unbiased distribution of grace and mercy to you and all who call upon Him. What's your proper response to His goodness in your life?

Week 34, Day 5: Who Gets the Credit?

When I see a football player do his "touchdown dance," pound his chest, and point to himself after a touchdown, I must wonder. It's as if he's saying, "I'm the only one who accomplished this task! I'm the greatest!" Wouldn't it be refreshing for a player to turn around and point to the linemen who placed strategic blocks so he could score, or perhaps running up to each linemen and shaking their hands for a job well done? And it's not just football players who have this problem. Too often our ego gets in the way of recognizing who gave us the opportunity to succeed.

It's true that God's Word tells us to take satisfaction in our efforts: "Be sure to do what you should, for then you will enjoy the personal satisfaction of having done your work well, and you won't need to compare yourself to anyone else." (Galatians 6:4 NLT) While God wants us to have a good self-image (we're children of the King!) and to take delight in our successes, we must remember that there are usually others involved in helping us reach our goals and accomplish our tasks.

Most of all, we need to give the glory to God. He is the one who has formed us, given us our gifts and abilities, and opened opportunities for us to succeed. The Apostle Paul stated, "I dare not boast of anything else. I have brought the Gentiles to God by my message and by the way I lived before them. I have won them over by the miracles done through me as signs from God—all by the power of God's Spirit. In this way, I have fully presented the Good News of Christ all the way from Jerusalem clear over into Illyricum." (Romans 15:18-19 NLT)

The Psalmist reminds us, "This is the Lord's doing, and it is marvelous to see." (Psalm 118:23 NLT). When we think about it, every idea we get, every dollar we earn, every relationship made, ultimately comes from our Creator. He can and does prosper us. When we take the credit, we rob Him of His glory.

Giving God the glory is the foundation of worship. It's saying, "It's not about me; it's about you. YOU are mighty and wonderful. YOU deserve the credit." When we take the credit, it's just self-worship.

The next time we see someone taking all the credit, may it be an opportunity to do a little self-check. Who gets the credit in my life, for my job, my kids, my home, my marriage? Let's humbly remember to be thankful that we have a loving God who equipped us with all our gifts, talents, and abilities. Without His abiding love and mercies, we would all still be dust. May God truly get the glory for the things He has done in our lives!

Scripture Reading: 1 Corinthians 1:26-31

Personal Application:

- Think of a victory or accomplishment you have in your life. Now, consider all who had a hand in helping you accomplish that victory. Take time today to thank them and the Lord for His gracious work in your life.

Week 34, Day 6: Flying Blind

Whenever I visit Alaska, I pray a lot and bring along an extra amount of antacids. While I enjoy flying, doing so around jagged mountain peaks in the fog and clouds adds a dimension of excitement that I could really do without.

My partner and I had just climbed aboard a small commercial plane that was going to return us from our hunting adventure near Lake Clark to the International Airport in Anchorage. The pilot was instructing his co-pilot on how to navigate through the tricky Inland Passage through the mountains. The pilots love to fly this route because of the scenery and the opportunity to show off their flying skills. The narrow passage calls for numerous changes in altitude and direction as they maneuver through the mountain range.

Shortly after taking off, the co-pilot guided our craft towards the notorious pass. Within minutes it became very apparent that the limited visibility would not let us proceed. We would've been flying blind. Beads of sweat began to pop out on my forehead as the plane became engulfed in clouds.

The co-pilot finally decided to climb to an altitude where he could pick up a navigational beacon that would direct us safely to our destination. That adventure reminded me of how the Holy Spirit guides us in all of life.

In Proverbs 3:5-7, we find a wonderful admonition, "Trust in the Lord with all your heart, and lean not on your own understanding. In all your ways acknowledge him and he will direct your path."

Our lives can be compared to a pilot making a flight through a cloudy mountain range. He must rely on someone else to keep him on track. The air traffic controller gives him his course and the best possible route to take, and eventually helps him land safety. The pilot may question the controller's judgment and contemplate going his own way, but this could lead him into dense fog, low-lying power lines, or oncoming air traffic that would end his trip in a hurry. The pilot must trust the controller because he sees the bigger picture, he knows what lies ahead, and he knows the way.

So, it is with us when we try to pilot our way through life instead of relying on God as our Omnipotent Controller. The future is history, not a mystery for God. He sees the way clear ahead of us, and guides us, with our best in mind.

Are you flying through some stormy problems or uncharted circumstances? Do you know the direction you wish to take? Check-in with the Master Controller-He will guide and direct your path.

Scripture Reading: Psalms 48:14

Personal Application:

- What course are you on? To what extent are you seeking guidance from the One who sees the whole plan and can give you the best directions?

Week 34, Day 7: Weekly Recap and Prayer

On the seventh day of each week, use the **ACTS** acronym to spend time with the Lord reviewing and assessing your week and praying to God. (**A**=Adoration; **C**=Confession; **T**=Thanksgiving; **S**=Supplication)

First, look back over the previous six days for this week to remind yourself what you read and agreed to. Then, follow the ACTS pattern for prayer below. Finally, use the space below to journal what God is doing in your life and share this with a trusted spiritual partner.

Adoration: Simply spend time in adoration of the Lord. Praise Him and glorify His name. (See 1 Chronicles 29:10-13; Psalm 100; Romans 11:33-36.)

Confession: Confess your sins and shortcomings before God. ("If we confess our sins, he is faithful and just and will forgive us our sins and purify us from all unrighteousness." – 1 John 1:9) To confess (or agree with God) about your sin, implies that you are repentant and desperately want Him to change you.

Thanksgiving: Thank God for what He has done and is doing in your life and the life of your family. Give Him credit, for everything you have comes from Him. (See Psalm 136.)

Supplication: Supplication is just a fancy word for making your requests known to God. Based on the devotions of this past week and the things going on in your life right now, what do you want to ask Him for? "If you, then, though you are evil, know how to give good gifts to your children, how much more will your Father in heaven give good gifts to those who ask Him!" (Matthew 7:11)

Journal: What is God doing in your life right now?

Week 35, Day 1: When We Fail

During the past two years I have listened to one of my hunting partners lament over some very disappointing adventures. Jeff is an excellent outdoorsman. Raised in the backwoods of Minnesota, he has taught me a lot about God's great outdoors. As a skilled hunter he has taken several animals with a bow and arrow in addition to scores of critters with a firearm. Whether I'm hunting for bear, deer, antelope, birds, or pigs I want Jeff in my camp. He is knowledgeable and carefully measures each opportunity with skill and precision. He rarely makes "rookie mistakes" that cause many hunters frustration and grief.

Yet for some reason, during the past few months good ole Jeff has arrowed two animals that would not go down and could not be found. He used a rifle and a bow on two separate trophy elk only to see his shots go astray because small limbs getting in the way. If that wasn't enough, he spotted a trophy mule deer in Mexico that ducked behind a bush. The guide directed him to shoot at the animal even though they could only see his hindquarters. He took the deer with one shot, but unfortunately, it was a different deer with only a small rack unworthy of mounting. While most hunters would have traded their rifle for a golf club by now, Jeff continues to persevere. Failure was not something that was going to bother him. Like Jeff, my feeling is we can't be afraid of failure. The only way we can grow and mature is to take risks that sometimes end in failure. Years ago, I came across these words from an unknown source:

You've failed many times, although you may not remember. You fell down the first time you tried to walk. You almost drowned the first time you tried to swim, didn't you? Did you hit the ball the first time you swung a bat? Heavy hitters, the ones who hit the most home runs, also strike out a lot. Babe Ruth struck out 1,330 times but he also hit 714 home runs. R.H. Macy failed seven times before his store in New York caught on. English novelist John Creasey got 753 rejection slips before he published 564 books.

Don't worry about failure. Worry about the chances you miss when you don't even try.

It is because of mankind's failure that we need a Savior. It is because of the grace of God we can fail and know that we are forgiven. First Chronicles 28:20 and Lamentations 3:22 remind us that God will never fail or forsake us.

Because of our trust and love for Him we have that eternal grace that forgives and forgets all our failures. Even the hunting mistakes and poor judgments we make are forgiven. Isn't it comforting to know that because He lives, we can deal with failure and disappointment without guilt and condemnation? Praise God!

Scripture Reading: Psalms 89:26-28

Personal Application:

• How do you react to failure? What do some of the Bible characters teach us about not letting failure destroy our dreams and goals?

Week 35, Day 2: Growing Old

Are you struggling with getting older? Someone once said, "As you get older you will understand more and more that it's not about what you look like or what you own, it's all about the person you've become."

When lamenting to a wise brother in the Lord about my aches and pains, frustrations, and yes even torment with not physically being able to do all the things I did when I was 40 or 50, he told me to begin a process of re-thinking aging. Yesterday's normal may not be today's reality. We desperately try to hold onto what we can no longer have. The rhythm and cadence of life must be different when we consider the aging process.

I am reminded of Genesis 18 when Sarah was listening to three visitors talking with Abraham. Her husband was 99 years old at the time, and these men were telling him about how he and Sarah would have a son out of whom an innumerable nation would flourish. When hearing these men talk about her becoming pregnant at age 90, she broke out in laughter.

Some reading this journal may feel a lot like Sarah, "What good can I do at my age?" When your pastor or a friend has asked you to serve in some capacity, you want to believe the age on your driver's license rather than prayerfully consider the request. Usually it is not the hardening of the arteries that's the problem, but the hardening of attitudes that keeps us on the sidelines. Maybe we give up on ourselves too soon.

Think about many of the biblical characters that had their best years of serving God *after* they were past 70 years of age.

- Adam enjoyed a long-life loving Eve and loving the Lord.
- Enoch maintained a close daily walk with God.
- Noah believed and obeyed the Lord to build the ark.
- Job endured severe hardships, repented, and trusted God.
- Abraham believed God for the impossible.
- Joseph trusted that God was with him in the darkest of times.
- Moses and Aaron led the Israelites out of Egypt.
- Joshua took courage in God and conquered Canaan.
- Jehoiada led the kingdom of Judah back to the Lord.
- Isaiah and Daniel prophesied about the coming Messiah.

By anyone's standards, these men were old when God used them so mightily. God can and does use people, even with physical limitations in far reaching ways that we might otherwise dismiss. The comic George Burns said, "You can't help getting older, but you don't have to get old."

Scripture Reading: 1 Corinthians 12:1-11; Ephesians 4:1-16

Personal Application:
- What gifts has God given you that you can still share with others?
- Who in your life needs your wise and godly counsel?
  How else can you serve God's Kingdom?

Week 35, Day 3: Can You Trust Your Conscience?

The conscience is an interesting human faculty. It defines the moral code by which a person lives, or at least hopes to live by. As far as I know, everyone had a conscience. But it's also clear that not everyone lives by the same standard of conscious morality.

When I was a boy, I asked for a BB gun one Christmas. I loved that BB gun and spent hours shooting at cans, flies, dandelions, and other innate targets. But one day I saw a sparrow land in a treetop. I didn't even aim. I just put the stock to my hip pointed the barrel upward and shot. I hit that defenseless bird and I can still see it plummet to the ground after all these years.

That incident pricked my conscience. I've never wanted to hurt one of God's creatures maliciously and pointlessly. Since then, I've had to deal with much more serious injuries to my conscience. Also, as I've matured, things that used to bother my conscience no longer do so and vice versa.

This demonstrates that our conscience is formed from life's experiences and inputs. By constantly rationalizing and entertaining actions and attitudes that conflict with our conscience, we manipulate and twist it. The Bible says that our conscience can become "corrupted" (Titus 1:15); "seared as with a hot iron" (1 Timothy 4:2); and "weak" (1 Corinthians 8:12).

The Apostle Paul makes the statement, "My conscience is clear, but that does not make me innocent. It is the Lord who judges me." (1 Corinthians 4:4) From all these things we see that our conscience is fallible. Our parents, teachers, coaches, friends, mentors, the media, and our culture in general all provide significant inputs to forming our conscience.

Therefore it's so important that we take care in what we watch, who we spend time with, and what we allow in our lives. On the positive side of forming our conscience, we need to abide in Christ, get a steady diet of His Word and the wise input of other brothers in Christ.

When we come to Christ, He cleanses our conscience from past sins (Hebrews 9:14). But this conscience-cleansing is not a singular event. Hebrews 10:22 urges, "Let us draw near to God with a sincere heart and with the full assurance that faith brings, having our hearts sprinkled to cleanse us from a guilty conscience and having our bodies washed with pure water."

Letting Christ form and mold our conscience and then living by that inner voice provides us with a clear conscience and a conscience we can trust.

Scripture Reading: 1 Corinthians 8:1-13

Personal Application:

- To what extent would you say your conscience is clear right now? What would it take to obtain and keep a clear conscience?
- If you're a father or grandfather, consider the weighty matter of providing inputs for the conscience of your children, your spouse, your grandchildren, and others whom you influence.

Week 35, Day 4: Isolation

The television series *Alone* provides one of the most interesting studies in human behavior. The premise of this reality program is that ten people volunteer to be dropped off in some remote wilderness area alone and must survive in total isolation off the land. When an individual can no longer take the isolation or conditions, they can "tap out" using a satellite phone. Then they are rescued and taken back to civilization.

The show is aptly named, because the number one issue that drives contestants to "tap out" is isolation. We are social people and suffer under prolonged isolation. There's a reason prisons use solitary confinement as a severe form of punishment.

But isolation occurs in more insidious ways as well. When we feel hurt, depressed, frustrated, or angry we often act like a wounded animal and crawl off into a hole somewhere by ourselves to lick our wounds. But isolating like this is a dangerous path to walk.

I've heard men counter that they're loners, introverts, and prefer being by themselves. It's true that some of us are more extroverted than others, but I can tell you on the authority of God's Word that He created us all to be social beings. We need relationship with Him *and* with others.

When we isolate, we remove ourselves from the support and influence of others. When we do this, we not only deprive ourselves of needed support and influence, but we deprive others of the same.

Also, isolating and seeking solitude are not the same thing. In solitude, we separate for a short time from others for the purpose of drawing closer to the Lord without distraction. Isolation, on the other hand, leaves us open to attack from Satan, renders us less effective in life, opens our minds to dark thoughts and sinful practices. Pornography is a destructive manifestation of isolation.

Ironically, one of the best ways to break free from the prison of isolation is to spend meaningful time with those who love you. Make a conscious effort to draw closer to Christ. Attend church and fellowship with others. Join a small group or form a spiritual partnership with another follower of Christ. Love your wife and spend meaningful time with her.

Hebrews 10:25 urges us, "Not giving up meeting together, as some are in the habit of doing, but encouraging one another—and all the more as you see the Day approaching."

Scripture Reading: Hebrews 10:19-25

Personal Application:
- When are you most prone to isolate? What safeguards can you put in place to avoid isolating?
- Think of another follower of Christ (a man) whom you trust and admire with whom you can form a spiritual partnership.
  Meet with each other regularly. Be open and honest with each other and propel each other into deeper relationship with Christ.

Week 35, Day 5: Never Give Up!

*"You need to persevere so that when you have done the will of God,
you will receive what he has promised."*
— Hebrews 10:36

During the peak of World War II Sir Winston Churchill encouraged the ally nations to continue their fight against the aggressors. In his famous speech at a critical time in the war, he proclaimed, "Never Give Up!"

This is not only good advice for a nation under siege, but for Christians and hunters alike. Dwight Schuh is one of the most well-known bow hunters in the country.

One of Dwight' favorite stories about not giving up, comes from a time when he was hunting Oregon's Blue Mountains on a blustery day in September. Dwight remembers, "I spotted a small four-pointer near some plumb bushes and was watching him feed. As I was looking through my spotting scope and thinking about how nice it would be to see a big deer, I had a startling surprise. My daydreaming was interrupted when a massive set of antlers rose into my view from behind the first buck."

Dwight studied the animal and landscape. He carefully began his stalk to this trophy mule deer. He took over an hour to circle around the canyon. Crawling and sliding on his belly, he kept out of view of the deer. Unfortunately, several snow squalls blew and whipped through the area from one end to the other. Then, as he crept up to the patch of plumb bushes where he thought the deer had been feeding, it appeared the deer was long gone.

"I couldn't see any sign of the deer and figured he had scented me and bailed out of the area." Dwight was cold and frustrated and willing to pack it in. As he was waiting out the snow flurry under a tree, a grouse jumped up on a rock 15 feet away. Clucking and chirping the bird began to tease our disappointed hunter. "I was freezing, hungry, and roast grouse seemed like just what the doctor would order to get over my case of blues." Convincing himself that the bucks were gone, Dwight shot a blunt point arrow at his future dinner. Missing the grouse, the arrow clanged off the rock.

Huge antlers erupted 20 yards away as two bucks sprang to their feet and vacated the area." Dwight had given up too soon. The largest mule deer he had ever seen was only 20 yards from his position. Like Dwight many of us give up too soon on those important "hunts" of life.

God gives endurance (Romans 15:5). He enables us to persevere. Cry out to Him to give you the strength to endure and persevere.

Scripture Reading: Romans 15:1-6; James 1:12; 5:10-11

Personal Application:
- When are you most likely to give up?
- What do you glean from the Scripture readings above that can help you persevere under trials?

Week 35, Day 6: Appreciate Others While You Can

"Therefore, as we have the opportunity, let us do good to all people, especially to those who belong to the family of believers."
– Galatians 6:10

In today's busy hustle-and-bustle world, genuine appreciation is rare. How often do you write a thank-you card, send flowers to your secretary, wife, or mother— or visit an older relative in a nursing home? Appreciation is something we should endeavor to show regardless of how busy we are or how saggy the economy or circumstances around us.

I recently heard a wonderful story that puts it all into perspective:

A busy middle-aged professional woman entered a floral shop to order a dozen roses for her mother who lived a couple hundred miles away. She'd wanted to do more for Mother's Day, but she'd been too busy and waited too long to send her a card and present. She hoped that the florist could help bail her out by wiring some nice flowers to her mother last-minute.

After paying for the flowers, the woman walked outside and was disturbed to find a little girl crying. Trying to comfort her, she asked her why she was crying. With crocodile tears streaming down her face she said, "I don't have enough money to buy my mom a flower for Mother's Day." The woman responded the way most of us would, guiding the little girl back into the shop and offering to pay for a flower.

The little girl picked out an exquisite red rose and carefully brought it to the counter. After paying for the rose, the woman asked the little girl, "Do you need a ride?" The girl looked up and nodded. They drove to the edge of town where the little girl pointed to a parking place across the street from an old cemetery. She got out of the car, walked up the hill to a fresh grave site, and placed the rose upon the newly placed turf. Kneeling, she began to pray and softly cry.

The busy professional woman decided then and there to drive back to the florist shop and cancel her order. Instead, she would pick out the biggest bouquet she could find and drive the two hundred miles to personally deliver the flowers to her mother. And that's exactly what she did.

Are you willing to break away from your busy life to become personally involved and communicate your love to someone? It's a struggle we all have. Sometimes it's the littlest gesture that can make someone's day. Showing gratitude and appreciation to our family is particularly important. Let's not wait for the funeral to tell everyone how much we have been blessed by our loved ones.

Scripture Reading: Acts 2:42-47; 1 Timothy 6:18

Personal Application:

- Think of someone in your life that you need to show appreciation and love for. Surprise them with a special visit, a call, a gift, or something to express your love for them.

Week 35, Day 7: Weekly Recap and Prayer

On the seventh day of each week, use the **ACTS** acronym to spend time with the Lord reviewing and assessing your week and praying to God. (**A**=Adoration; **C**=Confession; **T**=Thanksgiving; **S**=Supplication)

First, look back over the previous six days for this week to remind yourself what you read and agreed to. Then, follow the ACTS pattern for prayer below. Finally, use the space below to journal what God is doing in your life and share this with a trusted spiritual partner.

Adoration: Simply spend time in adoration of the Lord. Praise Him and glorify His name. (See 1 Chronicles 29:10-13; Psalm 100; Romans 11:33-36.)

Confession: Confess your sins and shortcomings before God. ("If we confess our sins, he is faithful and just and will forgive us our sins and purify us from all unrighteousness." – 1 John 1:9) To confess (or agree with God) about your sin, implies that you are repentant and desperately want Him to change you.

Thanksgiving: Thank God for what He has done and is doing in your life and the life of your family. Give Him credit, for everything you have comes from Him. (See Psalm 136.)

Supplication: Supplication is just a fancy word for making your requests known to God. Based on the devotions of this past week and the things going on in your life right now, what do you want to ask Him for? "If you, then, though you are evil, know how to give good gifts to your children, how much more will your Father in heaven give good gifts to those who ask Him!" (Matthew 7:11)

Journal: What is God doing in your life right now?

Week 36, Day 1: The Center of Gravity

My Friend Barney Barnes offered me some insight on a military term "Center of gravity." Center of Gravity (CG) is a term that applies to various realms such as physics, aerodynamics, warfare, and human anatomy. In all these realms an understanding of CG is helpful, sometimes critical. In war, the essence of a military campaign plan is to attack the enemy's CG while protecting your own. In the Gulf War '90 to '91, General Schwarzkopf's war planners determined that Iraq had three CGs: Strategic leadership, the Republican Guard, and Iraq's nuclear, chemical, and biological capability. The rapid unbalancing of these CGs made for the speedy defeat of the Iraqi military and Kuwaiti liberation.

In humans, CG is located behind and just below the navel. Much of martial arts is based upon keeping your balance while unbalancing your opponent. If we understand the spiritual warfare application, as taught by Jesus, we will have a clearer understanding of the authority of the Word and the proper exercise of this authority delegated to us for this purpose.

These two familiar Scriptures which perfectly describe this principle of CG in the spiritual warfare realm, Matthew 4:1-11 and Luke 4:1-13. The scenario, you will recall, is that Jesus has been led by the Holy Spirit into the wilderness. This is described as a place of fasting and of being tempted by the devil for 40 days.

The devil, knowing that Jesus was in human form, targeted the three major chinks in "man's armor": lust of the flesh, lust of the eyes, and pride of life. And Satan attacked deploying his major weapons of deception and half-truths. In the Luke 4 text, the devil said to Jesus, "If you are the Son of God, tell this stone to become bread." Jesus let the devil "throw the first blow." But when Jesus countered with truth, "It is written, man shall not live by bread alone," He had the devil's CG and had him off balance.

In response, the devil gave Jesus a visual image of all the kingdoms of the earth, "If You worship me, it will all be Yours." This time, Jesus struck an artful blow to the devil's CG of "deceiver." "It is written, worship the Lord your God and serve Him only." (Deuteronomy 6:13)

Then the devil moved to strike at pride, and at the temple in Jerusalem of all places. The devil hedged his move by quoting Scripture. But Jesus saw through his improper use of God's Word and blocked this blow with the clear truth, "It is written, do not put the Lord your God to the test." (Deuteronomy 6:16) The point is clear: to strengthen your CG and attack the devil's CG, know the Word, and apply its truths to your whole life.

Scripture Reading: Ephesians 4:17-32

Personal Application:

- How has Satan tried to trip you up lately? In what ways are you equipping yourself to resist Satan's temptations?
  Put on the full armor of God every morning.

Week 36, Day 2: The Footprint of God

Most successful deer hunters have learned the importance of looking for signs. A friend of mine once said, "Animals don't wear diapers and eat at McDonald's." Wherever game presents itself it will leave the tale-tell signs of disturbance. There may be a clear imprint of a track, a matted down area used as a bed, a thrashed tree on which a buck rubbed the velvet off its antlers, cool moist areas that the animals used to role in, feces droppings, and traces of urine flows. By analyzing these signs, you can predict the type of game, its gender and approximate size.

The Creator of the universe who made all things has also left His signs for us to follow. The Apostle Paul pointed out that the evidences of God's presence are so numerous and obvious that everyone knows something about Him. In His creation we see His majesty, His unfathomable wisdom, His power to give life, and His amazing creativity.

Consequently, no one has a valid reason for not acknowledging His existence. Paul points us to the reality of the Creator, "For since the creation of the world God's invisible qualities—His eternal power and divine nature—have been clearly seen, being understood from what has been made, so that men are without excuse." (Romans 1:20)

God has left the prints of His invisible fingers all over creation. David spent many years as a shepherd tending sheep on the hills of Palestine. I imagine he spent many a night wrapped in his cloak, laying of his back, staring at the heavens.

David wrote, "The heavens declare the glory of God; the skies proclaim the work of His hands. Day after day they pour forth speech; night after night they reveal knowledge. They have no speech; they use no words; no sound is heard from them. Yet their voice goes out into all the earth, their words to the ends of the world." (Psalm 19:1-4)

The greatest sign of all God gave when His Son Jesus Christ died on Calvary's cross, was buried in a tomb, and rose again on the third day. With an empty tomb and nail prints in His hands and feet, Jesus appeared to more than 500 witnesses after His resurrection.

When He ascended into heaven, He left His indwelling Holy Spirit who continues to testify about Jesus through myriads of His followers whose lives He is transforming. "And this gospel of the kingdom will be preached in the whole world as a testimony to all nations, and then the end will come." (Matthew 24:14)

Today, we all watch eagerly as we recognize the signs of His soon return!

Scripture Reading: Hebrews 1:1-4

Personal Application:
- What do you see in nature that testifies to the wonder of the Creator?
- How can you use your joy of the outdoors to share the wonders of the Creator with others?

Week 36, Day 3: You Are Never Alone

In Acts 18 we catch a glimpse into Paul's life as an activist and ambassador for Christ. As he spoke to the Jews about the Christ they had crucified, the crowds became furious with Paul. When Paul saw the intensity of those who opposed him and the Good News, he was sharing about the risen Christ it stirred fear in his spirit. He started to become afraid, but then he heard from the Lord.

While taking refuge in the house of a certain man named Justus, whose house was next to the synagogue, the Lord spoke to Paul in the night by a vision. The Lord said, "Do not be afraid, but speak, and do not keep silent; for I am with you, and no one will attack you to hurt you, for I have many people in this city." (Act 18:9-10)

Paul went on with his teaching in Corinth for another eighteen months. Rather than be paralyzed with fear Paul elected to speak out with boldness. Have you ever been paralyzed with fear? Maybe it was the fear of loss, rejection, ridicule, loneliness, or persecution that gripped your spirit. I think most of us have had the experience of allowing fear to control our thoughts and actions.

There's an acronym for FEAR that I can relate to: Fear is False Evidence Appearing Real. Jesus Christ is always with us. Have you noticed how brave you can become when someone else is with you? Allow the promises of God to help dispel fear and drive your courage to move forward in faith.

There are nine accounts in the Gospels of Jesus saying, "Don't be afraid." Four other times, He encouraged His followers with the promise of His presence. Three times during Christ's teachings on the Sermon on the Mount he told his disciples to not worry or be fearful (Matt. 6: 25-34). God's presence makes all the difference. His word, love, and grace drives out fear (1 John 4:18). Whatever you are facing you are not alone.

Scripture Reading: John 14, Matt. 6, 1 John 4

Personal Application:
- List the things that are most fearful to you. Seek out Scripture that rebukes the fear and focus on God's love and promises to stand with you.
- When fear grips your spirit – stop and recount the many times God's presence and word has helped you overcome your fear.

Week 36, Day 4: Pride

If there's one universal sin that we're all guilty of it would be pride. Pride is what caused Satan to fall and he used the same ploy to instigate the fall of mankind. He tempted Adam and Eve with the false promise, "You will be like God...." (Genesis 3:5) And ever since the fall, all of mankind has struggled with pride.

Pride is what prevents many from coming to Christ. Pride destroys relationships. Pride causes us to do stupid things.

Proverbs 6 lists seven things that the Lord hates. In fact, these are "detestable to Him." And guess what's at the top of the list—pride, or a haughty, arrogant attitude. (Proverbs 6:16-17)

But there's pride, and then there's *pride*. Here's what I mean. Taking pride in one's work, for instance, is a good and noble thing. What it means to have pride in our work is that we hold ourselves to a high standard, we have God-given abilities in performing our work, and we work in such a way that we glorify God, and please those for whom we're working. We put our name (and Christ's name) on our work.

Peter urges us to, "Live such good lives among the pagans that, though they accuse you of doing wrong, they may see your good deeds and glorify God on the day He visits us." (1 Peter 2:12) And Paul said he took pride in his ministry (Romans 11:13). Taking pride in our work and life is commendable from this standpoint. This kind of pride focuses on pleasing God and others.

But then there's the self-centered pride. In 2 Timothy 3:1-5, Paul warned Timothy about the end times and what people will be like, "People will be lovers of themselves, lovers of money, boastful, proud, abusive, disobedient to their parents, ungrateful, unholy, without love, unforgiving, slanderous, without self-control, brutal, not lovers of the good, treacherous, rash, conceited, lovers of pleasure rather than lovers of God—having a form of godliness but denying its power."

That passage is rife with pride. Pride oozes from every evil characteristic mentioned. How do we avoid this ugly, self-centered, ungodly pride? James explains, "'God opposes the proud but shows favor to the humble.' Submit yourselves, then, to God. Resist the devil, and he will flee from you. Come near to God and He will come near to you. Humble yourselves before the Lord, and He will lift you up." (James 4:6-8, 10)

So, take pride in your work. Glorify God in all you do and be thankful to Him. Serve others humbly and wholeheartedly. But avoid a prideful, arrogant spirit like the plague!

Scripture Reading: Micah 6:8; 1 Peter 5:5-7

Personal Application:

- To what extent do you take pride in your work and the way you lead your family? (Pride in the good sense)
- Where does pride and arrogance rear its ugly head in your life? Do business with God about it.

Week 36, Day 5: Fathers

"A good father is one of the most unsung, upraised, unnoticed, and yet one of the most valuable assets in our society." – Dr. Billy Graham

In 1924, President Calvin Coolidge proclaimed the third Sunday in June as Father's Day. The idea for creating a day for children to honor their fathers began in Spokane, Washington, near where I currently live.

Sonora Smart Dodd thought of the idea for Father's Day while listening to a Mother's Day sermon in 1909. Sonora was raised by her father, Henry Smart, after her mother died. Her father had sacrificed much, and was in her eyes, a courageous, selfless, and loving man. Sonora wanted her father to know how much he meant to her. Sonora's father was born in June, so she celebrated the first Father's Day on June 19, 1910, in Spokane.

My father went to be with the Lord many years ago. He was a gentle and quiet man who really didn't have much time to spend with me while I was young, but I loved him so much. His legacy to me was his kind heart and great integrity. I am so very grateful for him, and I really miss him.

It is human nature to assume and expect that those things we cherish most will always be with us. Many men are so caught up in their careers that they don't take time to really show their appreciation to others, especially their parents. I'm thankful that the Lord gave me six months during my dad's battle with cancer to "get things right."

Dad enjoyed going for rides, watching the A's games, and popping down to the donut shop to get a cup of coffee and a donut. None of these things were particularly favorites with me, but I knew dad enjoyed them, so they became important to me. My greatest regrets in life revolve around my dad. I wish I had taken more time to be with him and really know him.

If your relationship is strained, too painful, or simply estranged, ask God how you might reconcile. I have a friend who was raised by a very abusive father. My friend got into fistfights with his dad, trying to protect his mom from his dad's beatings. Later in life, my friend was praying one day when God told him, "Your dad is the best dad you'll ever have." This phrase shocked my friend, but he decided to visit his dad and tell him what God told him. Hearing those words, his dad broke down and wept and my friend was able to lead him to Christ!

If your father has died or you never knew him, consider showing your appreciation to an older man in your life who has modeled Christ for you and encouraged you.

Scripture Reading: Matthew 15:3-9

Personal Application:

- We don't have to wait for a national holiday to honor our dads or spend time with them. If your father is still alive, consider calling him today to let him know how much you love and appreciate him.
  Send him a note or take him to coffee.
- If you're estranged from your dad, pray for him,
  and seek to reconcile before it's too late.

Week 36, Day 6: God's Love Trumps Any Trial

I can't remember when so many of my friends and family members have experienced so many trials and tribulations. As I write this, friends of ours were on a trip of a lifetime in Australia when the whole COVID-19 pandemic occurred. They were scheduled to go to New Zealand, but that got canceled. Then they had to quarantine for 14 days in Australia. They tried for days to secure a flight back to the States and when they finally did, It took them days to get home.

When they got home, their furnace failed and had to be replaced; someone bashed in their gate; and finally, the wife's father became deathly ill. So, she drove to his hometown and spent two weeks with him before he died. That's a lot to deal with in such a short time span!

Scripture reminds us that in the last days the intensity of our pain and suffering will increase (2 Timothy 3:1). And so, it is. Things can look bleak. I'm sure glad we have the presence of the Holy Spirit and God's written Word to comfort us.

I heard the following poem preached at New Heights Church in Vancouver, Washington and is a beautiful reminder of our true reality. May it encourage you:

> God, I may fall flat on my face;
> I may fail until I feel old and beaten and done in.
> Yet, Your love for me is changeless.
> All the music may go out of my life,
> My private world may shatter to dust.
>
> No turn in the affairs of my fractured life can baffle You.
> Satan with all his braggadocio cannot distract You.
> Nothing can separate me from Your measureless love –
> Pain can't, disappointment can't, anguish can't.
> Yesterday, today, tomorrow can't.
> The loss of my dearest love can't.
> Death can't. Life can't.
>
> Riots, war, insanity, loss of identity, hunger, neurosis, disease –
> None of these things nor all of them heaped together
> Can budge the fact that I am dearly loved,
> Completely forgiven, and forever free through Jesus Christ Your beloved Son.

While the winds of destruction and despair blow all around us, let us keep our eyes fixed on our One true hope, our Deliverer—the One who will never leave us: Jesus Christ.

Scripture Reading: Romans 8:31-39

Personal Application:

- Consciously walk with Jesus every day. Talk with Him frequently. Read His Word. Fellowship with other followers of Christ and find comfort and encouragement from each other.

Week 36, Day 7: Weekly Recap and Prayer

On the seventh day of each week, use the **ACTS** acronym to spend time with the Lord reviewing and assessing your week and praying to God. (**A**=Adoration; **C**=Confession; **T**=Thanksgiving; **S**=Supplication)

First, look back over the previous six days for this week to remind yourself what you read and agreed to. Then, follow the ACTS pattern for prayer below. Finally, use the space below to journal what God is doing in your life and share this with a trusted spiritual partner.

Adoration: Simply spend time in adoration of the Lord. Praise Him and glorify His name. (See 1 Chronicles 29:10-13; Psalm 100; Romans 11:33-36.)

Confession: Confess your sins and shortcomings before God. ("If we confess our sins, he is faithful and just and will forgive us our sins and purify us from all unrighteousness." – 1 John 1:9) To confess (or agree with God) about your sin, implies that you are repentant and desperately want Him to change you.

Thanksgiving: Thank God for what He has done and is doing in your life and the life of your family. Give Him credit, for everything you have comes from Him. (See Psalm 136.)

Supplication: Supplication is just a fancy word for making your requests known to God. Based on the devotions of this past week and the things going on in your life right now, what do you want to ask Him for? "If you, then, though you are evil, know how to give good gifts to your children, how much more will your Father in heaven give good gifts to those who ask Him!" (Matthew 7:11)

Journal: What is God doing in your life right now?

Week 37, Day 1: Perspective

How we view life is called our perspective. It shapes our outlook, our decisions, and our actions. Whether we're on the job, shopping, working in the yard, leading a Bible study, or watching a football game, our perspective interprets what we see and experience. Like a pair of glasses, our perspective can either distort or finely tune reality.

As a follower of Jesus, I want God's perspective. Only God knows the beginning from the end and where this journey all leads. Only God knows the wonders of this world. Only God knows the heart and the motives of a man. He created us. He has a plan. He's on a mission, and I want to see life through His eyes. I want to gain God's perspective. How do I go about gaining the perspective of God as I navigate my way through life and all its pitfalls? As a man who truly enjoys God's creation, I have "How-to" books, field guides, manuals, and other books that I use to refine my skills as a hunter, fisherman, and all-around outdoorsman.

I have that same type of resource in God's Word. The great thing about the Word of God is that it's not limited to a hobby or a passion that I want to pursue; instead it is applicable to every situation, every moment of my life. The Bible is my manual for learning and attempting to understand God's perspective. It's full of answers for all of those "how to," "what if," and "I'm not sure" moments.

God's Word is His gift to us that we're able to use to gain God's perspective. Without His Word—without the truth it contains, we'll never be able to live out our faith in a way that honors Him. Psalm 119:105 declares, "Your word is a lamp to my feet and a light for my path."

If we hope to gain God's perspective, we need to incorporate three critical strategies into our life:

1. Hunger for His Word. We need to foster a desire to learn and know what the Bible says. We need to spend time in it, reading it and applying to our life. (Read Psalm 1:1-2)
2. Communication with God. We need to deepen our relationship with God through prayer. We need to be willing to confess the easy stuff AND the hard stuff to Him. We need to ask for guidance and His help to see what He wants us to do.
3. Accountability with other followers of Jesus. We need to surround ourselves with other men who desire to serve Christ with everything they have and mutually spur each other on to deepen our relationship with Christ.

I strive to be the best that I can be in God's strength and for His glory. Will you join me?

Scripture Reading: 2 Peter 1:3-9

Personal Application:
- To what extent do you think you possess God's perspective on your life?
- Of the three strategies above, which one needs your attention most? What will you do?

Week 37, Day 2: From Death to Life

My friend Rob is an avid hiker. He and his son, Jason, planned an early morning hike a few years ago in the Superstition Mountains northeast of Phoenix, AZ. It was a nine-mile loop with only 1,000 feet of elevation gain. Normally, they would've been able to complete the hike in three hours: at the trail head by 6am and out by 9am.

But due to unforeseeable events, they couldn't begin their hike until mid-morning. Neither of them had ever hiked this trail and theirs was the only vehicle at this remote trail head, and there was no cell service. The trail head was nicely developed, but the farther they got from the trail head, the more primitive and scant the trail became.

Finally, with no visible trail and spending too much time trying to identify a trail, they were five-to-six miles into the loop. It was 105 and they were running low on water. It would've been shorter to keep going, but there was no trail! The map they had with them was useless. Their only recourse was to backtrack. But soon, both began feeling the onset of hyponatremia—too low sodium. This condition can be deadly within a few hours.

Both were suffering horribly. Every muscle in Rob's legs was cramping violently and their depleted electrolytes rendered them weak and disoriented. The sun was relentless. They knew they were in a bad way and nearer death than they'd ever been.

Mercifully, they finally made it back to the car. It was now late afternoon. They stopped at a drugstore and sat in the air conditioned store for 45 minutes trying to replenish their electrolytes. When they left, they needed to stop for gas. On the way to the gas station, they saw a young man walking along the road with a white garbage bag of clothes slung over his shoulder. Rob remembers feeling sorry for the guy out there in that relentless heat.

They stopped for gas and Rob went in to buy a couple of bananas. When he got back to the car, the young man they had seen was asking Jason for a ride. They agreed to give the guy a lift, but Rob silently prayed, "God, please don't ask me to witness to him. I don't have the strength."

But Rob and Jason looked so bad, Rob felt he owed the young man an explanation. Then, the young man poured out his life story to them. He had just gotten out of prison that day after two years. His life was a wreck. All he owned was in that garbage bag. We were driving him to his girlfriend's house. He hoped she would take him in.

At this, Rob relented and shared the Gospel of Jesus Christ with this young man. When they arrived at the man's destination, Rob prayed with him and the guy wept uncontrollably. When they drove away, Rob and Jason looked at each other totally awe-struck by God's split-second timing in the day's events! God truly works all things together for good for those who trust Him!

Scripture Reading: Romans 8:28
Personal Application:
- What is it about this story that impacts you most?
  How is the Lord speaking to you through it?

Week 37, Day 3: Spiritual Gifts

In 1 Corinthians 12-14 Paul provides extensive teaching on spiritual gifts. He also offers instruction in Romans 12 and Ephesians 4. Spiritual gifts are skills that the Holy Spirit endows followers of Jesus with.

Spiritual gifts are specifically intended for the benefit of others. The Apostle Peter urges us, "Each of you should use whatever gift you have received to serve others, as faithful stewards of God's grace in its various forms." (1 Peter 4:10) And Paul says, "To each one the manifestation of the Spirit is given for the common good." (1 Corinthians 12:7)

At various times during my lifetime, spiritual gifts have been in the forefront of teaching. At other times, we hear almost nothing about them. I've also recognized that there is a lot of confusion around spiritual gifts—especially with tongues and the other so-called "sign" gifts.

Let me suggest an idea I've been pondering for some time. If you compare the various lists of spiritual gifts, not one of the lists matches the others, and some of the lists contain gifts that you won't find in another list. This suggests to me that the lists we have are not intended to be complete but merely representative of the spiritual gifts.

Then one day I was reading Exodus. In the latter part of Exodus, we find specific instructions about constructing the tabernacle. In Exodus 31:2-6, the Lord is speaking to Moses:

"Look, I have specifically chosen Bezalel son of Uri, grandson of Hur, of the tribe of Judah. I have filled him with the Spirit of God, giving him great wisdom, ability, and expertise in all kinds of crafts. He is a master craftsman, expert in working with gold, silver, and bronze. He is skilled in engraving and mounting gemstones and in carving wood. He is a master at every craft!

And I have personally appointed Oholiab son of Ahisamach, of the tribe of Dan, to be his assistant. Moreover, I have given special skill to all the gifted craftsmen so they can make all the things I have commanded you to make."

Clearly, the Holy Spirit endowed these men with all kinds of skills in a variety of crafts, and they used these skills to serve the Lord and the community of Israel.

What is it that you do well? I believe everything we have is a gift from God. What are your skills? Expand your mind regarding the spiritual gifts. Maybe your spiritual gift is something very down-to-earth like carpentry, plumbing, or electrical work. Perhaps your spiritual gift is more cerebral like accounting, managing projects or people, engineering, etc. However, God has gifted you, use your spiritual gift as a faithful steward of God's gifts and for the good of others.

Scripture Reading: 1 Corinthians 12:1-11

Personal Application:
- In what ways has God gifted you? How might you use your spiritual gifts to glorify Him and serve others?

Week 37, Day 4: Can We Ask God for That?

A friend of mine and his wife served as missionaries in Austria. One of the couples they were trying to lead to Christ was the Mittermeyers, who owned the local drug store. They had spent considerable time getting to know the Mittermeyers and spending time with them.

So, one Sunday, they invited the Mittermeyers to attend their small church with them. Because of the size of the church, an integral part of the service each Sunday was the sharing time. During this time, anyone who was there could share what God had been doing in their life the previous week.

Five or six people shared that morning. They didn't share anything monumental from the standpoint of the miraculous. But what they did share demonstrated the intimate, loving, trusting relationships that they enjoyed with their heavenly Father.

- A mother had prayed for her baby who was teething and in pain, and thanked God for soothing the child.
- A coupled prayed for their son who needed to pass his school exams and did.
- A wife had lost the diamond from her wedding ring and she praised the Lord for helping her find it.
- A man thanked God for helping him with a proposal he had written for work.

And there were other similar praises for answered prayer.

Following the church service, my friends took the Mittermeyers out for lunch. While they were sitting around the table, they asked the Mittermeyers what they thought of the service. Herr Mittermeyer grew self-righteously angry and said with disgust, "Who do those people think they are to trouble God with such petty issues? I find that proud and arrogant!"

My friend pointed out that God does indeed esteem humility. But how do we express humility toward God? The Lord tells us in 1 Peter 5:6-7, "Therefore humble yourselves under the mighty hand of God, that He may exalt you in due time, casting all your care upon Him, for He cares for you." (NKJV)

What the Mittermeyer's (and many others) don't understand is that our loving heavenly Father is honored when we humble ourselves by "casting all our cares on Him." Does God care about the small, petty issues in our lives? You bet He does!

And think about it, when a little child comes to us with a hurt finger, we don't reprimand the child for disturbing us with such a trite matter. We inspect the hurt, kiss their finger, and tell them it's all better. And that's the kind of Heavenly Father we have.

Scripture Reading: Luke 18:15-16

Personal Application:
- To what extent do you "cast all your cares" on Jesus? What have you been holding back because you thought it was too petty to bring to God?
  As a beloved son, entrust that to Him now.

Week 37, Day 5: Jesus Taught Us How to Pray

If you've ever wondered if you're praying "right," let me just state I don't believe there is a "right" way to pray. Prayer is simply communication, between you and God. Still, Jesus has much to tell us about prayer:

"And when you pray, do not be like the hypocrites, for they love to pray standing in the synagogues and on the street corners to be seen by men. I tell you the truth, they have received their reward in full. But when you pray, go into your room, close the door and pray to your Father, who is unseen. Then your Father, who sees what is done in secret, will reward you. And when you pray, do not keep on babbling like pagans, for they think they will be heard because of their many words. Do not be like them, for your Father knows what you need before you ask him. This, then, is how you should pray:

'Our Father in heaven, hallowed be your name, your kingdom come, your will be done on earth as it is in heaven. Give us today our daily bread. Forgive us our debts, as we also have forgiven our debtors. And lead us not into temptation but deliver us from the evil one. For thine is the Kingdom, power, and glory forever, Amen.'" (Matthew 6:5-13)

Verses 9-13 are commonly referred to as "The Lord's Prayer," but I think it should be called "The Disciples' Prayer," because Jesus was showing us how to pray. Notice the elements of this prayer:

- "Our Father in Heaven" – He gives us permission to call Him Father and wants us to approach Him as a child would His loving father.
- "Hallowed be Your name" – We honor God and esteem Him in His holiness. We revere Him and praise Him.
- "Your kingdom come, Your will be done on earth as it is in Heaven" – We surrender our will to Him and desire what He desires.
- "Give us today our daily bread" – We look to Him and thank Him for meeting all or daily needs.
- "And forgive us our debts (sins, trespasses), as we also have forgiven our debtors." – We come to Him with a repentant heart, confessing our sins and forgiving others who have sinned against us.
- "And lead us not into temptation" – By asking God to keep us from temptation, this implies that we will not deliberately place ourselves in situations we know would tempt us.

This "Disciples' Prayer" is not a formula, but a model. It teaches us about God, our relationship with Him, and how to talk with Him. Pray simply, personally, and in faith believing.

Scripture Reading: Philippians 4:6-7; Jeremiah 33:3

Personal Application:

- Spend time simply talking with the Lord each day.
  Bring Him all your requests in every situation and thank
  and praise Him for who He is and for all He has done in your life.

Week 37, Day 6: Do I Have Enough Faith?

For the past two days, we've been talking about prayer. Much about prayer is often misunderstood and one of those issues has to do with faith and doubting.

James 1:5-8 says, "If any of you lacks wisdom, you should ask God, who gives generously to all without finding fault, and it will be given to you. But when you ask, you must believe and not doubt, because the one who doubts is like a wave of the sea, blown and tossed by the wind. That person should not expect to receive anything from the Lord. Such a person is double-minded and unstable in all they do."

That passage seems to sound like if we pray and ask God for something, but don't have enough faith to believe we'll get what we ask for, then we should not expect God to answer. That would be very formulaic, wouldn't it? And if we're honest, we all ask God for help not knowing what the outcome should look like. So, of course, we may waver in our faith whether this or that will come about. In fact, often we don't even know how to pray regarding an issue.

We often think about faith as some intangible force that we must somehow muster or generate for our prayers to be answered. But this is not the meaning or intent of the James passage above.

The doubt or lack of faith that James is talking about is basically the kind of doubt that Herr Mittermeyer displayed in yesterday's devotional. He didn't believe that it was in God's character to even care about such petty issues in our lives. The doubt that James refers to is doubt in the goodness and love of our heavenly Father, or doubt in God's ability to do what we ask. Such doubt is what makes a man "double-minded and unstable in all he does."

When we come to the Lord with our requests, we don't need to drum up faith. Jesus said, "Truly I tell you, if you have faith as small as a mustard seed, you can say to this mountain, 'Move from here to there,' and it will move. Nothing will be impossible for you." (Matthew 17:20)

Faith is simply taking God at His word. We speak of having "childlike faith" because it is simple, unfettered, and uncluttered. Faith must focus on God and who He is, not on us and what we're able to muster.

The Psalmist displays this double-mindedness in Israel's attitude in the wilderness. "They spoke against God; they said, 'Can God really spread a table in the wilderness? True, He struck the rock, and water gushed out, streams flowed abundantly, but can He also give us bread? Can He supply meat for His people?' When the Lord heard them, He was furious." (Psalm 78:19-21)

When you pray, go to God believing in His love and infinite ability and simply ask.

Scripture Reading: Matthew 7:7-11

Personal Application:
- Rehearse in your mind the various character traits of God. Bring those traits to mind when you pray. Know that the Lord can do anything and that He delights in the prayers of His children.

Week 37, Day 7: Weekly Recap and Prayer

On the seventh day of each week, use the **ACTS** acronym to spend time with the Lord reviewing and assessing your week and praying to God. (**A**=Adoration; **C**=Confession; **T**=Thanksgiving; **S**=Supplication)

First, look back over the previous six days for this week to remind yourself what you read and agreed to. Then, follow the ACTS pattern for prayer below. Finally, use the space below to journal what God is doing in your life and share this with a trusted spiritual partner.

Adoration: Simply spend time in adoration of the Lord. Praise Him and glorify His name. (See 1 Chronicles 29:10-13; Psalm 100; Romans 11:33-36.)

Confession: Confess your sins and shortcomings before God. ("If we confess our sins, he is faithful and just and will forgive us our sins and purify us from all unrighteousness." – 1 John 1:9) To confess (or agree with God) about your sin, implies that you are repentant and desperately want Him to change you.

Thanksgiving: Thank God for what He has done and is doing in your life and the life of your family. Give Him credit, for everything you have comes from Him. (See Psalm 136.)

Supplication: Supplication is just a fancy word for making your requests known to God. Based on the devotions of this past week and the things going on in your life right now, what do you want to ask Him for? "If you, then, though you are evil, know how to give good gifts to your children, how much more will your Father in heaven give good gifts to those who ask Him!" (Matthew 7:11)

Journal: What is God doing in your life right now?

Week 38, Day 1: Battle-Ready

Lately, it has become more and more apparent to me that we are in a spiritual battle, and I was reminded of God's faithfulness to His people almost 3,500 years ago. Under the leadership of Moses, God had enabled the Israelites to endure many hardships during their 40 years in the wilderness. He regularly allowed opportunities for His chosen to prove their obedience and faith through the testing of their courage and commitment.

Some of the battles that Moses and Israel faced were actual, full-scaled military battles, like when the Amalekites attacked Israel. At other times, the people of Israel rebelled against Moses and challenged his God-given leadership. Moses must have been at his wit's end during such times. And like Moses, at times, we get tired in the flesh and weak of heart.

In the same way, sometimes our "battle" is dealing with the little things in life that demand our attention and distract us from what's truly important. At other times, we find ourselves consumed with weightier matters like navigating a rift in a relationship, trying to overcome some sin, or attempting to lead someone to Christ.

The Apostle Paul was right; we are in a spiritual battle that requires preparation, perseverance, and dependence on the Lord. He warns us to, "Put on the full armor of God so that you can take your stand against the devil's schemes. For our struggle is not against flesh and blood, but against the rulers, against the authorities, against the powers of this dark world and against the spiritual forces of evil in the heavenly realms." (Ephesians 6:11-12) nowing we're in a battle, we must constantly keep our communication lines open with the Lord and follow His battle plan. In Exodus 17:4-7, Moses does this very thing:

Then Moses cried out to the LORD, "What am I to do with these people? They are almost ready to stone me." The LORD answered Moses, "Walk on ahead of the people. Take with you some of the elders of Israel and take in your hand the staff with which you struck the Nile and go. I will stand there before you by the rock at Horeb. Strike the rock, and water will come out of it for the people to drink." So, Moses did this in the sight of the elders of Israel. And he called the place Massah and Meribah because the Israelites quarreled and because they tested the LORD saying, "Is the LORD among us or not?"

As God was with Moses, He is also with us. I love what Paul wrote in 1 Corinthians 16:13, "Be watchful, stand firm in the faith, act like men, be strong." (ESV) Men, we are in a spiritual battle. Be ready. Don't let your guard down. Keep relying on the Lord for His strength, courage, and plan.

Scripture Reading: Ephesians 6:10-18

Personal Application:

- What battles are you fighting right now? Pray and ask God for guidance and perseverance. Trust Him with whatever it is you're battling and find your strength in Him who is all powerful.

Week 38, Day 2: Giving through God's Provision

My friend Rob tells a touching story of faith from his childhood. The church Rob attended with his family was very missions minded. Once a year the church held a missions conference that featured missionaries and God's work from around the world.

The church also gave a very large amount of money to missions, but their giving to missions was not part of the church budget. Instead, they practiced what they called a "Faith Promise" that supplied the funds targeted for missions.

Here's how the faith promise worked: At the beginning of the conference each year, they passed out Faith Promise cards and asked the congregation to go home and pray throughout the week. They were to ask God to show them an amount of money they could trust Him to provide for them above and beyond their regular giving.

Then, on the final Sunday of the conference, everyone would turn in their Faith Promise cards and the elders would total the amounts on the cards and that amount became the church's missions budget.

Rob was twelve years old the first time he participated in the faith promise campaign. He took the challenge personally and after a week of praying, he filled out his card pledging $4.00 each week for 52 weeks. This was 1964, so $4.00 was considerably more than it is today.

On the way to church that morning, Rob's mom saw that he held a Faith Promise card in his hand. She asked if she could see it. She said, "Rob, how are you going to give this much money? You only get $1.00 for allowance each week." And with the faith of a child, Rob simply replied, "God will provide." And that morning in the service, Rob excitedly turned in his Faith Promise card with the full expectation that God would provide.

After lunch that afternoon, Rob excused himself and told his parents he was going out to drum up some business with the neighbors. That afternoon, Rob landed three weekly lawn-mowing jobs that would more than cover his pledged $4.00 each week. And God provided Rob with other jobs during the year raking leaves, shoveling snow, and planting flowers. One elderly man even hired Rob to go fishing with him so Rob could carry his tacklebox and outboard motor.

By the end of that year, God had provided that $4.00 faithfully every single week. But even more important than the money, God demonstrated His absolute faithfulness and provision; assurance that Rob has carried with him into adulthood. Rob loves Philippians 4:19, "And my God will meet all your needs according to the riches of His glory in Christ Jesus."

Scripture Reading: 2 Corinthians 9:6-15

Personal Application:
- In what ways does this story challenge you?
- What is God asking you to trust Him for right now?
  In what ways could you bless others by trusting
  God to meet your needs?

Week 38, Day 3: In Christ

When the Apostle Paul was in prison in Rome, among other letters, he wrote to the church in Ephesus. A common theme in that letter is the concept of us being "in Christ." Paul wrote, "In Him we were also chosen, having been predestined according to the plan of Him who works out everything in conformity with the purpose of His will, in order that we, who were the first to put our hope in Christ, might be for the praise of His glory." (Ephesians 1:11-12)

The phrase, "in Christ," or, "in Him" is repeated numerous times in Ephesians:
- God has "blessed us in the heavenly realms with every spiritual blessing in Christ." (1:3)
- "For He chose us in Him before the creation of the world to be holy and blameless in His sight." (1:4)
- God has freely given us His glorious grace in Christ. (1:6)
- "In Him we have redemption through His blood, the forgiveness of sins." (1:7)
- God "made known to us the mystery of His will according to His good pleasure, which He purposed in Christ." (1:9)
- "In Him we were also chosen." (1:11)
- We have put our hope in Christ. (1:12)
- "And you also were included in Christ when you heard the message of truth." (1:13)
- "When you believed, you were marked in Him with a seal, the promised Holy Spirit." (1:13)

I think you get the picture! But what does it mean to be "in Christ"? In John 15, Jesus described our relationship with Him as "organic." Jesus likened our relationship with Him as branches on a vine. "I am the vine; you're the branches. If you remain in Me and I in you, you will bear much fruit; apart from Me you can do nothing." (John 15:5)

And using the analogy of marriage and that the husband and wife become one flesh, Paul explains, "Whoever is united with the Lord is one with Him in spirit." (1 Corinthians 6:17)

To be "in Christ" means so much more than merely to say, "we're Christians." We truly become one with Him. As a branch on the vine, we are totally and utterly dependent on Him. We take on His DNA. Our sustenance comes from Him and the "fruit" we bear comes from Him.

When Paul met Jesus on the road to Damascus, Jesus so identifies with His church (us) that Jesus asked Paul, "Why do you persecute Me?" (Acts 9:4) "In Christ" we are His family, His children, and therefore one with Him and with each other (John 17:21). In fact, just as Christ is one with the Father, so are we with Him and with each other.

Scripture Reading: Ephesians 2:1-22

Personal Application:
- When you read the Scripture reading above, what else do you learn about what it means to be "in Christ"? What impact does being "in Christ" have on the way you live? When you have time, read the rest of Ephesians to understand more of what it means to be "in Christ."

Week 38, Day 4: No Wasted Time

Many men I know struggle with priorities and balance. As they measure their passion for success considering God's Word, they begin to question their perspective. Some highly successful business leaders have shared with me their personal stories about the price they paid pursuing what the world defines as being important. They reached the top of their profession only to find emptiness, loneliness, regret, and often deep grief for "time wasted."

I admit, especially during the early years of parenting, I struggled with finding balance—and still do at times. As a young father I knew that the most important responsibility God had given me was being a godly father to the twin sons Louise and I had been blessed with. However, knowing what really counts doesn't necessarily make setting appropriate priorities easy. I had to pray for wisdom and ways to effectively measure the impact of my life. God used the following story to challenge me regarding the time I set aside for my wife and sons.

James Boswell was a renowned Scottish author and lawyer who is best known for writing the biography of his friend Samuel Johnson. His biography is acclaimed as "the best biography ever written in the English language." Boswell also kept a diary that he began writing at a very early age.

In his diary, Boswell often refers to special days during his childhood when his father routinely took him fishing. As an adult, Boswell often thought back fondly on those times spent with his father and treasured the many things his father had taught him while they fished together.

Years later, a researcher took note of Boswell's frequent mentions of his fishing trips with his father. The researcher knew that Boswell's father had also kept a journal and wondered what his father had thought of their fishing excursions. But when the researcher found journal entries to that effect in Boswell's father's journal, all it said was, "Gone fishing today with my son; a day wasted."

I find it somewhat tragic that what Boswell's father took as wasted time, his son found unforgettable and rich with learning the lessons of life. How grateful Boswell was for his father's attentions, even though his father was apparently unaware of how impactful those times were in the life of his young son.

Similarly, I can't help but reflect upon the many days my boys and I enjoyed the early fishing season or a chance to water ski. Each adventure was a time of great conversation and bonding. If you're spending more time trying to be important rather than doing what's important—stop! Consider what really counts and reprioritize.

Scripture Reading: Proverbs 2:1-15

Personal Application:

- What are your most memorable times your dad spent with you? Why are they memorable?
- If you're a dad, what ways can you spend meaningful time with your children? If you're not a dad, who could you invest your time in?

Week 38, Day 5: Triumphant Love

A friend of mine shared a touching story of boots-on-the-ground love. Fred was a pastor at a large church. A fringe couple in his church was very needy and often came to the church asking for financial aid. Both parents were disabled, though ambulatory, and they had two teenage kids who were following in their parents' footsteps.

Late one Thursday afternoon, the husband called Fred announcing that they had to vacate the house they were renting by that weekend. He had reserved a U-Haul truck and they had another house they could move into on the other side of town.

Wanting to minister to this needy couple, Fred told him he'd try to muster a moving crew to show up on Saturday and help them move. But it was summer, and no matter who he called, Fred couldn't find anyone who was available to help. Fred confesses that he was becoming less and less excited about helping this family move.

Furthermore, based on his history with this couple, Fred wanted to establish some boundaries. He asked that the family have everything packed in boxes so that when the crew showed up on Saturday morning, they could simply load the truck and make the move. The couple assured him this would be done and kept saying that they didn't own much.

Meanwhile, Fred kept calling for volunteers and by Friday evening, he had only found two other helpers and they wouldn't be available until mid-morning on Saturday. On Saturday morning, Fred was not looking forward to spending his day moving this family, especially since he knew the burden of the work would fall on him.

When he arrived at the couple's home at 7am, it took him several minutes pounding on the front door before he could rouse anyone—they were still all in bed! When the dad finally came to the door and let Fred in, Fred looked around in horror. Nothing was packed and the family were hoarders. It was impossible to distinguish between their trash and their belongings.

The dad suggested they go get the truck first, so they drove to U-Haul. But when they got there, they discovered that it wouldn't be open for another 45 minutes. By now, Fred was seething inside! He felt taken advantage of, lied to, and manipulated. However, as the two of them sat in his car, the Lord spoke to Fred and prompted him to ask this man to tell him his story.

While they waited, this man poured out his heartbreaking story and the Lord filled Fred's heart with compassion for him and his family. The move was fraught with difficulties and took them two full days. But because of the love that God poured into Fred's heart, the Lord sustained him with joy and Fred could count it a privilege to have been worthy of serving this family.

Scripture Reading: Romans 12:9-21

Personal Application:
- Who in your life do you find it difficult to love? Imagine Jesus sitting down with that person and getting to know them. What would Jesus say and do in that situation? Now ask the Lord for the grace to do the same with that individual you find it hard to love.

Week 38, Day 6: Take a Stand

I remember when former NFL Commissioner Paul Tagliabue stated that there is a "Crisis of character in the NFL." Good character needed to become more important than terrific times in the 40-yard dash or great moves in the open field. The NFL admittedly couldn't afford to ignore the importance of character when rating a prospective player's potential.

That was years ago, and still, too often we see famous athletes compromising good decency, embarrassing their teams, and disgusting their fans. Whether it's lying, cheating, taking drugs, carousing, or picking fights, we must draw the line. Someone must take a stand for what is good and right and true. I think it starts with you and me.

When I was in public service for twenty years, frequently, I had to strive for the middle ground on difficult political issues. I fought for win-win scenarios, providing positive outcomes for the agency I served as well as the citizens who ultimately paid my salary. The same negotiating skills make good coaches and agents. However, in negotiation we must not compromise our faith.

If we identify fully with what it means to be a true disciple of Christ, and submit ourselves totally to God's authority, and if we humbly serve Him in all our endeavors, then we will find ourselves in direct conflict with Satan...and often the culture around us. There are simply times when we must take a stand...no matter how unpopular it makes us. That's when our true character shows. We are either aligned with the Kingdom of God and His Lordship in our lives, or we are aligned with Satan's kingdom and under his control.

Whether we face the lures of this culture, pressure from our peers, or our own lustful desires, as believers, we are given the power to resist the devil—to take a stand against his ways and anything he represents—and to walk in truth.

The Holy Spirit gives us conviction, truth, and strength to stand firm against our enemy and to resist the temptations the devil brings. God often allows trials and temptations in our lives to build our character and grow us into the godly men He intends us to be. If he doesn't remove the struggle, He provides a way out. "No temptation has taken you except what is common to man. And God is faithful; he will not let you be tempted beyond what you can bear. But when you are tempted, he will also provide a way out so that you can stand up under it." (1 Corinthians 10:13)

Temptation is just a test of our character. Are we really who we say we are? Do we really believe what we think we believe? Who are we when no one is looking? It's not just athletes that are in a crisis of character. We all need to choose where we stand.

Scripture Reading: 1 John 4:1-6

Personal Application:

- What tests of your character are you currently facing?
- What aspects of your character are at risk? How will you take a stand?

Week 38, Day 7: Weekly Recap and Prayer

On the seventh day of each week, use the **ACTS** acronym to spend time with the Lord reviewing and assessing your week and praying to God. (**A**=Adoration; **C**=Confession; **T**=Thanksgiving; **S**=Supplication)

First, look back over the previous six days for this week to remind yourself what you read and agreed to. Then, follow the ACTS pattern for prayer below. Finally, use the space below to journal what God is doing in your life and share this with a trusted spiritual partner.

Adoration: Simply spend time in adoration of the Lord. Praise Him and glorify His name. (See 1 Chronicles 29:10-13; Psalm 100; Romans 11:33-36.)

Confession: Confess your sins and shortcomings before God. ("If we confess our sins, he is faithful and just and will forgive us our sins and purify us from all unrighteousness." – 1 John 1:9) To confess (or agree with God) about your sin, implies that you are repentant and desperately want Him to change you.

Thanksgiving: Thank God for what He has done and is doing in your life and the life of your family. Give Him credit, for everything you have comes from Him. (See Psalm 136.)

Supplication: Supplication is just a fancy word for making your requests known to God. Based on the devotions of this past week and the things going on in your life right now, what do you want to ask Him for? "If you, then, though you are evil, know how to give good gifts to your children, how much more will your Father in heaven give good gifts to those who ask Him!" (Matthew 7:11)

Journal: What is God doing in your life right now?

Week 39, Day 1: The Guidance of the Holy Spirit

Getting lost is never fun. As a fisherman or hunter, being able to locate our exact position and areas where fish and wildlife frequent is a critical consideration. In the early 1990s, Hummingbird Corporation put out a portable depth-finder with Global Positioning System (GPS) that utilized commercial satellite receivers to help the sportsman precisely define their coordinates anywhere in the world. What an amazing tool!

Today, the market is saturated with all types of GPS units of various sizes, shapes, and prices. In fact, most of us probably have one in our phone and in our car. No more fumbling through the road atlas or fold-out maps! Built-in base-maps cover all major roads and cities and can guide us to any location. I like the advertisement one manufacture placed in the fishing catalogs, "The world is a big place, but finding yourself in a big world isn't a problem anymore thanks to …GPS."

We spend a great deal of time and resources trying to find our way in the world, but what are we using to guide our spiritual life? If God is not at the center of our internal guidance system, what has replaced that void? Many try to fill it with the pursuit of power, fame, or fortune. Others seek out New-Age philosophies or Eastern religions that promise peace and harmony but have no power to guide one through this life, much less to eternal life.

If you have accepted Jesus Christ as your Savior, your internal guidance system is the Holy Spirit, who is always with you. On the day of Pentecost, the Apostle Peter urged the assembled multitudes, "Repent and be baptized, every one of you, in the name of Jesus Christ for the forgiveness of your sins. And you will receive the gift of the Holy Spirit" (Acts 2:38).

The guidance of the Holy Spirit isn't limited by low battery power, dead zones, or sunspots. He is with us 24/7 and always available. Yet many of us go through our daily life without even considering that He is with us and ready to guide us when we are lost, comfort us when we are lonely, teach us when things are confusing, direct us in the right path, and convict us when we sin. But… we must listen.

Jesus also said of the Holy Spirit, "He will testify about me." (John 15:26) And, "He will glorify Me." (John 16:14) My point is that the Holy Spirit wants to testify about Jesus and glorify Him through our lives. His purpose gives us purpose.

Let's not wander through this life confused, discouraged, and lost. Let's stop and listen and depend on the teaching and guidance of the Holy Spirit to show us the way. Often, God's ways are not what we would choose, but they're always what's best for us!

Scripture Reading: John 14:15-18; 15:26-27; 16:12-15

Personal Application:
• Where do you need guidance in your life right now? Trust the Holy Spirit to lead you. Sometimes that involves waiting—even when we feel hard-pressed to decide. Just relax and trust Him to lead you.

Week 39, Day 2: Division in the Church

As I write this, we're 15 weeks into the coronavirus shutdown. Some things have opened, but others remain closed or significantly curbed in their operations. One of my chief concerns in this is for the church, Christ's body of believers.

Many churches have decided to open again despite governors' mandates prohibiting it. Consequently, we find ourselves in a situation that is creating division within the body of Christ. Emotions often run high during the fray preventing us from seeing clearly.

Christians on one side are insisting that we obey our civil leaders because the Scripture tells us to (e.g., Romans 13:1ff.). Meanwhile, other followers of Jesus point out that the governors' mandates defy our first amendment rights and God's command "not to forsake the assembling of ourselves together." (Hebrews 10:25)

Some Christians are listening to the news reports and are fearful of catching the virus or giving it to others. They feel that the government has established these mandates to protect us. And to go against the mandates is careless—if not unloving and disrespectful of others.

Other Christians are listening to their doctors and other health professionals who debunk these precautionary mandates, claiming they are unnecessary and may cause harm in other ways.

My point is this whole mess has the church divided and we're not treating each other with love and respect in the midst of it. Romans 14 and 1 Corinthians 8 guide us through situations like this where Christians "quarrel over disputable matters." The matters back then were different, but the principle is the same. Let's see what the Lord says:

Accept the one whose faith is weak, without quarreling over disputable matters. One person's faith allows them to eat anything, but another, whose faith is weak, eats only vegetables. The one who eats everything must not treat with contempt the one who does not, and the one who does not eat everything must not judge the one who does, for God has accepted them. Who are you to judge someone else's servant? To their own master, servants stand or fall. And they will stand, for the Lord is able to make them stand. (Romans 14:1-4)

And in 1 Corinthians 8:1, Paul says, "Now about food sacrificed to idols: We know that 'We all possess knowledge.' But knowledge puffs up while love builds up." Bringing this forward to the present, "We all have knowledge." We all think we know what's best, right, and proper. But to focus solely on our "knowledge" only makes us arrogant and divides. Instead, we must follow God's way of love and accept each other in Him.

Scripture Reading: Romans 14:12-19

Personal Application:
- Hopefully, by the time you read this, the whole coronavirus pandemic will be behind us. However, there are always "disputable matters" over which we Christians seem to fight. What are those for you right now and based on God's Word, how will you respond?

Week 39, Day 3: Life's Perspective

Look around. What do you see? Life is happening everywhere. People get up, go to work, go to school, take care of business, take care of kids, take out the trash…. but what's it all about?

How we view the world affects how we experience life. How we answer the big questions in life determines how we approach life. Is life just a big free-for-all? Grab what you can while you can and have a good time? Is it about leaving the world a better place, leaving your mark, making lots of money, impressing mankind, seeing the world, or raising a bundle of kids? Are we just molecular sludge, evolved over billions of years?

There are many perspectives. If we look at Hollywood, we might think life is just all about wealth, fame, and indulgence. If we look at Washington, DC, we might think it's about power, prestige, and popularity. If we look at Wall Street, it seems to be about high-powered greed. If we look at professional sports—strength, achievement, and glory. If we look at many churches, we might think it's about size and appearances.

If life is about getting, achieving, looking good, and self-gratification, there's no room for love—at least no room for loving anyone other than ourselves. And even if you throw in a little kindness, it's still just a self-serving journey that ends at the grave. We live our own little story, where we are the main character… and then we die. No thanks!

I know we are created for something greater than that. We're players in a grand story. We have key roles, but we're not the key players. This story has no end. It is an exciting drama, full of adventure, romance, tragedy, irony, humor, and challenge. Each day we're invited to enter in with curiosity, wondering where The Great Author will lead us, what new things we'll experience, what we'll learn about Him, and how we'll be changed.

In this story we are greatly flawed but forgiven. We play a variety of roles, but we're also a child of the King, serving Him, fighting for Him, and watching for His return. We are painfully aware that we have an enemy who tempts and threatens to destroy us and those we love. We know that the pleasures and treasures of this world are temporary. So, we press on, reaching for the prize of spending eternity with our Lord and Savior. And there the story will surely continue.

What's it all about? "For God so loved the world that he gave his one and only Son, that whoever believes in him shall not perish but have eternal life." (John 3:16)

Want some perspective? Look at Jesus. Let's enter His story daily, experiencing His love, wonder, beauty, grace, mercy, and faithfulness. There is so much more to come!

Scripture Reading: 2 Corinthians 5:1-10

Personal Application:
- Take some time to quietly sit before the Lord and consider your life and the perspectives you're living by. What do you see?
- Ask the Lord to give you His perspective for your life and pursue Him daily to follow it.

Week 38, Day 4: The Product of Pain

We all love our comfort. Americans spend lots of money on plush recliners, deluxe mattresses, luxurious sheets, and even swanky shoes—all promising "ultimate comfort." Life isn't always comfortable though. In fact, a lot of life is just plain hard. If we respond poorly, tough times can turn us into people we don't want to be.

Pain can produce anger, bitterness, loneliness, and despair, or it can produce humility, compassion, determination, and endurance. A friend shared the following story about adversity with me:

"The Coffee Bean"

A young woman went to her mother and told her about her life and how hard things were for her. She did not know how she was going to make it and wanted to give up. She was tired of fighting and struggling. Whenever one problem was solved a new one took its place.

Her mother took her to the kitchen. She filled three pots with water. In the first, she placed carrots, in the second she placed eggs and the last she placed ground coffee beans. She let all three pots boil without saying a word. In about twenty minutes she turned off the burners. She fished the carrots out and placed them in a bowl. She pulled the eggs out and placed them in a bowl. Then she ladled the coffee out and placed it in a bowl.

Turning to her daughter, she asked, "Tell me; what do you see?" "Carrots, eggs, and coffee," she replied. Her mother brought her closer and asked her to feel the carrots. They were soft. She then asked her to break one of the eggs. It was hard-boiled. Finally, she asked her to sip the coffee. The daughter smiled, as she tasted its rich aroma. The daughter then asked. "What's the point, mother?"

Her mother explained that each of these objects had faced the same adversity—boiling water—but each reacted differently. The carrot went in strong, hard, and unrelenting but came out soft and weak. The egg went in fragile but emerged hard. But the ground coffee beans were unique, for they transformed the water into something wonderful.

"Which of the three are you?" she asked her daughter. "When adversity knocks on your door, how do you respond? Are you a carrot, an egg, or a coffee bean? Don't tell God how big your storm is. Tell the storm how big your God is!" (Author Unknown)

Only God can bring fullness out of adversity. He loves to turn adversity into something beautiful… if we'll let Him.

Scripture Reading: 2 Corinthians 12:7b-10

Personal Application:

• What are your current struggles and challenges? We seldom know ahead of time how the Lord will use our trials for our good or the good of others but be assured that He will. So, how will you respond to your current challenges?

Week 39, Day 5: Learning to Be a Godly Father

I have a friend who is in his 70s. He has struggled with his self-image, depression, and a warped view of God all his life. Though I wouldn't be so bold as to put all the blame on his father, clearly his father had a lot to do with the way my friend has struggled through life.

It might surprise you to know that my friend's dad was a pastor and Bible scholar. Others revered him as a spiritual and godly man. But his view of God was twisted, for he portrayed God as an ever-present, ever-critical judge, waiting for us to get out of line, and quash us.

My friend's dad showed no physical affection like hugs or kisses—even when his kids were young. Compliments and encouragement were rare. He was strict in the many rules he laid down and he used his religion like an emotional whip to punish his kids when they got out of line. Because, "After all, they weren't just answering to Dad, they were answering to God!"

As fathers, we bear a huge responsibility to provide for and protect our wives and children. And providing and protecting go well beyond going to work and providing a home, food, and clothing. Our kids need our presence and love. Boys need a strong role model. Unlike my friend's father, so many fathers are simply absent from the upbringing of their children.

Ephesians 6:4 tells us, "Fathers, do not exasperate your children; instead, bring them up in the training and instruction of the Lord." To exasperate means to frustrate or provoke to anger. Obviously, sometimes when dealing with teens, they are going to get angry and feel exasperated. But this should not be our MO.

I'm a father of two sons and I know how hard being a father can be sometimes. It's easy to fall into the trap of expecting too much from our kids, especially when they're young. We walk a fine line between being too strict and too lenient. We tend to either over-discipline or under-discipline.

I think down deep we all want to be good fathers. We want to bring our kids up "in the training and instruction of the Lord." We want to be a godly influence in our kids' lives. The best way I know to do that is to follow Jesus and engage our kids in following Him. Show them that following Jesus is your way of life. Also, surround yourself with men who are great role models of fatherhood. Be honest with them about your struggles and listen to their advice.

To the extent possible, we want to portray to our children what their heavenly Father is like. Let your kids see your vulnerability and need for the Lord. Apologize to them when you blow it; they'll love and respect you for it.

Scripture Reading: Matthew 7:7-12

Personal Application:
• What is your biggest struggle as a dad? Seek counsel from older godly men who are fathers. Confide in them and pray for each other.
  Ask the Lord to help you follow Jesus and learn from Him how to be a godly father.

Week 39, Day 6: It Is Finished!

After enduring the excruciating pain and suffering on Calvary's cross, in his finale breath, Jesus declared to the world, "It is finished" (John 19:30). Perhaps there would be no more appropriate time in history for the "Halleluiah Chorus" to break out... except maybe when He rose again and when He returns!

What immeasurable strength, courage, and love it must have taken to bear the weight of all our sins, the torture of being nailed to a cross, and the separation from His Father. And yet, because "It is finished!" we need never say, "I'm finished!" His finished work of redemptive grace means that we can never be conquered by sin, fear, anxiety, frustration, temptation, failed relationships, or even death!

His finished work of salvation has accomplished forgiveness and deliverance from our sins. We no longer must fear judgment or feel the anguish of guilt and shame. Our relationship with God through Christ allows us the freedom and liberty that only grace can provide.

And respecting the price of that freedom, we honor Christ through submission, obedience, and worship of Him. As the Apostle Paul wrote, "What shall we say, then? Shall we go on sinning so that grace may increase? By no means! We died to sin; how can we live in it any longer?" (Romans 6:1-2) And again he urges us, "You, my brothers, were called to be free. But do not use your freedom to indulge the sinful nature; rather, serve one another in love." (Galatians 5:13)

Even our faith in Christ is a gift, and through that faith, we know that God has renewed, restored, cleansed, purified, blessed, and freed us from the power of sin. "It is finished!" Satan no longer has a grip on our souls or a claim on our lives. We are free to love and serve others, free to hope and forgive, and free to obey and worship our merciful Savior. We may not know what tomorrow brings, but we know how this story ends... and He wins!

Because "it is finished," the Lord invites us to enter His rest—rest from our own striving and rest from the self-imposed burden of religion. Jesus beckons us, "Come to Me, all you who are weary and burdened, and I will give you rest. Take My yoke upon you and learn from Me, for I am gentle and humble in heart, and you will find rest for your souls. For My yoke is easy and My burden is light." (Matthew 11:28-30)

Let's take a break away from the concerns of war, from the sorrows and disappointments of life, from the sadness of failed relationships, and from the rush of busy schedules. Let's not be overcome by the weight of this world, but rather be overwhelmed with the reality that Jesus has conquered it all. "It is finished!" Rejoice and be glad!

Scripture Reading: Revelation 12:10-11

Personal Application:
- In what ways does Jesus' cry, "It is finished!" mean to you personally?
- Share your testimony of Christ's power in your life with someone today.

Week 39, Day 7: Weekly Recap and Prayer

On the seventh day of each week, use the **ACTS** acronym to spend time with the Lord reviewing and assessing your week and praying to God. (**A**=Adoration; **C**=Confession; **T**=Thanksgiving; **S**=Supplication)

First, look back over the previous six days for this week to remind yourself what you read and agreed to. Then, follow the ACTS pattern for prayer below. Finally, use the space below to journal what God is doing in your life and share this with a trusted spiritual partner.

Adoration: Simply spend time in adoration of the Lord. Praise Him and glorify His name. (See 1 Chronicles 29:10-13; Psalm 100; Romans 11:33-36.)

Confession: Confess your sins and shortcomings before God. ("If we confess our sins, he is faithful and just and will forgive us our sins and purify us from all unrighteousness." – 1 John 1:9) To confess (or agree with God) about your sin, implies that you are repentant and desperately want Him to change you.

Thanksgiving: Thank God for what He has done and is doing in your life and the life of your family. Give Him credit, for everything you have comes from Him. (See Psalm 136.)

Supplication: Supplication is just a fancy word for making your requests known to God. Based on the devotions of this past week and the things going on in your life right now, what do you want to ask Him for? "If you, then, though you are evil, know how to give good gifts to your children, how much more will your Father in heaven give good gifts to those who ask Him!" (Matthew 7:11)

Journal: What is God doing in your life right now?

Week 40, Day 1: A Case of Mistaken Identity

More and more these days I meet people who say, "I'm a Christian, but I don't go to church." Some who say this communicate a sense of liberty—that they've been freed from the burden of attending a church. Some people have been so wounded by a church that they swear they'll never go back. Others simply hold the belief that church-going isn't an important part of being a Christian. Many Christians who choose not to identify themselves with a church say things like: "I can worship God better in the woods or at the lake." "I pray and read the Bible, though not as much as I should." "I've accepted Christ." "I live as best as I can." And so on.

Researcher George Barna wrote, "American Christians are not as devoted to their faith as they like to believe. They have positive feelings about the importance of faith, but their faith is rarely the focal point of their life or a critical factor in their decision-making." But what does God think? Is church unimportant to Him? Can Christians do without the church after all?

Jesus declared, "I will build My church, and the gates of Hades will not overcome it." (Matthew 16:18) But we've been taught about the "universal church" of believers and the "local church" of believers. And many readily claim membership in the universal church, while abandoning the local church. Is that valid?

The word "church" in the New Testament appears over 100 times. The Greek word *ekklesia*, simply means "an assembly of people." In its meaning in Scripture, it clearly denotes a local gathering of Christ-followers who meet to hear God's Word, to pray, worship, serve, and fellowship with each other. All the New Testament letters were written to or about local churches.

The church was not man's idea but Christ's. When Saul was persecuting the church, Jesus so identifies with the church that He asked Saul, "Why are you persecuting Me?" (Acts 9:4) Furthermore, we need each other. We cannot grow in Christ without the input and relationships with other followers of Christ.

To shun the church is to shun Christ. The writer of Hebrews warned us, "And let us consider how we may spur one another on toward love and good deeds, not giving up meeting together, as some are in the habit of doing, but encouraging one another—and all the more as you see the Day approaching." (Hebrews 10:24-25)

Going to church doesn't make a person a Christian. But could it also be that claiming to be a Christian, yet forsaking Christ's church may be a case of mistaken identity?

Scripture Reading: Acts 20:28-31a

Personal Application:

- What has been your attitude and practice regarding church? If you're not currently attending a local assembly of Christ-followers, I urge you to find a church where you can worship and serve.
  See what Christ does in and through you there.

Week 40, Day 2: Seven Ways to Revitalize Your Marriage!

A marriage is like a garden. A beautiful garden needs constant attention. It needs to be watered regularly. It requires the skilled pruning of the master gardener. Weeds must be pulled. And the plants need fertilizing. But a garden left to itself will soon be overrun by weeds and thistles. Bugs, though small, will come in and devour what could have been beautiful.

In the same way, we must tend to our marriage. Here are seven ways to cultivate a healthy marriage:

1. Recognize that marriage is hard work, so give it your best efforts! A young family was discussing marriage around the dinner table. The older two children said they wanted to get married someday. But the youngest child said, "I don't know if I'll get married. Marriage is awful hard work. I think I'll get a job instead!" After the laughter subsided, the parents had to agree with this six-year-old psychiatrist—marriage is hard work!

2. Tell your wife you love her often (multiple times every day). She not only needs to hear it, but you need to hear yourself say it. Keep your romantic spark alive!

3. Date your wife regularly. This is especially important once you have kids. Contrary to popular belief, the child is not the center of the universe. If he/she grows up believing that, you'll have even bigger worries to deal with. As one a man said, "The best thing a father can do for his children is to love their mother!"

4. Look for concrete ways to serve each other selflessly. One of the biggest reasons that marriages get stale is because we become self-absorbed. The best way out that downward spiral is to serve your spouse lovingly, joyfully, and selflessly.

5. Listen to each other attentively. Learn to listen to your wife attentively and caringly. And when your wife shares problems with you that you can't fix, don't try to fix them. Simply love her, reassure her, hold her, and tell her things will be alright.

6. Eat a meal together daily. We often allow life to get so hectic that we don't even share a meal together. Mealtime (especially supper) offers a great opportunity to catch up.

7. Pray with each other. These need not be lengthy prayer meetings! Simply stop and pray with each other. Draw each other into God's presence daily and rely on Him.

Marriage is so holy, so special that God uses marriage to describe His relationship with us.

Scripture Reading: Ephesians 5:25-33

Personal Application:

- Which of these seven tips needs your immediate attention? Consider sharing this list with your wife and work on your marriage together.

Week 40, Day 3: The Lord's Supper

A pastor friend of mine related to me the following story:

One Sunday a few years ago, I had the privilege of leading people in communion at our church. It struck me that the Lord's Supper is a practice that we are meant to participate in *together*. Communion is not an individual but a corporate activity that demonstrates our unity in Christ as we remember His substitutionary death for us. On that Sunday, this truth was impressed on me in a graphic and unexpected way.

"When we bless the cup at the Lord's Table, aren't we sharing in the blood of Christ? And when we break the bread, aren't we sharing in the body of Christ? And though we are many, we all eat from one loaf of bread, showing that we are one body." (1 Corinthians 10:16-17 NLT)

That morning when we observed the Lord's Supper, I looked around and saw that Christ not only died for me, but for these—my brothers and sisters there gathered with me. At the Lord's Table we are all on a level plain. We all come humbly before Him in need of His grace and love that He extends freely toward us. The Lord's Supper brings us together like nothing else.

Well, during communion on that Sunday a few years ago, I was blessed to observe something so tender and sweet. Such an occurrence could have only been caught in the context of sharing Christ's meal together. A mother and her son came forward to the table with about six or eight others. I could see that her son had down's syndrome.

That Sunday we had people take a piece of bread, dip it into grape juice and then eat it. This boy followed the others' example. He took some bread and dipped it into the juice. But he wasn't satisfied with the conservative single dip that the others practiced! Instead, he sloshed the bread back in forth in the grape juice to ensure it was well saturated.

Then he lifted the bread into his mouth, closed his eyes and savored his sacred morsel. Audibly we heard him exclaim, "Mmm, that's good!" And I thought to myself, this boy in his simplicity understands more deeply than the rest of us what it means to enjoy the Lord in his Supper! I could sense God's pleasure over this young man and this cluster of Christ-followers who witnessed this holy scene.

When we come together to observe the Lord's Supper, may we fully enjoy our Lord and His people with whom we share His meal together.

Scripture Reading: 1 Corinthians 11:23-28

Personal Application:
- I encourage you to keep this story in mind the next time you celebrate the Lord's Supper. Enter the experience with the simple joy of this young man and let Christ fill you with love for those around you.

Week 40, Day 4: Pursuing God

When my wife, Louise, and I were sophomores in high school we first met in a Spanish class. I was so absolutely knocked over with this dynamic girl! Each day I woke up, she'd be the first thing on my mind. I would see her in several classes, in student government programs, and at various sports events. I'd wonder if she would ever have the same feelings for me as I had for her.

I looked so forward to my time with her, curious, wondering where we'd go, what we'd do and talk about. And I wanted to know everything there was to know about her. I fantasized about spending our entire lives together and wondered what that would be like.

After five years from that first meeting, Louise agreed to become my bride! That was fifty-five years ago next month. Wow – how time flies! While there were difficult times (primarily because I was a rock-head) we worked through our stuff together. Over the past five-and-a-half decades my love for her has grown as my understanding of God's love and grace for me has developed.

When courting Louise, nobody ever had to ask me if I was spending time with her regularly. I didn't have to make a special effort to schedule time with her. I could hardly wait to spend time with her. And I told her everything—my hopes, dreams, fears—even dumb stuff.

While in college we were apart. Long distance calls were expensive and we missed each other a lot, we tried to write each other daily. We'd mail our letters back and forth to try to fill in the lonely times between visits.

Now, imagine if we each pursued God like that. And why shouldn't we? He wants us to be completely smitten with Him. God doesn't want to be just another priority among priorities. He wants to be on our hearts and minds all day long every day.

The Psalmist expressed his longing for God like this: "As the deer pants for streams of water, so my soul pants for You my God. My soul thirsts for God, for the living God. When can I go and meet with God?" (Psalm 42:1-2)

Sometimes I think we pursue God like a college degree—way too structured, forced, and impersonal. He wants a relationship with us, not an appointment. Let's stop putting God on our list of things to do today and start pursuing Him from our heart. And by the way, He's coming back for us. I can hardly wait!

Scripture Reading: Psalm 16

Personal Application:
- What are some ways you can develop this kind of relationship with the Lord?
- If you already enjoy this kind of relationship with the Lord, what advice could you give others? Share this devotional with someone and describe for them how you pursue God.

Week 40, Day 5: Cheap Grace

Salvation involves being delivered from the eternal consequences of sin. It requires that we acknowledge and accept the sacrifice made on Calvary's Cross by the God-man Jesus. God provided the perfect sacrifice to save us from ourselves, our sin, Satan, and our Godless world. It is only by God's grace that we are saved. Jesus paid a tremendous price for an indescribable gift.

Still, some would try to cheapen it. They try to water down the message of salvation, saying there are many ways to God and Jesus is just one of the ways. Many people believe they don't need Christ's sacrifice—that they're basically a good person and that's good enough. Others say they can counter the effects of their sins by performing acts of kindness or good works, ignoring Jesus' sacrificial death for them.

This reminds me of a story I heard from Chuck Swindoll:

One of the largest department stores in our nation took on a commercial venture that proved to be disastrously unsuccessful. It was a doll in the form of the baby Jesus. It was advertised as being unbreakable, washable, and cuddly. It was packaged in straw with a satin crib and plastic surroundings, and appropriate biblical texts added here and there to make the scene complete.

It did not sell. The manager of one of the stores in the department chain panicked. He carried out a last-ditch promotion to get rid of those dolls. He brandished a huge sign outside his store that read: "Jesus Christ–Marked Down 50%! Get Him While You CAN!"

God's Word tells us that salvation is not something we do; it's something that only God can do. When we try to earn our salvation, we cheapen Christ's sacrifice and minimize our sin. Isaiah wrote, "Your iniquities have separated you from your God; your sins have hidden His face from you, so that He will not hear." (Isaiah 59:2) And if we accept the gift but just walk away, we act like spoiled, ungrateful children who don't appreciate its value.

Imagine a drowning person who is pulled from the ocean. It's not merely about being saved from drowning but being given a fresh opportunity at life. When we come to Christ in true humility and sorrow over our sin, we are completely redeemed, washed white as snow.

What about you my friend? Have you accepted the gift of salvation? If you have accepted the gift of eternal life, live like someone who has been saved from drowning. Value Christ's sacrifice! Quit floundering and walk in new life.

Scripture Reading: Acts 3:11-26

Personal Application:

- Spend time in prayer thanking God for His gift of salvation through Jesus Christ. Worship and praise Him. Live each day as a gift from Him.
- Tell someone else today about God's grace and forgiveness through Jesus. Perhaps the best way to do this is to simply share your story of how you came to Christ.

Week 40, Day 6: The Game of Life

Football has long been considered "The Game of Life" by many who philosophize. Dr. Larry Wilhite, a management consultant, supports that theory.

Larry's first experience playing organized football came his freshman year of high school, in a small Idaho town, with only about 25 boys eligible to play varsity. He was big for his age—220 pounds and six feet tall! Bucking hay bales for his uncle during the summer, he had developed muscles in places most kids just dreamed about. But he was just like any other kid his age, wanting to look and be like someone else.

Given the sparse pickings, Larry was a welcomed sight when he turned out for the varsity team and began preseason conditioning. He knew little about football, but his enthusiasm and drive made him extremely coachable. If his coach said, "Jump," he'd ask, "How high?" and double his efforts on the way up. He took in the coach's game philosophy, too: "The first hit is the most important hit of the game. Hit the other guy harder and more times than he hits you. Do your job better than the other guy 85% of the time, and you will win!"

Building up the team's confidence and courage, the coach also warned them that the game isn't without pain and sacrifice. Especially with their limited numbers, they should be prepared to play hurt. Larry understood and was eager to do his best.

As the first game day approached, it was time to gear up. Most of the equipment was hand-me-down, and the freshmen had last pick. Everything about Larry's uniform was wrong. His shoulder pads were half the size he needed, and the helmet was so big it wobbled when he ran! Despite all this, on game day, Larry was ready.

The game began with a flurry, and soon he had his first big hit on the opposing lineman. But as the pile of players began to unfold, he knew something was wrong. He couldn't see out of his left eye and had tunnel vision in the right eye. He thought he was probably hurt badly but determined to press on. Feeling his way to the next play, suddenly he heard the coach bark, "Wilhite! Turn your helmet around! You're looking through the ear hole!!"

Though he may have had a lot to learn about football and the proper use of his gear, Larry learned a great deal about life that day! He learned that attitude has a powerful impact on how well you do.

Chuck Swindoll said, "I am convinced that life is 10% of what happens to us and 90% how we react to it." On the first play of each day, let's project our best attitude, and sustain it at least 85% of the time—even when we've "gotta play hurt!"

Scripture Reading: 1 Thessalonians 5:12-24

Personal Application:

- The Scripture reading for today offers some characteristics of a great attitude. Which of these characteristics do you find most challenging? These attitudes are all qualities of Christlikeness. As you abide, or remain in Christ, He will enable you to display these attitudes as well.

Week 40, Day 7: Weekly Recap and Prayer

On the seventh day of each week, use the **ACTS** acronym to spend time with the Lord reviewing and assessing your week and praying to God. (**A**=Adoration; **C**=Confession; **T**=Thanksgiving; **S**=Supplication)

First, look back over the previous six days for this week to remind yourself what you read and agreed to. Then, follow the ACTS pattern for prayer below. Finally, use the space below to journal what God is doing in your life and share this with a trusted spiritual partner.

Adoration: Simply spend time in adoration of the Lord. Praise Him and glorify His name. (See 1 Chronicles 29:10-13; Psalm 100; Romans 11:33-36.)

Confession: Confess your sins and shortcomings before God. ("If we confess our sins, he is faithful and just and will forgive us our sins and purify us from all unrighteousness." – 1 John 1:9) To confess (or agree with God) about your sin, implies that you are repentant and desperately want Him to change you.

Thanksgiving: Thank God for what He has done and is doing in your life and the life of your family. Give Him credit, for everything you have comes from Him. (See Psalm 136.)

Supplication: Supplication is just a fancy word for making your requests known to God. Based on the devotions of this past week and the things going on in your life right now, what do you want to ask Him for? "If you, then, though you are evil, know how to give good gifts to your children, how much more will your Father in heaven give good gifts to those who ask Him!" (Matthew 7:11)

Journal: What is God doing in your life right now?

Week 41, Day 1: Troubling Times

The present economy has created great uncertainty for many. Believers re-defining their future often struggle, trying to understand God's will for their lives. It's easy in times like this to allow anxiety and uncertainty to overwhelm us. No matter how unstable our environment, though, we can rest in knowing God loves us and He is in control. We must remain faithful as we trust Him.

History reveals that seasons of unrest and poverty often follow years of peace and prosperity. Mankind finds it easy to forget God when all is going well, but often return to Him when times are tough. During the days of the prophet Micah, times had grown tough. Micah began his ministry about 735 BC. His "calling" was to help the nation of Israel turn its attention back to God. Read the first six chapters of Micah and you'll see that the religious condition of Israel had deteriorated. The rich turned their backs on the Lord and began to imitate the lifestyles of pagan nations. When the peasant farmers couldn't produce the required luxury goods, the rich landowners took over their holdings, perverted justice, and took advantage of the poor. The poor then drifted to the cities seeking shelter. For the first time in Hebrew history, serious overcrowding threatened their cities. Squalor and disease soon accompanied poverty.

The situation grew quite bleak, but Micah told the nation of Israel exactly what God desired from them. God wasn't interested in mindless lip service or a religious façade. God wanted them to obey Him out of desire, devotion, and love for Him and not from mere obligation. Obedience was never meant to be a burden.

The prophet Micah stated God's expectations clearly and concisely in Micah 6:8. God saw their suffering and gave them instructions, explaining how to make things right again. He gave them the antidote to their bleak situation, "To act justly and to love mercy and to walk humbly with your God." Micah's ancient message aptly applies to us today as well. They are certainly words to live by, not as a formula for a "good life," but as template for a pure and loving heart. God wants us to be fair in our dealings with others, follow through on our commitments to others, and pursue Him humbly.

Justice, mercy, and walking humbly with God are all intertwined—the result of loving God and loving others. As Jesus explained, "All the Law and the Prophets hang on these two commandments:" to love God and love others (Matthew 22:37-40). Living in this manner is not merely the antidote for troubling times, but for all times.

Scripture Reading: Matthew 23:1-12

Personal Application:
- In what ways is the message of Micah 6:8 speaking to you? Spend time humbly before the Lord in prayer and ask Him to express His love, mercy, and justice through you today.

Week 41, Day 2: Pretenders

The media is full of scandalous stories of deceit. Whether in big cities or small towns, our society is filled with pretenders—people who have forgotten about integrity. Still, when everything is stripped away, all a person really has is his faith and his character. I believe that keeping a humble spirit while seeking God's purpose for our lives is so critical. Temptations that could compromise our integrity are all around us. Our principles and honor must remain strong and pure if we are to endure the struggles and challenges life brings.

I remember hearing about a fellow who purchased a record-breaking white tail deer rack from an "old timer." While the rack had never been officially recorded, some folks were familiar with its existence. The new owner decided to give the head a new cape and display it at several sports shows. He regularly boasted about the stalk and the harvesting of this animal. Having won many awards for "his new record deer," he and his trophy soon became very popular among hunters. Then, one fateful day, someone recognized the head for what it was. Officials were contacted and the pretender was properly reprimanded and fined for his actions.

When we try to take the credit for something God has done, we are no better—worse. When we flaunt our good deeds for all to see or pretend to be something we're not, we become hypocrites—pretenders of the worse kind. Eventually we're sure to be found out.

Jesus had much to say about hypocrisy. He will not tolerate it. When confronting the pious pretenders of His day, he exclaimed, "Woe to you, teachers of the law and Pharisees, you hypocrites! You travel over land and sea to win a single convert, and when he becomes one, you make him twice as much a son of hell as you are." For this reason, Peter urges believers: "Therefore, rid yourselves of all malice and all deceit, hypocrisy, envy, and slander of every kind." (1 Peter 2:1)

God's Word tells us, "True humility and fear of the LORD lead to riches, honor, and long life." (Proverbs 22:4 NLT) I believe true humility and fear of the Lord comes from understanding who we are and who God is. Both will keep us from pretending to be something we're not.

An old country preacher put it this way: "Be who you is, cuz if you ain't who you is, you is who you ain't." We can't expect to be the "light of the world" or the "salt of the earth" if our character is flawed with hypocrisy. We must approach each day with integrity, knowing full well that any good that we do is in God's strength, by His grace, and through His will.

Let's not be pretenders, but keep our focus on Christ, bringing Him glory, and bringing others to Him through a life of integrity.

Scripture Reading: Proverbs 10:9; 12:9; 13:7

Personal Application:
- Spend time in prayer thanking God for all He has blessed you with—
  your family, your health, your gifts, skills, strengths,
  your possessions, your job—everything you can think of.
  It's all a gift from Him.

Week 41, Day 3: "And Such Were Some of You"

When Paul wrote his first letter to the church at Corinth, it was not a letter glowing with praise for their faithfulness and purity in following Jesus. Instead, Paul had to reprimand them for falling back into worldly ways and for living to please their fleshly desires instead of pleasing God.

Paul's letter exposed their pride; a case of incest in the church that they willingly tolerated; lawsuits among church members; marital problems; fighting within the church, and a host of other sinful issues.

In chapter six, Paul reminded them that "wrongdoers will not inherit the kingdom of God." Then, he went on to list despicable sins—sins which God's judgment will rightly condemn. But immediately following that list of awful sins, Paul wrote some remarkable words, "And such were some of you. But you were washed, but you were sanctified, but you were justified in the name of the Lord Jesus and by the Spirit of our God." (1 Corinthians 6:11 NKJV).

Forty-five years ago, I met a man in the church I attended. He was married with two children. He prided himself in how much he read and studied the Bible, and he knew God's Word quite well—in his head. But through a series of events, it came out this this man, who was a long-haul truck driver, had mistresses all along his route. Additionally, he had pedophile tendencies and had sexually molested his young niece.

When his deeds came to light, he spent time in prison for his crimes. He lost his family and friends. For many years, he simply disappeared off anyone's radar. Then, a few months ago, he asked to meet with me. At first, I was repulsed by the idea, knowing what he had been. But when I met with him, I found a transformed man.

This man who had formerly been brazen in his sexual sin and spiritual pride, is now humble and contrite. He is a broken man—but in a good sense, for he had humbled himself before God. Today, he is a man who is fully aware of how depraved and sinful he had been and how merciful and gracious God is. As a result, he praises God daily for His forgiveness and cleansing.

So, now it could be said of him too, "But you were washed, but you were sanctified, but you were justified in the name of the Lord Jesus and by the Spirit of our God." But isn't that the situation with each of us? For we have all sinned and fall short of God's glory. We all deserve God's judgment and death. But praise God! "We are washed, we are sanctified, we are justified in the name of the Lord Jesus and by the Spirit of our God!"

Scripture Reading: 1 Corinthians 6:7-11

Personal Application:

- Where do you stand in your relationship with Christ? Are there sins in your life that you still engage in, knowing how much they displease the Lord?
  If so, confess those sins. Humble yourself before the Lord, and
  by His Spirit, live for Him in all you do, walking in freedom
  knowing that you are forgiven and cleansed.

Week 41, Day 4: Change

Change is inevitable! With change often comes more change, as we adapt to new circumstances, new technology, or new ideas. Whether they're minor or drastic, the fact is, "adapting" has become a routine part of our daily existence. And it can be quite rattling. We wonder, "Am I just too old-fashioned, too set in my ways, or too black and white? Am I even up to this?" Whether we decide to "go with the flow," or not often takes a lot of sorting out… and sometimes we simply have no choice.

Change seems to be happening faster than ever in this country. The pace with which we live creates an environment of constant change. It often leads to what I call a "hurried sickness." Consider the computer industry alone: what's current technology or efficient today, probably won't be tomorrow, and certainly won't be a few months from now.

Also, people's values and perceptions are rapidly changing. What we blushed at only a few years ago is now viewed as common and acceptable behavior. What were previously "unmentionables" are now discussed openly on television, radio talk shows, and the internet.

Sometimes change means losing a job, a home, one's health, or a loved one. Some things change for the better, and some for the worse, and sometimes it's hard to tell which is which. Yes, we live in a fast-paced, ever-changing world that often leaves us wondering who and what we can trust. With the constant flux around us, we can get discouraged.

Here's some good news; some things will never change… and they're the most important things! As those who trust in Jesus, we know:

- He will never change: "I the LORD do not change." (Malachi 3:6a)
- His love for us will never change: "I have loved you with an everlasting love; I have drawn you with loving-kindness." (Jeremiah 31:3b)
- His Word will never change: "The grass withers and the flowers fall, but the Word of our God stands forever." (Isaiah 40:8)
- His purposes will never change: "But the plans of the LORD stand firm forever, the purposes of his heart through all generations." (Psalm 33:11)

Jesus told us, "In this world you will have trouble. But take heart! I have overcome the world." (John 16:33) In this world change is inevitable and often means trouble. But in Christ, we too have overcome the world and its onslaught of change. So, let's put our trust in Him who never changes.

Scripture Reading: Romans 8:38-39; Hebrews 13:5

Personal Application:
- What changes are you facing in life right now?
- Find stability and constancy in the Lord who can help you navigate the changes you face. Thank Him that His love and care for you never change.

Week 41, Day 5: Be a Godly Example to Others

Godly examples of men and women in our life provide us with a powerful motivation and pattern for pursuing Christ. Especially when we are young, we simply mimic the example of others, often without conscious thought for what we're doing. We simply do what they do. My friend Rob shared with me some of the men who served as examples in his life.

When he was in the first grade, a girl in his class invited him to attend the Boys Brigade meetings at her country church. Rob attended and met her dad and his brother. The two McClellan brothers were carpenters by trade, lived exemplary lives and invested in boys and young men training them how to follow Jesus. Rob was deeply impacted by their example.

Then, in the sixth grade, Rob's Sunday school teacher was a man named Buzz Sawyer. Rob remembers Buzz as "a machinist who always had dirty fingernails," but he loved God and he loved the boys he ministered to. Buzz was humble and sincere as he taught God's Word to these young men. Rob gained a love for God's Word from watching Buzz.

In high school, Rob's Sunday school teacher was a man named Dick Plaep. Dick was a probation officer and volunteered for Youth for Christ. He was a big guy who had played tackle on a college football team. Dick's manner was loving but direct and he challenged Rob in his walk with Jesus.

Dick introduced Rob to Larry Anderson, who was Director of Youth for Christ in Minneapolis at the time. Larry invited Rob and some other teenage boys on a canoe trip in the Boundary Waters area in northern Minnesota. One night in camp as the boys sat around the fire, Larry challenged them to go all out for Jesus. Rob declared before the others that night that he would follow Jesus whole-heartedly.

Some years later, Rob was in basic training in the Army. He was selected for the Special Leadership Training Program. One of his instructors was a veteran combat soldier, a Black man named Drill Sergeant Roosevelt. Rob held this man in high esteem and learned much about leading men from him.

I hope you see a pattern here. All these men were regular guys from a variety of backgrounds and walks of life. They all lived their lives with integrity and purpose knowing that the way they conducted their lives would help lead others closer to Christ. Their lives made a difference.

Paul was Timothy's example and mentor. He wrote to Timothy, "Don't let anyone look down on you because you are young, but set an example for the believers in speech, in conduct, in love, in faith and in purity." (1 Timothy 4:12)

I wonder, who is watching you or me today?

Scripture Reading: 1 Timothy 4:6-16

Personal Application:

- To what extent do you conduct your life knowing that you serve
  as an example to others in following Jesus? It's never too late
  to start living an exemplary life as a Christ-follower.

Week 41, Day 6: "What We're Doing Is Not Right!"

There's a remarkable story of God's deliverance in 2 Kings 7. The Aramean army had laid siege to Samaria, the royal city of Israel. (This was after the nation of Israel split into two kingdoms.) The siege had gone on so long that there was no more food in the city and the people began resorting to cannibalism to stay alive. Israel had been very evil in the years leading up to this siege, but God wanted to demonstrate His mercy and power to them so they might turn from their evil ways and trust Him. Here's what happened:

"The Lord had caused the Arameans to hear the sound of chariots and horses and a great army, so that they said to one another, 'Look, the king of Israel has hired the Hittite and Egyptian kings to attack us!" So, they got up and fled in the dusk and abandoned their tents and their horses and donkeys. They left the camp as it was and ran for their lives." (2 Kings 7:6-7)

Meanwhile, the Israelites had no idea that the Arameans had fled. But there were four leprous men in the city. They conferred with each other and decided to surrender to the Arameans rather than starve to death in the city. So that evening they went out to the camp of the Arameans intending to give themselves up. But when they got there, they found the camp deserted. We pick up the story again in verses 8-9:

"The men who had leprosy reached the edge of the camp, entered one of the tents and ate and drank. Then they took silver, gold, and clothes, and went off and hid them. They returned and entered another tent and took some thing from it and hid them also. Then they said to each other, 'What we're doing is not right. This is a day of good news and we are keeping it to ourselves. Let's go at once and report this to the royal palace.'" And that's what they did.

I love that story not only because it displays the mercy and power of God, but because it also reminds us about the good news of Jesus Christ that we possess. Many who come to Christ and taste the riches of relationship with Him, merely go and hide what they've found, keeping it to themselves.

But we dare not hide this Good News from others. We must not keep it to ourselves but tell others what God has done on their behalf through His Son Jesus Christ.

Someone has said, "Sharing the Gospel of Jesus Christ is like one beggar showing another beggar where to find food." Let's be as free and generous at sharing the Gospel with others just like those were who shared the Gospel (Good News) with us.

Scripture Reading: Matthew 5:13-16

Personal Application:
- One of the simplest, most natural ways to share the Gospel of Jesus Christ with someone is to share your story. You can tell your story in three simple parts: what your life was like before Christ; how you met Christ; and how He has changed your life.
- Pray and ask God to give you a clear opportunity to share the Gospel with someone today.

Week 41, Day 7: Weekly Recap and Prayer

On the seventh day of each week, use the **ACTS** acronym to spend time with the Lord reviewing and assessing your week and praying to God. (**A**=Adoration; **C**=Confession; **T**=Thanksgiving; **S**=Supplication)

First, look back over the previous six days for this week to remind yourself what you read and agreed to. Then, follow the ACTS pattern for prayer below. Finally, use the space below to journal what God is doing in your life and share this with a trusted spiritual partner.

Adoration: Simply spend time in adoration of the Lord. Praise Him and glorify His name. (See 1 Chronicles 29:10-13; Psalm 100; Romans 11:33-36.)

Confession: Confess your sins and shortcomings before God. ("If we confess our sins, he is faithful and just and will forgive us our sins and purify us from all unrighteousness." – 1 John 1:9) To confess (or agree with God) about your sin, implies that you are repentant and desperately want Him to change you.

Thanksgiving: Thank God for what He has done and is doing in your life and the life of your family. Give Him credit, for everything you have comes from Him. (See Psalm 136.)

Supplication: Supplication is just a fancy word for making your requests known to God. Based on the devotions of this past week and the things going on in your life right now, what do you want to ask Him for? "If you, then, though you are evil, know how to give good gifts to your children, how much more will your Father in heaven give good gifts to those who ask Him!" (Matthew 7:11)

Journal: What is God doing in your life right now?

Week 42, Day 1: Go After Sin Proactively

A pastor friend of mine shared with me how he used to get very angry in traffic. He didn't participate in road-rage but considered himself "the cosmic referee of all traffic etiquette." One day he left the church early to go home and get a hike in before going back that evening to teach a Bible study. On the way home, another driver rudely cut him off and he was livid! He gave the guy an angry blast of his horn and a nasty look. Then, instantly, the Holy Spirit convicted him of his sin. My friend knew this angry behavior was sinful, displeasing to the Lord, and unbefitting a follower of Jesus.

But until that day, my friend admits that he had always approached this recurring sin *reactively* and not *proactively*. Here's what I mean: by merely reacting to an angry outburst he would feel remorse, confess his sin to the Lord and hope it didn't happen again, which it inevitably did!

This time was different. My friend went on his hike, but for that hour he meditated on and prayed through 1 John 1:9, "If we confess our sins, He is faithful and just and will forgive us our sins and purify us from all unrighteousness." During his hike and extended conversation with the Lord, he experienced the refreshment of God's forgiveness and was reminded again of the amazing grace and mercy of the Lord toward him. He also recognized that this time he needed to proactively root this sin from his life. He knew this wouldn't be easy because it had been his go-to reaction for many years.

That same day, my friend contacted his spiritual partner or comrade in arms, Ed, and told him about the above incident and his resolve to ask Christ to remove this from his life. He gave Ed permission to hold him accountable and asked him to pray for him as they met each week. Additionally, my friend told his wife and asked the same of her. The above incident occurred 15 years ago and my friend reports that God has done a marvelous work of grace in his life. The Lord has replaced his anger with patience and peace. In fact, every time he gets in the car, he asks the Lord to help him drive cautiously, courteously, and patiently.

My friend went after his sin proactively and he knew that he could only do so in Christ's strength and with the assistance of his spiritual partner and his wife. Paul urges us, "Just as you used to offer yourselves as slaves to impurity and to ever-increasing wickedness, so now offer yourselves as slaves to righteousness leading to holiness." (Romans 6:19)

All of us, at some time, have some niggling sin that we can't seem to shake. Stop dealing with it *reactively*. Instead, follow my friend's example and watch the Lord remove it from you.

Scripture Reading: Romans 6:1-14

Personal Application:
- What sin has been troubling you? With the Lord's help and assistance from a spiritual partner, go after it proactively.

Week 42, Day 2: Faithfulness

When someone asked a well-known NFL coach why he always had a pastor on the sideline during a game, he explained, "I'm not even sure if I believe in God, but in case there is one, I want Him on my side."

In a similar way, King Nebuchadnezzar seemed to use the prophet Daniel as a spiritual rabbit's foot or lucky penny. But Daniel had a tremendous testimony and demonstrated time and time again how people who have great faith in the one true God manifest great character. Nebuchadnezzar learned to admire and respect Daniel's character because of his faithfulness and his obedience to "his God."

Nebuchadnezzar believed in many gods; he didn't believe that the God of the Hebrews was the only true God. He even went so far as to set up an image of himself and demand that everyone in his kingdom bow down to it or be thrown into the fiery furnace.

But Daniel's three friends Shadrach, Meshach, and Abednego refused to bow down to his idol. When Nebuchadnezzar heard of their defiance, he had them thrown into the fiery furnace. But God sent His angel to protect His three faithful followers. And when Nebuchadnezzar saw how the God of Shadrach, Meshach, and Abednego protected them, this reluctant king acknowledged that the Lord is the one true God.

"Then Nebuchadnezzar said, 'Praise be to the God of Shadrach, Meshach, and Abednego, who has sent his angel and rescued his servants! They trusted in him and defied the king's command and were willing to give up their lives rather than serve or worship any god except their own God." (Daniel 3:28)

Eventually, Nebuchadnezzar blessed the God of Shadrach, Meshach, Abednego, and Daniel and decreed that anyone speaking an offense against their God would be destroyed.

I humbly wonder if I would have had the courage to defy the king's command and bow down to his image. After all, it would be so easy to rationalize, "Lord, I'm just bowing down to this idol to save my skin. I don't really mean it. How can I be a witness for You if I'm dead?"

God doesn't always rescue His children when they exhibit courage and faithfulness like this. Sometimes their blood speaks louder than if they were saved. But God was and continues to be honored when we are faithful.

Scripture Reading: 2 Corinthians 4:1-12

Personal Application:

- Few of us will find ourselves in a situation as grave as Shadrack, Meshach, and Abednego. Sometimes it's easier to take a stand when the heat is turned up or the stakes are high. So how do we define and demonstrate faithfulness to the Lord in our lives here and now?

Week 42, Day 3: Delighting in the Lord

When I was a kid, Bible memory was a common spiritual discipline at Sunday school, summer camp, and youth group. One of the verses that I committed to memory back then was Psalm 37:4, "Delight yourself in the Lord, and He will give you the desires of your heart." (ESV)

But I must confess that I didn't understand what that verse meant. I had this vague sense that if I kept the Lord as my one chief focus, then He would basically give me whatever I wanted. This was a twisted, genie-in-a-lamp view of God, but not altogether that unusual even today I wager.

Fast forward many years and one day I was meditating on that verse, "Delight yourself in the Lord, and He will give you the desires of your heart." I was having a conversation with the Lord about this verse. I really wanted to understand it and live by it. I asked, "What does it mean to 'delight in You, Lord'?"

I know I delight in my wife, my children, and grandchildren. My thoughts went to synonyms for "delight": "Take pleasure in," "find joy in," "enjoy," "desire…" I hit on the word "desire" and plugged it in instead of "delight" to see what happened. "*Desire* the Lord, and He will give you the desires of your heart."

Immediately, a light went on. "If I sincerely desire the Lord, He will fulfill that desire." We're talking about the Almighty God who created all that exists! "If we truly desire Him, He will grant our desire! He will fill us with His fulness!" Let that truth soak in!

It was about the same time that I read a little book by John Piper, *The Dangerous Duty of Delight*. Perhaps his most well-known quote from that book is, "God is most glorified in us when we are most satisfied in Him." In other words, to enjoy God is to glorify Him. But despite my Christian upbringing, I was unfamiliar with the concept of enjoying God.

Between my meditation on Psalm 37:4 and reading Piper's book, my walk with the Lord took a mammoth stride forward. We know we're to love the Lord, but one of the purest expressions of love for someone is true enjoyment of them. In an earlier devotional I shared with you about my courtship with my wife. I truly enjoyed being with her every possible moment (and I still do)!

I realized that when I enjoy and long for the Lord's company, He fulfills my deepest desire for Him in ways beyond description. I urge you too to learn what it means to "delight in the Lord."

"You make known to me the path of life; You will fill me with joy in your presence, with eternal pleasures at your right hand." (Psalm 16:11)

Scripture Reading: Psalm 100

Personal Application:

- To what extent would you say that you enjoy God? How do you cultivate that enjoyment and desire for Him? (Hint: His Word, prayer, and spending time with others who enjoy Him are significant means for cultivating enjoyment and satisfaction in the Lord.

Week 42, Day 4: You Are Called as a Disciple

When a quarterback drops back to pass, the one thing he doesn't want to do is to throw an interception. Unfortunately, in the heat of the battle, what a quarterback wants and what happens to the pigskin may be two different things. The possibility of an interception shouldn't keep him from throwing the ball, however. An experienced quarterback is quick and decisive. Of course, there's always the risk of interception, but nothing ventured, nothing gained.

A successful passer must constantly refine and perfect his skills while taking some risks. It takes practice and commitment to throw the pigskin into very tight spots and accuracy is essential. Great quarterbacks aren't born; they're made. Success comes from devotion, a great deal of hard work and the refinement of great mentors—coaches that help shape and mold these young men into valuable players.

So, it is with being a disciple. Jesus is perpetually perfecting us for the work of ministry. You and I, as disciples, are called to live like Jesus and make other disciples who can, in turn, live like Him and make other disciples. Discipleship is apprenticeship—the process of sharing, encouraging, modeling, teaching, listening, and serving.

Living like Christ and leading others comes from devotion to the Lord, time in His Word, time conversing with Him, and spending time with others. Like any skill, we become better with practice. Representing Christ is both simple and hard. It's simple because we simply tell our story and let Christ shine through us. It's hard because we and our sin can get in the way. We can become distracted by the things of the world that quench our fervor and choke our witness.

I love what Ken Carpenter, editor for *Spirit of Revival* magazine, has to say about discipleship: "Discipleship is a process. God's desire is to etch into our lives the imprint of His Son, Jesus. He is responsible for the construction process of making us like Christ. But He needs yielded, available individuals willing to be shaped, molded, and carved by His hands." And so, it is.

Speaking truth and leading others to a saving knowledge of Christ can feel risky, but the victory is so sweet! The daily practice of living a Christlike life will help keep us from having our intentions and actions thwarted by the evil one. Thankfully, God's grace cuts through our own inadequacies. He just asks for a heart that is fully devoted to Him and willing to take the risk!

Scripture Reading: Luke 8:26-39

Personal Application:
- What strikes you most about verses 38-39 from the above passage?
- Let me challenge you with the following: Every day, when you rise, ask the Lord to help you represent Him well today through your life and words. Ask Him to lead you and give you opportunities to show His love to others.

Week 42, Day 5: "What Is Truth?"

The title of this devotional are the words spoken by Pontius Pilate when he was listening to Jesus' defense at His trial. Jesus had just told Pilate, "In fact, the reason I was born and came into the world is to testify to the truth. Everyone on the side of truth listens to Me." And that's when Pilate retorted, "What is truth?" (John 18:37-38)

Perhaps Pilate's words were prophetic, for our culture in America today sarcastically poses the same question, "What is truth?" The very word "truth" means something that is true. It speaks of the veracity of a statement or incident. Truth and facts go hand in hand.

But today, our culture says truth is merely what you believe it to be. Truth has become relative, so we hear people say things like, "That's your truth, but not my truth. My truth is different." I hope you see that from the standpoint of reality, such thinking is insane. If all truth is relative then mathematics, science, history is all lost and up for grabs.

It's like saying, "If you want to believe that two plus two equals four that's fine. That's your truth. But I like to believe two plus two equals five." Try using this ridiculous logic next time a police officer pulls you over for speeding or running a red light. Do we really think truth is relative?

Paul explained in Romans, "The wrath of God is being revealed from heaven against all the godlessness and wickedness of people, who suppress the truth by their wickedness, since what may be known about God is plain to them, because God has made it plain to them." (Romans 1:18-19) Then, Paul adds, "They exchanged the truth about God for a lie…." (Romans 1:25)

Sin not only separates us from God, but it blinds us to the truth. When we choose to continue in sin, we must suppress the truth, or we'd feel real guilt and shame for our evil practices. Living in sin, we don't like the truth, so we simply say (insanely) that truth doesn't exist. "If we claim to have fellowship with Him and yet walk in the darkness, we lie and do not live out the truth." (1 John 1:6)

Jesus declared, "I am the way and the truth and the life. No one comes to the Father except through Me." (John 14:6) And earlier in his Gospel, John said of Jesus, "The Word became flesh and made His dwelling among us. We have seen His glory, the glory of the one and only Son, who came from the Father, full of grace and truth." (John 1:14)

As followers of Christ, we must not deny the truth but cling to it, stand on it, and proclaim it. Jesus Christ is God. He gave Himself up for our sins. He rose from the dead and ascended into heaven. And as sure as you are reading these words, He is coming back again soon!

Scripture Reading: John 8:31-32

Personal Application:
- How would you respond to someone who says truth is relative?
- Meditate on the Scripture Reading for today.
  In what way does the truth set a person free?

Week 42, Day 6: The Last Word

In a similar vein with yesterday's devotional, our culture seeks to discourage believers by trying to dispel the claims of the Bible. Many of the iconic personalities in this nation openly blaspheme God. Our societal norms have been adjusted to accept all kinds of behavior that only two decades ago would have been ludicrous. Some of those running for political offices around the country deny that our moral compass is off. Getting the vote is more important than taking a stand, and that charisma is more important than character.

As long as we're in this world, we want to represent Christ well to others in hopes that they will come to the knowledge of the truth and receive Christ as their Savior. But we also know that those who thumb their nose at God or ignore Him will discover the truth—but too late—and God will have the last word. He will be vindicated.

It reminds me of what was happening in Jerusalem during King Hezekiah's reign. The Assyrian army had already conquered the northern ten tribes of Israel, and now they had their sights on Judah. King Sennacherib's army had surrounded Jerusalem and the situation looked grim. We'll pick up the story here:

Sennacherib's officers spoke further against the LORD God and against his servant Hezekiah. The king also wrote letters insulting the LORD, the God of Israel, and saying this against him: "Just as the gods of the peoples of the other lands did not rescue their people from my hand, so the god of Hezekiah will not rescue his people from my hand." Then they called out in Hebrew to the people of Jerusalem who were on the wall, to terrify them and make them afraid to capture the city. They spoke about the God of Jerusalem as they did about the gods of the other peoples of the world—the work of men's hands. (2 Chronicles 32:16-19)

Sennacherib's words were boastful and proud. He belittled God and thought Him no different than the gods (idols) of the other nations he had already conquered. But God would have the last word.

Upon hearing all this King Hezekiah cried out in prayer to God, "Lord, the God of Israel… You alone are God over all the kingdoms of the earth. You have made heaven and earth. Giver ear, Lord, and hear; open your eyes Lord, and see; listen to the words Sennacherib has sent to ridicule the living God." (2 Kings 19:15-16)

In response to Hezekiah's prayer, the Lord sent an angel that night who put to death 185,000 of Sennacherib's troops. Then, Sennacherib went back to Assyria and two of his sons murdered him while he was worshiping in the temple of his god Nisrok, an idol. So, God had the last word.

Scripture Reading: Matthew 24:27-31

Personal Application:

- Think of a loved one, a co-worker, or a neighbor who doesn't yet know the Lord. Pray for them today that they might come to know Him before it's too late.

Week 42, Day 7: Weekly Recap and Prayer

On the seventh day of each week, use the **ACTS** acronym to spend time with the Lord reviewing and assessing your week and praying to God. (**A**=Adoration; **C**=Confession; **T**=Thanksgiving; **S**=Supplication)

First, look back over the previous six days for this week to remind yourself what you read and agreed to. Then, follow the ACTS pattern for prayer below. Finally, use the space below to journal what God is doing in your life and share this with a trusted spiritual partner.

Adoration: Simply spend time in adoration of the Lord. Praise Him and glorify His name. (See 1 Chronicles 29:10-13; Psalm 100; Romans 11:33-36.)

Confession: Confess your sins and shortcomings before God. ("If we confess our sins, he is faithful and just and will forgive us our sins and purify us from all unrighteousness." – 1 John 1:9) To confess (or agree with God) about your sin, implies that you are repentant and desperately want Him to change you.

Thanksgiving: Thank God for what He has done and is doing in your life and the life of your family. Give Him credit, for everything you have comes from Him. (See Psalm 136.)

Supplication: Supplication is just a fancy word for making your requests known to God. Based on the devotions of this past week and the things going on in your life right now, what do you want to ask Him for? "If you, then, though you are evil, know how to give good gifts to your children, how much more will your Father in heaven give good gifts to those who ask Him!" (Matthew 7:11)

Journal: What is God doing in your life right now?

Week 43, Day 1: Too Many Sticks

My friend Rob Fischer tells a humorous story with a poignant moral:

Some years ago, I took my grandson Parker on his first hike in the woods. He was just four years old at the time. We had no sooner gotten into the forest when Parker spied an interesting stick that he just had to have. He picked it up and we walked on.

Parker was soon distracted with all the wonderful sticks he was finding on the ground. I tried to limit him to three, but he would have none of it. Soon he was having difficulty walking because he now had a sheaf of sticks clutched to his chest with both arms.

So, I tried the safety ploy and explained to him that I didn't want him to trip while trying to carry all those sticks. He thought about it for a moment, looked at me and saw that I wasn't carrying anything. So, he asked me with his puppy-dog eyes if I would carry some of his sticks for him and ease his burden.

I consented to carry some of his sticks but asked him to refrain from gathering any more. Also, I secretly decided that for every new stick he picked up, I would surreptitiously discard one.

The climax came as we were nearing the end of our hike. We were climbing through a labyrinth of large rock formations and Parker picked up yet another stick. In response, I placed one of the sticks I was carrying on a high ledge of rock, hoping that Parker hadn't noticed. But to my dismay, he had caught me in the act!

Parker asked me very seriously, "Grandpa, what did you just do?" I chuckled as I confessed that I had discarded one of the sticks I was carrying. He asked me to show him which stick it was, so I reached up for it and showed it to him. And Parker, in all seriousness, said, "Grandpa, that was my favorite stick!" I had to laugh out loud as I handed Parker his favorite stick!

When I got home, I started thinking about our hike together and the fact that Parker's infatuation with sticks is not much different from what we do as adults. We constantly fill our lives with the next best "shiny" thing that we just must have, and we load our calendars to the hilt with so many activities that we don't have time to breathe.

The result is that we're so weighed down by all our stuff and our over-booked schedules that we become distracted and unfruitful. Jesus warned, "The worries of this life and the deceitfulness of wealth choke the word, making it unfruitful." (Matthew 13:22)

How about you? Are you trying to pick up too many sticks?

Scripture Reading: Luke 21:34-36

Personal Application:

- Take a good long look at your life right now.
  To what extent have you become distracted and unfruitful?
  Pray and ask God what you can give up or give away.

Week 43, Day 2: Fishing for Men

For some years, we lived in a home overlooking the beautiful Spokane River, where I would daily receive inspiration from God's creation. The Spokane River was famous for its "caddis hatch" each June. I would regularly see drift boats and a few bank fishermen whipping the water with their fly rods hoping that their imitation bugs would tempt some unsuspecting trout.

While watching them one day, it occurred to me that with my busy travel and speaking schedule, and the numerous chores around the yard, I hadn't taken the opportunity to participate in this seasonal event. It is hard to call yourself a fisherman if you are not fishing.

In a similar sense, it is hard to call yourself a disciple if you are not fishing for men. As former U.S. Senate Chaplain, Peter Marshall, once said, "Fishing for fish is pulling fish out of life unto death. Fishing for men is pulling men from death into eternal life." When Jesus said, "Follow me and I will make you fishers of men," to a group of common fisherman, He ignited a passion for evangelism that still burns in the hearts and minds of His disciples today.

We can learn a great deal from Andrew, one of the very first fisherman/apostles called into service by Jesus. Before he met Jesus, Andrew was a follower of John the Baptist. But when John introduced Andrew to Jesus, "The first thing Andrew did was to find his brother Simon and tell him, 'We have found the Messiah' (that is, the Christ)." (John 1:41)

It was also Andrew who brought a little boy from the crowd to Jesus: "There is a lad here who has five barley loaves and two fish…" John 6:9a. Miraculously, Jesus used this introduction, and the boy's lunch, to feed the entire crowd.

In John 12:20-22, we read about another time when Andrew introduced others to Christ. This time Andrew brought some Greeks to Jesus. Andrew was just a common fisherman, but he knew how to introduce others to Jesus Christ.

Andrew shows us how to lead others to Jesus simply and matter-of-factly. With his brother Peter, Andrew simply shared his experience with Jesus. Telling your story and how you met Jesus is one of the easiest yet most powerful ways to introduce others to Jesus Christ.

As we share our personal story of salvation with friends and neighbors, we give them an appetite to know Jesus. Our hope is that, like Andrew, we can bring people to know Jesus and that when they meet Him, they too will be captivated with Who He is and what He has done for them.

Scripture Reading: Matthew 4:19; 28:18-20

Personal Application:

- I encourage you to write out your story of how you came to know Jesus. Keep it short—perhaps just half-a-page. Then, rehearse it so you can tell it easily from memory. Now, share it with someone you know.

Week 43, Day 3: Suffering for Christ

Gus Bess is one of the most dynamic pastors I have ever had the opportunity to work with. He manifests a passion for everything he does, including bow hunting. When Gus was pastoring near Bellingham, Washington, he regularly saw some large elk feeding next to a small wooded area. Whenever he stopped his car and got out, they made their way through the woods and escaped to the open area on the other side.

One day Gus decided to have Danny, his 14-year-old son, help him set a trap for the wary elk. They both piled out of the car and looked around, but no elk were visible. Gus told his son, "You give me about 10 minutes to walk around to the back of the woods, then you start walking to the front part where we've previously seen them feeding. Maybe they're back in the woods and you'll scare them to me when they run out."

Gus moved quickly to his position and nocked an arrow. Then, he waited and waited, wondering if his young son was ever going to walk through the woods. Suddenly he heard the familiar beat of hoofs running across the forest floor. But as he listened, it became apparent that the elk moving away from him. Concerned for his son, Gus ran through the woods to see Danny standing perfectly still, eyes bulging out of his head.

"Son," Gus yelled, "Are you all right?" "Yeah Dad, I'm just scared." Gus could see the fright in the boy's face. "What happened?" "Well Dad, I did just what you said. I waited about ten minutes and started walking towards the woods when I stepped right into the middle of an entire herd of elk bedded down. The six big bulls jumped to their feet, acting like they wanted to fight me. They were snorting and digging at the ground. I was scared stiff; I didn't know what to do."

Gus figures that, once the elk scented the boy, they ran off away from both Danny and Gus. As the two men now recall this adventure, they are reminded how, even in obedience, we can find troubles. Danny was obedient to His father, but things didn't turn out the way he expected.

We often suffer as a consequence for our disobedience, but to suffer for righteousness is a special blessing. Suffering for good, for obedience to God's Word, can still be very difficult: we don't get the promotion, we're left out of a group gathering, or we're mocked, simply because we're trying to live a righteous life as a follower of Christ.

Peter wrote, "It is better, if it is God's will, to suffer for doing good than for doing evil. For Christ died for sins once for all, the righteous for the unrighteous, to bring you to God..." (1 Peter 3:17-18) Let us be obedient to our Father, knowing that He loves us especially when we suffer.

Scripture Reading: 2 Timothy 2:1-10

Personal Application:

- Most of us in America do not routinely suffer due to our witness for Christ. But thousands throughout the Muslim world and in countries like India, China, North Korea, and Nepal suffer harassment, imprisonment, confiscation of goods, and even torture and death. Spend time praying for them today.

Week 43, Day 4: Compromise

If you're married and you and your wife are at a stalemate over a decision, a compromise can be a good thing. But applying compromise to our faith in Christ can be deadly.

In Jesus' letters to the seven churches in Revelation 2 and 3, He called on five of those churches to repent. Why? Because they had compromised their faith in Christ in one way or another. Here's what we find there, and keep in mind that "church" is simply a collective name for a gathering of those who claim Christ as Savior:

- The church in Ephesus had compromised her love for Christ, "You have forsaken the love you had at the first. Consider how far you have fallen! Repent and do the things you did at first." (Revelation 2:4-5)
- The church in Pergamum had compromised both its doctrine and its behavior that resulted from false doctrine, "Nevertheless, I have a few things against you: There are some among you who hold to the teaching of Balaam, who taught Balak to entice the Israelites to sin so that they ate food sacrificed to idols and committed sexual immorality. Likewise, you also have those who hold to the teaching of the Nicolaitans. Repent therefore!" (Revelation 2:14-16)
- The church in Thyatira compromised by tolerating a wicked woman in their midst who was leading people in this church into sexual immorality and the eating of food sacrificed to idols. Jesus also calls these people to repent.
- Jesus' message to the church in Sardis is also sad. "I know your deeds; you have a reputation of being alive, but you are dead. Wake up! Strengthen what remains and is about to die, for I have found your deeds unfinished in the sight of my God." (Revelation 3:1-2)
- Finally, to the church in Laodicea He wrote, "I know your deeds, that you are neither cold nor hot. I wish you were either one or the other! So, because you are lukewarm—neither hot nor cold—I am about to spit you out of My mouth. You say, 'I am rich; I have acquired wealth and do not need a thing.' But you do not realize that you are wretched, pitiful, poor, blind, and naked. So be earnest and repent." (Revelation 3:15-17, 19)

We see that these churches, those who called themselves followers of Christ, compromised their faith due to lack of love for Christ and others, immorality, false doctrine, self-satisfaction, complacency, and sin.

Jesus calls us to remain faithful by remaining in Him. Don't compromise your faith. A small rock can cause a large landslide. Remain true to Christ and His Word. Maintain your integrity in Christ.

Scripture Reading: 2 Timothy 3:1-5

Personal Application:
- Spend time considering what Christ wrote to the five churches above and pray asking Him to cleanse you and protect you from falling into the same forms of compromise.

Week 43, Day 5: I Want to Grow Old Like Caleb

As I write this, I'm now in my 70s and depending on your perspective, there are a couple of different ways to take that statement.

First, many younger people would think, "Wow! That's old!" Some of them might tend to write off someone my age as being feeble, senile, forgetful, fuddy-duddy, "shelved," "past the expiration date," or something else useless.

Others more my contemporary might say with a sense of futility, "Seventies, huh? Welcome to the club. Now you can retire, live on a fixed income, take lots of medications, and sit around swapping stories about what ails you." They see growing old as the inevitable bummer of life.

I've begun to realize that in our culture, one of worst prospects of growing old is becoming invisible. By "invisible" I mean is that old people don't seem to matter. Others don't seem to notice them. Their ideas and views no longer carry weight. We don't see the elderly as the building blocks of a church, a business, or even a family. We tend to feel sorry for them. They're consigned to a soft chair in the corner.

I have other plans for growing old *when I do*. I want to grow old like Caleb. Only Caleb and Joshua had a vision and faith for what God wanted Israel to do: go in and take the land of Canaan. Sadly, because they were in the minority, the majority overruled them. And so, along with the entire vast company of Israel, Caleb and Joshua had to wander in the wilderness for 40 years—because of someone else's sin and lack of faith!

But Joshua and Caleb didn't let that minor setback (40 years) change their view of God or of themselves. Here's Caleb's testimony at the age of 85:

Now then, just as the LORD promised, he has kept me alive for forty-five years since the time he said this to Moses, while Israel moved about in the wilderness. So here I am today, eighty-five years old! I am still as strong today as the day Moses sent me out; I'm just as vigorous to go out to battle now as I was then. Now give me this hill country that the LORD promised me that day. You yourself heard then that the Anakites were there and their cities were large and fortified, but the LORD helping me, I will drive them out just as he said. (Joshua 14:10-12)

Wow! No soft chair in the corner for Caleb! By Caleb's own admission, God did this for him. Following Jesus and trusting God doesn't guarantee long life and robust health. But it does guarantee a life worth living, a life of meaning and purpose, a life devoted to serving Christ and others. That's why I want to grow old like Caleb!

Scripture Reading: Philippians 3:7-14 (Paul was old when he wrote this.)

Personal Application:

- In what ways did today's devotional speak to you? What action will you take because of being reminded of these things?

Week 43, Day 6: Living Large

"I used to think God guided us by opening and closing doors, but now I know sometimes God wants us to kick some doors down." – Bob Goff

If you knew that you had unlimited resources at your disposal, what would you attempt that otherwise wouldn't even enter your mind?

We forget that as followers of Christ, we *do have* unlimited resources at our disposal! Jeremiah prayed, "Ah, Sovereign LORD, you have made the heavens and the earth by your great power and outstretched arm. Nothing is too hard for you." (Jeremiah 32:17)

Shortly after Jeremiah prayed that, the Lord responded, "I am the LORD, the God of all mankind. Is anything too hard for me?" (Jeremiah 32:27)

Jesus said much the same thing. In His parting words to His disciples, He said, "All authority in heaven and on earth has been given to me. Therefore, go and make disciples of all nations..." (Matthew 28:18-19)

When Jesus says that all authority in both heaven and earth has been given to Him, it embraces all other authority. Everything is subject to Him. Nothing happens outside the scope of His authority.

Sure, sometimes it feels like things are out of control. Plenty goes on in our world politically, economically, and even personally that runs counter to God's character and purposes. But He is not subject to those negative or evil circumstances. He is Lord overall.

So where does that leave us? On what basis do we live our lives, conduct business, or engage in ministry? Do we live as though we're confined and limited by our circumstances or by others? Or do we live and work knowing that our Lord possesses all authority and all resources?

In Romans 8:37-39, Paul wrote, "No, in all these things we are more than conquerors through him who loved us. For I am convinced that neither death nor life, neither angels nor demons, neither the present nor the future, nor any powers, neither height nor depth, nor anything else in all creation, will be able to separate us from the love of God that is in Christ Jesus our Lord."

By "living large," I'm not talking about a prosperity gospel. I'm talking about trusting a BIG God for BIG results. Again, God told Jeremiah, "'Call to Me, and I will answer you, and show you great and mighty things, which you do not know.'" (Jeremiah 33:3)

Scripture Reading: Numbers 11:21-25

Personal Application:
- In what big ways do you need to trust the Lord right now?
- How else is the Lord speaking to you from His Word in this devotional?

Week 43, Day 7: Weekly Recap and Prayer

On the seventh day of each week, use the **ACTS** acronym to spend time with the Lord reviewing and assessing your week and praying to God. (**A**=Adoration; **C**=Confession; **T**=Thanksgiving; **S**=Supplication)

First, look back over the previous six days for this week to remind yourself what you read and agreed to. Then, follow the ACTS pattern for prayer below. Finally, use the space below to journal what God is doing in your life and share this with a trusted spiritual partner.

Adoration: Simply spend time in adoration of the Lord. Praise Him and glorify His name. (See 1 Chronicles 29:10-13; Psalm 100; Romans 11:33-36.)

Confession: Confess your sins and shortcomings before God. ("If we confess our sins, he is faithful and just and will forgive us our sins and purify us from all unrighteousness." – 1 John 1:9) To confess (or agree with God) about your sin, implies that you are repentant and desperately want Him to change you.

Thanksgiving: Thank God for what He has done and is doing in your life and the life of your family. Give Him credit, for everything you have comes from Him. (See Psalm 136.)

Supplication: Supplication is just a fancy word for making your requests known to God. Based on the devotions of this past week and the things going on in your life right now, what do you want to ask Him for? "If you, then, though you are evil, know how to give good gifts to your children, how much more will your Father in heaven give good gifts to those who ask Him!" (Matthew 7:11)

Journal: What is God doing in your life right now?

Week 44, Day 1: Comforting Others

During the past several years it seems like our country has faced tragedy after tragedy. With TV, internet, and cell phones, we're bombarded daily with devastation and despair in the news. How many floods, mud slides, fires, hurricanes, snow and ice storms, tornados, earthquakes, shootings, plane crashes, pandemics, and freeway pileups can we take before we simply start to lose heart? We can debate endlessly about why these things happen, but the bottom line is simply this: God uses tragedy to draw us closer to Him.

Col. Mike Anderson looked at life with a unique spiritual insight. As you may recall, he was the second African American astronaut and one of those lost on the re-entry of the Columbia space shuttle in 2003. Col. Anderson was from Spokane Washington, where he attended a small Baptist church. Through the years, we have heard a great deal about this man's rich spiritual heritage and abiding faith. God has used Mike's story to touch thousands of lives. Prior to going on the Columbia mission, his pastor asked him if he was ever frightened about venturing into outer space. Mike said, "If something were to happen in space, I'm just that much closer to God... Instead of coming down, I'll just be going up to my home in Glory." That's the kind of attitude and assurance God wants us to have. Mike's death was a great loss to His family, friends, and this nation. His family has not only been comforted, but over the years, they have used this tragedy and their great faith to comfort others.

The Apostle Paul reminds us: "Praise be to the God and Father of our Lord Jesus Christ, the Father of compassion and the God of all comfort, who comforts us in all our troubles, so that we can comfort those in any trouble with the comfort we ourselves have received from God... If we are distressed, it is for your comfort and salvation; if we are comforted, it is for your comfort, which produces in you patient endurance of the same sufferings we suffer." (2 Corinthians 1:3–4, 6)

Tragedy is inevitable in our broken, sin-sick world. But God uses tragedy to draw us to Himself and He offers us comfort and encouragement. Once we have dealt with our hurt, He often brings someone across our path who also needs comforting. And because the Lord has equipped us, we can now comfort them. This is part of God's strategy in maturing us and spreading the Good News of salvation. God is in the business of developing comforters of those who have struggled with pain or sorrow themselves and have emerged from that experience victorious. Let's go out and comfort those who do not yet know of our loving and merciful God. Pass it on!

Scripture Reading: Philippians 2:25-30

Personal Application:
- In what ways has the Lord comforted you following tragedy in the past?
- Who do you know right now who could benefit from the comfort you might offer them? Call or visit that person today and give them hope.

Week 44, Day 2: "Call on Me!"

In Isaiah 55:6 we read, "Seek the Lord while He may be found; call on Him while He is near." In fact, frequently in Scripture the Lord invites us to call upon Him.

Don't ever think that your issue is too insignificant or trivial for the Lord to address. He wants us to "cast all our cares on Him." (1 Peter 5:7) And He delights in coming to our rescue.

My good friend Jim Knuppe is a great pilot and holds many aeronautical records. He has flown around the world in his private planes several times. I remember Jim once shared a story of an incident he had with a powerful thunderstorm just outside Denver.

The unusual air currents caused the plane to momentarily loose power and fall from the sky. Jim told me what came to mind was just that simple desperate prayer of a believer, "Jesus Help Me!" Scripture records the same prayer used by numerous kings, prophets, and disciples.

Jim was spared from tragedy and he was able to land the plane safely and without incident.

There's a story in Mark 10 about a blind man who cried out to Jesus for help in a similar way. This man was sitting beside the road begging when he heard the commotion of a large crowd. He asked what was going on and someone told him it was Jesus of Nazareth passing by.

Apparently, this blind man had heard about Jesus and His ability to heal, so he called out to Him, "Jesus, Son of David, have mercy on me!" (Mark 10:47) Many around the blind man told him to be quiet and not to trouble Jesus, but he cried out more.

When Jesus heard him, He asked the crowd to call the blind man to Himself. "So, they called to the blind man, 'Cheer up! On your feet! He's calling you.' Throwing his cloak aside, he jumped to his feet and came to Jesus. 'What do you want Me to do for you?' Jesus asked him. The blind man said, 'Rabbi, I want to see.' 'Go,' said Jesus, 'your faith has healed you.' Immediately he received his sight and followed Jesus along the road." (Mark 10:49-52)

Even above the noise of the crowd and despite Jesus' agenda, He heard this man's plea, He stopped, and He healed him. Don't ever think you're troubling the Lord or keeping Him from something more important by calling on Him. He delights in hearing from His children. He won't ignore your call.

He even responds to our pleas for help when we've done something dumb, foolish, or simply unfortunate. I think of the young man Eutychus who fell asleep during one of Paul's lengthy sermons. Eutychus was sitting in a third-story window when he fell asleep and fell to his death. Paul cried out to the Lord and the Lord gave the young man his life back. (See Acts 20:7-12.) In the same way, let us always call on Jesus to help us whatever the situation.

Scripture Reading: Psalm 55:22

Personal Application:
- What do you need to call on the Lord for today?
  Don't delay, call upon Him in prayer right now.

Week 44, Day 3: On Being a Disciple

Throughout the New Testament we read about disciples. To be a disciple means to be a follower of Christ, a learner or apprentice of His, and a devoted believer in Him. Over the years, I've had the privilege of delivering scores of messages and writing several books on discipleship.

A close review of Scripture reveals that a disciple must not only accept the promises of Christ by faith but must also be willing to apply those truths to his life. There must be a resulting action from the commitment or conversion experience. As Jesus tells us, "By their fruit you will recognize them." (Matthew 7:16) There are always godly by-products from living a Spirit-filled life.

The Apostle Paul wrote the letter to the Roman followers of Christ prior to his visit to Rome. He begins Romans by surveying the spiritual condition of all mankind, especially as he understood it to be in Rome. If you look at what Rome was like back then, it was much like America is today.

The first eleven chapters of Romans explain that sin is a problem we all share, salvation through Christ is the only answer, the Holy Spirit indwells us, and we serve a grace-filled God who wishes none to perish.

Then, in Romans 12, Paul offers a clear picture of what a disciple or follower of Jesus looks like:

- He is surrendered to God and seeks to please Him. (Vs. 1)
- He is not to be of this world, but rather be transformed by God. (Vs. 2)
- He has an accurate picture of himself: "God made me for His glory!" (Vs. 3)
- He is a member of the body of Christ. (Vs. 5)
- He has gifts from God with which he is to serve others. (Vs. 6)
- He loves others and hates evil. (Vs. 9)
- He is "joyful in hope, patient in affliction, faithful in prayer." (Vs. 12)
- He serves others—allowing God's love to pass through him. (Vs. 13)
- He lives in harmony with and acceptance of those around him. (Vs. 16)

In short, a disciple of Jesus lives like Jesus. The above bullets aren't a list of rules to live by but express the character of Christ that His followers should seek to imitate.

We cannot walk with God and stand still at the same time. God is on a mission and He asks us to join Him. When we spend time with Christ, we become more like Him. It's that simple. Let's endeavor to be a Romans 12 disciple.

Scripture Reading: Romans 12:1-16

Personal Application:

- Spend time with Jesus each day, asking Him to make you more like Him. Then look for opportunities to express His character as you spend time around others.

Week 44, Day 4: "Some Days, I Don't Even Like My Wife"

Do those words shock you? Those were the words that a married man confessed to me. However, I think if we're honest with ourselves there are probably days when every married man could admit to thinking those words.

We hear the word "compatibility" thrown around a lot today with respect to marriage. I hear couples who have resigned themselves to divorce simply say, "We were no longer compatible." They speak of compatibility as though it were an immutable trait.

However, based on Scripture and the experiences of countless couples, I believe that compatibility is a choice and not some inherent trait over which we have no control.

When asked about divorce, Jesus quoted Genesis 2:24, "'For this reason a man will leave his father and mother and be united to his wife, and the two will become one flesh.' So they are no longer two, but one flesh. Therefore what God has joined together, let no one separate." (Matthew 19:5-6)

My point is that every marriage has its rough spots. It simply stands to reason that when two sinners of the opposite gender agree to spend the rest of their lives together, of course there will be disagreements and friction. There will probably even be times when you don't like each other. But feelings are fickle and change like the wind.

But the currency of marriage is love. We're told to love each other—not because we're both so lovable—but precisely because only love can overlook all our faults. And believe me, both my wife and I have plenty.

The true test of a good marriage is not how compatible a couple is, but how compatible or loving they *choose* to be despite conflict and differences. This is why the marriage covenant is such a big deal. Rightly seen, incompatibility is a refusal to work on one's marriage. But under the covenant of marriage we mutually agree to work towards compatibility and genuinely enjoying one another.

Perhaps you've been hurt by your spouse and you're in a place where it's quite an effort to even liker her. The best way I know to overcome that is: through prayer ask God to give you a genuine love for your wife; and to engage in doing and saying loving things. When you speak lovingly and perform acts of love for your spouse, your feelings will follow, and you'll reignite the flame of love that attracted you to this lovely woman in the first place.

Regardless of the state of your marriage, don't wait to put these actions into play!

Scripture Reading: Ephesians 5:25-33

Personal Application:

- If you are married, don't leave the health of your marriage to chance. Begin actively pursuing an ever-growing love relationship with your wife. If you're not yet married, consider what you read here and tuck it away for the day that you are married.

Week 44, Day 5: A Most Unusual Miracle

Of all the miracles of Jesus recorded in Scripture, the one that seems most unusual to me is when Jesus walked on water. (See Matthew 14:22-33; Mark 6:45-51; John 6:16-21.) All His other miracles have intrinsic value—healing the sick, feeding the multitudes, casting out demons, even turning water into wine at a wedding.

Forgive me for saying so but walking on the lake to His disciples almost sounds like—well—showing off! But of course, showing off doesn't sound like Jesus at all. So, what was going on?

These are some of the questions I sought to answer when I studied this miracle a few years ago. Here's what I discovered. This event took place early in Jesus' ministry. He had just taught a great multitude the day before in a remote place. And feeling compassion for them, Jesus had fed this large crowd of five thousand, besides women and children, on five loaves of bread and two small fish. Afterwards, He instructed His disciples to pick up the leftovers and they gathered twelve baskets full, one for each disciple.

But even after witnessing this amazing miracle, Mark's Gospel tells us, "For they had not understood about the loaves; their hearts were hardened." (Mark 6:52) Following the feeding of the five thousand Jesus sent His disciples across the Sea of Galilee in a boat. Then, He went up a mountain to pray.

I cannot prove this, but I pondered the question, "What was the Lord praying about?" Based on Mark's admission of their unbelief and hardheartedness, I believe Jesus was asking the Father what He might do to bring His disciples to faith in Him. I purpose that Jesus received the following answer, "This is a group of common men. Show them something visceral, unbelievable, that only God could do, like walking on water."

From His perch on the mountain, Jesus could see His disciples in the boat "straining at the oars, because the wind was against them." (Mark 6:48) So, just before dawn, Jesus walked out on the lake coming toward them. When they first saw Him, they were frightened and supposed Him to be a ghost. But He calmed and assured them that it was He.

But notice this: When Jesus climbed into the boat, "Then those who were in the boat worshiped Him, saying, 'Truly You are the Son of God.'" (Matthew 14:33) This is the first recorded instance where His disciples acknowledged who He is and worshiped Him! It took this crazy miracle of walking on water to convince these hardened men that Jesus is the Son of God.

How about you? What did it take to convince you that Jesus is the Son of God and to accept His gift of Salvation? Isn't the Lord wonderful to craft specific events like this to bring people to Himself?

Scripture Reading: Matthew 14:22-33

Personal Application:

• Thank the Lord for the way He reached out to you
  and revealed who Jesus is and worship Him.

Week 44, Day 6: A Clean Heart

It's funny how God can speak to us during some of the most mundane things we do. Like today when I went through the car wash. My car was unusually dirty—I mean embarrassingly so. It's been one of those particularly messy weeks with rain, wind, and lots of slop on the roads. I kept meaning to get the car washed, but I was just too busy. I try to keep my vehicle in good shape.

As I approached the car wash, I looked around at the other cars in line. Some were in "show room condition" and needed little to restore their beauty. Others were a real mess like mine. As I waited for the car wash to run through its cycles, I thought it really doesn't matter how dirty my car is when I enter; it always comes out nice and clean. It doesn't matter if I get it washed twice a week or twice a winter; when I pull out, it looks like new.

It dawned on me that this is a lot like worship. When I humble myself before God, recognizing my filth and need for His cleansing, He makes me clean. Like King David, I too can cry out to the Lord, "Wash away all my iniquity and cleanse me from my sin." (Psalm 51:2) No matter what I've done, how ugly my heart has been, or "sideways" I've gotten, when I enter into God's presence, the precious blood of Jesus washes away my sins, and God sees me as righteous. Unlike a car wash though, He cleans me from the inside out.

I must admit there have been too many times in my life when busyness has kept me from spending quality time with God. The longer the lapses, the more "grime" I seem to collect. I get flustered more easily, feel impatience bubbling up, and am in general more irritable. If I stay away from my daily routine of Bible study, prayer, and meditation my heart can get ugly. Sometimes it doesn't even take that long. One minute I'm feeling really on track, at peace with God, in a pleasant mood, and focused on God's will; the next minute I'm plowing through messy circumstances and my attitude shifts. I can too easily focus on the crisis or struggle and lose perspective.

When we see the ugliness in our hearts but put on a phony smile and try to come across like everything is fine, we become like the Pharisees of old. "Woe to you, teachers of the law and Pharisees, you hypocrites! You clean the outside of the cup and dish, but inside they are full of greed and self-indulgence. Blind Pharisee! First clean the inside of the cup and dish, and then the outside also will be clean." (Matthew 23:25-26) I need to remember that only God can clean the inside.

There's no doubt that life can be messy. I'm so glad that, because of the sacrifice of Jesus Christ, we can approach God anytime, anywhere. He may not clean up our circumstances or rescue us from certain consequences, but He takes us just as we are, washes away our sins, and makes us clean. In His presence, we are made new.

Scripture Reading: Hebrews 10:19-22

Personal Application:

- Come to Jesus daily—even moment by moment—for cleansing. Trust in His shed blood and forgiveness and move forward in the joy of a clear conscience.

Week 44, Day 7: Weekly Recap and Prayer

On the seventh day of each week, use the **ACTS** acronym to spend time with the Lord reviewing and assessing your week and praying to God. (**A**=Adoration; **C**=Confession; **T**=Thanksgiving; **S**=Supplication)

First, look back over the previous six days for this week to remind yourself what you read and agreed to. Then, follow the ACTS pattern for prayer below. Finally, use the space below to journal what God is doing in your life and share this with a trusted spiritual partner.

Adoration: Simply spend time in adoration of the Lord. Praise Him and glorify His name. (See 1 Chronicles 29:10-13; Psalm 100; Romans 11:33-36.)

Confession: Confess your sins and shortcomings before God. ("If we confess our sins, he is faithful and just and will forgive us our sins and purify us from all unrighteousness." – 1 John 1:9) To confess (or agree with God) about your sin, implies that you are repentant and desperately want Him to change you.

Thanksgiving: Thank God for what He has done and is doing in your life and the life of your family. Give Him credit, for everything you have comes from Him. (See Psalm 136.)

Supplication: Supplication is just a fancy word for making your requests known to God. Based on the devotions of this past week and the things going on in your life right now, what do you want to ask Him for? "If you, then, though you are evil, know how to give good gifts to your children, how much more will your Father in heaven give good gifts to those who ask Him!" (Matthew 7:11)

Journal: What is God doing in your life right now?

Week 45, Day 1: The Lure of Fishing

What is a fisherman? Some would say a fisherman is a jerk on one end of the line waiting for a jerk on the other end. Most people would describe a fisherman as a committed person who pursues his sport with dedication and zeal. For some it's competition, for others it's relaxation, many use it as a sport to bring together family and friends, and for sure it is a wonder way to appreciate God's great outdoors.

Our character and performance are shaped in part by our passions. For centuries there has been a unique bond with people who share the challenges and opportunities that this wholesome sport presents. There is something intriguing about a fisherman. I'm continually amazed about the number of parallels and correlation's that exist between the first century disciples and fishermen. I believe it was no coincidence that Jesus picked eight fishermen to be among His twelve disciples (John 21). Jesus related to fishermen for several reasons. In the following paragraphs, notice the similarities between fishing for fish and fishing for men as a disciple of Jesus.

- Fishermen have a sense of adventure and exploration. Likewise, the disciple sees every opportunity to share Christ as an adventure.
- Fishermen are incredibly patient, waiting for long stretches to catch the big one. In the same way, a disciple patiently represents Christ to others through his life and words and waits expectantly for God to work in their lives.
- Fishermen have faith that every cast could produce a fish. They believe that just one more cast could be the one. Fishers of Men also live by faith not by sight (2 Corinthians 5:7).
- Fishermen are passionate about their sport and persistent in pursuing it. They will spend countless hours preparing, analyzing, and evaluating their beloved sport. Similarly, a disciple attacks his mission with dedication and zeal.
- Fishermen know and study the habits and habitats of the fish and routinely practicing their casting skills. Likewise, fishers of men are keenly aware of the culture they live in and prepare themselves to share Christ with others.
- Finally, fishermen catch fish. They're not content to let some "trained professional" do it for them. The same can be said of the true disciple of Jesus!

Scripture Reading: Matthew 4:18-22

Personal Application:

- You may or may not enjoy fishing for fish. But there's real joy in the privilege of leading someone else to Christ. If you know Jesus, you don't need any special training to share your story with someone else. Ask God to give you an opportunity to do so today.

Week 45, Day 2: The Power of a Dad's Influence

Tim and Sharon were driving in heavy traffic one afternoon. Their young son, Daniel, was sitting in his car seat in the back. His car seat was equipped with a pretend steering wheel complete with horn so he could "drive like daddy."

Tim and Sharon were deep in conversation when suddenly, they heard Daniel pounding on his little car horn. Tim looked in the rearview mirror to see what was happening. Then, little Daniel threw his clenched fist in the air and yelled, "Watch out where you're going, you stupid idiot!"

Tim's heart sank as he turned to his wife and said with his voice filled with sarcasm, "I wonder where he learned that?"

Our children (and grandchildren) are great mimics. Whatever they see us doing, they imitate. They do this for two primary reasons. First, they're soaking up everything their little eyes see, their ears hear, and their hands handle. This is how they learn.

Second, most children, especially boys, want to be like their daddy. Our children imitate us because they want to be like us. This is a very daunting responsibility to consider! But rather than fear the bad habits they might learn from us, there's another way to look at this role we play in their young lives.

As followers of Jesus, we want to be like Him. Through reading His Word, praying, being a part of a church body, and engaging in other spiritual disciplines, we're seeking to draw closer to Him so He can transform us and make us more like Him.

In the same way, we can show our children what it looks like to pursue Jesus. But we must not put on a false front, for our kids see right through pretense. Instead, they know we're still sinners, so when we sin or blow it, we can take that opportunity to demonstrate humility and repentance. If we've offended or unjustly disciplined our child, we should humbly ask their forgiveness and assure them of our love.

And what a joy it is to watch your child or grandchild begin to follow Jesus by watching you and imitating you in the Christlike way you deal with others.

Being a dad or grandfather can be a daunting role, especially considering how much our children mimic us and want to be like us. But being a dad or grandpa can also be hugely rewarding from the standpoint that you've got a captive audience right in your home learning how to follow Jesus. Men, there's no greater joy than watching your kids pursue Christ like you are.

Scripture Reading: Proverbs 3:1-8

Personal Application:

- To what extent would your children (or grandchildren) know that you are pursuing Christ?
- In what ways would you like them to imitate you?
  How will you make this happen?

Week 45, Day 3: The Lord Provides!

In the late 70s, my friend Rob and his wife Linda were attending college in preparation to go to Austria as missionaries. Rob was taking a full load of credits at school and working two part-time jobs. At the time, they had two small children, ages four and two.

One of Rob's jobs was serving a small church as their part-time pastor. Part of his salary included free rent in the church parsonage. But the church treasurer was a young single man with more of an accounting head than a compassionate heart.

The parsonage was a beautiful home, nicer than anything Rob and Linda had ever lived in. Because of this, the young treasurer reasoned that the church was fulfilling their obligation to pay Rob chiefly in rent. Subsequently, the church paid him just $200/month salary—hence the need for Rob to work a second job.

Early one June, Rob got home from work and discovered that they didn't have anything in the house to eat for supper. It was the day before payday, and the cupboard was bare except for a couple chicken bouillon cubes, a little flour, and some milk.

Rob immediately went out to the garden knowing full well that it was too early to harvest a meal from it. Instead, he walked around the garden calling out to God. He reasoned that he could easily have gone without a meal or two, but he didn't want to ask his wife and two young children to go without.

Rob was really struggling. "Why wasn't God providing?" Yet, he knew that God is good and cares for His children. As Rob continued to walk around the garden praying, he affirmed his trust in God's tender care and prayed for His provision.

On one of his laps around the garden, he noticed that there were a few radishes ripe enough for harvesting, so he mindlessly picked them and continued his prayer walk. Suddenly, Rob stopped and looked at the small bunch of radishes in his hand. Out loud he asked, "Radishes! What can you do with radishes?" Then a thought came to him that he knows came from the Lord. "Cream of radish soup! That's what we'll have for dinner!"

Excitedly, Rob ran in the house and showed his wife the radishes. "We're going to have cream of radish soup for supper tonight, and I'll make it." To which Linda responded, "I've never heard of cream of radish soup." Rob smiled and replied, "Neither have I, but it might be good."

This young family of four sat down that night to hearty bowls of cream of radish soup. They thanked the Lord, grateful for His amazing provision, and Rob insists that the soup was quite good. In fact, from time to time, they serve cream of radish soup now for their grandchildren, so they can share with them the goodness of God.

Scripture Reading: Exodus 16:1-12

Personal Application:

- Cast all your cares on the Lord and express to Him your thanks f or all He provides!

Week 45, Day 4: Living with Integrity

Disgrace and scandals fill the headlines of media. Our society is filled with examples of people who have forgotten about character. Whether in business, on a sport's field, at a sports show, in the White House, on a fishing outing, or in nearly any other context you can spot the people who care about character. When all else is gone, a person is left with his faith and character.

Someone once said, "The heart of a man is his humility. The soul of a man is his integrity. And the righteousness of a man is in God."

Whether it is within the church or part of a sports show, hypocrisy eats at the soul of our character like a cancer. I can't tell you how many times a non-Christian has told me that he/she doesn't want anything to do with Christ or the church due to the hypocrisy of some so-called Christian in their life.

There is nothing as devastating to a church member than to see church leaders who lack good character. Hypocrisy was severely criticized by Jesus during His ministry. The Sermon on the Mount is one example of how Jesus warned His followers about the dangers of straying from godly character. He continually reminded the early church not to be caught up in the entanglements of hypocrisy.

But there are some bright spots. Recently, I heard about a young man, a follower of Jesus. He accidentally backed his truck into another man's truck doing considerable damage to this tricked-out truck. The young man admitted he was at fault and turned the incident over to his insurance company.

But when the victim received a check from the insurance company, it was far short of what it would cost to repair his truck. So, this young follower of Jesus took cash to the victim to make up the difference. The man whose truck he hit was awestruck by this act of integrity!

An old country preacher put it this way: "Be who you is, 'cuz if you ain't who you is, you is who you ain't." What he meant was, if you claim to follow Jesus, then follow Him!

We can't expect to be the "light of the world" or the "salt of the earth" if our character is flawed with hypocrisy. Each day we need to focus upon the ideal model of a Christlike life. As we continue to grow in our faith and obedience to God's Word our character will be refined and God will be glorified.

Proverbs 4:25-27 says, "Let your eyes look straight ahead, fix your gaze directly before you. Make level paths for your feet and take only ways that are firm. Do not swerve to the right or the left; keep your foot from evil."

Scripture Reading: Colossians 1:9-14

Personal Application:

- To what extent would those around you characterize you as a man of integrity? If you have some doubts about that in areas of your life, confess that sin and get right with God.

Week 45, Day 5: How's Your Aim?

Recently, I visited one of my hunting partner's archery range in his large back-yard. I had been shooting very consistently on my own 20-yard target, hitting the bull's-eye nine out of ten times. But when I extended my range to the 40- and 50-yard targets, my shots became very inaccurate. Shortly after release, I noticed my arrow would take off to the right. When I corrected my bow sights to allow for that deviation, my arrow would go radically to the left. My shots were all over the place!

I asked my friend what I was doing wrong? He said the problem wasn't with the bow or the sights but with my aim. Apparently, I was not anchoring on my cheek-bone in the same way each shot. My anchor point was inconsistent; therefore, my aim was off. Once I corrected my anchor point, my aim became accurate and the arrows began to hit their mark.

So, it is in life. As believers, Jesus is our anchor point. if we get away from our anchor point, we flounder and miss the mark. Jesus described our anchor point using a different metaphor—that of a branch on a grapevine.

Jesus explained, "I am the vine; you are the branches. If you remain in Me and I in you, you will bear much fruit; apart from Me you can do nothing." (John 15:5) "Bearing much fruit" in the context of this passage has to do with our whole life and becoming more like Jesus. We don't become more like Jesus by striving on our own. We will always need to stay connected with (abide in or remain in) Him.

When we are missing the mark in our lives, it could be for a variety of reasons:

- Maybe we are trying to do everything on our strength rather than rely on God's wisdom and might to empower us.
- There may be unresolved sin in our life, which is standing in the way of our relationship with Christ and others.
- We could have broken fellowship with someone who is close to us thereby impeding our prayers.
- We may be "aiming" at the wrong things. Sometimes the worries of this life and the lure of power, prestige, fame, and fortune can get us off track.

Whatever the reason, our anchor point is off. To correct the problem, we must return to Jesus and remain in Him. Spiritual disciplines like reading God's Word, praying, meditating, worshipping, fellowshipping with other believers, and con-fessing our sins to the Lord all have one primary purpose: to help us deepen our relationship with Jesus Christ.

How about you? How's your aim? Who is *your* anchor point?

Scripture Reading: John 15:9-17

Personal Application:

- What are you aiming at in life? To what extent are you abiding in Jesus? Meditate on the Scripture reading for today and follow Jesus' instructions.

Week 45, Day 6: Joy!

The winsome personality of Jimmy Houston has won the hearts of many anglers. His captivating positive attitude is infectious to anyone encountering this black bass tournament champion and television sports show host.

Over the years, I have enjoyed Jimmy's approach to life and his Christian testimony. Samuel Shoemaker once said, "The surest mark of a Christian is not faith, or even love, but joy."

What is joy? Joy is an attitude that is characterized by a feeling of satisfaction, pleasure, and fulfillment. It is contentment and calmness resulting from a strong and abiding faith in the power and grace of the Almighty.

"Joy is prayer. Joy is strength. Joy is love. Joy is a net of love by which you can catch souls. God loves a cheerful giver. He gives most who gives with joy. The best way to show our gratitude to God and the people we serve is to accept everything with joy. A joyful heart is the inevitable result of a heart burning with love. Never let anything so fill you with sorrow as to make you forget the joy of the Christ risen." – Mother Teresa

Joy appears 218 times in The New International Version. Joy is the currency of our faith. Joy is a deep inner peace that projects a sense of well-being, contentment, and confidence in the Lord.

Happiness on the other hand is fickle, dependent upon our circumstances. We are happy when the job promotion comes in on time. We feel cheerful when our financial dreams are met. We are glad when our favorite team wins a game and especially happy when they go to a Bowl game. These feelings temporarily comfort a person until the next trial or failure occurs. With happiness there is no lasting or enduring significance to any event or material possessions.

True joy is centered on the Lord and emanates from the Lord. "The joy of the Lord is your strength." (Nehemiah 8:10) "You make known to me the path of life; You will fill me with joy in Your presence, with eternal pleasures at Your right hand." (Psalm 16:11) Jesus said, "These things I have spoken to you, that My joy may be in you, and that your joy may be made full." (John 15:11)

Joy recognizes that pain and suffering are part of life and therefore is not contingent on our circumstances. Because joy comes from Him who never changes, joy is ever available no matter what befalls us.

Joy is a fruit of the Spirit. When we are filled with the Spirit, following in His steps, we exude the joy that He freely gives.

Scripture Reading: Romans 12:12; 14:17; 15:13

Personal Application:

- Yield to the leading of the Holy Spirit in your life and cultivate joy by focusing on Him and all He has done for you and your loved ones.

Week 45, Day 7: Weekly Recap and Prayer

On the seventh day of each week, use the **ACTS** acronym to spend time with the Lord reviewing and assessing your week and praying to God. (**A**=Adoration; **C**=Confession; **T**=Thanksgiving; **S**=Supplication)

First, look back over the previous six days for this week to remind yourself what you read and agreed to. Then, follow the ACTS pattern for prayer below. Finally, use the space below to journal what God is doing in your life and share this with a trusted spiritual partner.

Adoration: Simply spend time in adoration of the Lord. Praise Him and glorify His name. (See 1 Chronicles 29:10-13; Psalm 100; Romans 11:33-36.)

Confession: Confess your sins and shortcomings before God. ("If we confess our sins, he is faithful and just and will forgive us our sins and purify us from all unrighteousness." – 1 John 1:9) To confess (or agree with God) about your sin, implies that you are repentant and desperately want Him to change you.

Thanksgiving: Thank God for what He has done and is doing in your life and the life of your family. Give Him credit, for everything you have comes from Him. (See Psalm 136.)

Supplication: Supplication is just a fancy word for making your requests known to God. Based on the devotions of this past week and the things going on in your life right now, what do you want to ask Him for? "If you, then, though you are evil, know how to give good gifts to your children, how much more will your Father in heaven give good gifts to those who ask Him!" (Matthew 7:11)

Journal: What is God doing in your life right now?

Week 46, Day 1: Skunked!

Russell Thornberry, the Executive Editor of *Buckmaster Magazine*, has many years' experience as a professional guide and outfitter. One of his favorite fishing memories was about a time when he got skunked… literally.

One summer Russell was guiding two fly fishermen for trout on the famous Bow River. This river flows out of the Canadian Rockies and onto the prairies of southern Alberta. "Things were not going well at all." "You could not even buy a fish; it was that bad!" says Russell. The combination of high winds and changing weather proved to be a prescription for difficult fly-fishing. After a morning of frustration, the weary anglers took a break to eat their lunch prior to taking a short nap. Normally, Russell would never fish while guiding his clients. His job as a guide was to find the fish and coach the clients on their techniques. Because the conditions were so tough, he figured that maybe his experience and persistence could charm a fish into hitting one of his secret fly patterns. Russell figured that catching a fish might be the very thing to renew the spirits of his clients that fish really do exist in the Bow River.

He made his way down to a section of river where the grass banks formed a high wall on one side of the waterway. However, the wind was overpowering his efforts and whipping his back cast onto the grassy bank. This determined fisherman was not about to quit. Cast after cast; snag after snag he persevered.

After losing six flies, Russell figured that the prairie grass once again snagged his cast. With a mighty tug to free the line, he jerked his rod forward. When he pulled he felt something odd. As he turned his head to check out the line, Russell noticed a ball of black and white fur flying down off the bank and heading right toward him. He ducked in time as the poor skunk landed in the river! Apparently, the skunk mistook the imitation grasshopper for the real thing and sampled a bit of his streamer fly.

We have all experienced those skunked days. Some days it just seems that it would have been better to stay in bed. It is good to remember that our God is a mighty God who encourages us to fight the good fight. We are to keep on keepin' on!

The Apostle Paul in his first letter to the church in Corinth encouraged Christ followers to fight the good fight. Corinth was a center for open and unbridled immorality. The moral laxness plagued this young church. Paul uses the figure of a boxer to represent the struggles in a Christian life. "I do not fight like a man beating the air. No, I beat my body and make it my slave so that after I have preached to others, I myself will not be disqualified for the prize." (1 Corinthians 9:27)

Scripture Reading: 1 Corinthians 9:24-27

Personal Application:

- What is the battle you are fighting? You can have victory over the temptations in your life if you rely on the Holy Spirit, remain faithful to His Word, and persist in the fight.

Week 46, Day 2: A Charging Moose!

My friend Rob lived in Alaska for some years. Being an avid hiker and mountaineer, he had countless encounters with moose that are so prevalent there.

One time in the fall during rutting season, he and his friend Ed were hiking in the woods near Anchorage. They were coming down a hill toward the junction of another trail when they heard a huge crashing noise coming from the brush on their left. Out came a full-grown cow moose at a trot. More people are killed by moose every year in Alaska than by bears.

As soon as she was in the junction, she turned to look back from where she had come, and a huge bull moose emerged from the brush. His strong instincts drove him to pursue this cow, but she would have none of it. Her ears were laid back and the hair on the back of her neck was bristled with warning.

With this angry cow in the way, Rob and Ed decided to take another trail and put some distance between them and the cow. They resumed their conversation as they took the turns and twists of the trail. Eventually, the trail took them up a steep rise but just as they were nearing its crest, there was the angry cow coming up the other side directly towards them!

She was still in a bad mood, for the moment she saw them, her ears went back, the hair on her neck went up, and she charged! Rob yelled at Ed, "You take the tree to the right and I'll go to the one on the left!" But as the two of them split, this must have confused the moose and she stopped, looking bewildered. The two hikers watched from behind their respective trees as she turned and stomped away.

Hiking in Alaska can quickly turn into an adventure. For this reason, there are a couple of cardinal rules when hiking in Alaska: Never hike alone, and always be vigilant and prepared.

In the same way, "hiking" through life can also turn into an unexpected adventure. The same two cardinal rules apply: First, don't "hike" alone. Meet regularly with another man, a comrade in arms, to watch your back and share your struggles with. Pray with and for each other.

Second, always be vigilant and prepared. Arm yourself with the Word of God and in His strength. In life, an angry cow moose is nothing compared with our enemy the devil.

Peter warns, "Be alert and of sober mind. Your enemy the devil prowls around like a roaring lion looking for someone to devour. Resist him, standing firm in the faith, because you know that the family believers throughout the world is undergoing the same kind of sufferings." (1 Peter 5:8-9)

Scripture Reading: 1 John 3:7-10

Personal Application:

- Who is another Christian man in your life with whom you can partner spiritually? Meet with him regularly and share your joys and challenges with each other. Pray with and for each other.
- To what extent are you prepared for the unexpected in life by relying on the Lord and being armed with His Word? Make this preparation a daily habit.

Week 46, Day 3: The Fish Test

Competitive sports allow us to test our skills against a known opponent. Coaches spend hours strategizing on how to effectively match the challenges of a rival. After careful evaluation there is a certain level of predictability associated with a field or court that has precise rules and regulations.

The great outdoors is not as predetermined. The various surprises awaiting the sportsmen can test your courage, stamina, wisdom, creativity, and preparedness. Most importantly it will test your character.

On a trip to Mexico searching for the elusive marlin, my fishing partners Hugh and Greg, joined me as we trolled a variety of lures for miles on end. The charter boat captains became increasingly frustrated with the lack of action due to the "El Nino" conditions that had prevailed for the previous two years.

The tour group we booked with was equally determined and disappointed as each evening they would take their frustrations out on a bottle of tequila. As Christians we tried to accept the circumstances and take them as a test of character. The question we had to ask ourselves each night was, "Would we give in and join the crowd of discontents or honor our Lord?"

The last day arrived and trolling the deep blue water was again unproductive. In frustration, I told the captain to take us along the rugged coastline. I rigged our team up with a potpourri of saltwater flies and small black bass soft plastic lures. We began to fish the rocks in about 70 feet of water when schools of fish began attacking our offerings. As we continued to move about the shoreline, we found schools of wahoo and dorado (dolphin fish) that joined in on all the fun.

Each time we set the hook, the skipper and his mate let out a yell and reached for another pennant to tie on the mast. It's customary for a skipper to declare his catch to the fleet as they arrive back in port. Our boat was one of the last to come in that evening with dozens of pennants, rags and even toilet paper blowing in the breeze to signify our large and varied catch. The test of our attitude and perseverance proved to be a character-building exercise that provided a testimony to the entire village.

In Peter's first letter we quickly recognize that the major theme of his letter was "Hope for the Hurting." Throughout the book we see how Peter's audience was tested again and again through various trials and suffering. Peter explains, "These have come so that the proven genuineness of your faith—of greater worth than gold, which perishes even though refined by fire—may result in praise, glory and honor when Jesus Christ is revealed." (1 Peter 1:7)

Scripture Reading: 1 Peter 2:1-5

Personal Application:
- In every test of life, continue to trust that God is faithful, and He will use each situation to refine and perfect your life.

Week 46, Day 4: This Pig Is Yours

My hunting and fishing activities during 1997 can be summed up with the word: "slim." With the responsibilities of a growing ministry, writing two books, training a new employee (J.D.), and having two of my hunting trips canceled due to weather related problems, my opportunities to enjoy the great outdoors were very limited.

Perhaps one of the best excursions of the year was a trip I took with a co-worker and my hunting partner, Jeff. We journeyed up to a cattle ranch located in Northern California. Our goal was to bag a wild boar. We all had the need to shoot at something and clamored for the glimpse of a moving black dot on the landscape.

After a day of some serious hiking and glassing, Jeff spotted an animal and called me on my radio. We met and began our climb on his ATV to the top of the mountain. I asked him why he passed up the shot? "Jim, I knew you really needed the opportunity and wanted to give it to you." During our short ride I thought about his generosity. There was nothing I did that deserved this chance and felt honored and unworthy for the gift.

As we rounded the last bend there stood my forlorn partner in ministry, J.D., with a sad look on his face. His past big game hunting experience had been minimal with little or no results. I knew that a chance for the pig would mean even more to him. I said to Jeff, "Stop the ATV and let's give J.D. the chance." Jeff said, "But this pig is yours." But I told him I wanted to share my gift in the same way Jeff had shared with me.

Unfortunately, J.D. missed the shot and the pig scrambled for the nearest bush where he quickly disappeared. While we were all disappointed with the empty game bag, there was a certain positive spirit in the truck on the way home. We had all experienced the rewards of grace, a gift that we don't deserve and cannot earn, and it compels us to share it with others.

"To show grace is to extend favor or kindness to one who doesn't deserve it and can never earn it. Receiving God's forgiveness and reconciliation by grace stands in sharp contrast to attempting to earn it based on works. Every time the thought of grace appears, there is the idea of its being undeserved. In no way is the recipient getting what he or she deserves. Favor is being extended simply out of the goodness of the heart of the giver." – Chuck Swindoll

God has freely extended grace to us. "For it is by grace you have been saved, through faith—and this is not from yourselves, it is the gift of God—not by works, so that no one can boast." (Ephesians 2:8-9) The question we ask ourselves today is what kind of grace are we extending to others?

Scripture Reading: Ephesians 2:1-10

Personal Application:
- Spend time thanking God for His generous, unmerited grace He has given you.
- Look for concrete ways to extend God's grace to others today—especially toward your family.

Week 46, Day 5: Motorcycle Wisdom

A couple of my friends have been avid motorcyclists all their adult lives. They love the rumble of a big twin idling and the exhilaration of going through the curves at break-neck speed. These bikers have traveled all over the northwest enjoying its back roads and unparalleled scenery.

Clad in their black leather and boots, these hearty souls stopped at a local dive for a hot cup of coffee. It was cold outside and had been raining on and off, but their spirits were not dampened. In fact, they seemed to revel in the thrill of the adventure with its hardships.

Sitting around the table they shared stories about the stubborn bull moose they encountered on that two-lane highway that would not let them pass. They recalled riding the length of Vancouver Island and seeing five black bears on that stretch. One of them boasted about the time he chased three Ducati's up Rattlesnake Grade in northeastern Oregon.

Yes, hardcore motorcyclists are a unique breed. But they also have some wisdom to share with us from the sport of motorcycling. One of the greatest dangers in flying through remote, curvy roads on two wheels is hitting debris on the road. A rock, a small animal, or other object in the road could mean a serious accident and a very abrupt end to a joy-filled ride.

But it's the way to avoid hitting that debris that is so intriguing. One veteran motorcyclist put it like this, "If you're ridin' fast through mountain switchbacks and suddenly you see a rock in the road ahead, you have to force your eyes away from the rock and focus on the path you'll take around the rock instead. Because if you focus on the rock, the bike will go where you're looking, and you'll hit the rock."

For the rest of us, there are things on the "road of life" that we want to avoid. It may be a habit we're trying to kick, a temptation, a past failure, or something negative or unpleasant in our lives. Using motorcycle wisdom, if we focus on that habit or temptation, we will fall prey to it. Instead, we need to focus our attention on a path around it.

And that path around that obstacle in our lives involves keeping our eyes on Jesus. It does no good to focus on that habit or temptation telling ourselves, "I'm not going to do it! I'm not going to do it!" For surely, we will. Instead, focus on Jesus and He will provide a way around it so we can get that troublesome sin in our past.

"Let us throw off everything that hinders and the sin that so easily entangles. And let us run with perseverance the race marked out for us, fixing our eyes on Jesus, the pioneer and perfecter of faith." (Hebrews 12:1-2)

Scripture Reading: 1 Corinthians 10:6-13

Personal Application:

- What "debris" in your life right now is tripping you up?
  Instead of focusing on it, fix your eyes on Jesus.
  Trust Him to take you on a path around that obstacle.

Week 46, Day 6: Courage

All pro tight-end Brent Jones is one of the most courageous football players to have ever played the game. But it was during many outdoor adventures that Brent learned courage from the man he most admired. Brent's granddad was a very accomplished athlete who regularly took Brent and his brother Craig to the outdoors to teach them lessons of life.

Once, on a family fishing outing with his granddad and brother their canoe overturned in the swift current of Hat Creek in northeast California. The icy water temporarily paralyzed the fishermen as they tried to hang on to their gear and the side of the canoe.

The fast current pushed the men toward shore where they stumbled onto dry land. "Granddad did not come out until everyone was safely on shore and the gear had been secured. After he reclaimed all our equipment, Granddad guided us to an area where we caught several nice trout. He wouldn't let us go back to camp empty handed, wet and licking our bruises. We continued on to conquer our fears and accomplish the goal of catching some fish for dinner."

Brent had seen this feisty spirit before as he watched his grandfather participate in sports and attack his daily work. His fearless nature and courageous heart provided Brent with a model that would help guide his life.

There are a least two types of courage. First there is the attitude or ability to deal with anything dangerous, difficult, or painful, instead of running from it. Next is having boldness to do what one thinks is right. Both definitions fit the profile of Brent Jones.

I think of people like Joshua as he faced the trials of leadership; Abraham, leaving his homeland to follow God and seek out a country he had not known; Gideon, attacking the armies of the Midianites and Amalekites; Daniel, being persistent in prayer despite a conspiracy to cast him into the lions' den; Nehemiah, refusing to cow to the threats of those who wanted to stop the rebuilding of the temple; James, being willing to die for Jesus; Paul, going to Jerusalem, despite knowing that bonds and imprisonment awaited him; and David, challenging Goliath who defied the armies of Israel.

In the land of Israel, on the football fields of America, and in your home or workplace there will be those who will challenge your faith and strength. There will be people like Goliath who defy God and everything good. No matter who you are, your calling as a follower of Christ is a courageous one. To truly follow Jesus is not for the faint of heart. Get in the game with courage!

"Be on your guard; stand firm in the faith; be courageous; be strong. Do everything in love." (1 Corinthians 16:13-14)

Scripture Reading: Acts 14:21-22

Personal Application:

- Someone once said, "Courage is not the absence of fear, but the conquest of it." What are you facing in your life right now that requires courage? Also, courage is contagious, so hang around other courageous people.

Week 46, Day 7: Weekly Recap and Prayer

On the seventh day of each week, use the **ACTS** acronym to spend time with the Lord reviewing and assessing your week and praying to God. (**A**=Adoration; **C**=Confession; **T**=Thanksgiving; **S**=Supplication)

First, look back over the previous six days for this week to remind yourself what you read and agreed to. Then, follow the ACTS pattern for prayer below. Finally, use the space below to journal what God is doing in your life and share this with a trusted spiritual partner.

Adoration: Simply spend time in adoration of the Lord. Praise Him and glorify His name. (See 1 Chronicles 29:10-13; Psalm 100; Romans 11:33-36.)

Confession: Confess your sins and shortcomings before God. ("If we confess our sins, he is faithful and just and will forgive us our sins and purify us from all unrighteousness." – 1 John 1:9) To confess (or agree with God) about your sin, implies that you are repentant and desperately want Him to change you.

Thanksgiving: Thank God for what He has done and is doing in your life and the life of your family. Give Him credit, for everything you have comes from Him. (See Psalm 136.)

Supplication: Supplication is just a fancy word for making your requests known to God. Based on the devotions of this past week and the things going on in your life right now, what do you want to ask Him for? "If you, then, though you are evil, know how to give good gifts to your children, how much more will your Father in heaven give good gifts to those who ask Him!" (Matthew 7:11)

Journal: What is God doing in your life right now?

Week 47, Day 1: Bear Attack!

Randy had been a long-time resident of Alaska and an avid outdoorsman who loved to fish and hunt. One summer his mom came to visit him and expressed the desire to experience a true Alaskan fishing trip in the backcountry. Randy arranged for a bush pilot to take them to a remote river in the interior of Alaska. When they arrived, they set up camp and fished that afternoon and into the evening. It had been a long day, and despite the perpetual daylight of an Alaskan summer, they decided to turn in.

Sometime in the middle of the night, Randy's mom woke him swinging Randy's short-barreled shotgun around the tent. Frantically, she whispered that there was a bear prowling around their campsite. Randy pushed the barrel of the shotgun down and tried to assure his mom that they would be alright, and that the bear would go away.

Randy drifted off to sleep—but not for long, for the bear stepped on his elbow that was tucked into the corner of the tent. Randy awoke with a start and slid his other hand onto the 45-caliber pistol under his pillow as he prayed. The bear finally stepped away releasing his elbow. Then he told his mom, "Okay, on the count of three we're going to grab the tent-poles and shake the tent while yelling. Hopefully, that will scare the bear away." On the count of three, they shook the tent and yelled. Then, they stopped and listened with all their senses on high alert. Suddenly, the bear swiped at the flimsy fabric of the tent slicing a gaping hole in it, bringing it down on Randy and his mom! Then they could see the bear wander off into the brush.

In a commanding voice Randy told her, "Grab the gun and your sleeping bag and come with me." They both scrambled from the ripped tent and headed for the two porta-potties that were chained together at the campsite. They barely got into one of the units and closed the door when the bear was upon them, pushing on all exposed sides of the porta-potty trying to get in. Eventually, the bear sauntered off and then they could hear it trashing their gear. After a fitful and frightful night's sleep in the john, they peeked outside and determined that the grizzly bear was gone. But when they got to their campsite, the bear had chewed and demolished every piece of equipment they had—nothing was salvageable! There was nothing more to do but call the bush pilot on his satellite phone and ask for him to pick them up. Their fishing trip was a bust, but memorable none-the-less, and they were thankful to be able to walk away alive! Randy's experience drew him closer to the Lord and highlighted his need to trust Him always. There are times for all of us when, despite our plans, everything goes wrong. It's times like those, however, when we recognize the sovereign hand of God protecting and guiding us.

Scripture Reading: Psalm 27:1-6

Personal Application:

• Commit today and each day to the Lord and trust Him with your safety and all your needs.

Week 47, Day 2: It's Been One of Those Days

There are days that I agree with those who claim, "The two happiest days for a boat owner are when he buys his boat and when he sells it!"

It was just one of those days. I had already lost two great fish and scuffed my beautiful bass boat on some unsuspecting reinforcement rods. Now I was headed back to the marina at full speed when I remembered that my favorite tackle box was still open on the back deck. As I pulled back on the throttle, I looked over my shoulder to see the tackle box flying out of the boat. The only good news was that all my surface lures remained afloat.

Have you recently had one of those days? You know the kind. A day when it seems like it may have been better to have stayed in bed. You knew you were going to have a bad day when you stepped on a Lego barefoot on the way to the bathroom.

I'm glad that God placed a number of incidents in the Bible to remind us that "bad days" are just a part of life and living. Without the dark days we couldn't really appreciate all the days when things just seem to go our way. Our Lord reminds us that it isn't the circumstances but our response to them that determines the depth of our faith and character.

There are times when I complain to God like King David, "Help, Lord, for the godly are no more; the faithful have vanished from among men. Everyone lies to his neighbor; their flattering lips speak with deception.... The wicked freely strut about [and] what is vile is honored among men...." (Psalm 12:1, 2, 8). At other times, I simply cry out, "Lord, get me out of here!"

During our melancholy days we can relate to David's despair and pain. There may be times when we feel alone and adrift in a sea of muck and mire. And yet we are not alone. Our Heavenly Father is there to help us ride out those tough times. It is the assurance of His Word that can bring us out of our hopeless attitude and into a joyful spirit. As the great song writer Andre Crouch encouraged us, "Through it all, I've learned to trust in Jesus, I've learned to trust in God."

Despite those rough days, we can rejoice like David, "Let all who take refuge in You be glad; let them ever sing for joy. Spread Your protection over them, that those who love Your name may rejoice in You. For surely, O Lord, You bless the righteous; You surround them with Your favor as with a shield...O righteous God, who searches minds and hearts, bring to an end the violence of the wicked and make the righteous secure." (Psalm 5:11, 12; 7:9)

Put your hope in God. Our life here and now is not all there is, so we can respond to tough situations in the hope and assurance of spending eternity with Him.

Scripture Reading: Romans 15:5-6, 13
Personal Application:
- When everything goes wrong, how do you typically react?
- Prepare yourself for those days by establishing a firm foundation for faith and hope in God through His Word.

Week 47, Day 3: Rescued!

I opened the Christchurch morning newspaper to the article that read "Copter missing over N. Canty." It was difficult to swallow my gulp of coffee when I realized that this article was about our ordeal the night before.

We had been hunting in the mountains of New Zealand for the elusive Tahr (a type of mountain goat). At one point, the pilot set the helicopter down on top of a mountain. In the process of organizing our gear my rifle barrel accidentally struck the rotor blade. Because of the dented blade, the pilot rendered the helicopter unfit to fly. He set the transponder of the helicopter to alert the world that we were in a desperate situation.

Our guide decided we needed to try to get off the mountain to avoid the freezing temperatures that would come with nightfall. The moonless night added to the worry, as we wondered if there was enough light to see our way down the steep slopes.

We were neither dressed nor prepared for an extended mountain climb. We had to survive with what we had. Quietly, we each prepared for the arduous climb off the mountain. We were at 9,000 feet and needed to climb down approximately 4,000 to 5,000 feet to reach the valley floor, where we hoped to find an abandoned shepherd's hut.

I suggested that we pray and ask God's guidance and direction. Then, with limited light, we began to climb down the mountain. After passing the dangerous cliffs, we endured the thick brush that whipped and thrashed us on our descent.

I had little to eat or drink during the day due to an upset stomach. The lack of reserve energy added quickly to my fatigue, and my body became so weary that on three separate occasions I had to sit down and evaluate whether I could go on.

At about 11 p.m. the temperatures fell below freezing. Cold and frightened we finally reached the hunter's hut. We were able to start a fire and dry out our wet clothing while trying to recuperate from the ordeal.

About 1:30 a.m. that night we heard the familiar sound of a helicopter. As we peered out the window into the blackness of night, we could see the searchlights of a rescue helicopter that responded to our transponder. This rescue crew had flown out through the darkness of night and jagged mountain passes to search for our party.

Except for some bruises and minor cuts, we miraculously escaped severe injury or death. Once again, I realized that my salvation (both physical and spiritual) is was due to the mercy and grace of God Almighty.

Scripture Reading: Psalm 46:1-3

Personal Application:

• The Lord truly is our "refuge and strength." Trust Him and rely on Him in all that you do today.

Week 47, Day 4: Where's Your Focus?

The mind is a powerful thing. Wherever it's focused, we seem to follow. Legendary Alabama coach, Bear Bryant, told of a unique moment in "Bama History" when, with two minutes remaining in a critical game against their rival, a miracle of the mind happened.

Alabama was first and ten on the opponent's twenty-yard line. With a five-point lead and no time-outs remaining for either team, the starting quarterback took the ball on a quarterback sneak and was hit hard. He was in too much pain to continue. Coach Bryant found his rookie quarterback and instructed him, "This game is ours if you do what I say. Rush the ball all three downs. Do not under any circumstance put it up in the air. Even if we don't make a first down, there will be so little time left on the clock, that our defense will hold them until the game is over. Do you understand? I don't want you to put the ball in the air."

With a big gulp, the quarterback responded, "Yes sir; I understand. Don't put the ball in the air." He ran onto the field, and immediately called an off-tackle play, gaining no yards. On the third down, he executed a quarterback sneak, gaining one yard. On the last down, with just seconds remaining in the game, he once again called an off-tackle play. This time the running back missed the hand-off, leaving the ball in the quarterback's hands. The frightened rookie looked up to see his tight end frantically waving his arms in the corner of the end zone—wide open. He knew all he had to do was lob a pass to the end zone and the game would be over.

What he didn't know was that it was a trap! An All-American safety had intentionally let the split-end roam free, hoping the quarterback would throw in that direction. The safety had lightening quick speed and planned to intercept the ball. As the pass was released the safety moved towards the ball with the speed of a cheetah. The graceful defensive back snatched the ball and began his 100-yard journey to Bama's end zone. The quarterback was the only person who had a chance to tackle the elusive defender… which he finally did… on his own two-yard line… just as the whistle blew, ending the game.

After the game, the two coaches met on the center of the field to exchange handshakes. The perplexed coach of the opposing team asked Coach Bryant, "According to our scouting reports your rookie quarterback is not very swift on his feet. How on earth did he catch our All-American safety—one of the quickest guys in college football?" Coach Bryant responded, "Your All-American safety was running for six-points. My boy was running for his life!"

As Christians, even with the best of intentions, we can become distracted and easy prey to temptation. However, when our focus is on God, we can be unstoppable! God's Word tells us to be single-minded in purpose, focusing our thoughts on what is good, and sticking with it!

Scripture Reading: Philippians 3:10-14

Personal Application:
- Where's your focus? What has you distracted? What's consuming your thoughts?
- Keep your focus on Jesus and His Word.

Week 47, Day 5: "The Lord Is My Shepherd"

Louise and I really enjoy summer. As we take a-week-or-two break from the work of our calling, we seek God's renewing Spirit upon our lives and ministry, saturating ourselves with His Word and enjoying His presence.

The second verse of Psalms 23 reminds us of the importance of physically resting—removing ourselves to the "quiet waters" of life where we can "drink in" the peace and comfort of God. Read on to verse three and you'll notice that it's only after we have rested and meditated that we can be restored and refreshed. If we have the appropriate time with God to contemplate His majesty and glory, we will experience and notice His goodness and mercy in our lives. And this reminds me of a cute story that is bound to make you smile.

Timmy's mom loved her five-year-old son very much and worried about him walking to school when he started Kindergarten. She walked him to school the first couple of days. Then he came home one day and told his mother he didn't want her walking him to school anymore; he wanted to be like the "big boys." But she wasn't so sure.

He protested loudly, so she finally got an idea how to handle it. She asked her neighbor, Mrs. Goodnest, if she would surreptitiously follow her son to school—at a distance behind him that he would not likely notice, but close enough to keep a watch on him. Mrs. Goodnest said that since she was up early with her toddler anyway, it would be a good way for them to get some exercise as well, so she agreed.

The next school day, Mrs. Goodnest and her little girl Marcy set out, following behind Timmy as he walked to school with another neighbor boy he knew. She did this for the whole week. As the boys walked and chatted, kicking stones and twigs, Timmy's friend noticed the lady following them—the same lady who had seemed to follow them all week. Finally, he said to Timmy, "Do you know that lady who's following us? I think she's been following us all week."

Timmy nonchalantly replied, "Yeah, that's just Shirley Goodnest with her daughter Marcy."

"Shirley Goodnest? Why is she following us?"

"Well, I'm not exactly sure," Timmy explained, "but every night my Mom makes me say the 23rd Psalm with my prayers 'cuz she worries about me so much. And in one part it says, 'Shirley Goodnest and Marcy shall follow me all the days of my life,' so I guess we'll just have to get used to it." – Author Unknown

As believers we appreciate God's protection and encouragement. He watches over us. We know that nothing can touch us unless it first passes through the loving hands of our Heavenly Father.

Scripture Reading: Psalm 23

Personal Application:

- Meditate on Psalm 23 today and let its message wash over you and encourage you. Share your insights with your spouse or a friend.

Week 47, Day 6: The Wrong Crowd

A friend of mine tells a funny story about his grandson Jack:

When Jack was about four years old, he and his mom were doing some last-minute Christmas shopping at large department store.

Jack was sitting in the shopping cart when an elderly gentleman walked up to him and said, "I bet you're excited that Christmas is coming!" Jack's eyes brightened and he nodded in agreement.

Then the man asked, "Is Santa going to bring you lots of toys?"

To which Jack replied, "I don't believe in Santa."

"What?" the man cried. "If you don't believe in Santa, you must be hanging around the wrong crowd."

To which Jack replied, "I think I'm hanging around the wrong crowd right now."

At that, the man laughed and rushed off to tell his wife what this cute little boy had just said to him.

In Jack's case, "hanging out with the wrong crowd" was harmless. But in life, especially as a teen or an adult, hanging out with the wrong crowd can bring serious consequences. I can't tell you how many stories I've heard especially of young men who go off the deep end morally because they've gotten involved with the wrong crowd.

The apostle Paul warned, "Do not be misled: 'Bad company corrupts good character.'" (1 Corinthians 15:33) The truth is, we become like those with whom we spend time. The character, attitudes, actions, and beliefs of those we associate with rub off on us.

This doesn't mean we can't or shouldn't have unsaved friends or Christian friends who are struggling in some area. But we must be careful to maintain our character and integrity when we're with them. We must not let others drag us down. And God forbid that we should take others down who spend time with us.

We want others to follow our example as we follow Christ's example. Paul also wrote, "Be wise in the way you act toward outsiders; make the most of every opportunity. Let your conversation be always full of grace, seasoned with salt, so that you may know how to answer everyone." (Colossians 4:5-6)

Scripture Reading: 1 Peter 3:15-16

Personal Application:
- Who are your closest friends? Who wields the greatest influence in terms of Christlike character, you, or them?
- Purpose to represent Christ well for others in any and every situation and context.

Week 47, Day 7: Weekly Recap and Prayer

On the seventh day of each week, use the **ACTS** acronym to spend time with the Lord reviewing and assessing your week and praying to God. (**A**=Adoration; **C**=Confession; **T**=Thanksgiving; **S**=Supplication)

First, look back over the previous six days for this week to remind yourself what you read and agreed to. Then, follow the ACTS pattern for prayer below. Finally, use the space below to journal what God is doing in your life and share this with a trusted spiritual partner.

Adoration: Simply spend time in adoration of the Lord. Praise Him and glorify His name. (See 1 Chronicles 29:10-13; Psalm 100; Romans 11:33-36.)

Confession: Confess your sins and shortcomings before God. ("If we confess our sins, he is faithful and just and will forgive us our sins and purify us from all unrighteousness." – 1 John 1:9) To confess (or agree with God) about your sin, implies that you are repentant and desperately want Him to change you.

Thanksgiving: Thank God for what He has done and is doing in your life and the life of your family. Give Him credit, for everything you have comes from Him. (See Psalm 136.)

Supplication: Supplication is just a fancy word for making your requests known to God. Based on the devotions of this past week and the things going on in your life right now, what do you want to ask Him for? "If you, then, though you are evil, know how to give good gifts to your children, how much more will your Father in heaven give good gifts to those who ask Him!" (Matthew 7:11)

Journal: What is God doing in your life right now?

Week 48, Day 1: A Pebble in My Boot

Have you ever been hiking and get a pebble in your boot? If you're like me, at first, I'm annoyed, because I don't want to stop and unlace my boot, so I try to ignore it. I may even hike for awhile with that pebble digging into my insole. But now I notice I'm limping and ignoring that pebble is no longer an option. So, reluctantly, I stop, unlace my boot, pull it off and empty it. I'm often amazed at how tiny that pebble is that caused me so much discomfort.

Sin is like that in our life. There may be some niggling sin in our life that is annoying, but we try to ignore it and keep going. The sin may be a wandering eye, anger behind the wheel, an unreconciled relationship, bitterness toward someone, or some dumb habit.

In our minds we may view our "pebble" of a sin to be minor and insignificant, but the longer we tolerate it, the more damage it does. This also reveals some misconceptions about our sin. We tend to view sin's weightiness in terms of comparison. "I'm better than most." Or, "I'm not as bad as people who do that...." But we must come to grips with the fact that Jesus died for ALL sin, even that little "pebble" of a sin I'm carrying around with me. To recognize and acknowledge this can be life changing.

If what I'm talking about resonates with you, it's time to stop, unlace your boot and empty it. Get that "pebble" out of your life. How do you do this?

First, go after it proactively. Confess it to the Lord and tell Him you want His help in getting rid of it. Read and follow 1 John 1:9. I can't emphasize enough how vital it is that we lean into the Lord in this regard and rely on His strength (John 15:5). You cannot beat the flesh by attacking it in the flesh (or in your own strength). You'll find yourself frustrated and inadequate to the task.

Second, share your resolve with a spiritual partner—another man, who is a follower of Jesus—someone you trust. Be transparent and honest with him. And ask him to pray with you and hold you accountable.

Third, if possible, replace that sin—whatever it is—with a Christlike attitude or action. For instance, if that niggling sin in your life is anger, ask the Lord to give you patience, humility, and kindness in its place.

Sometimes that "pebble" sin in our life is a past hurt that we've inflicted on someone. In that case, go to that individual and ask them to forgive you. But do so in humility and genuineness. Even the smallest of sins can greatly hinder our walk with the Lord.

Scripture Reading: Colossians 3:5-14

Personal Application:

- Perhaps in the reading of this devotional the Lord has brought some niggling sin to your mind. Follow the actions above to rid yourself of this annoying, hindering sin.

Week 48, Day 2: Hang in There!

It took three trips to New Zealand, hours of climbing and glassing, a near death experience with a helicopter, plus a whole lot of persistence before I finally got my Record Book Tahr (a large mountain goat). Did you ever notice that the more challenging things in life do not come easy?

Many hunters pull themselves out of a warm, comfortable bed and hike through overgrown trails in freezing weather so they can sit in a cramped tree stand next to a pond full of mosquitoes. All this to possibly bag a trophy deer elk, or other species.

Typically, those hunters who eventually score are very persistent. They are willing to make the sacrifices needed to experience the challenge of the hunt and the satisfaction of taking the trophy animal.

Similarly, as Jesus was traveling from village to village in Galilee, He taught His disciples the parable of the sower as a way of encouraging them to persevere. He said, "The seed on good soil stands for those with a noble and good heart, who hear the word, retain it, and by persevering produce a crop." (Luke 8:15)

He reminded His band of followers that to be spiritually fruitful they must persevere and give themselves wholeheartedly to the challenge. In other words, fruitfulness does not come easily.

When Paul and Barnabas traveled all over the Mediterranean spreading the Gospel, they encouraged these new followers of Jesus with the following words, "We must go through many hardships to enter the kingdom of God." (Acts 14:22) The Lord makes it clear that following Him and producing fruit for Him will be a struggle, a challenge requiring perseverance or endurance. So, how do we obtain this perseverance?

Paul tells us how in Romans. First, he explains that, "suffering produces perseverance." (Romans 5:3) At first this might sound like circular reasoning, but it makes sense that we can't learn to persevere without opportunity to do so. We learn perseverance by enduring suffering. Paul also explains that God has given us His Word, the mind of Christ, and hope of success to help us endure. Why persevere if there's no hope of success? But in Christ, we are guaranteed success.

"For everything that was written in the past was written to teach us, so that through the endurance taught in the Scriptures and the encouragement they provide we might have hope. May the God who gives endurance and encouragement give you the same attitude of mind toward each other that Christ Jesus had." (Romans 15:4-5)

Let me leave you with this word from Hebrews 10:36, "You need to persevere so that when you have done the will of God, you will receive what he has promised."

Scripture Reading: James 1:3-4, 12; 5:11

Personal Application:

- What is God calling you to endure right now? Grab hold of His Word, His hope, and the mind of Christ to persevere under your current trials. Hang in there! God is faithful!

Week 48, Day 3: Don't Hesitate!

One of the outdoorsmen I most admire is the host of "God's Great Outdoors," Gerry Caillouet. Gerry is a gifted communicator and woodsmen who has encouraged many Christian sportsmen's organizations throughout the country.

Some years back, Gerry was shotgun hunting in the hills of southeast Ohio. "I was still-hunting up the logging road, the prevailing wind was in my face and deer sign was everywhere." Gerry knew these woods well and figured this was his day to take a nice trophy buck, "It was a perfect day to still-hunt, wet leaves and an overcast sky with occasional spitting of snow showers."

At midday Gerry was halfway up the road when a nice 8-point buck descended off the ridge top. The deer headed towards an area where the old road and ridge met.

"The buck stopped just before dropping onto the flat. I prepared to shoot just as soon as he came into my shotgun range." The buck continued to move into range, but Gerry still didn't pull the trigger. "It wasn't buck fever or a sudden feeling of guilt, I really can't explain why I didn't drop the animal when I had the chance."

Moving to close the gap even more, Gerry slowly moved down to the animal by quietly crossing a small depression. This time the deer turned broadside and presented the prefect shot. As Gerry pulled up on the animal, he again hesitated. The wind began to swirl and the buck winded him and within seconds spotted Gerry.

"Emotion rushed upon me and screamed 'SHOOT!'" I still could not pull the trigger. The animal spun and headed across the overgrown logging trail when Gerry placed his sights on the chest of the runaway critter. "As I led the animal, I squeezed off a shot, Boom! Unfortunately, a 10-inch diameter poplar tree took a direct hit as the buck ran between me and the tree."

"I kicked myself many times for blowing the opportunity," states Gerry. Continuing to analyze his misfortune he laments, "I often think about how many times I could have taken that deer. I will probably never have another chance to take a trophy animal that close again."

When was the last time you hesitated to take advantage of a sure thing? Maybe your missed opportunity was a chance to build a relationship, or to assist someone in need, or to encourage a child. What about the last time you could have shared your faith but didn't?

Almost every day we have opportunities to tell people about Jesus. Many seem to feel that talking about Jesus is the pastor's job. Scripture indicates otherwise. We're all to be His witnesses. Don't get frigid about sharing your faith! Pull the trigger on the next opportunity.

Scripture Reading: Acts 8:26-40

Personal Application:
- Sometimes when the Holy Spirit nudges us to talk to someone, give a gift, or help someone we hesitate. And in that moment of hesitation we doubt and then fail to act.
Next time the Holy Spirit prompts you, don't hesitate—act!

Week 48, Day 4: Spiritual Myopia

I've had the privilege of being around a few NFL coaches and players who can legitimately critique quarterbacks. A player's ability to "scan the opponent's defense" is a critical element in play selection and execution. Many very athletic quarterbacks have been rendered "functionally nearsighted" when it comes to seeing potential opportunities or problems on the playing field.

Nearsightedness (myopia) causes people's eyes to focus the parallel rays of light in front of the retina. They can clearly see things right in front of them, but the farther out they look, the more out of focus objects become. With this condition comes a selectivity of vision that doesn't always consider the things that can bring about harm to a person – like a blitzing 215-pound safety.

When the ball is snapped and chaos ensues in front of the quarterback, if the plan dictates a pass, he's got to look past the commotion before him and seek out that open receiver, even if it means he'll be tackled right after throwing the ball. But without this ability to scan distant opportunities, the quarterback will be sacked or not able to move the ball down the field.

"Spiritual nearsightedness" is even more concerning. Professed believers become unfruitful when they are spiritually nearsighted. When they focus on self, the worries of life, or all the lures of materialism, the big eternal issues of life become blurred—a distant reality; they can't see the dangers or opportunities right in front of them.

People who are spiritually myopic risk being consumed with sinful behavior; it can easily sneak up on them. The blitzing addictions of life brought about through lustful thoughts, pornography, substance abuse, uncontrolled anger, out-of-control spending, and unbalanced lives can cause the person to miss the lasting blessings God intended.

Solomon coached his son, "Let your eyes look straight ahead; fix your gaze directly before you. Give careful thought to the paths for your feet and be steadfast in all your ways. Do not turn to the right or the left; keep your foot from evil." (Proverbs 4:25-27)

When "all hell breaks loose" around us, it's easy to take our eyes off the goal. It's easy to feel overwhelmed and to be entirely focused on the problems and challenges in front of us. When we feel this happening, it's time to withdraw momentarily and pray, asking the Lord to give us focus and perspective about what we're experiencing.

Additionally, if our focus is on ourselves, then our sight will be very limited. Psalm 121 is called a "Song of Ascents." As the Children of Israel would go up to Jerusalem to worship, they would sing this song in anticipation of meeting with the Lord. The first verse says, "I lift my eyes to the mountains—where does my help come from? My help comes from the Lord, the Maker of Heaven and earth." My we continually lift our eyes to the Lord!

Scripture Reading: Psalm 121:1-8

Personal Application:

- Who or what has your focus right now? "Look to Jesus, the Author and Finisher of our faith."

Week 48, Day 5: Getting Older

Each morning I wake up and begin the process of stretching out the stiff muscles and tendons to the rhythm of bones and joints cracking as they reset for another day of activity. As I make my way to the mirror in our bathroom, I discover more grey hair, another reminder that I'm getting older.

The aging process isn't for the faint of heart as we reflect upon all the things we use to do that required agility, strength, and flexibility that abound with a younger body.

The venerable alumnus of baseball Satchel Paige said, "How old would you be if you didn't know how old you were?" An honest answer to that question depends on an honest admission of one's attitude. It has nothing to do with one's age.

As the year's pass by I'm more convinced that our major battle in life is not with the aging process but with choosing the right attitude and character to glorify our Lord. Rather than focus on aches and pains, bitterness and apathy, regrets and loss we can choose each morning to develop an attitude of thanksgiving and grace.

God's desire is for us to mature as wise and committed leaders to help transform a broken world with the spiritual gifts, talents, and experience He has given us. No matter how old we are, our goals is to become more like Christ.

My good friend and mentor Chuck Swindoll gives us three things we can focus upon when it comes to aging:

1. Look within...and release. What is it down inside you that is stunting your spiritual growth? When you probe around and find something you are hanging onto too tightly, deliberately let go...

2. Look around...and respond. Don't wait for someone else. Act on your own, spontaneously... is there a need you can help meet? Risk responding.

3. Look up...and rejoice. You are the recipient of God's riches, so enjoy them! Realize anew all He has done for you; then rejoice in the pleasure of getting involved with others... and stay involved! You will never regret it. Furthermore, it will help you grow up as you find yourself growing old. And the more involved you remain, the less concern you will have for how old you are.

By the way, how old would you be if you didn't know how old you were?

Scripture Reading: Philippians 4:19; Ephesians 4:17-5:2

Personal Application:

• Regardless of how old you are, wake up each day in anticipation of what the Lord has for you today. Thank Him and look for ways to represent Him well to others.

Week 48, Day 6: A Symbol That Can't Be Taken from Us

If the year 2020 wasn't already one of the craziest year's I've ever seen with the pandemic, flooding in the south, and social and political uprisings – now protestors have decided to tear down, destroy, or mutilate many of our cherished monuments and historical statues that have been with us for hundreds of years. This is absolute insanity.

While mistakes were made in the original thinking of our founding fathers on such issues as slavery and woman suffrage, a wonderful mechanism was put in place to amend the Constitution. To date, twenty-seven amendments have been ratified and put in place to help better govern our country and correct the mistakes of the past.

What will the protestors take down next? Will it be symbols of our faith such as the Cross or the Star of David? These are the most precious and sacred of all symbols. It was the Judeo/Christian values that were used to form the Constitution and Declaration of Independence. Half the Declaration's signers had divinity school training. Many were pastors or lay leaders in their churches.

The cross is an influential symbol of our Christian faith. It speaks to any on-looker of the grim realities of suffering and death. Christ and many of His followers endured pain and agony as they hung on a cross. As God entered the world to live and die in the flesh, Calvary's Cross became the ultimate sacrifice for sin and to bring us newness of life. The cross is a sign of the glory within the Old Testament that was concealed but revealed in the New Testament.

It stands as a symbol of hope and assurance to a world distracted by its pride, apathy, and self-indulgence. Regarding those who don't yet know Christ, let's pray that through your witness and mine they may come to faith in Jesus and embrace the significance of the Cross He died on. For without the cross of Christ, there would be no forgiveness of sins, no reconciliation with God, and only the bleak outlook of eternity in hell.

Many stumble over the cross seeing it only as a symbol of death and suffering. But the cross represents the great lengths to which God went to free this dark and sick world from its sin and despair. Next time you look at a cross keep in mind the importance of this symbol. It is everything to all who believe and trust Christ for the forgiveness of sin.

And pray that the wonderful symbols of America's past can be reclaimed, preserved, and protected. As we look upon these relics of the past may we learn from history and repeat the positive but shun the negative.

Scripture Reading: 1 Corinthians 1:18-2:5; Ephesians 2:11-22

Personal Application:

- Let God's Word wash over you as you read about the significance of the Cross of Christ. Then, spend time in prayer thanking God for what He did for you through Christ.

Week 48, Day 7: Weekly Recap and Prayer

On the seventh day of each week, use the **ACTS** acronym to spend time with the Lord reviewing and assessing your week and praying to God. (**A**=Adoration; **C**=Confession; **T**=Thanksgiving; **S**=Supplication)

First, look back over the previous six days for this week to remind yourself what you read and agreed to. Then, follow the ACTS pattern for prayer below. Finally, use the space below to journal what God is doing in your life and share this with a trusted spiritual partner.

Adoration: Simply spend time in adoration of the Lord. Praise Him and glorify His name. (See 1 Chronicles 29:10-13; Psalm 100; Romans 11:33-36.)

Confession: Confess your sins and shortcomings before God. ("If we confess our sins, he is faithful and just and will forgive us our sins and purify us from all unrighteousness." – 1 John 1:9) To confess (or agree with God) about your sin, implies that you are repentant and desperately want Him to change you.

Thanksgiving: Thank God for what He has done and is doing in your life and the life of your family. Give Him credit, for everything you have comes from Him. (See Psalm 136.)

Supplication: Supplication is just a fancy word for making your requests known to God. Based on the devotions of this past week and the things going on in your life right now, what do you want to ask Him for? "If you, then, though you are evil, know how to give good gifts to your children, how much more will your Father in heaven give good gifts to those who ask Him!" (Matthew 7:11)

Journal: What is God doing in your life right now?

Week 49, Day 1: God Is Not through with You

In 1985 Bill Rhodes of North Huntingdon Township in Pennsylvania was on a roll. He was on the cutting edge of medical science as a technician and operator of heart and lung machines. His wife Marcia was a special education teacher who also brought home a good salary. The Rhodes were card-carrying members of the American dream and middle-class suburbia.

As an avid archer, Bill was setting local archery records by shooting at least one-trophy buck four years in a row. Then on that fateful day in July 1985 Bill took a short motorcycle ride on his brother's bike. As he rounded a corner approach to a bridge, he knew he was in trouble. He misjudged his speed going into the curve and hit his right shoulder on a large girder. In a split second, the nerves in his right arm were torn away from his spinal column. The resulting paralysis was immediate, permanent, and life changing. After three life-saving operations, Bill faced his long recuperation with thoughts of despair, denial, and deep grief. "You mourn the loss of your arm the way you would the death of a friend or a family pet," states Rhodes.

As Bill began to wrestle with God in prayer over his situation, he realized that God wasn't through with him yet. Despite the fact he lost his occupation, altered his physical appearance and now was unable to do all the things he used to do, he was determined to move ahead with life. Bill claimed God's promises, "I can do all things through Him who strengthens me." (Philippians 4:13) With that assurance he began to think about his favorite pastime—archery. He contacted another disabled person who told him how to modify a compound bow to accommodate a nylon month piece on the string. By using his teeth and a modified anchor point, Bill now shoots a 60-pound compound bow and is again taking some nice deer.

Each time he pulls back the bowstring and feels the power of the draw, he is reminded of God's power. Bill now appropriates God's strength in place of his energy.

King David was no stranger to pain, anxiety, suffering, threats, fear, and despair as the lines in this Psalm testify to. "God is our refuge and strength, an ever-present help in trouble. There we will not fear, through the earth give way and the mountains fall into the heart of the sea, though its waters roar and foam and the mountains quake with their surging." (Psalm 46:1-3) We have a BIG God! Whatever it is we're going through; God is infinitely bigger. His grace is more than sufficient to deal with any and every challenge.

Scripture Reading: Luke 12:22-31

Personal Application:

- What challenge are you currently facing that you can trust God with? Make David's prayer in Psalm 46 your own and trust the Lord with your situation. Ask Him to align your emotions and responses with the reality of His presence and power in your life.

Week 49, Day 2: Suffering for Christ

In December 2015, just days before Christmas, Petr Jasek was standing in line at the airport in waiting to board his plane bound for his home in the Czech Republic. He had spent the last four days in Sudan as a representative of Voice of the Martyrs. He had been visiting, encouraging, and interviewing Christians who had been persecuted under the heavy hand of this radical Islamic state.

Petr could hardly wait to get home to his wife, son, and daughter—especially at this time of year when being together as a family is so special. While waiting to board his flight, he called his wife Vanda one more time. Hopefully, it would only be a few more hours and they'd be together.

But suddenly, he felt someone tap him on the shoulder, and two Sudanese secret service officers demanded that he come with them. Petr was used to being singled out as a foreigner and suspected this was just a routine search. The guards ushered him to a secluded room in the airport and began interrogating him.

Time rolled on and their questions continued. Soon Petr heard his name being called to report to his gate as his plane was leaving. He knew now that he would miss his flight. The guards escalated the intensity and depth of their probes into Petr's intentions and movements in Sudan. Petr was beginning to get concerned.

During the day, Petr soon found himself arrested and sent to prison pending a trial. He was put in a cell designed for one or two men, but which he shared with six others. The cell was all that the imagination could conceive of as "squalor" and more. But imagine Petr's surprise and dread when he discovered that his six cell mates were convicted ISIS terrorists—and they knew he was a Christian.

Petr suffered unspeakable deprivations, harassment, and beatings from his cell mates. Numerous times he cried out to God to save him. He couldn't understand why he was being subjected to such torture. Eventually, the guards intervened and transferred Petr to another cell. There he shared the Gospel and was able to lead twelve inmates to the Lord.

After spending fourteen-and-a-half months in several prisons in Sudan, Petr was finally released despite receiving a life sentence through a mock trial. Petr reflects on his time in prison, "I was so thankful to the Lord—deeply thankful— for allowing me the privilege of suffering dishonor for the name of my Savior. Sometimes, while being beaten by my ISIS cellmates, all I could do was groan. But during those awful moments, the Holy Spirit was groaning with me, interceding on my behalf (Romans 8:26)." (Petr Jasek, *Imprisoned with ISIS* (Washington DC: Salem Books, 2020), pp. 209-210.)

Scripture Reading: Acts 20:22-24; 21:10-14; Philippians 1:29

Personal Application:
- In what ways does Petr Jasek's story challenge and encourage you?
  To what extent are you willing to suffer for Christ's sake?
  Pray for Christians around the world who suffer persecution.

Week 49, Day 3: What's Your Hurry?

Over the past five decades I have enjoyed every opportunity to share with folks my passion for fishing and hunting. One of the common disciplines that is required to master both sports is patience.

Whether you are slip hunting from tree to tree, sitting in a tree stand, or dunking a bait in your favorite fishing hole, it is critical to practice a great deal of patience if you hope to be successful. A frantic or hurried approach to these activities usually chases off game.

In our fast-paced, instant-everything society, it's refreshing when we're forced to take life at God's pace rather than ours. Fish and wildlife do not fret about the diseases and emotions associated with stress. Undisturbed, animals are rarely hurried or anxious. To be successful in the outdoors and life we must slow our pace down and listen to God.

God's plan for all His creation is one of balance and order. It is difficult for us to listen to God through the noise and competition of technology, the media, and an over-committed schedule. We need those special quiet times of communication and fellowship with the Lord; times to recreate, reflect, rest, and restore.

Many sportsmen have experienced the wonderful tranquility the outdoors provides. Through the rustling of the trees, chirping of the birds, and rushing of water over the falls we can hear God's quiet, still voice.

I am continually amazed that during Christ's three and a half years of ministry, He was never in a hurry or a rush. He was always that perfect model of "balance."

In the Gospel accounts, we discover that Jesus often took time to get away from the crowd to be alone with His Father. Luke 5:16 says, "But Jesus often withdrew to lonely places and prayed."

Jesus lived in constant communion with the Father. And if Jesus, the Son of God, needed that level of connection with the Father, how much more do we need fellowship with Him? Jesus still bids us, "Come away by yourself to a lonely place and rest a while" (Mark 6:31)

So often we simply shoot up a prayer to God in haste on our way to another meeting or at mealtime. I'm as guilty as the next person for neglecting to spend the time alone with the Lord that I truly need. But during those times when I'm in the woods, on the water alone, or simply walking my dog, I've had some deep, meaningful times with my Lord.

Purpose to follow Jesus' example and withdraw to "lonely places often to pray."

Scripture Reading: Psalm 9:1-10
Personal Application:
* Take out your calendar and schedule a time to be with the Lord alone in the next few days. When you meet with Him, praise Him, thank Him, enjoy Him, commune with Him, simply talk to Him. Intercede on behalf of others.

Week 49, Day 4: Coming Clean with God

Many go through life without any consciousness of God's presence and purposes in their life. But God wants to be totally involved in our lives and we won't begin to experience the fulness of our relationship with Him until we acknowledge His presence and live accordingly.

King David recognized this when he wrote Psalm 139. He began this Psalm by speaking to the Lord, "You have searched me, Lord, and You know me. You know when I sit and when I rise; You perceive my thoughts from afar. You discern my going out and my lying down; You are familiar with all my ways. Before a word is on my tongue You, Lord, know it completely." (Psalm 139:1-4)

What David acknowledged in that prayer is true for each one of us as well. Think about that for a moment: The Lord knows you and me intimately. Nothing about us is hidden from Him. He knows everything about us: our plans, our goals, our thoughts, our words—everything. This is both comforting and sobering depending on how we're living.

David shifts his prayer in verse 7 where he prayed, "where can I go from Your Spirit? Where can I flee from Your presence?" And in the next verses he concludes there is nowhere he can go where God is not present. Think about this too. Whether you're at home, at work, at play—no matter where you are, God is present with you.

During several times in my life I've found myself in circumstances where the Lord seemed distant or even absent. This feeling can especially prevail during times of suffering and grief. Yet, I realize that my feelings are fickle, and if stop to consider what is happening to me, I see God's presence and power in my life despite what I'm experiencing and feeling.

Many years ago, I underwent a life-threatening surgery. I went under the knife not knowing whether I'd wake up again. I didn't know whether I'd leave my wife a widow and my boys fatherless. This was a frightening time, but God was with me and my family. He knew the outcome before I even knew there was a problem.

That was a life-changing experience. As a result, I strongly identify with David's closing prayer in this Psalm. In verses 23-24 he prayed, "Search me, God, and know my heart; test me and know my anxious thoughts. See if there is any offensive way in me and lead me in the way everlasting."

This prayer brings the Psalm full circle to a sweet conclusion. For if God already knows everything about us, then when we invite Him to know us thoroughly and to expose anything harmful in us, we're humbly submitting to His will and His way in our life. We're asking Him to have His way in our lives, for that's what we ultimately desire. Is this your desire?

Scripture Reading: Psalm 139

Personal Application:

- Read Psalm 139 aloud to the Lord, making it your own prayer. Then, listen to Him. As you invite Him to search your heart, what is God revealing to you?

Week 49, Day 5: Worship

On my second excursion to New Zealand, I had the opportunity to hunt three beautiful trophies including the famous Red Stag. New Zealand is in the South Pacific about 1500 miles from Australia and is without a doubt the most beautiful and friendly country I have ever experienced.

During my hunt in a pristine wilderness area, I had the experience of stalking and evaluating several "world class" animals. Because the cost of a hunt is determined by the size of your trophy, I decided to limit my choice to an SCI Bronze level (approximately 225-250 scoring points).

After two days of viewing several possible prospects, I began to stalk a beautiful 15-point, 450-pound stag. It was my first time to take an animal of this size. As we approached this stately beast my heart began to beat like a drum. I could feel the beads of perspiration forming on my brow. Closer and closer we crept keeping tight to the brush until we were within 125 yards. The guide nodded, as if to say, "It's all up to you!"

After dispatching the animal, I felt an enormous sense of gratefulness that God would allow me the opportunity to harvest one of His majestic creatures. I was equally excited that the meat would be used to feed the needy. All this welled up within me so that I felt the overwhelming need to bow down and worship the Creator.

I later learned through Dr. Tom Rakow's writings on Old Testament hunting, that worship was part of the hunter's tradition. Also, in Scotland they continue to honor God in a form of worship after each hunt.

Worship is an exercise that many of us engage in on a regular basis. Sometimes it is on a Sunday morning, evening, or on a Wednesday night. But it is also something each sportsman should do as part of their experience in honoring and praising God for His provision and the wonder of His creation.

Worship is something that involves the total person. It is not just the songs we sing before the message the pastor gives. Nor is just the quick "nod to God" in the field. We worship Him with our lives, our words, our thoughts, and our actions.

Are you allowing yourself the full experience of worship? Are you letting your personal hang-ups and/or inhibitions create a barrier between yourself and God? Why not enjoy all the facets of worship there are to experience even in the field?

Scripture Reading: Psalm 104

Personal Application:

- Use Psalm 104 as a blueprint for worshiping the Lord today.
- What part of this Psalm did the Lord use most impactfully in your life?

Week 49, Day 6: Fishing on the Right Side of the Boat

I try to stay away from large charter boat operations because of the crowded conditions. But occasionally, I will help guide a men's group on one of these excursions. It never ceases to amaze me how one side of the boat will do better than the other. There can be several reasons for this phenomenon. The shadows cast into the water will provide better action to those fishing on the shaded side. The boat could be sitting on a contour allowing one side to be at a more preferred depth. The drift of the bait due to currents or boat maneuvering will also change the action and depth of baits on separate sides of the boat.

In John 21 we find a wonderful story of how the resurrected Jesus directed his disciple fishermen to "cast their nets to the right-hand side of the boat." The fish were on that side because God directed them to be there. He used this miracle to reintroduce Himself to the distraught band of believers who faltered after His crucifixion.

When the disciples recognized that it was Jesus, they hurried ashore and found that He had already prepared a fish barbecue with all the trimmings. After breakfast He answered the disciples' questions then pulled Peter aside to ask him a few critical questions.

Three times He asked Peter, "Do you love Me?" Remember, it was Peter who denied Jesus three times during His trial before Caiaphas. Our loving Savior asked Peter to confirm his love for Him. Each time Peter affirmed his love with a deeper sense of passion and commitment.

There are at least three facets to Christ's questioning that we can apply to our daily lives. First, Jesus wants us to know that love requires both an attitude and action. Many believe that saying "I Love You" is enough. But if we truly love sacrificially, then we take on Christ's attitude and actions by "tending His lambs." We demonstrate our love in acts of kindness and service.

Secondly, Christ indicates that there is an intensity to our love. With a Christlike love we bear with each other and forgive each other. Grace and mercy abound when our love is deep.

Finally, when we truly love the Lord, we have His glory and His concerns foremost in our minds. We value Him above all else. He is the "pearl of great price." He is the "treasure hidden in a field" for which we are willing to forfeit all else. As the Psalmist declared, "Whom have I in heaven but You? And earth has nothing I desire besides You." (Psalm 73:25)

If you're fishing on the wrong side of a relationship and not receiving or giving Christlike love, then follow Jesus' approach. It worked for those first century disciples, and it will work for you.

Scripture Reading: John 21:15-19

Personal Application:

- If the Lord were to ask you, "Do you love Me?" What would be the proof of your response?
- In what ways would you like to grow in your love for the Lord and for others?
- Ask the Lord to give you His love.

Week 49, Day 7: Weekly Recap and Prayer

On the seventh day of each week, use the **ACTS** acronym to spend time with the Lord reviewing and assessing your week and praying to God. (**A**=Adoration; **C**=Confession; **T**=Thanksgiving; **S**=Supplication)

First, look back over the previous six days for this week to remind yourself what you read and agreed to. Then, follow the ACTS pattern for prayer below. Finally, use the space below to journal what God is doing in your life and share this with a trusted spiritual partner.

Adoration: Simply spend time in adoration of the Lord. Praise Him and glorify His name. (See 1 Chronicles 29:10-13; Psalm 100; Romans 11:33-36.)

Confession: Confess your sins and shortcomings before God. ("If we confess our sins, he is faithful and just and will forgive us our sins and purify us from all unrighteousness." – 1 John 1:9) To confess (or agree with God) about your sin, implies that you are repentant and desperately want Him to change you.

Thanksgiving: Thank God for what He has done and is doing in your life and the life of your family. Give Him credit, for everything you have comes from Him. (See Psalm 136.)

Supplication: Supplication is just a fancy word for making your requests known to God. Based on the devotions of this past week and the things going on in your life right now, what do you want to ask Him for? "If you, then, though you are evil, know how to give good gifts to your children, how much more will your Father in heaven give good gifts to those who ask Him!" (Matthew 7:11)

Journal: What is God doing in your life right now?

Week 50, Day 1: Fishing the Depths of God's Word

I don't know that you could find anyone in the fishing industry more loved and appreciated than the late Uncle Homer Circle. Long before "professional sports fishermen" came to be, and at a time when this country needed uplifting, along came Florida's Homer Circle. As a former sports editor/tackle manufacture executive, Homer became the primary author for *Sports Afield Magazine*. For decades this publication has provided timely insights and warm humor that has cheered and inspired sportsmen everywhere.

I knew Homer for many years and received inspiration and encouragement from his wise counsel. Many folks got a glimpse into this patriarch's warm personality through the award-winning film "Big Mouth." This project involved Uncle Homer and Glen Lau, a world renown videographer/producer. These two men were able to share the secrets of black bass fishing by spending thousands of hours filming fish underwater in their natural habitat. They worked hard and dove deep to retrieve priceless footage for our edification. To really know how fish would react to selected presentations they had Uncle Homer fish a variety of lures, carefully studying the nature of the fish. Many helpful theories about bass fishing came from the lessons learned from their months of research.

In some ways, I like to approach God's Word like I approach learning to fish for a species. Sure, a cursory reading of the Bible will provide you with many wonderful insights. But when you cast deep and study God's Word, you begin to "catch" some significant truths. For instance, you begin to see amazing correlations between the Old and New Testaments.

Years ago, when I first started studying Scripture, there were just a few translations to choose from. Today we have dozens of translations and paraphrases of the Bible that can provide a clear understanding of the message God is proclaiming. When I think about Christians in China and other countries who may have to share one tattered Bible among a whole church congregation, I realize how truly blessed we are.

A frayed and worn Bible is a well-read one. What is the condition of yours? When was the last time you picked up a Bible? If you are uncomfortable with the translation you currently have, ask a Christian friend to help guide you to a translation of the Bible you can really get into. he Apostle Paul reminds us regarding God's Word, "For everything that was written in the past was written to teach us, so that through the endurance taught in the Scriptures and the encouragement they provide we might have hope." (Romans 15:4)

Scripture Reading: Psalm 119:9-16

Personal Application:
- If you're new to reading the Bible, the Gospel of Mark in the New Testament is a good place to start. Always go to the Word with the intent to meet with God and not just to learn "stuff." Make Bible reading a daily habit. You can also get the You Version App on your phone and read or listen to God's Word anywhere, anytime.

Week 50, Day 2: God Will Supply All Your Needs

Throughout our four decades of ministry, God has abundantly supplied the resources for our needs. Many faith-partners have been encouraged by the Holy Spirit to support the vision and goals God has put before us of reaching men for Christ.

We marvel at the faithfulness and generosity of our large contributors, and we are humbled by the sacrificial giving of those who have so little.

The following story is a beautiful illustration of God's creativity and sovereignty in using all our gifts, large or small, to further His Kingdom:

In the latter part of the 17th century, German preacher August H. Francke founded an orphanage to care for the homeless children of his town, Halle.

One day when Francke desperately needed funds to carry on his work, a destitute Christian widow came to his door begging for a *ducat* – a gold coin. Because of his financial situation, he politely but regretfully told her he couldn't help her.

Disheartened, the woman began to weep. Moved by her tears, Francke asked her to wait while he went to his room to pray. After seeking God's guidance, he felt that the Holy Spirit wanted him to give to this widow after all. So, trusting the Lord to meet his own needs, he gave her the money.

Two mornings later, he received a letter of thanks from the widow. She explained that because of his generosity she had asked the Lord to shower the orphanage with gifts.

That same day Francke received twelve ducats from a wealthy lady and two more from a friend in Sweden. He thought he had been amply rewarded for helping the widow, but he was soon informed that the orphanage was to receive 500 gold pieces from the estate of Prince Lodewyk Van Wurtenburg. Upon hearing this, Francke wept in gratitude.

In sacrificially providing for that needy widow, he had been enriched, not impoverished. – Author Unknown

What an inspiring story! God is so good! I'm reminded of 2 Corinthians 9:6, "Remember this: Whoever sows sparingly will also reap sparingly, and whoever sows generously will also reap generously."

May this challenge us to ask God how much He wants us to give, and to whom… not from our abundance, but from compassionate and generous hearts.

Scripture Reading: 2 Corinthians 9:6-15

Personal Application:

- To what extent have you experienced the joy of giving? Be generous and always hold material things with an open hand.

Week 50, Day 3: The Great Hunt

Over the years, I have tried to bridge the gap between hunters and non-hunters. I appreciate that some regard hunting as barbaric and that it has no relevance in modern civilization. But the fact remains that over 20 million Americans still consider hunting a wholesome outdoor activity that tests a person's fiber and puts food on the table. Many also enjoy the unique and intimate fellowship opportunities that come from sharing in a thrilling stalk and brilliant campfire.

I have a deep love for all that God has created. I'm also vitally concerned about what is happening to the wildlife around the world. God created the heavens and earth with a divine plan. The only thing He created with a soul was man. He gave man dominion and stewardship over all His creation so that we might enjoy and use creation to sustain life. Animals have served the purpose of sacrifice, food, clothing, recreation, and companionship.

God did not put animals on the earth for us to worship them. His Son died on the cross for man not animals. He also demanded that we be good stewards and managers of His resources. There are numerous countries that have severe problems maintaining their vegetation and agricultural resources because of an imbalance in wild animal management. Without controlled hunting we could not sustain healthy populations of animals. Overcrowding and disease would settle in on the wild and domestic animal populations threatening the balance God intended.

We hunt not to brag or boast, not to wastefully slaughter game, nor to destroy or devour for selfish gain. Outdoorsmen should respect God's creation as they carefully and selectively take animals that are in abundance.

Hunting is among the most ancient of outdoor skills. While the Israelites were known more for their pastoral skills, archeological evidence and the Scriptures identify several well-known people who participated in the sport of hunting. For example, Esau was a "skillful hunter" (Genesis 25:27), and King Solomon loved wild game as provisions for his royal court, including "deer, gazelles, roebuck, and choice fowl." (1 Kings 4:23)

It was God Himself who told Noah, "Everything that lives and moves will be food for you. Just as I gave you the green plants, I now give you everything." (Genesis 9:3). God also made it permissible under Jewish law to hunt and eat wild game: "The deer, the gazelle, the roe deer, the wild goat, the ibex, the antelope and the mountain sheep." (Deuteronomy 14:5 and 12:15)

My intent in this devotional isn't to make hunters of us all, but rather to demonstrate the breadth and depth of God's Word and its wisdom for living and answering the tough questions of life. Remember, God is the greatest hunter of all. He has been hunting for men to worship Him and fellowship with Him since the Garden of Eden.

Scripture Reading: Genesis 1

Personal Application:

- As we participate in this wonderful sport, lets us remember to give thanks to Him who made all that we enjoy. Praise Him for His amazing provision!

Week 50, Day 4: The Iditarod

Each year in Alaska, Iditarod, the annual long-distance sled dog race takes place in early March. The grueling course spans 938 miles from Anchorage to Nome. Mushers endure horrific arctic conditions of gale-force winds, white-out conditions, and subzero temperatures with windchills plummeting to minus 100 degrees!

Mushers generally take between 8 and 15 days, and often longer to complete the course. Each musher starts with 14 sled dogs and must cross the finish line with at least five of their dogs.

Each year there is a ceremonial start in Anchorage, but the official start occurs in Willow 80 miles north of Anchorage. To date, Mitch Seavey holds the record run in 8 days, 3 hours, 40 minutes, and 13 seconds, mushing over 100 miles per day.

If you ever have the chance to be present at the ceremonial start in Anchorage, it is a sight and sound to behold! Imagine 50 or more dogsled teams of 14 dogs each. These dogs are bred to run and pull a sled and it's abundantly clear that's what they love to do.

Before the race begins, the mushers are busy getting their dogs tethered to the sled. The dogs are so hyped up that this is no small feat. In their excitement, the dogs jump all over each other, yipping, and even playfully biting each other—all from pent-up energy and the anticipation of the run.

As the start draws near, the canyon of buildings in downtown Anchorage echo with the cacophony of dogs barking, yipping, and snarling. But when the start gun goes off and mushers give the command to mush—everything grows unearthly quiet. The only sound you hear is that of the sled runners shooting across the snow and the soft pat of the dogs' paws as they engage in what they were made to do. It's quite a sight to behold!

I can't help but think that the church is a bit like that Iditarod start. When we're not doing what we were designed to do, we're "barking, snarling, yipping and biting" each other. But when we're dialed in, all doing what God gifted us to do and commanded us to do, all you hear and see is the beautiful rhythm of the church functioning as a coordinated, effective unit.

In writing to the Thessalonian church, Paul praised them for doing just that, "You became a model to all the believers in Macedonia and Achaia. The Lord's message rang out from you not only in Macedonia and Achaia—your faith in God has become known everywhere." (1 Thessalonians 1:7-8)

In Christ, the Lord has groomed us to function with other believers as a unified team. We are to represent Christ well to others through our life and words and make Him known.

Scripture Reading: Ephesians 4:1-16

Personal Application:

- What church family are you a part of? How do you fit in?
  What gifts and skills has God given you with which to help build
  up His body, the church?

Week 50, Day 5: True Confession

Anyone who is even casually acquainted with professional football has no doubt witnessed all the ways teams celebrate a touchdown. Sometimes the entire offensive line performs a carefully choreographed routine around the player scoring the touchdown. The more flamboyant receivers or running backs may simply perform a signature jig or dance.

For every offensive celebration, however, there is a demonstration of sheer disappointment from the defensive team—often full of blame and finger-pointing. Maybe they're embarrassed, but they've sure got lots of excuses for what went wrong: somebody called the wrong play, a critical block or tackle was missed, there was an overlooked assignment, or a defensive player was simply physically miss-matched with his opponent. Sometimes players hang their heads, walking dejectedly off the field. Some literally point the blame at someone else.

While we should be slow to point the finger at others and quick to examine our own hearts and behaviors, this sort of show-case confession is embarrassing. True confession eliminates the whole blame game. Confession is the first step in defeating sin and eliminating blame. Sometimes the hardest part of dealing with a problem is admitting that we have one.

Much like some of our embarrassed NFL stars, many times we want to deny our own responsibility for our failings. We want to blame our parents, the culture, a lack of a proper education, or even God—that He's somehow just against us. But Jesus urges us to take a second look when we're ready to point the finger at someone (or something) else: "Why do you look at the speck of sawdust in your brother's eye and pay no attention to the plank in your own eye?" (Matthew 7:3)

Confession is simply agreeing with God about our sin. It affirms that God is just when He deals with our sins. By confessing we realign ourselves with God's purposes and our joy is restored. Ongoing confession of sin to God is necessary and characterizes a follower of Jesus. As Christians, we are also to confess our sins to one another so that we can pray for each other.

God's people have always recognized the importance of confession. David acknowledged to Nathan the prophet, and then to God, "I have sinned against the Lord." (2 Samuel 12:13) When Isaiah saw the holiness of God he declared, "Woe to me…I am ruined! I am a man of unclean lips, and I live among a people of unclean lips.…" (Isaiah 6:5) Daniel confessed his sins and the sins of his people (Daniel 9:20) True confession takes honesty and humility, but it sure beats the "Blame Game" for grace and healing.

Scripture Reading: 1 John 1:5-10; James 5:16

Personal Application:

- Let the Lord expose any sin or bitterness (blame) in your life.
- Now confess this sin or bitterness according to the pattern in 1 John 1:9. And if you're struggling to shed a habitual sin, confess that sin to a brother whom you trust. Ask for prayer and support as you seek to break free from that sin.

Week 50, Day 6: Tips for Parenting

Several years ago, I received the following from a dear friend and national Christian counselor, Dr. Karen Johnson. No one is ever going to be a "Perfect Parent." However, there are some ways to be a successful parent—a parent whose child can make it in this world. Here's what she sent:

T— Time with you is more important to your child than money and gifts.

I— Interest must be shown in what your child is interested in.

P— Patience in letting them be kids, not little "grown-ups."

S— Say "I'm sorry" when you are wrong and expect them to do the same.

F— Forgiveness, fun, and flexible must be ever most at the top of your mind.

O— Offer encouragement in your words, attitudes, and actions.

R— Responsibility is what a parent must teach and a child must have.

S— Strokes (positive, verbal) are something every child needs, along with hugs.

U— Understand and accept who your child is despite what he/she does and/or how he/she looks.

C— Caring and careful with your comments will be an encouragement to your child.

C— Commitment to what is best for your child, not what makes you look good.

E— Establish boundaries and stick with them.

S— Surprise your child with a special treat just because he is special and loved.

S— Stay in love and in a healthy relationship with your mate.
  That's the best security for a child.

F— Faith is a crucial aspect of a child's life. Make sure yours is strong.

U— Utilize your experiences & listening skills when your child talks to you.

L— Love them.

P— Pray for them, protect them, and provide for them.

A— Ask good questions.

R— Rules, when broken, have consequences; rules, when kept, have rewards.

E— Enforce the boundaries and the rules—both parents must do this consistently.

N— Never try to be your child's best friend—be his/her parent.

T— Take the initiative to know what is happening with your child & who he/she is hanging out with.

I— Imitating you is what kids do—make sure you're providing a good example.

N— Nothing makes for a successful child like a positive, godly parent.

G— God wants to be known by your child—be sure you introduce him/her to Him.

Our children are a gift from God entrusted to our care. Please take the above as sound advice and not a cumbersome list of rules to follow.

Scripture Reading: Ephesians 6:4; Colossians 3:21

Personal Application:

• Select three of the above tips that especially speak to you and begin applying them with your children today. Also, pray daily for your kids and trust God with their lives.

Week 50, Day 7: Weekly Recap and Prayer

On the seventh day of each week, use the **ACTS** acronym to spend time with the Lord reviewing and assessing your week and praying to God. (**A**=Adoration; **C**=Confession; **T**=Thanksgiving; **S**=Supplication)

First, look back over the previous six days for this week to remind yourself what you read and agreed to. Then, follow the ACTS pattern for prayer below. Finally, use the space below to journal what God is doing in your life and share this with a trusted spiritual partner.

Adoration: Simply spend time in adoration of the Lord. Praise Him and glorify His name. (See 1 Chronicles 29:10-13; Psalm 100; Romans 11:33-36.)

Confession: Confess your sins and shortcomings before God. ("If we confess our sins, he is faithful and just and will forgive us our sins and purify us from all unrighteousness." – 1 John 1:9) To confess (or agree with God) about your sin, implies that you are repentant and desperately want Him to change you.

Thanksgiving: Thank God for what He has done and is doing in your life and the life of your family. Give Him credit, for everything you have comes from Him. (See Psalm 136.)

Supplication: Supplication is just a fancy word for making your requests known to God. Based on the devotions of this past week and the things going on in your life right now, what do you want to ask Him for? "If you, then, though you are evil, know how to give good gifts to your children, how much more will your Father in heaven give good gifts to those who ask Him!" (Matthew 7:11)

Journal: What is God doing in your life right now?

Week 51, Day 1: Marital Faithfulness

Malachi was the last prophet in Old Testament times. Despite all that God had done for Israel and even after their return to their homeland after 70 years of exile, they had become indifferent toward God.

Like Israel in Malachi's day, we too can become indifferent toward God. We may still call ourselves Christians. We may still attend church—at least occasionally. But we fail to recognize that our lives are one whole, not a collection of separate parts. When we neglect our relationship with God, it profoundly impacts every other area of our life and vice-versa.

So, it was in Israel. Among other issues, Malachi exposed the following sin in their lives:

Another thing you do: You flood the Lord's altar with tears. You weep and wail because he no longer looks with favor on your offerings or accepts them with pleasure from your hands. You ask, "Why?" It is because the Lord is the witness between you and the wife of your youth. You have been unfaithful to her, though she is your partner, the wife of your marriage covenant. Has not the one God made you? You belong to him in body and spirit. And what does the one God seek? Godly offspring. So be on your guard, and do not be unfaithful to the wife of your youth. "The man who hates and divorces his wife," says the Lord, the God of Israel, "does violence to the one he should protect," says the Lord Almighty. So be on your guard, and do not be unfaithful.

Men, perhaps never in history have we been inundated with so many temptations in this regard: pornography, R-rated movies, the prevalence, ease and acceptance of divorce, business travel, spending much time with female co-workers, etc.

None of us is immune to such temptations. Marital disharmony and even divorce can seem to sneak up on us. I also recognize that responsibility for a healthy marriage rides on both husband and wife. Lately, I've heard of so many wives who engage in extra-marital affairs, often to the surprise of their unsuspecting husbands.

For this reason, we must do as the Lord warns in Malachi to "be on our guard, and not be unfaithful." This requires active, deliberate effort on our part. Cultivate love for your wife every day. Never take her for granted. Allow her to blossom in her own right. Encourage her, love her, provide for, and protect her. Serve her. Involve her in your life. Be willing to sacrifice for her (Ephesians 5:25) and continue to woo her your whole life.

Be faithful to her, your partner, the wife of your marriage covenant.

Scripture Reading: Ephesians 5:25-33

Personal Application:

• Tell your wife every day that you love her. Compliment her on her looks. Plan things you can do together and make great memories. Spend time with other couples who love each other and offer healthy examples of marriage.

Week 51, Day 2: How Tests Help Us Grow

I have never liked tests. Whether in an academic setting, a medical evaluation, or a test of one's courage while being stranded on a remote mountain lake, testing is rarely pleasant. But I must admit that testing is often necessary for building character.

My hunting partner John and I had saved all year to be able to afford our 1996 Alaska Caribou/Bear hunt. But shortly after our bush plane dropped us off at the small lake in front of our camp, John began to have trouble breathing. It seems that the molds and fungi surrounding our area had activated some old allergy problems. He quickly became weak and needed to be evacuated. On top of everything else, a heavy storm began to bludgeon our little tent and pelt our equipment with branches.

Periodically, I left camp to survey the area for game. But it seemed that the foul weather had even caused the animals to hide out. Our supplies were limited and most of our matches were wet. Despite efforts to medicate John's asthma, he became weak and fearful.

Finally, we placed a distress signal on the ground and hailed down a small plane. The pilot was able to contact our operator and within hours he picked us up. After landing at the lodge, the proper medicine, shelter, and grub soothed us both.

Trials have a way of refining and perfecting our faith. God sends trials to the righteous, for it causes them to grow rich in the things of the Lord. If we believe that everything is under God's control and divine guidance, then our trials like our blessings are traceable to His providence. As beautiful as a rose is, it grows among thorns. There cannot be a rainbow without a storm. Most of us cannot find that 6x6 bull elk without the rigors of a long hike in the woods.

The grand ole preacher, Charles H. Spurgeon, gives us some insight about trials:

One may drown in seas of prosperity as well as in rivers of affliction. Our mountains are not too high, and our valleys are not too low for temptations. Trials lurk on every road. Everywhere, above, and beneath, we are beset and surrounded with danger. Yet no shower falls unprompted from the threatening cloud. Every raindrop has its orders before it falls. The trials that come from God are sent to prove and strengthen our graces. They illustrate the power of divine grace to test the genuineness of our virtues and add to their energy.

Dear friend, know that nothing touches us that is unknown by our Heavenly Father. The Apostle James reminds us that, "Consider it pure joy, my brothers, whenever you face trials of many kinds, because you know that the testing of your faith develops perseverance. Perseverance must finish its work so that you may be mature and complete, not lacking anything."

Scripture Reading: Mark 6:45-51; James 1:2-3

Personal Application:

- The next time you encounter a test or trial of any kind, apply James 1:2-3 to that trial. Additionally, pray and ask God what He wants you to experience through this trial.

Week 51, Day 3: Light Attracts

During daylight hours most fish will try to avoid light as they hide in shadows or dive to deeper depths. But in the evening many species find that light is a friendly invitation to finding an easy meal. The baitfish, insects and algae will concentrate around a well-lit area.

Such was the case when Dick Gaumer (former editor and outdoor writer) and I fished the Stockton, California Delta late in the evenings. The big striped bass, black bass, American shad, and crappie would gather around the marina areas to attack our surface plugs and mini jigs. The late spring and summer evenings were always a good time to find a calm, well-lit bay.

The first century disciple/fishermen also did most of their fishing at night. They would build a fire in a highly polished brass pan sitting in the middle of their boats. The reflection of the light would draw the fish from some distance. When the schools came to the surface the fishermen cast their nets out and brought the catch aboard.

Jesus used the metaphor of light to describe Himself. He declared, "I am the light of the world. Whoever follows me will never walk in darkness but will have the light of life." (John 8:12) Jesus is "the true light that gives light to everyone." (John 1:9)

Of course, many refuse to come to the Light of the world. The reason is simple, as Jesus explained in John 3:19-20: Men love darkness instead of light because their deeds are evil. They shun the light lest the light expose their evil deeds. But when someone repents of their sins and comes to Jesus His light illuminates their life. "I have come into the world as a light, so that no one who believes in me should stay in darkness." (John 12:46)

And when we put our faith in Jesus Christ, He makes us "children of light." This designation describes our calling in terms of the holy way God wants us to live. "For you were once darkness, but now you are light in the Lord. Live as children of light." (Ephesians 5:8) And, "You are all children of the light and children of the day. We do not belong to the night or to the darkness." (1 Thessalonians 5:5)

But being children of the light also pertains to our calling regarding our witness. Just like fishing at night with a light, many people are attracted to Jesus by the light He radiates through us. "In the same way, let your light shine before men, that they may see your good deeds and praise your Father in heaven." (Matthew 5:16)

So, let us live as children of the light and may others come to faith in Jesus through the light of our life and witness.

Scripture Reading: Ephesians 5:3-20

Personal Application:

- Let the light of Jesus shine in every corner of your life. And let Him shine through you to others that they too may come to faith in Him.

Week 51, Day 4: War Footing

Veteran Barney Barnes, Promise Keepers National Ambassador for the Military and Prisons was a fine pilot and officer during the Vietnam War. He is an inspiration to me and many others. I love his stories from his prestigious military background including his comments about "war footing."

"War footing" describes the condition of being prepared to undertake or maintain war. As I write this, the President recently ordered the nation onto a "war footing." This should prompt all Americans to check their footing and evaluate where and how they will make this stand.

"Footing" refers to how securely your feet are placed on the ground. For example, if you lose your footing, your feet may slip, and you could fall. This reminds me of what Paul advised, "So, if you think you are standing firm, be careful that you don't fall." (1 Corinthians 10:12)

It is critical that we assume a war footing especially in view of the fear that grips so many due to the threat of the Coronavirus, or the civil unrest we're facing, or the possible threat of war with a Middle-Eastern country.

First, we must be clear about what fear is: "A distressing emotion aroused by impending danger, evil, pain, etc., whether the threat is real or imagined." It is significant that the threat can be either real or imagined for fear to emerge.

Secondly, let's be clear on the meaning of courage: "mental or moral strength to venture, persevere, and withstand danger, fear, or difficulty." Courage comes from the same root word as coronary (i.e., having to do with the heart). So, courage is a heart issue… not a head issue. "A fearful world needs a fearless Church." – A.W. Tozier

Moses ordered war footing complete with strategy in Deuteronomy 31:6-8. He urged, "Be strong and of good courage, do not fear nor be afraid of them; for the LORD your God, He is the One who goes with you. He will not leave you nor forsake you." (Deuteronomy 31:6)

As Christians, we too are called to a war footing. But "our struggle is not against flesh and blood, but against the rulers, against the authorities, against the powers of this dark world and against the spiritual forces of evil in the heavenly realms." (Ephesians 6:12)

In this season in which we find ourselves, we should be greatly encouraged and filled with courage rather than fear because our God is an Awesome God. Remember, "He lifted me out of the mud and mire; He set my feet on a rock and gave me a firm place to stand." (Psalm 40:2) This fact is true for every Christian. We have a "rock" on which to stand and that "rock" is Christ. So, don't move off the rock!

Scripture Reading: Isaiah 40:28-31; 41:10

Personal Application:
- As you read today's Scripture reading, take it to heart, believe it, claim it for yourself and live accordingly.

Week 51, Day 5: Hiking through Life

Most people I know enjoy a nice hike in the woods. There's something about trekking in the forest—getting away from all the noise, concrete, and things that distract us—that breathes life back into a man's spirit. Hiking also provides some great applications for our spiritual lives.

I remember hiking in a remote area one time following a severe windstorm. About a dozen huge trees had fallen across the trail in a monstrous tangled heap. Climbing over them was a chore in and of itself, but then I realized that the debris they brought down with them had completely camouflaged the trail making it difficult to find. Unexpected disasters in life pose similar challenges, but we must find our way back to the trusted main trail.

Sometimes a well-used game trail can also lead us astray. Animals often don't use the same hiking trails provided for humans and develop their own trail networks that usually lead to their food, water source, a bedding area, or sometimes nowhere. It's possible to inadvertently follow a game trail instead of keeping to the often-over-grown hiking trail. Occasionally, people even get lost in the woods, usually resulting in confusion, frustration, and fear. In life we sometimes get sidetracked by the lure of a "game trail" as well that has led us on a wild goose chase.

And then there are the hazards of the trail itself. We need to be attentive to loose rocks, tripping hazards, snakes, poison oak, and potholes on the path. Carelessness can quickly turn an enjoyable hike into a turned ankle, a twisted knee, or worse.

Sometimes, trail workers will cut in a new trail and cover the old, familiar trail with brush to force hikers onto the new trail. It's amazing to me that within a few short weeks, hikers pack down the new trail so that it looks well-worn, forgetting the old trail ever existed. Our culture does that, changing our old ways and replacing them with new. Sometimes this is for the better, but often it is not.

Life is often like taking a long hike on an unfamiliar trail. As we journey through life, there are unexpected hazards threatening to trip us up or cause harm. They may be moral traps Satan puts in our path or just worldly temptations that cause us to stumble. Then there are those trails that cross our pathway that could mistakenly redirect our plans. Sometimes the new trails that our culture forges can lead us into sin (i.e., the ways of the wicked).

In choosing the right path, often our struggle is not between picking a good path vs. an evil path, but rather in simply picking God's best, and for that we must regularly communicate with God and listen to His voice.

For the best "hiking experience" possible as we go through life, we need to follow in Jesus' steps, obey His Word, and listen to the promptings of His Holy Spirit in our lives.

Scripture Reading: Psalm 25; Psalm 119:105

Personal Application:

- Today and each day, ask the Lord to lead you in the way you should go. Trust Him and stick to His trail even when the going gets tough.

Week 51, Day 6: Asking God for a Fish

As a young man Adrian Rodgers felt called to the ministry. From the onset he was a very dedicated and hardworking man of God. After a year and half of ministry in his first church, one of his men insisted that he take a break and go fishing with him. They packed up their gear and drove to a restricted area near the primary launch pad of Cape Kennedy. They received clearance to enter a small beach area, where they could wade and fish in the shallow water.

Within minutes each man went his own way and Adrian started casting a Mirror-Lure with his old Mitchell spinning combo. With the big Florida blue sky above and numerous water birds filling the air, Adrian soaked up the peace and quiet.

Several hours passed without a single strike. Where were the fish? Each step and cast brought new anticipation but without success. Adrian looked up and said, "Lord I have tried to be obedient and have sought to faithfully serve you. It would really do my heart good, that out of your kindness I could catch a fish - any 'ole fish will do." As Adrian lowered his head, he spotted a dark-deep pocket located just ahead of him. He moved a few steps toward the sinkhole and placed his lure right in the center.

Unsure of the depth, he allowed the lure to settle for several seconds, then began to slowly reel. Just as the lure was about to clear the dark hole, he spotted another shadow; this one was moving at a fast rate of speed. The large yellow mouth of a speckled trout opened and engulfed the Mirror-Lure.

The spunky seatrout took off, peeling several yards of frayed line from the dusty reel. After several runs and some shouts of joy, Adrian wrestled the trophy size trout ashore. "The thrill and adrenaline rush that comes from such a battle is one of the things that inspires all anglers." Adrian recounts. "It was one of those awesome experiences that you never forget."

"I really felt it was more than a coincidence that this fish hit right after I prayed, so I thought I would try it again. I said 'Lord that was wonderful, I really enjoyed the experience and wonder if you could provide another one of those monster fish for me. If you can guide that miracle fish to the Apostle Peter's hook, then I believe you can do the same for me."

Adrian made a second cast into the same spot and again allowed the lure to settle. Just like before the lure came out of the pocket only to be swallowed up by another giant trout. The ensuing fight was exciting, and Adrian landed the fish right next to the one already beached.

While some may see this as a trivial thing to a God who created the universe, Adrian believes, "God doesn't see things as big or small. He hears the prayers of a small child with the same compassion and care as He listens to a great theologian."

Scripture Reading: Matthew 7:7-11

Personal Application:
- God is not a genie in a lamp, but He does hear and answer the prayers of His children. What do you need to ask God for today?

Week 51, Day 7: Weekly Recap and Prayer

On the seventh day of each week, use the **ACTS** acronym to spend time with the Lord reviewing and assessing your week and praying to God. (**A**=Adoration; **C**=Confession; **T**=Thanksgiving; **S**=Supplication)

First, look back over the previous six days for this week to remind yourself what you read and agreed to. Then, follow the ACTS pattern for prayer below. Finally, use the space below to journal what God is doing in your life and share this with a trusted spiritual partner.

Adoration: Simply spend time in adoration of the Lord. Praise Him and glorify His name. (See 1 Chronicles 29:10-13; Psalm 100; Romans 11:33-36.)

Confession: Confess your sins and shortcomings before God. ("If we confess our sins, he is faithful and just and will forgive us our sins and purify us from all unrighteousness." – 1 John 1:9) To confess (or agree with God) about your sin, implies that you are repentant and desperately want Him to change you.

Thanksgiving: Thank God for what He has done and is doing in your life and the life of your family. Give Him credit, for everything you have comes from Him. (See Psalm 136.)

Supplication: Supplication is just a fancy word for making your requests known to God. Based on the devotions of this past week and the things going on in your life right now, what do you want to ask Him for? "If you, then, though you are evil, know how to give good gifts to your children, how much more will your Father in heaven give good gifts to those who ask Him!" (Matthew 7:11)

Journal: What is God doing in your life right now?

Week 52, Day 1: Reflecting the Light

My wife and I thoroughly enjoy the Christmas season. The smells, the music, the giving, the wonderful food, and the beautiful multi-colored Christmas lights all add to the rejoicing and celebration of the new-born King - Jesus. The next best thing to do besides seeing many great Christmas church programs is driving through decorated neighborhoods and looking at the array of Christmas lights. It occurred to me that without the lights people could not really appreciate or enjoy the festive ornaments.

I'm reminded of a story about a little village tucked away in Rjukan, Norway. The sheer mountains surrounding the village, coupled with its location in the far northern latitude, prevent the sunlight from reaching the village from October to March. This rendered Rjukan was a pretty bleak and depressing place to be during the winter months.

Some enterprising citizens decided to install some large mirrors on the mountainside to reflect the sunrays and beam sunlight into the town square to add life and joy to the otherwise dark community. They also mechanized the mirrors so they could stay aligned with the sun, blessing the citizens with energizing sunlight for at least twelve hours a day.

As Christians it's our joy and privilege to reflect the true Light that came into the world over 2,000 years ago – Jesus the Christ. Jesus said, "I am the light of the world. Whoever follows Me will never walk in darkness but will have the light of life." (John 8:12) He gave mankind the greatest gift of all - eternal life. The joy, peace, passion, gifts, talents, and hope that is within us is the light we need to share with a lost world.

In Matthew 5:14, Jesus told His followers that we are, "the light of the world." We are to reflect the light of Jesus to a dark world. Christ is the true light that "shines in the darkness." Friends, there is darkness all around us. Don't leave the reflection of Christ to the paid professional pastors and missionaries. It is the responsibility of every Christian to be the light in our families, communities, places of business, and especially to those friends and extended family members who do not know Christ.

Jesus challenges us, "Let your light so shine before men, that they may see your good works and glorify your Father in heaven." (Matthew 5:16) It seems like our world is getting increasingly darker. But you and I can tell others about the One who can bring light into darkness through a personal relationship with Jesus!

Scripture Reading: Matthew 5:14-16

Personal Application:
- Why do you think Christ uses the metaphor of light to represent Himself?
- What are some specific ways you can reflect the light of Christ to others today?

Week 52, Day 2: The Lord Is Our Security

Security is a big deal and a huge money maker in today's economy. But home security systems, vehicle air bags, passwords, birth control pills, yearly physicals, savings accounts, and pension plans provide only temporary peace of mind. As Americans, we spend billions of dollars on hi-tech self-protection equipment to find that they are often rendered obsolete even before the warrantee expires.

We are obsessed with attempting to remove all possible inconveniences, accidents, thefts, and unwanted consequences from our lives. In essence, we are seeking the absence of trouble. We want peace of mind and that is what many of these security devices and measures claim to offer.

Gadgets break, stock markets crash, and people let us down. Despite all the precautions we take, life dishes out its share of calamity. But the only fully dependable and lasting peace comes from our security in Christ—knowing that we never have to face life alone. God is in control and always present with us. That is really the only absolute security we can count on.

Although it is prudent to take safety precautions and plan wisely for our future, we must ultimately put our trust in God. Depending on man or the things of this world for our security makes about as much sense as anchoring ourselves to the rear bumper of a city bus. Sure, it feels strong and stable right now, but wait till it takes off!

The Psalmist, King David, understood this. As a shepherd, he carried a sling. As a soldier, he carried a sword. As a general, he had an army. As a king, he had his mighty men. Ultimately, though, he knew in his heart that only God's presence would protect Him, and that is where he found peace.

David declared, "Lord, you alone are my portion and my cup; you make my lot secure. I keep my eyes always on the Lord. With him at my right hand, I will not be shaken. Therefore my heart is glad and my tongue rejoices; my body also will rest secure." (Psalm 16:5, 8-9)

Trusting the Lord puts us in the lap of the One who will protect us, watch over us, help us through our problems, and make us better people because of them. We can rest in the peace and presence of a caring, loving God who will never leave or forsake us—even when it seems that the world is crashing down on us.

God has given us His Holy Spirit. "When you believed, you were marked in Him with a seal, the promised Holy Spirit, who is a deposit guaranteeing our inheritance until the redemption of those who are God's possession—to the praise of His glory." (Ephesians 1:13-14) You are in God's watch-care and so am I. Praise God!

Scripture Reading: Psalm 18:1-19

Personal Application:

- Spend time in prayer thanking the Lord for the security you enjoy in Him. Practice resting in Him and His peace when things go sideways.

Week 52, Day 3: Out of Control

"A fool gives full vent to his anger, but a wise man keeps himself under control."
— Proverbs 29:11

Outdoorsmen are known to be passionate about their sport. Some individuals will spend more time, effort and resources trying to perfect the ballistics of their ammunition or tying a species fly than improving relationships within their homes. I've seen professional bass fishermen sacrifice everything in their quest to attain success. At one time or another we have all suffered from the addiction of our passions.

Here are seven humorous warning signs that your fishing may be out of control:

1. Your refrigerator drawer is full of night-crawlers.
2. You carry pictures of the fish you've caught in your wallet.
3. You named your kids Gill, Rod, and Stinkbait.
4. Cats follow you everywhere you go.
5. You practice casting in the bathtub.
6. Selling your gear could put the kids through medical school.
7. You leave your hot spot on that important lake to someone in your will.

I think you would agree that it is important to have your life under control. Throughout the New Testament the Apostle Paul reminds us that we should have control and authority over our bodies, minds, and tongues. The reason he can speak with such conviction is that prior to accepting the Lord as his personal Savior, Paul was an out-of-control guy.

James urges us, "My dear brothers and sisters, take note of this: Everyone should be quick to listen, slow to speak and slow to become angry, because human anger does not produce the righteousness that God desires." (James 1:19-20) A person with an uncontrolled spirit is unpredictable, difficult to live with, and an embarrassment to God and his family.

Many Christians are angry today. They're angry at politicians, at the injustices in this sin-sick world, and even with other Christians. But Christ calls us to a life of mercy, grace, and love. If any man ever had the right to express his anger it was Jesus when He was unjustly crucified. Yet, upon the cross He prayed, "Father forgive them!"

If we identify with Christ, then we desperately want His Spirit to control our lives and our emotions. King Solomon said it like this, "He who is slow to anger is better than the mighty, and he who rules his spirit than he who takes a city." (Proverbs 16:32 NKJV)

Scripture Reading: Ephesians 4:17-32

Personal Application:

- If someone were to ask your wife, children, or closest friends whether you frequently display anger, how would they respond? If you struggle with anger, ask the Lord to replace it with patience, mercy, and compassion.
Ask a spiritual partner to pray for you and hold you accountable.

Week 52, Day 4: Do Not Be Deceived

Have you ever noticed how often we use deception in various sports? Whether we're talking about hunting, fishing, football, or some other competitive sport, there's always some degree of deception involved in playing that sport. With hunting, it's camouflage, a blind, or a call. With fishing it's artificial bait and playing the line to make it look alive and enticing. With football it's the dodge to the right, then running left, or a fake hand-off to a runner, followed by a pass.

In some ways, we might even suggest that the better we are at deception, the more successful we'll be at those sports. But after all, deception is just part of the game. It's the way we take that animal, fish, or beat our opponent. But there is another far more insidious kind of deception.

Just days before Jesus went to the cross, His disciples asked Him about end times and the sign of His return. In Luke's Gospel, chapter 21, the first thing Jesus warned His disciples was, "Watch out that you are not deceived." (vs. 8) It's notable that Jesus said this to His disciples. He didn't say it to those who don't know Him. He said to us who know Him, "Watch out that you are not deceived." So, even we His children can be deceived.

How do we avoid being deceived? It has oft been said that the way to distinguish counterfeit money from the real thing is to be fully acquainted with the real thing. I believe this is true in spiritual matters as well. Make it your life goal to know Jesus thoroughly. There have been times in my life when I've been tempted to act or respond to a situation in a certain way, but realized, "That's not like Jesus." "That's not how Jesus would respond." And I know that because I know Him.

Another way we avoid being deceived is by knowing His Word. That doesn't mean we have to be a Bible scholar, but it means that we spend time in God's Word, not just learning facts, but getting to know its Author. When Satan tempted Jesus in the Wilderness, at one point the devil even quoted Scripture trying to trip up Jesus (Luke 4:9-11). But Jesus recognized he was twisting Scripture to make the temptation plausible. But Jesus replied with Scripture, demonstrating its true intent (Luke 4:12).

Tragically, soon after Jesus warned His disciples about being deceived, Judas, who was one of the twelve disciples, succumbed to the deception of the devil and betrayed Jesus. This should sober us. Here was a man who had spent at least three years with Jesus, yet he allowed himself to be deceived. We need to take Jesus' warning to heart.

"Watch out that you are not deceived. For many will come in My name, claiming, 'I am he.'" (Luke 21:8)

Scripture Reading: Matthew 24:3-14

Personal Application:

- How well do you know Jesus? How well do you know His Word?
  Make it your life's goal to know Him and His Word thoroughly.

Week 52, Day 5: Be Ready!

We talked yesterday about deception, especially in the context of Jesus' return. Jesus also urges us to "be ready" and to "keep watch" for His return. The concept of being ready also has ties to outdoor sports as well as team sports. The player on the field of a football game will quickly put himself and his team in jeopardy if he's daydreaming and not paying attention. The same can happen with fishing.

My friend Jack was fishing for Kokanee off a dock on a lake in Eastern Washington when his son Jason was still a small boy. On the dock were Jack, his son, and Jack's friend Mike. All three of them had a line in the water.

Suddenly, Jason's pole started jerking violently and the young boy didn't know what to do, so Jack quickly set his pole on the dock and turned to give Jason a hand. But while Jack was reeling in Jason's fish, two more fish hit both Mike's and Jack's lines almost simultaneously!

Jack was busy with Jason's rod and Mike was reeling in his own, when both Jack and Mike looked down and watch a fish pull Jack's pole off the dock and into the lake. Quickly, Mike shoved his pole at Jack, kicked off his shoes, and dove in after Jack's pole.

Jack landed both Jason's and Mike's fish just in time to watch Mike surfacing holding the pole toward Jack on the dock. Jack grabbed it and reeled in his fish as well. It had been a frantic five minutes that none of the three had been ready for. It was only their good fortune that they were able to land all three fish.

Again, those were just fish. What Jesus is talking about is far more serious. "Therefore keep watch, because you do not know what day your Lord will come. But understand this: If the owner of the house had known at what time of night the thief was coming, he would have kept watch and would not have let his house be broken into. So you also must be ready, because the Son of Man will come at an hour when you do not expect Him." (Matthew 24:42-44)

And in Luke's Gospel, Jesus warns about letting our hearts becoming "weighed down with carousing, drunkenness and the anxieties of life. Be always on the watch, and pray that you may be able to escape all that is about to happen, and that you may be able to stand before the Son of Man." (Luke 21:34 & 36)

How do we keep ready for Jesus' return? By anticipating and expecting His soon return for one thing. We don't know when He will come, so we must watch for Him expectantly. We also stay ready by avoiding thoughts and activities that can distract and defeat us. Therefore, "Be ready!"

Scripture Reading: 2 Peter 3:3-14

Personal Application:

- To what extent would you say you are ready for Christ's return? What would you want to change or do differently if you knew He was coming tomorrow?

Week 52, Day 6: Living More Simply

Whenever I backpack or go on an extended hunt, I like to travel as light as possible. Even a few pounds of unneeded weight can really make a difference when you're climbing a significant elevation gain. A friend of mine got into ultra-light backpacking and had his three-day backpack down to 18 pounds!

I confess that I've never been able to get my backpack that light but it's still very manageable. You don't want to scrimp on essentials either and it's only by experience that you can determine what's too much and what's too little to take along. It's important to have some necessary survival gear in case of emergencies, but you simply can't prepare for every contingency.

But I find there's something very satisfying about the simplicity of backpacking and knowing that I'm able to carry everything I need for survival or can find it in the wilderness.

I have often thought of Jesus regarding the simplicity with which He lived while on earth. In Luke 9:57-58, for instance, we read, "As they were walking along the road, a man said to Him, 'I will follow you wherever you go.' Jesus replied, 'Foxes have dens and birds have nests, but the Son of Man has no place to lay his head.'"

And toward the end of Jesus' earthly ministry, Luke records, "Each day Jesus was teaching at the temple, and each evening He went out to spend the night on the hill called the Mount of Olives." (Luke 21:37) It sounds like Jesus was simply sleeping under the stars during that time.

And, "Do not worry about your life, what you will eat or drink; or about your body, what you will wear. Is not life more than food, and the body more than clothes?" (Matthew 6:25)

I'm not suggesting that we sell everything and live like hermits and I don't believe that's Jesus' desire for us. But there is great wisdom in paring down and seeking to live a simpler lifestyle.

For instance, I know Christians who have so many toys, they struggle to decide whether to go camping in their RV, boating, kayaking, or take the motorcycle out for the weekend. Others have gotten themselves so deep into debt that they live from paycheck to paycheck and have no reserve or savings. Being shackled with debt also severely limits options. Paul wrote, "The time is short… I would like you to be free from concern." (1 Corinthians 7:29 & 32)

Let me challenge you to consider living a simpler life. Take inventory of your stuff. If it's collecting dust and you haven't used it in a year, consider selling it or giving it away. For others, it's primarily a very cluttered calendar. Life doesn't have to be that cumbersome! Just think of how much simpler life could be and how much freer you could be to follow Jesus and serve others.

Scripture Reading: Matthew 6:25-34

Personal Application:

- If you're married, sit down with your wife. Share with her what you read here today and challenge each other to think of three ways you could simplify your life. Then do it!

Week 52, Day 7: Weekly Recap and Prayer

On the seventh day of each week, use the **ACTS** acronym to spend time with the Lord reviewing and assessing your week and praying to God. (**A**=Adoration; **C**=Confession; **T**=Thanksgiving; **S**=Supplication)

First, look back over the previous six days for this week to remind yourself what you read and agreed to. Then, follow the ACTS pattern for prayer below. Finally, use the space below to journal what God is doing in your life and share this with a trusted spiritual partner.

Adoration: Simply spend time in adoration of the Lord. Praise Him and glorify His name. (See 1 Chronicles 29:10-13; Psalm 100; Romans 11:33-36.)

Confession: Confess your sins and shortcomings before God. ("If we confess our sins, he is faithful and just and will forgive us our sins and purify us from all unrighteousness." – 1 John 1:9) To confess (or agree with God) about your sin, implies that you are repentant and desperately want Him to change you.

Thanksgiving: Thank God for what He has done and is doing in your life and the life of your family. Give Him credit, for everything you have comes from Him. (See Psalm 136.)

Supplication: Supplication is just a fancy word for making your requests known to God. Based on the devotions of this past week and the things going on in your life right now, what do you want to ask Him for? "If you, then, though you are evil, know how to give good gifts to your children, how much more will your Father in heaven give good gifts to those who ask Him!" (Matthew 7:11)

Journal: What is God doing in your life right now?

Week 53, Day 1: (or Day 365) O for a Thousand Tongues to Sing

"I, even I, am He who blots out your transgressions."
– Isaiah 43:25

One of my historical heroes was the great song composer Charles Wesley. He has given us hundreds of great hymns and praise choruses to enjoy. He and his brother, John, have provided so much inspiration to the evangelical community.

While I really appreciate many of the new praise and worship music, I prefer listening to those theologically rich old hymns and black gospel music. It sometimes feels like some younger worship leaders do not give the proper credit and listening time to the "old hymns" of the faith. Wrapped in the mystic of trying to be "seeker sensitive" too many new age worship leaders devaluate the wonder and majesty of the old hymns that teach us Scripture and many lessons about life.

When Charles Wesley experienced the joy of divine forgiveness through God's grace, he told a Moravian friend of his new sense of pardon, and added, "I suppose I had better keep silent about it." His friend responded, "Oh, no, my brother. If you had a thousand tongues, you should go and use them all for Jesus."

Wesley went home and penned the great hymn: "O for a thousand tongues to sing/ MY great Redeemer's praise, /The glories of my God and King, /The triumphs of His grace!"

In a world filled with wickedness, God says to all who believe, I'm the One who can blot out your sin. That is called grace my friend. Amazing Grace – it is that unmerited favor we seek and receive from God Almighty.

Whatever our sin, whatever our failures, whatever we feel about ourselves we must remember that the gift of forgiveness is a wonder of our faith. It is God saying that the sacrifice of His son on The Cross covered the sins of mankind. The one condition He placed upon His gift is that it would be received.

In order to believe we must receive. Have you received God's gift? Open your heart and ask Him to forgive and receive you into His Kingdom. Amen

Scripture Reading: Romans 3:24, 5:2

Personal Application:
- How are you showing grace to others; especially, people who seem ungrateful?
- What could you do to be a person who better exemplifies a grace-filled life?

Leap Year Bonus Day: A Renewed Mind

As I close this devotional book with a final entry, we're into our ninth month of the COVID-19 pandemic and folks are beginning to wonder if life will ever go back to normal. I can't foresee what will be happening in your life when you read this, but life has a way of throwing curve balls at us. What I have found in life is that our *response* to what happens to us is as important, if not more so, than the actual trials we face. Because we know that God's presence and power are with us, it makes total sense that we can respond to trials with joy. In Christ, we can renew our minds. One of my favorite stories is about a man who reflects this kind of joyful attitude in the face of trouble. Dave was the kind of guy you love to hate. He was always in a good mood and speaking positive words of encouragement to help motivate others. When someone would ask him how he was doing, he would reply, "If I were any better, I would be twins!"

He was a unique person who had several hunter friends who followed him around the fields as he participated in his favorite past time—pheasant hunting. Dave's positive energies flowed through the whole experience. The hunting partners, dogs, and farmers all loved Dave and his upbeat way of living. And when It would grate on others how genuinely positive Dave was, he would say, "Life is all about choices, so I choose to be happy."

But then one day, Dave had a very unfortunate accident. While pheasant hunting with a friend, he placed his loaded shotgun against the fence as he climbed over the barbed wire. The gun fell against a fence pole and discharged, shooting Dave in the chest.

He was rushed to the nearest trauma center and evaluated for surgery. There were several pellets logged in critical areas and Dave was losing a lot of blood.

While still conscious Dave noticed the worried and frantic attitudes of the medical personnel. It felt like they were treating him as if it was a foregone conclusion that he would die. As they debated his chances of survival, one burly nurse asked him, "Are you allergic to anything?" Dave took a deep breath and yelled, "Yes, I'm allergic to lead!"

Over the laughter of the doctors and nurses, a quiet peace fell among the team as if to say, "Dave is not about to quit; he wants to live. So, let's operate on him if he's going to live."

By God's grace and the skill of his doctors Dave lived, but it was his amazing positive attitude that put the doctors in the right frame of mind to work on him.

Scripture Reading: Ephesians 4:20-24; 1 Peter 4:1

Personal Application:

- There's a world of difference between mustering a positive attitude by one's own strength and will and tapping into the power of Christ and taking on His character and attitude. Whatever comes your way, focus on Christ and His presence and power within you.

Topics Alphabetically

ABOUT THE AUTHOR

Dr. Jim Grassi is an award-winning author, communicator, outdoorsman, pastor, and former television co-host. He has presented hundreds of messages and programs around the world that helped equip people to fulfill the Great Commission (Matt. 28). He brings a sense of challenge, wisdom, excitement, and humor to his presentations, as he connects with people of various cultures and backgrounds. Through his multi-media outreach ministry, he encourages participants toward a greater understanding and appreciation of evangelism, discipleship, and the development of creating vibrant men's ministries. His practical approach to teaching biblical truth has captivated audiences around the world.

Jim Grassi is the founder and president of the culturally strategic Men's Ministry Catalyst, an organization he incorporated in 1981. Grassi is also the recognized author of several books, including *The Ultimate Fishing Challenge, Heaven on Earth, In Pursuit of the Prize, The Ultimate Hunt, Crunch Time, A Study Guide of Israel, The Ultimate Men's Ministry Encyclopedia, Crunch Time, Crunch Time in the Red Zone, Guts, Grace, and Glory—A Football Devotional, The Spiritual Mentor,* and *Building a Ministry of Spiritual Mentoring, More Than a Fisherman,* and *Finishing Well – Finishing Strong,* and *Act Like Men – Be Strong.* Jim has also written numerous magazine articles, booklets, and tracts. His popular booklet series on men's issues is utilized in many churches and Christian counseling centers.

Dr. Grassi has appeared on many radio and television programs including *Hour of Power, The 700 Club, The Carol Lawrence Show,* Cornerstone Television, Southern Baptist Television—*Cope,* Chicago Television 38, *The Dick Staub Show, Getting Together, In-Fisherman, Fishing Tales, Jimmy Houston Outdoors, Home Life, Focus on the Family, FOX Sports,* and *CSN.* He is the host of a weekly men's radio program called *Man Up!*

Dr. Grassi was born and reared in the San Francisco Bay area. Known for his evangelistic heart, he teaches people from a background of an outdoorsman, public administrator, Hall of Fame fisherman, college professor, businessman, community leader, and pastor. He has served in the capacity of a chaplain with the San Francisco 49ers, the Oakland Raiders, Hurricane Katrina relief efforts, and local police and fire departments. His life experiences, study of discipleship, and work with hundreds of churches has given him a unique perspective on helping men to know God and make Him known.

Contact Dr. Jim Grassi at:
contact@mensministrycatalyst.org
www.mensministrycatalyst.org

NOTES:

NOTES:

Made in United States
Orlando, FL
16 April 2024

45866156R00212